IN PHENOMENOLOGY

PHILOSOPHY OF EXPERIENCE

James M. Edie

Quadrangle Books 1969

Library of Congress Catalog Card Number: 76-78309

CONTENTS

INTRODUCTION

The studies in this volume were originally read at the sixth and seventh annual meetings of the Society for Phenomenology and Existential Philosophy.[1] Most of them have been revised and some of them considerably changed and developed by their authors since their first oral presentation. This necessary revision and rearrangement carries with it certain hazards. Abstracted from the atmosphere of discussion and debate for which they were originally produced, they may lose in vivacity and impact what they gain through the second thoughts of scholarly restriction and qualification. At the same time, while each of these papers represents an original effort of research and discovery in some personally chosen area of interest in contemporary American phenomenology, their being collected together here does not make them into a unified or systematic treatise on the subject as a whole. They are not meant to cover all the problems, or even all the major areas, of phenomenology. Each bears the stamp of the particular concerns of its author and his particular public. They represent no monolithic agreement in method, argument,

1. The sixth annual meeting of the Society for Phenomenology and Existential Philosophy was held at Purdue University, October 26–28, 1967, and the seventh annual meeting at Yale University, October 24–26, 1968.

or conclusions. On the contrary, they are frequently written in deliberate, and often more than partial, disagreement with one another. None would attempt a universal definition of phenomenological method or claim to vindicate its use as his own exclusive right.

Having described what these essays are not, it is time to be more positive. It will be seen through a glance at the Contents that the interests of contemporary American "phenomenologists" are sufficiently capacious and open to cover the most opposed and conflicting viewpoints: metaphysicians and antimetaphysicians, existentialists and structuralists, historians and logicians. What unifies these studies are not so much doctrines and arguments held in common but, rather, a series of themes or problems which tend to recur in different perspectives and a shared excitement for, and interest in, exploring the methods and tasks of phenomenology. It is this communality of interest and intention alone which justifies the publication of these studies and which inspires the hope that this collection, like those which have preceded it,[2] will contribute to the phenomenological fecundation of contemporary American philosophy.

The papers in Part One center on the experience of meaning,

2. *An Invitation to Phenomenology* (Chicago, 1965) and *Phenomenology in America* (Chicago, 1967). If the editor of this and the previous volumes has made any decisive contribution to their contents, apart from selection and arrangement, it lies in his efforts over the past seven years to encourage contributions that were directed to the problems and concern of the main stream of contemporary American philosophy. What has distinguished the Society for Phenomenology and Existential Philosophy during this period from the various other quasi-closed (and sometimes secret) Husserl and Heidegger conventicules which have begun to meet in this country— with restricted membership and cut off from the criticism and debate which they would face in open confrontation with the major philosophical currents—is a firm decision to engage other schools of thought and other methodologies in discussion, to open the doors of membership to all, and to test the relevance of phenomenology in the open forum of American philosophy as it exists in the second half of the twentieth century. In all these collections of articles from the recent meetings of the Society, we have tried to avoid the stuffy atmosphere of the philosophical chapel in which an elite group of exegetes related to the European fathers either by certified discipleship or direct apostolic succession, expound achieved doctrine. Phenomenology in this country has already been accused of becoming a new form of dogmatism; it is to be hoped that the contents of these volumes, and others like them, will show that such an accusation is unjustified.

through perception, through language, through art. Most of the papers are phenomenological, though some of them also pose questions concerning the ontology of meaning. Collectively, they begin with *aesthetics,* first in the classical sense of Plato, Baumgarten, and Kant, as the analysis of that fundamental *aisthesis* in which form is discovered, distinguished, and justified within the primary and most primitive layers of sense experience, and then in the more modern sense of the fusion of meaning and form in language and works of art. The first two papers, by Todes and Lingis, can be read as an attempt to rehabilitate sensation, to account for the "positivism" and "realism" of phenomenology. Both are concerned with the relation of categorial thought to perception—Todes to account for the necessity and intrinsic limits of all "theory" in the face of the invitations and possibilities of "sensuous abstractions," Lingis to reestablish the hyletic data beneath the level of "relational predicates" and practical interests as primarily "elements of enjoyment."

Perhaps the one problem which unifies all the papers in Part One, and which is the central theme of discussion in several of those that treat of language and art, is that of the relationship of meaning to the expression of meaning. Is the linguistic expression of meaning coextensive with experience, or is there something more? In how many languages—behavioral, ecological, gestural, productive—can meaning be expressed? How many are the languages of man?

Casey argues that art, like man, is in essence condemned to meaning; it cannot *not* mean, and the most irrationalist experiments of Dada, which were meant to mean nothing, are so charged with meaning that their significance is still being explored. Such meaningfulness, it is implied, can be thematized linguistically but is primarily nondiscursive and prelinguistic. McDermott's reflections on aesthetic "ecology" also discover the "taken for granted," unexpressed, and subunderstood ground of affective qualities which determine the texture and value of human existence prior to reflection; it sometimes takes urban renewal and the destruction of neighborhoods to raise such pre-reflexive meaning contextures to the level of expression—and then it is too late. Bulldozers carry meaning as well as words.

Erickson and Ihde pose the *aporia* in its clearest form, but most of these papers make some contribution to the discussion: does language alone give form and meaning to experience, or are there sources of meaning which are prior to, or at least outside of, language? Is this source consciousness? The world of things? The sense of the transcendental turn to consciousness in Husserl and the consequent primacy of the meaning-structures of consciousness over their verbal thematization leads in one direction. Heidegger's turn to embodied existence and then to language seems to point toward, or at least permit, the direction taken by Wittgenstein. In fact, the most pervasive influences in these chapters are Heidegger and Wittgenstein together, names that are not always so closely associated in philosophical discussions. No one would claim this discussion has settled the point at issue, or even that this is the best way to approach what is most original in each of the papers presented here, but this focusing on the problem of linguistic versus nonlinguistic (or extralinguistic) meaning seems to me one of the best avenues of approach to phenomenology provided by this remarkable and rich collection of essays.

Several of the papers in this volume were the result of symposia directed toward the examination of specific themes or problems from new and divergent points of view. This is the case with the papers in Part Two. They explore the terrain of two "categories" which loom large in existentialist literature: nihilism and the absurd. The discussions in each case range in character from the historical to the semantic to the prophetic, as becomes the topic, and, while they are in no sense exhaustive, together they give us a good *status quaestionis* on the basis of which to prosecute the discussion.

The papers in Part Three are more diversified in aim and structure. The first three were delivered at a symposium on William James and contribute to the James renaissance which is now well under way as a result of recent reinterpretations of his philosophy by various phenomenologists.[3] The rapidly growing

3. Cf. Alfred Schutz, *The Problem of Social Reality*, The Hague, 1962; Aron Gurwitsch, *The Field of Consciousness*, Pittsburgh, 1964; James M. Edie, "Notes on the Philosophical Anthropology of William James" in *Invitation to Phenomenology, op. cit.*, pp. 110–132, and "William James and the Phenomenology of Religious Experience" in *American Philosophy*

literature on this subject is one of the more striking instances of the influence of phenomenology on American philosophy in the second half of the twentieth century. The final papers, on Sartre, on Kant, on the philosophy of history, likewise face the work of historical philosophers, and history itself, witih questions and expectations specific to contemporary existential philosophy; and they provide us with some fresh answers which open paths for further research. I am sure that the authors who contributed their work so generously to this volume claim no greater unity either of purpose or achievement than this, nor can I, as their editor, rightly claim less.

I wish to thank the editors of *Philosophy East and West* for permission to reprint "On the Consciousness and Language of Art" by Albert Hofstadter. All the other papers in this volume are printed here for the first time.

JAMES M. EDIE

Northwestern University

and the Future, New York, 1968, pp. 247–269; Johannes Linschotten, *On the Way Toward a Phenomenological Psychology*, Pittsburgh, 1968; Bruce Wilshire, *William James and Phenomenology*, Bloomington, Ind., 1968; John Wild, *The Radical Empiricism of William James*, New York, 1969.

PART ONE

MEANING: PERCEPTION, LANGUAGE, AND ART

Samuel J. Todes

SENSUOUS ABSTRACTION AND THE ABSTRACT SENSE OF REALITY

Theoretical interpretation poses a paradox: it is somehow responsible both *to* and *for* the facts to which it refers, viz., facts consisting of what is shown by interpreted data. The interpretation is responsible to these facts since it may be true or false as fitting or failing to fit the data. Yet the interpretation is also responsible for the facts because interpreted data first gain factual significance (whether properly or misleadingly) by being subjected to interpretation. To be sure, we cannot in practice consider a datum (e.g., the color of a precipitate or the reading of an instrument or punch card) strictly by itself, apart from all interpretation. For we would have no stable context in which to identify "this" datum again and again over the course of one or more experiments. But we can distinguish the datum from its interpretation for purposes of understanding it as a datum, even though we cannot do so for purposes of treating it as an objective event. So considered, apart from all interpretation, an interpretable datum is a purely qualitative presence (or, by extension, the record of such a presence). It is the presence of a nonqualifying quality. As such it has two striking features. First of all, it is thoroughly clear evidence, but of . . . nothing in particular. It is uninformative evidence pointing to no conclusion. It testifies not to elementary facts but to no facts at all. In short, apart from its interpretive context, it is unintelligible as a too-pure form of evidence. But the scientific datum, considered by itself, is equally unintelligible in a second respect, viz., as a too-isolated form of presence. That the theoretician is presented with certain data rather than others appears as a "brute" fact into which no insight is possible. Theory, of course, makes the internal relations in the body of evidence taken as a whole remarkably lucid. The data as a whole are strictly explicable as precisely coherent. The favorable comparison of theory to unaided perception in this respect is so widely recognized and honored as to be platitudinous. But a price is paid for this advantage, a price which goes generally unnoticed. *What* the facts are is made luminous by theory. But *that* these are the facts is plunged by theory into a darkness just as extraordinary as the light shed on their nature. Even a body of theoretically understood data remains a body of evidence for "brute" facts which we understand might just as intelligibly have been quite otherwise. Our hypothetical way of conceiving the given facts makes plain that they might equally conceivably have been quite different.

So in theoretical data pure qualitativeness is associated with brute givenness. Theoretical interpretation overcomes the former limitation by assigning to data a factual significance. But the latter limitation is not overcome; theoretical facts remain brute facts. There is something objectively unsatisfying about this. Philosophers have perennially sought to peek behind this "facade" of brute facticity to discover, like Leibniz, some sufficient reason for the facts being just as they are, or, like Plato and Descartes, some self-evidently necessary principles from which they follow. Nonphilosophers have been equally tenacious in seeking to understand the seemingly brute facts of life as deliverances of some God or Fate or Destiny working secretly behind the scenes of experience, though they avoid the question of the brute facticity of these agents themselves, these supposed puppeteers of existence. But many philosophers, like Hume, and many tough-minded nonphilosophers have insisted that whether it is satisfying or not, the existence of what exists, the existence of this world rather than some other, is unintelligible. Like it or not, facticity *is* brute facticity. This latter view is shared by all those who believe that all real or responsible knowledge of matters of fact is scientific knowledge.

Ordinary noncontrolled experience offers some reason to doubt this conclusion of scientism. To be sure, sometimes in the course of uncontrolled experience things appear as they do in science to be the "brute" facts of the matter. The facts in such cases may be reasonably clear. They may even display a consistent pattern so that any few are readily placed in light of the others. Still, in such cases, it seems strikingly unfathomable that the facts are just these rather than some others. We are struck at such moments not with our ignorance of why things are as they are but with our knowledge of the intrinsic unintelligibility of things being just as they are. But normally in our uncontrolled experience things appear somehow to be "naturally" there; the semiautonomous facts of our local situation do *not* appear to be "brutely" given. One must first adopt or fall into a special unnatural attitude in order that it come to appear startling, surprising, inexplicable that one's local situation happens to be the way it is rather than some other way. The very abnormality of this attitude renders the appearance suspect.

In particular, one must "step back" from one's situation through an inhibition or destruction of interest and involvement in order that the appearance of brute facticity pervade uncontrolled experience. With moderate inhibition or disillusionment one's surroundings appear "curious" and perhaps "interesting" as an object for disinterested scrutiny. Severe disengagement, however, makes one's situation appear "strange" and even repulsively alien so that its special character ceases to be noticed and tends to be submerged in the sheer obtrusive *presence* of the unwanted and not otherwise differentiated situation. Only extreme disaffection of this sort produces shocked awareness and surprised questioning such as, "What am I doing here (rather than elsewhere)?" "Why am I alive (anywhere) at all?" "Why here, not there?" "Why now, not then?" "Why me, not another?" "Why this, not that?" In sum, "Why are things the way they are rather than some other way?" Or, in the limit of disaffection from reality, "Why is there anything rather than nothing at all?" Under such conditions of abnormal disengagement the fact or facts of one's personal life do take on the air of "brute" facts. But with normal concern and hope, and with the resulting normal degree of participation, the fact and facts of daily life do not seem arbitrary and surprising.

So the sense of brute facticity is normal in scientific understanding and abnormal in the everyday understanding of reality. Which sense of reality is more fundamental, which more to be trusted? Is our everyday sense merely an unreliable impression, or our theoretical sense merely an elegant fiction? Both senses of reality seem too weighty to be discarded. One is right at this point to be at least as perplexed about such questions as about their answers. For the connection between the "brute facticity" of science and the "brute facticity" of ordinary disillusionment is not yet made sufficiently clear to demonstrate any conflict or contrast between the norms of scientific and ordinary understanding. The brute facticity of science is bound up, as we have seen, with the abstractness of its data. But ordinary disillusionment seems to have nothing to do with abstraction. So perhaps its brute facticity is not significantly related to that of science. Perhaps the "natural" facticity of normal (as contrasted to disillusioned) experience is quite compatible with "brute" facticity in the specifically theoretical sense. The matter is decidable only by discovering how sensuous abstractions are produced; how we turn from perceiving things of a certain sort to entertaining just their sort, just the qualities they display.[1] For the question whether there is a significant link between the two modes of brute facticity is the question whether there is some function clearly related to ordinary disillusionment and also clearly essential to sensuous abstraction.

I shall try to show that such a function does exist. The pervasive appearance of brute facticity in ordinary experience is effected, as we have seen, by a comparatively rough or complete

---

1. The question is philosophical, concerning the logic of the formation of sensuous abstractions; it is not psychological, concerning how we come to notice qualities initially given as such in sense experience. Kant, for example, considers sense experience to be initially given as sensation (*Empfindung*). For him the problem arises in regard to the constitution of appearance (*Erscheinung*) out of sensation. He treats the problem in the first portion of the subjective deduction of the categories.

disengagement from one's situation. Sensuous abstractions with their air of brute givenness are effected, I shall argue, by a mild, incomplete, and delicately controlled inhibition of the perception of the particular object having the abstracted sense-quality. The "standing back" which produces sensuous abstractions is not the spontaneous total disengagement of a Husserlian or Kantian transcendental attitude, which is required rather for the theoretical interpretation of these previously formed sensuous abstractions. Nor is it the forced total disengagement effected by a loss of reality which for early Heidegger discloses the pure sense of what is lost. It is rather a "standing back" of the *bodily* man who remains, however tentatively, in touch with his real material rather than detached from it. Conceptual abstractions are formed by the transcendental subject, but sensuous abstractions, I shall try to show, are formed by the embodied subject in the world, viz., the percipient.

Perception normally has three stages: (1) In the first stage we prepare ourself to perceive an object by getting into a proper position or attitude in respect to it. For example, we reach toward something so as to be able to touch it; we place something in our mouth so as to be able to taste it; we sniff to smell; we look and listen for something in order to see and hear it. (2) Having prepared ourself to perceive it, we next ready the object to be perceived. This is done by "getting at" the object in some essentially preliminary, tentative, and easily reversible way which allows us to test with comparatively light consequences the desirability of going on to fully perceive the object. For example, we touch something preparatory to taking hold of it; we taste before eating; we get a whiff of something before smelling it by taking in a deep breath; we look at or listen to something in order to see or hear it. (3) In the third stage we finally perceive the object. We finally "get" what we have "gotten at." We finally receive what we have made receivable by establishing an affinity between our readied self and our correspondingly prepared object. Thus eating is the consummation of tasting what we have put in our mouth; getting hold of something is the fulfillment of having reached for and touched it; seeing is the fruition of looking at something looked for; hearing is the successful outcome of listening to something listened for. The second stage, getting-at things, gives us evidence for tentative conclusions. But the real nature of the object is not fully established till the third stage of getting the thing itself. Taste is a guide; but the proof of the pudding is in the eating.

So perception is a form of motivated objectification having a natural terminus. But man is no more a slave to his nature in perception than in his other affairs. We make a frequent, enjoyable, and highly significant practice of holding back the course of perception so as to prevent its natural completion. We indulge in a kind of perceptual foreplay, stimulating our senses for stimulation's sake without regard to their natural end of consummation in the founding of an objectified reality. The sensualist makes this practice a way of life. As a gourmet, he does not taste to eat but eats to taste. Such preliminary tasting, when done unnaturally for its own delightful sake, is called "savoring." Similarly the unnatural sensualist-lover concentrates as long as he can on the dallying touch. Nor is the method restricted to the practical arts of the contact-senses of hand and mouth. It is equally central to the fine arts of the distance-senses of sight and hearing. Not only the grossest sensualists but also the most refined do it. For sight and hearing the method is practiced by retaining attitudes of looking and listening even after what is sought presents itself. Thus one hears sounds, but *listens to* music. And one sees things, but *looks at* paintings. One remains before a work of art in a state of sustained receptivity which at its fullest is wonder. This state of rapt attention is achieved by looking-at or listening-to things seen or heard with that attitude of attentiveness normally reserved for looking-for and listening-for things not yet seen or heard.

In all these cases of skillfully inhibited perception—perception carefully preserved, as it were, in a state of delightfully prolonged adolescence or immaturity—one becomes aware of *qualities* rather than things. Thus we ordinarily taste the food, but the gourmet savors the flavor. We ordinarily feel the thing, but the buyer may lightly stroke the fur to feel not it but its texture. To the aesthetic eye, similarly, a painting is not a material thing like what it is on but a pure surface of visual forms. And music is not listened to as a real sound made by real things but as a pure sound of tones and timbres sounding, as it were, by themselves. Savoring, stroking, looking-at, listening-to, and other forms of inhibited perception are "studied" ways of perceiving because they are ways of bringing out and noticing the forms of things while disregarding the things themselves.

So perception is a systematically achieved outcome of a multi-staged effort, and sensuous abstraction is founded on the inhibition of this effort. Sensuous abstractions must therefore be deficient in whatever intelligibility comes to experience from the completion of normal perception. What sense does come from the completion of normal perception? "I conceive x" is quite consistent with "X does not exist." The same is true for "I imagine x," "I desire x," "I intend x," etc. "I *perceive* x," however, is *in*consistent with "X does not exist." Acceptance of the latter statement requires correction of the former to "I *seem* to perceive x." "I remember x" also implies the (past) reality of x in all cases. But only if x is taken as *my previous consciousness of* something, rather than the thing itself.[2] Thus I may remember imagining y. This implies I really did imagine y, but it does not imply the (past) reality of y. Perception, I conclude, is essentially and distinctively our knowledge of the *existence* of existing things. Perception is perception of existing things *as* existing as what they are. This knowledge of the existence of things comes, however, only with the completion of perception and must therefore be lacking in all experience of sensuous abstractions. Since sensuous abstractions in the form of "data" comprise the only scientific evidence of matters of fact, the theoretical sense of facticity must be deficient in the same respect. Sensuous abstractions occur, we have seen, when the normally transient stage of anticipatory presence is maintained. Thus for theory, which

2. In the special case in which my previous consciousness was perceptual, memory does of course imply the reality of a remembered thing. But only because it implies the reality of a previous experience which in turn implies the reality of its object or referent. But essentially— that is to say, in the general case—memory is not of things but only of our consciousness of things; the existence of a memory does not imply the reality of past things but only of our past consciousness of things. Memory may then be regarded as the "perception" (because implying the reality of its object) of our past consciousness of things.

understands matters of fact only by way of such abstractions, facticity is understood in terms of the presence of a form (or sort) of possibility. But in perceptually rooted experience facticity is understood in terms of the complete presence of a particular actual thing.

Now the scientist is, of course, also a man. Though his perceptual knowledge cannot be cited as scientific evidence, it remains with him as his primary sense of reality. He understands facticity as "brute" facticity from a theoretical point of view only because he also understands perceptually that there is more to facticity than he can theoretically comprehend. Specifically he understands that the particularity and actuality of things, in general the "thisness" of things, systematically eludes his abstract comprehension. All perception is the coordinated knowledge of four particular actualities, four "thises": this thing in this local situation in this world as presented to this individual percipient. None of these "thises" is theoretically comprehensible. So theory assigns to "thing," "situation," "world," and "knower" a new sense which (as the price paid for a wonder-fully lucid insight into the nature of things) barters their natural facticity for a brute facticity. (1) The particular thing is understood as a purely logical, rather than real, conjunction of its properties. So its existence is entirely unfounded in its nature. (2) The local situation is the context of relevance in perception; it is the vehicle of perceptual comparison among distinct perceptual objects. The "constancy phenomena" of perception depend upon some pervasive character of the local perceptual field as a parameter in respect to which objects may be perceived to vary among themselves. Thus, for example, an object appears to be "bright" because it is *relatively* bright in a given field of illumination. But from a theoretical point of view the autonomy of a particular circumstance is as obscure as the particularity of a single object. So the form-alization of things is accompanied by a univers-alization of their context of relevance. Objects are theoretically interrelated not by constancy phenomena of local range but by formal laws of universal scope. The local situation as a context of relevance *within* the world is simply eliminated. (3) The world is perceived to be "the" world—that is to say, the one and only actual world. It is not perceived to be a sort or kind of world. For a "sort" admits of a variety of possible specifications, and things of a given sort are correspondingly variable. But the world is perceived to be the unconditioned, hence invariant, condition of all variable conditions in the world. Since the actuality and particularity of "this" world are theoretically unintelligible, the real world is conceived as one sort of world among many other equally possible worlds. The actuality of this possibilized world rather than another is then understood as a "brute" fact—that is to say, as ununderstandable. (4) Perception understands "this world" as the setting of all settings, the context of all contexts. But theory understands "this world" as one specific context among others, viz., the context of possibilities conforming to certain universal laws held to be, in brute fact, true of Nature. The role of the context of all contexts is then assigned to the knower himself in whose mind the various possible worlds are envisaged. But the knower has no content of his own. Theory leaves the existence of the knower's formally all-encompassing mind not merely unintelligible but unacknowledged.

The sensuous abstractness of theoretical data is associated with a "bruteness" of fact because sensuous abstraction is produced by inhibition of the perceptual consummation in which our intelligible sense of reality is founded. The "natural" contingency of perceptual things and events does not imply that their existence is *un*founded but only that it is *locally* founded in a certain highly skillful way.

Alphonso Lingis

THE ELEMENTAL BACKGROUND

For phenomenology, seeing is believing: phenomenology is profoundly positivistic. It takes philosophical understanding to be an operation that elucidates, that founds, that grounds, not by moving from the given fact to its cause, or to its reason, or to its premise, but by moving from the simply envisaged to the vision itself, from the intuitively empty to the intuitively fulfilled. In this philosophy the pursuit of reason, of the legitimizing, is the pursuit of the intuited.

This positivism requires and produces a rehabilitation of sensation. To be sure, phenomenology first shows that the notion of an intuition that is sensible has not been rendered intelligible through the notion of passivity. Sensation is not reducible to a manifold of impacts or impressions recorded on the passivity of the mental apparatus; the intentional analysis is the discovering of sense, of meaning, in sensible experience. The sensible experience is a veritable presentation of sense, of meaning; the sensation is the particularization of a configuration of meaning in a Gestalt. But the primordial dator intuition is also sensuous. This sensuousness of sensation is not just the opacity that makes meaning obscure and indistinct to a thought. It is what makes the intuited be there *leibhaft*, and in the original.[1]

What fulfills the intuition with sensuous *Leibhaftigkeit* is

1. Edmund Husserl, *Logische Untersuchungen*, Halle-sur-Saale, 2nd ed., 1921, II, 1, pp. 81–84.

brought forth out of the background or horizon into the high noon of optimal and plenary presence. The discovery of the operation of the background or horizon is one of the essential contributions of phenomenology. In this intuitionist philosophy it has come to play a role equivalent to that of the concept in classical philsophy. In order to understand the passage from the merely signified to the sensuously present we have to understand how the background operates, how it pro-duces, brings forth, the sensuousness of what fulfills intuition. What, then, is in the background of intuition? What is the background?

I. *The Background as a Fund of Objects and as Context*

Because intentional analysis is an explication teleologically proceeding toward the actualized intuition, it first discovers the background in the form of a horizon of nonactualized potentialities for intuition, upon which subsidiary intentions already open. It is a reservoir or fund of not yet evident objects of intuition.

As long as it is the mode of presence of the content of intuition that differentiates the background from the center, the background is characterized negatively, privatively, as the margin or fringe of the implicit, the inactual, the unclear, the indistinct, the inarticulate, the inadequately evident manifold of objects of possible intuition. Its sole positive determination is that it appears as an infinite or inexhaustible fund of objects. Husserl said that perception is ex-ception; to perceive is to extract a figure out of the background-fund of available figures. But the plenitude of the background is not diminished by what is extracted. The background extends beneath the figure: it is not interrupted, not limited by the figure.

In order to thematize the form and essence of the background as such, and no longer the mode of presence of its content, a certain liberation from the intuitionist teleology of natural consciousness is required. This yields a second stage of understanding of the background, where a functional relationship is discovered between the structure of the background and the very intuitability of the figure. The background emerges as the *context* of the intuited.

This means: (1) that not only a qualitative contrast in clarity and distinctness but also a difference in functional articulation, in coherence and cohesion, endows a figure with its own contours, and thus with its identity. (2) The figure maintains its intuitive identity across time because the background—and not the connecting operation of the synthesizing understanding nor an explicit memory—retains whatever is once given, or only portended, of it.

We thus come to understand that the high-noon visibility of evidence is not possible without the latency of the background. This is not simply the negative and privative contingency that but one object at a time would fill with plenary presence the limited diaphragm of a consciousness factically finite. It is that the figure owes not only its relief but its very identity to the occultation of the background.

The intuition, then, that aimed at the evidence of the figure finds itself—after the event—borne upon noematic horizons that have already anticipated its trajectory. It is for this that intentionality is openness upon being in the original: the being that already founds and bears the very intention that constitutes it. In the *Cartesian Meditations* [2] Husserl spoke of an "exceeding of the intention by the intention." The spontaneity of consciousness is borne by a founding passion which has no longer anything to do with the passivity of a given nature in consciousness or a facticity—but which is due to the very excess of its spontaneity. What is this prior possession of the horizon upon which the intuition itself is founded? Upon what more foundational passion is the intuition itself borne?

II. *The Background as a Field of Routes and as Void*

For Heidegger the cognitive intuition teleologically receptive of evidence is a founded mode of consciousness: founded upon *Umgang*—"concernful, circumspective dealings"—which is the

2. Edmund Husserl, *Cartesianische Meditationen und Pariser Vorträge*, The Hague, 1950, p. 84.

true primordial dator phase. It is in this phase that *Dasein* enters into the prior possession of the background of intuition. And it is, then, this phase that we must scrutinize to see how intuition is founded in its double structure, as exhibition of meaning and as penetration into sensuous materiality.

The background with which *Umgang* deals is revealed first as a field of routes, and secondly as void.

A. Heidegger's exposition of the background as a field of routes follows directly from his conception of the primordial form of the givenness of entities. In the primordial dator phase, prior to the intuitive and cognitive consciousness, what is given is not really objects, but *Zeuge*—gear. The *Zeug* is not fundamentally an instrument; it is not really defined by technical and axiological predicates. Rather its defining characteristic is a double openness. *Zeuge* are entities open to *Dasein* and open to one another. This double intrinsic openness is the minimum necessary for an entity to be able to emerge into the Open. It is open to *Dasein;* it is *zu-Handen,* open to the hand before the mind; it is within-reach. Secondly, *Zeuge* are open to one another: each *Zeug* leads to, gears in with, the rest, refers to the next, involves the next—such that one cannot emerge into the Open without a system, a referential complex emerging.

Thus the background is from the start veined with determinate routes along which *Zeuge*—equipment, gear—gear in with one another. Indeed the background is nothing but this system of *Um-zu* references, channels of assignation. But *Zeuge* are what they are only by opening upon one another: the form of the background therefore forms all possible mundane objects. The background now assumes a transcendental and no longer simply psychological role, and the passage of attention from the figure to the background is a veritable passage from the ontic to the ontological. The background formed by routes of involvement is an expanse preceding the form of objective space; it is an expanse of directions, not dimensions; of settings, not points; of itineraries, not lines; of regions, not planes; of routes, not distances. Likewise it is a sort of temporal expanse. A route differs from a line in that it leads to the future while it leads to the elsewhere; the *Zeug* in the distance gleams like something expected or hoped for. But this temporal cast is not the result of its being inscribed in the time taken as the constituted order of the succession of nows.

This field of routes is at the same time already the field of meaning, of significance; in it the ideal order is already inscribed. The background is the realm of ideas. . . . For beneath the order of meaning there is not first a register of facticity where particulars would occupy here-now sites univocally and would have to be connected with the synthesizing operation of the spontaneity of the mind. The particular is from the first open to the system, open upon system: involvement is its constitutive characteristic. Heidegger thus discovers a sort of radiation of things, which are there only by referring beyond themselves. The background is the very spread of their dimensionality, their involvement, their signifyingness.

What opens upon, and opens, this field is *Umgang*: a going round, a moving down the routes of the world, moved by concern and illuminated by *Umsicht*—circum-spection—that sort of looking round, looking about, that precedes cognitive perception. Heidegger thus discerns a "kinesthetic" substructure to intuition. It is a teaching already foreshadowed by certain texts of Husserl—in *Ideen II*, and in the text on the constitution of space edited by Alfred Schutz and published in *Philosophy and Phenomenological Research*,[3] where space was presented as an idealized order founded upon a prior intentional layer constituted in kinestheses. But this is absolutely not an empirical explanation of the ideal. For these kinestheses are no longer qualitative motor images of corporeal movement recorded or reflected in the immobility of subjectivity. In fact the real function of this introduction of movement into the very subjectivity of the subject is to anchor the idea of the submittedness of *Dasein* to the system it discloses. The routes of involvement open only in the measure that one travels those routes: it is only by traveling the route that the route is a route, and leads. *Dasein* is thus delineated not as a subjectivity whose ability to apprehend the form of objectivity as an infinite given magnitude expresses its own infinite distance from objectivity, but as a

3. Vol. 1 (1940), 21–37, 217–226.

finite ex-istence geared into the very system it opens, blazing the routes into the ground only in the measure that it is itself oriented by them. This structure of being oriented by, this essential submittedness to the very realm it constitutes, is the most fundamental trait by which the Heideggerian *Dasein* differs from subjectivity.

B. If the first characterization of the background as a field of routes answers to the "kinesthetic" substructure of intuition, *Umgang* is not only kinesthetic; it is "concerned"—it has an affective infrastructure. Our dealings along the routes of the world are concerned because it is affectivity—mood—that directly opens us to the background as such. For Heidegger, mood effects a radical transcendence prior to every intentional act; it is affective disposition: it discloses how one is affected, how one is disposed, with regard to the background. It discloses *Dasein* to itself as already affected by the Clearing of the world, already cast upon it, delivered over to the empty horizon of one's future and one's death. *Dasein* is the *lumen naturale* that *empties* the Clearing across which a spectacle spreads, about which a system of faces can phosphoresce. The background, first discovered as the skein of routes according to which *Zeuge* are open upon one another, is in its essence openness itself: void. The *Grund* is *Abgrund*: Abyss.

This extraordinary and highly original identification of the background with Nothingness is prolonged in the doctrine according to which *Dasein*'s absorption with entities, its concerned pursuit of the routes that lead from entity to entity, is interpreted as a flight from the Abyss. The finding oneself at home in the world is disclosed within the authenticating mood of anxiety as a flight from uncanniness, the being not at home here, which Heidegger asserts must be conceived as the more primordial phenomenon.[4] The falling of *Dasein*, its falling up against the proximate entities of everydayness, is thus explained in terms of the vertigo before void that propels *Dasein*.

How has this Heideggerian archeology of intuition founded intuition as apprehension of meaning in sensuous plenitude?

4. *Sein und Zeit*, 8th ed., Tübingen, 1957, p. 189.

In exhibiting the background not as a halo about the center of intuition but as a field of referential routes along which entities devolve in one another and signifiy one another, Heidegger makes us understand how the entities first given for intuition are already charged with sense (meaning).

At the same time the idea of founding intuition on *Umgang* —on concernful, circum-spective dealings—would seem to account for the sensuousness of intuition, without undermining the transcending intentionality of intuition by afflicting it with an immanent hyletic passivity. This is what was precisely not possible as long as intuition was taken as primordial, and the explanation for its fulfillment sought in subjectivity. Intuition, in its disinterested, immobile, nonmanipulative beholding, when founded on the idea of subjectivity, which in its position and its metaphysical constitution is defined by the op-position with which it posits ob-jectivity before itself, can be conceived as an intentionality that aims at objectivity across distance, across the distance constituted by its own nature. But in what sense subjectivity could be filled, fulfilled by the plenitude of sensuousness, cannot be explicated. Heidegger's idea of *Umgang*, with its kinesthetic infrastructure, is rather founded in the idea of *Dasein*, the idea of a Being that is there, that opens the routes of the ground only in the measure that it travels them. This approach leads toward an essentially new conception of sensation in which the meaning and the sensuousness involved are no longer analyzed in terms of the ancient categories of matter and form. It aims to make us understand that intuition is an *in*sight, movement into the density of things, penetration and involvement in them. Sensation, then, is not blurred thought, nor thought laden with passivity: it is an entry into the world. Thought posits; sensation penetrates.

In addition, the sensuous intuition is born in sentiment, inasmuch as the movement of *Umgang* is moved by, affected by, what its initiative will disclose. This is so because *Dasein* is out of its very being delivered over beforehand to the Abyss of the world, horizon of its future and its death. It is even this submissive attunement to the structure of the world that Heidegger finds at the ground of the conformity characteristic of predicative truth: the conforming of the statement to the state of affairs it states is possible, finally, because *Dasein* in its affective essence is tuned in and submitted to the world.[5]

Yet it seems to me highly doubtful that we have here a sound explanation for the sensuous structure of intuition. It is flamed first because for Heidegger transcendence is conceived as the very essence of disclosure. It is then doubtful that the Heideggerian affectivity is indeed affective. Mood discloses *Dasein* to itself in its dereliction, its being cast into and delivered over to the world. This peculiar form of self-disclosure, this immanent circuit characteristic of affectivity, turns out to be a specific type of disclosure of *Dasein's* past, its having been delivered over beforehand to the world.[6] But this means that the very tone of mood is being construed as a mode of transcendence, in the very sense in which, for Husserl, reflection is intentional and transcendence: the act that discloses is separated, by its very being, from that which it discloses, even though that which it discloses is a moment of the same temporal flux. Because the disclosure of *Dasein* to itself that occurs within affectivity is a disclosure across time, this disclosure is itself a mode of separation and a transcendence across a separation. But how is this affectivity and not comprehension; how is this a tone and not a view?

In other words, Heidegger does not tell us what is the *suffering* of anxiety. *Dasein* is, in anxiety, cast open upon its own being-there, upon its thrownness, its dereliction in the Openness of the Abyss. But because this revelation is a temporal ek-stasis, a specific type of openness upon *Dasein's* past, *Dasein* is brought into proximity with itself across a distance—the distance of time. It is senescence. But we cannot understand how it is sensuous.

The Heideggerian account is flawed, secondly, because the background upon which sentiment opens is void. *Dasein* flees in the face of itself, Heidegger says.[7] The fascinated movement from entity to entity that closes the diaphragm of open-

5. *Vom Wesen der Wahrheit*, 3rd ed., Frankfurt, 1954, pp. 18–19.
6. *Sein und Zeit*, p. 340.
7. *Ibid.*, p. 184.

ness and that characterizes everydayness would accomplish a
flight from the anxious apprehension of one's dereliction in the
openness of the world; the finding oneself at home here would
be a flight from uncanniness, the not being fully at home
here; fallenness is exposed as a flight from anxiety. This doctrine
is surely very strange. It is as though, then, the relaxation of
our everyday absorption with *Zeuge* would inevitably be a
relapse into anxiety, into the vertigo before void. But at the
end of the day and its cares, to loosen our frenzied concern with
everyday preoccupations is not to find ourselves once more
prey to the uncanniness of not being at home here; it is to be
received into the intimacy, the familiarity of finding oneself at
home.

I shall, then, in the final section of this paper, endeavor to
exhibit a format of the background that is not void, and to
exhibit, beneath intuition, a substructure of relationship with
that background that is not transcendence but a certain kind of
intimacy.

III. *The Background as Levels and as Element*

In order to thematize the positive consistency of the background and its operation, I propose first to introduce a conception of the background as a system of levels. We can find a
concept of a sensorial level at work in three places in Merleau-
Ponty's *Phenomenology of Perception:* in the discussion of vision
in the light, the distribution of spatial forms and dimensions, and
the segregation of motion and rest.

Let us consider the relationship between vision and the light.
There is a sort of field logic governing the distribution of
tones and hues in the visual field at each moment: a color can
segregate itself and condense into visibility—as a surface color,
or a color volume, or glow, or gleam, or haze—only in accordance with a general system of distribution at work in the field.
At the limit a color glow, or haze, or volume, functions no
longer as a certain color within the system and begins to function as illumination. Simultaneously it tends to the zero of
visibility, to the neutral, and the visible surfaces of the field
acquire color tone and density according to the degree and

modality of their divergence from this level of neutrality, as
sounds acquire a melodic position and direction in function
of the degree of their divergence from the tonic, which is no
longer a particular tone but the level at which the melody
plays.

What is the meaning of this becoming-invisible of the illumination? The illumination is a sensuous datum that no longer
holds the gaze, that effaces itself, that yields before the gaze,
that opens before the gaze. One does not see the light, but
according to, or with the light (this consciousness is not a
consciousness of . . . , but a consciousness with . . . , or according to . . .). The light leads the gaze and no longer holds it.
It is not understood by a mind like a law immanent in a pattern of distribution, but induces a certain movement of the
gaze. To look is to follow the light, is to move the gaze according to its directions and sense, to circumscribe the reliefs and
contours according as they are segregated by the *a priori*
action of the light.

There are, then, two senses to the "kinesthetic" substructure
of vision: (1) The free play by which the gaze sees by looking,
by displacing itself freely across the field. It is an intentional
movement because it can freely vary itself while maintaining
its objective fixed, and thus constitute its object as an ideal
pole of identity across the fluctuation of perspectives upon it.
(2) A lateral movement of concordance or attunement with
the level of the lighting, produced in a sort of sympathetic
vibration. But this second movement precedes and makes
possible the first. In order that there be vision it is not enough
that there occur the auto-nihilation by which the light, effacing
itself, empties the void about which a system of faces can
be ex-hibited; the light is not sensuous data nihilated, but
become dimensional.

We begin to perhaps understand, then, why it is that the
sole seer we know of is itself something visible, why the
being that is sensitive is itself something sensible. For the
sort of being that can be solicited by a sensorial level without
understanding it, that can be drawn by the light as it veers
from being a visible something to being a dimension or level,

can no longer be conceived by op-position to the being it posits before itself. The inaugural act of vision, then, is not the power of nihilation and of distance that inhabits our eyes inasmuch as they are the organs of consciousness, nor is it a synthetic or connecting power operating across the pure manifold given to sensibility, charging what is just sensorial matter with significance; the inaugural movement of vision is produced in that move by which the gaze, out of its own mobility, captures the scheme and level of illumination that command the articulation of a spectacle in gradients.

Just as the light functions as the level according to which colors are systematically distributed before the gaze, so also a system of levels governs the distribution of size and shape in appearances. Without a unilateral orientation of the spectacle according to verticality, horizontality, and depth, no coherent distribution of forms is possible. These axes are not given *de facto* within the empirical space of the body, which of itself has no unilateral orientation, and acquires one only inasmuch as it assumes a stance in a spatially coherent setting. Spatial axes function in the background that encompasses not only the objects of intuition but the body posited before them also. They are invisible in the sense that light is invisible; they do not function as a law we understand but as levels we join in the movement by which we rise to meet a spectacle.

But there are levels that command the exhibition of each thing. Each thing is recognizable only according to a certain orientation and itinerary; a photograph or a face explored in the reverse is no longer intuitively recognizable. This is intelligible only if we admit that the unity of a sensible thing is not constituted by collating its diverse sensory aspects in ascribing them to an ideal identity, that the unity of each thing takes form under the movement along a determinate itinerary that effects the merging of sensory facets. It is the movement of the gaze that effects the passage from one aspect to the next as it follows the reverberation of a smile across a face. Thus there must arise on each object certain fixed itineraries, certain orientations that solicit a determined movement of exploration. This is possible only if the things *open* forth in the very sense the light opens forth to illuminate: by veering into the background, where they function as pivots about which the gaze may turn, as levels along which there is gradation and differentiation of visibility.

In opening upon the background the gaze does not slip into void; it moves to join a positive system of levels, dimensional sensuous data, along which particulars—colors, forms, sizes, shapes, and surfaces—take form. And it is only in merging with the dimensional sensuous data, the levels, that the gaze can then intend objects across the particular sensuous data.

But there is yet another kind of positive plenitude in the background.

The Elemental. The light illuminates. Effacing itself, it empties space, and opens before the gaze, leads the gaze upon the exhibited relief of things. But also: the light shines. It is radiance, vibrancy, incandescence, phosphorescence. It is not about the illuminated like a context or a system of operational references. Nor is it the void before which anxiety trembles. In seeing, we enjoy the light. It has its own sensuous consistency. But its sensuous aspect is not an *Abschattung,* an adumbration of anything; it does not refer to other sensuous aspects that would confirm or undermine an ideal identity. On the other side of the luminosity of the light there is only the light: it is without profiles; it is nothing but depth. The light is quality that qualifies no thing, quality without substance, property without substrate, adjective without noun, content without form. This type of sensuous datum, irreducible to *Abschattungen,* I should like to name, following Emmanuel Levinas,[8] the Elemental.

Without profiles to eclipse other profiles, the elemental light is fully in the present, without inner horizons, without secrets. It is not at the term of a trajectory of intentionality intending the identity of objects across sensuous data; it is always at the beginning. It is not involved, not geared in with the referential system that delineates the world of *Zeuge.* There are no routes

8. *Totalité et infini,* The Hague, 1965, pp. 103 ff.

to the light; it is immediately there, it is too familiar to be found, it is not the object of exploration but of enjoyment. It neither approaches nor passes; it waxes and wanes. It is nothing but presence; it comes from no where. It is the incessance of oncoming; it is from the first as close to us as our own sleep, which comes by stealth and cannot be pursued through directions. It is there, unfounded, gratuitous, a chance.

Wholly presence and oncoming, there without routes nor surveyable, the light fills the void and obliterates its terror; the light is not disclosed in anxiety but in enjoyment. What is the specific trajectory of the intentionality of this enjoyment? While the cognitive intuition passes through the light as through nothing toward the things to be found in the light, a specific noncognitive intuition opens upon the sensuous as upon an end; it is the contentment that finishes in immediacy, in the plenitude of an expanse without distances. Here the intention does not exceed the intention; it does not exceed the finite sensuous datum toward the infinity of references inscribed as inner and outer horizon. Enjoyment is an intentional movement that is going nowhere, steeped in a medium coming from nowhere; its finitude consists in finishing in the present.

There is a like elemental presence of the earth; it was divined already by Husserl in a text of 1934.[9] The earth as a theoretical object is a globe, a planet. But the earth is also constantly present in the background of our sensorial experience, as the original reservoir of solidity and repose, upon which landscapes are at rest. Lacking profiles, its contours being impossible to encompass with our gaze, unexplored, it is not susceptible of becoming an object of perception. Its presence is elemental. It is not really in space, it is beneath space; it sustains everywhere the spread of a spectacle extended along spatial axes before our upright stance. It is not at a distance, and we approach it no more than we approach or quit our own body. Whenever we go we find ourselves here, on the one same earth. It is one without its unity being constituted in ideality

9. *Umsturz der kopernikanischen Lehre in der gewöhnlichen weltanschaulichen Interpretation. Die Ur-Arche Erde bewegt sich nicht,* May 7–9, 1934.

across perspectives. It does not spread across a perspective; it is always at the "here," the primordial "here," where we are. It is not in motion as objective bodies are, but not at rest either, for they are at rest by being supported on it, while it is supported on nothing further. It is pure depth of supporting solidity and repose, a property without substrate, a content without form. Its solidity is not the resistance of matter; it does not resist our effort, but on the contrary sustains every exertion. The relationship with the earth is not one of simple contact of mass upon mass, but involves an original intentionality of assumption of the repose of the elemental. It is a relationship enacted in our stance. To see an object is to have a point of view, to be oriented; it is to have a position that is an attitude, that is, to have a stance. We stand upright by conjoining the background as the system of levels of verticality and horizontality. But the firmness and support that qualifies our position, our stance, our movement, and our repose is the very mode of sensorial presence of the elemental earth. Its presence is adverbial: it modifies or qualifies, and is revealed by, our movement, our stance and our position before all objects. In assuming a stance we *enjoy* the support of the earth.

There is thus an elemental background to intuition. It is the depth of the earth, the atmosphere, the luminosity of the light, the muffled depth of sonority. If we hesitate to say that these sensuous phenomena have a "structure," at least their "format" awaits our elucidation.

The element is sensuous in an entirely new sense: it is not simple opacity, due to the significance of a thing being confused in the maze of its infinite references, or due to the consciousness being encumbered with inert hyletic matter within itself. This opacity obscures the consciousness without solidifying the things. Nor is it due to the affectivity by which the consciousness, that transcendence, would find itself in an immemorial past already submitted to the facticity of the world. The element is sensuous, and fills the routes by which the things are open, because it is simple presence.

Husserl tells us that the things are present *leibhaft* when they confirm the expectation of intentionality; present by incessant oncoming, the element is the plenitude of presence formed by no *a priori,* and thus filled beyond anticipation, beyond all expectation. This presence that neither approaches nor passes would be the primordial presence of the *Urimpression,* the self-constituting presence.

Sense is possible only if sensuous presence is taken as an *Abschattung,* across which ideality is intended. This is possible only if a minimal distance opens between the intention and its term. This minimal spacing is produced as a dephasing, when the intuition aims at its term across a sensuous datum that has already passed, that is only retained, that is now an *Abschattung,* an adumbration of something yet to come. To intuit objects is to take one's distance from the present; it is to age. In its senescence intuition separates itself from the absolute presence of sensuousness, and seeks sense, seeks things out of the incessant oncoming of the element.

Phenomenology has been unable to account for the density and thickness of things except as a maze of relational references that refer whatever is given to the infinity of possible profiles it already portends, and to the infinity of connections and routes that open forth from them. The objects of sensorial intuition do not just arise out of a system of references and involvements and out of meaning, and they are not just stages of routes. And they do not arise out of the nothingness of void. They take form in a medium. They are found immersed in an atmosphere, sustained by the solidity of the earth, bathed by the elemental light. They are *Dinge*—condensations of the elements. They are not just networks of relational predicates. They are not first *Zeuge;* they were first the elements of enjoyment.

Stephen A. Erickson

LANGUAGE AND MEANING

Discussion of a phenomenological approach to language is pregnant with intriguing possibilities. Not the least of these is the temptation to define such an approach dialectically—construing the phenomenology of language as a discipline which stands both *over against* and at the same time *beyond* linguistic analysis. That the phenomenology of language conceptually *can* and historically *will* attain this status, I believe, is true. But its concrete results at this stage of its development do not justify such honorific description. What I wish to accomplish within the limited context of this study is to suggest (a) some of the perils the phenomenology of language faces and (b) some of the promise to which these perils, when properly confronted, give rise.

My first point concerns the concept of meaning. Not only can we say that language "conveys" meaning and thus that a phenomenology of language is inseparable from a description of various sorts of meaning. We must also assert that it is primarily *extralinguistic* meaning to which language gives us access. In fact in terms of transcendental priorities, the meaning of (extralinguistic) entities and events, experiences and situations *precedes* the various meanings which find their metaphorical residence in our language.

Let me first comment on the weaker and twofold thesis implicit in this assertion, viz., that there is such a thing as extralinguistic meaning and thus, by implication, that there are at least two basic sorts of meaning, viz., the linguistic and the extralinguistic. Though this thesis may not sound controversial and may in fact sound perfectly harmless, there are some philosophers who would take great exception to it. Fortunately the phenomenology of language—here construed simply as a careful, straightforward *look* at the way language actually functions—comes to my aid. In ordinary language, the term "meaning" (and its variants) often functions in a way which supports my position—at least to the extent of admitting the existence of extralinguistic meaning. Consider the following examples:

1. She means everything to me.
2. For those with no background in industrial psychology, his decisions have very little meaning.
3. What do you take their presence to mean?
4. I found the [Paul] Klee exhibition quite meaningful.
5. The sacraments mean nothing to some churchgoers.
6. Just having the opportunity means a great deal to him.
7. A red light means that you must stop.
8. The meaning of those events was not yet clear.
9. Nature is much more meaningful to some than to others.

On the surface at least, meaning is here ascribed to such disparate items as persons, acts, paintings, religious rites, objects produced by modern technology, nature, and abstract entities. Meaning, in short, is ascribed to a wide variety of extralinguistic entities. Though commonplace, these statements do raise some difficulties for "ordinary language" and some other forms of linguistically oriented philosophy. Philosophers of these persuasions often assert, implicitly if not explicitly, that meaning has its exclusive residence in language, that meaning is a property of words or complexes of words, and that meaning is to be understood solely in terms of the roles various words play. But this simply will not do, as can be seen from an examination of language itself. If meaning is a property solely of language, the concept of meaning ought to be a metalinguistic concept and that alone. Rather than applying to items in the world, it ought only to apply to the language we use in talking about these items. If this is the case, the statements I have just offered, which embody the concept of meaning, are ill formed and terribly misleading. More particularly, the statements must be capable of being translated, as possibility-statements more successfully are, into what the philosopher Carnap and others refer to as a formal mode of speech. A translation of any of these statements into a formal mode of speech, however, presents all but insuperable difficulties. What these translations must produce are statements in which the term "meaning" is no longer predicated of—or ascribed by indirection to—the various entities mentioned in the original statements. The term "meaning" must in effect drop out of the straightforward statement made in the "object" language—the language by means of which we refer to extralinguistic items—and reappear, if it is to reappear at all, as a metalinguistic notion embodied in a metalinguistic statement which serves as a commentary on the (now modfied) object language statement. Quite clearly, however, this is a formula which licenses the abuse of ordinary language remarks. Such abuse, I believe, has grave philosophical consequences. Since our ordinary language remarks reflect the manner in which we experience the world, contrived modifications of ordinary language are bound to lead us away from our experience.

I turn now to the stronger, transcendental thesis, viz., that the meaning of (extralinguistic) entities and events, experiences and situations precedes the various meanings which find their metaphorical residence in our language. I construe this thesis to entail (a) that a gap exists between extralinguistic meaning and its linguistic appropriation, (b) that through our "creative" uses of language we are constantly trying to overcome this gap, and (c) that the phenomenology of language, in recognizing the existence of this gap, finds itself in a peculiar quandary, viz., that as a *phenomenology* of language it cannot but appeal to a prelinguistic, extralinguistic context if its descriptions of the functions of language are to be concrete and credible, but

that as a phenomenology of *language,* which proceeds by means
of the *use* of language, its appeal to this context can at best
be oblique.

No account of meaning other than this transcendental one
does justice to a number of phenomenologically accessible linguistic facts. Consider a few of the more obvious ones. With
changes in human attitudes and concerns come changes in the
quality and structure of human experience. The advent of
romanticism represented such a change, as did the development
of the therapeutic dimension of contemporary psychiatric
theories. Whether modifications in the pattern of human experience are cause, effect, or neither is of no concern. In any case,
in periods of transition, people, individually and in groups,
find themselves having to grope for words to *describe* their new
experiences. Old metaphors die, and new ones come to take
their place. Some phrases are found to be appropriate, others
inappropriate. This distinction cuts across the distinction between old and new uses of words, old and new words. In
periods of transition people judge the appropriateness of expressions in terms of the accuracy of those expressions with respect
to the experiences they are used to describe. In short, experience
itself, prior to its linguistic appropriation, serves as a (linguistically) mute criterion for its own decription. If meaning were
not in some respects antecedent to language, these obvious facts
could not be. Modifications in human experience, its description
and explanation, would be incomprehensible, and the (phenomenological) analysis of these modifications would be a curious
blend of convention and caprice. If meaning were not in some
respects antecedent to language, the labors of a number of
serious poets, scientists, and contemporary novelists would be
equally incomprehensible.

To be sure, linguistic phenomenology, that aspect of the
phenomenology of language which has as its task the careful
description and classification of the conceptual behavior of terms
as they function in various "language games," is an important
dimension of the phenomenology of language as well. The
fact that most of the significant work in this area has been
accomplished by philosophers of analytic persuasion should not

obscure this truth. But linguistic phenomenology is, after all, only a dimension of the phenomenology of language. In recognizing a prelinguistic human world of meaning, which language seeks to appropriate, the phenomenology of language opens itself to various aspects of human experience, which, I would argue, are basic to the fabric of human presence. Since Freud it has been seen, though not often enough by philosophers preoccupied with *linguistic* considerations, that *practical* action and the language which adumbrates, articulates, and expresses it are not necessarily fundamental with respect to the mechanisms of human agency and awareness. To reach the basic dimensions, I believe, is to reach something transcendentally fundamental, something which is at the heart of human presence. These basic dimensions, it seems to me, can be grasped by a linguistic phenomenology which (a) works within the broad context of the phenomenology of language and (b) resorts to certain nonpraxis-oriented linguistic paradigms. I wish to offer a few of these paradigms for your consideration—pointing out in the process that they are much more concrete and "practical" than our traditional philosophical notion of praxis. First, however, I need to make two parenthetical points.

The first concerns the doctrine—perhaps for some it has congealed into dogma—that "the limits of our language are the limits of our world." Given, if nothing else, the simple fact that the metalinguistic vocabulary of ordinary language recognizes the distinction between a real and a nominal definition, this doctrine is surely remarkable. When we hear it said that we cannot transcend the limits of our language, the term "language" is clearly being used in an unusual and speculative sense—not in an ordinary sense open to concrete analysis. Experience has given way to abstraction. This may all be for the good, but then the term "language" requires careful redefinition. I do not believe that such redefinition has been provided by expounders of this linguistically based variant of idealism.

My second parenthetical point is closely related. A standard argument *against* the view that we have access to extralinguistic meaning seems to me lacking in force. A philosopher holding this view is often challenged to state and describe those struc-

tures which transcend language. Once he has stated and described them, it is then pointed out that language was employed
in this process. Further grammatical parallels are exhibited which
are said to be the covert source of the characteristics attributed
to the presumed structures. Thus, it is argued, the structures are
not extralinguistic after all. It strikes me that this argument
simply fails to take seriously the consequences of ascribing intentionality to language. If language is, as philosophers claim,
intentional in nature and no items in the universe are in principle unknowable, then various structures should be describable
in language. Language should, in describing these structures
perspicuously, mirror their characteristics in some of its grammatical properties. This of course is not an argument for the
picture theory of meaning. If there are structures which get
expressed in language but are themselves extralinguistic, the
verification of their existence must perforce take one beyond
simple linguistic analysis. At this point material modes of
speech become necessary. This, I take it, is what primarily distinguishes the phenomenology of language as an enterprise from
linguistic analysis and makes phenomenology slightly more
empirical and in its methodological commitments less idealistic
in orientation.

I turn now to some nonpraxis-oriented linguistic paradigms.
Here I shall refer to *existential* uses of terms within certain
linguistic contexts. My use of the term "existential" is merely
for classificatory purposes. Consider the term "in." I suggest
that this term functions most straightforwardly and in the
most philosophically perspicuous way in statements such as
"John is *in* philosophy,'" or "George is *in* trouble," or "Ralph
is *in* love." I hold that existential uses of terms, such as the
use of the term "in" I have just illustrated, are paradigmatic.
Other uses I take to be extended, sometimes metaphorical, but
always more abstract applications of the terms. The consequences
of an unequivocal reliance on this view, I admit, are somewhat
peculiar. Presumably, for example, a perspicuous phenomenological comprehension of space and the spatial dimensions of
the human world is best gained through a careful study of
statements such as these:

They were never *close* to each other.
Keep in *touch*.
He's lost *contact* with himself.
He was *beside* himself with grief.
She was feeling *low*.
He had no *room* in his life for others.
She was rather *shallow*, but his thoughts were *deep*.

To understand space one must analyze the concept of space as an ingredient in one's discourse and experience. This I take to be a minimal and justifiable Kantian requirement. The requirement does not go far enough, however. One must also describe space as it is experienced prelinguistically—that is to say, space must be described with respect to those of its features which form part of the structure of one's world. If the conceptual behavior of spatial terms is to be clarified and understood, all sophisticated theoretical notions of space must thus in the end be related back to this experiential context of meaning, this transcendentally fundamental locus of human presence, which in large measure is prelinguistic. What follows from an espousal of this strategy is the relegation of more theoretical notions of space to secondary status. They might in fact be viewed as *abstract*, perhaps even metaphorical *extensions* of the concept of space. Even the statement "The chair is *close* to the window" must come to be understood to be an exemplar of a relatively abstract understanding of space—compared, for instance, to a statement such as "They are *close* friends."

And here I arrive at a major point I wish to make. The way in which men express themselves linguistically concerning space, I am suggesting, must be understood in terms of the model of the "closenesses" and "distances" of people from one another, and these notions, in turn, in terms of people's capacities for *openness* and their tendencies toward *closedness*. These latter notions, openness and closedness, are of course primordially *interpersonal* notions which have their locus in the intersubjective life-world of a community. In short, I suggest that in human experience, as reflected in our language, spatiality is first and foremost a means of establishing contact with, and setting limits to, the interaction between and among human beings. The data at our disposal as the result of the researches of various psychiatrists and anthropologists, it seems to me, establish this point rather convincingly.

But I must add a few qualifications and comments. First, to understand, say, Newtonian spatiality *in terms of* what I might call existential or interpersonal spatiality is neither to *reduce* the former to the latter nor to imply that, in some mysterious sense, the former really *"is"* the latter. Rather, it is to suggest that a proper *grounding* of spatial concepts, and of their corresponding experiential contexts, requires that these be construed as rising out of an interpersonal context of human communion, confrontation, and withdrawal.

Second, and rhetorically, why should spatiality be construed primarily in terms of the mileage to Chicago? Practical as such spatial measurements are, it seems to me that more practical *qua* primordial is the "distance" which separates me from myself and from others. This distance cannot be measured in miles, though I suspect it has a measurability of its own. I suggest that this sense of distance and of the term "distance" is fundamental in a transcendental sense. It creates the realm (*Spielraum*) within which and in terms of which my awareness operates.

I can perhaps illustrate the intimate connection between spatiality and the interpersonal and at the same time exhibit the dependence of language, both spatial and nonspatial, upon the interpersonal by means of a brief phenomenological description. What I shall describe is a man's response, put in the first person, to a situation in which he wishes to speak of himself, but feels that the other party is not interested in his remarks. I shall label this the experience of linguistic self-alienation. Its spatial overtones should be obvious.

> When the man turns his head away from me and glances out of the window, when he drums his fingers on the desk, when he fidgets with his folders and looks at his watch, I find myself losing contact with what it was I had wanted to tell him concerning myself. My voice becomes ever so slightly higher in pitch. I speak a little faster, and I feel as if I were

talking to and for myself—though not completely. I no longer hear distinctly nor comprehend fully what I am saying. I no longer know exactly what it was I wanted to say. The man is not sympathetic, for that matter not even open to me, so it seems at least, and suddenly—no, perhaps it is gradually—I find that I am closed off from myself. To be sure, I can say what I intended to say if I had thought it out beforehand, but when I say it, I fail to feel its force. It comes out mechanically. I do not grasp the meaning of my own remarks. I experience a disorientation with respect to myself. Neither does what I say seem to belong to me, nor do I seem to relate to it. I find myself alienated, as it were, from the very language in which I express myself. The words I speak are "there" before me, but I do not find myself in these words. Oddly enough, what is said comes as somewhat of a surprise to me. It is as if someone else were speaking. Not that I usually think out what I say before I say it, but what I say usually does not surprise me. There is an element of unreality to my remarks, and in the room the objects I view, particularly the man, waver ever so slightly. My world begins to shrink.

I might sum up my brief remarks concerning space in this way. Take the following two statements: (a) The chair was *close* to the wall, and (b) They were *close* to each other— close to each other in the sense of being close friends. Statement (a) exemplifies a quantitative conception of space; statement (b) a qualitative, though no less "measurable" conception. Clearly the same set of concepts cannot be used to explicate both statements. The phenomenology of language, I would argue, ought to take statements of the (b) type more seriously than has so far been done in philosophy, analyze them and the experiences they articulate, and forge meaningful conceptual means of sorting out the significant interrelations of the phenomena intended through these statements. By doing this a proper transcendental foundation will be laid for the phenomenon of spatiality.

Time, no less than space, needs to be analyzed more existentially—in both its linguistic and its extralinguistic dimensions. Consider ordinary language statements such as these, together with the extralinguistic situations they adumbrate:

He lives in the *past*.

The *past* weighs heavily on her.
The *past* had engulfed him.
Having no *future* in the firm, he tendered his resignation.
Some people live too much in the *future*.
It is difficult to live in the *present*.

Though in each of the first three statements a chronological—that is to say, clock-measurable—interpretation of "past" is possible, an existential interpretation is possible too. The latter interpretation is philosophically most suggestive. A man "living in the past" need not be characterized as a person whose attention is for the most part directed toward events having transpired chronologically prior to the time they capture his attention. He may be a man the focus of whose concern is the chronological present, yet who deals with this present as if the same conditions determined it as determined situations whose temporal locus is in the chronological past. A similar analysis of the second statement is equally plausible. For the past to "weigh heavily on one" may be for the *effects* of the chronological past upon one's "world" to constrict one's comprehension and response to events and situations in the chronological present. A strict chronological interpretation of "past" in this statement, in fact, is conceptually implausible. It suggests that chronological time can accumulate on a person in much the same way that dust accumulates on a windowsill. A past which "engulfs one," finally, may be construed as a set of continuing effects of a chronological past, which bring about cognitive and volitional paralysis in the chronological present.

In neither of the two statements which employ the term "future" is a chronological—that is to say a clock-measurable—interpretation of "future" plausible, if taken as exhaustive. An existential analysis, though not sufficient, is clearly necessary. This analysis, clearly, involves both a description of experiences of lived time and a linguistic consideration of the terms which adumbrate these experiences.

Consider finally the statement: "It is difficult to live in the present.'" A chronological interpretation of this statement is conceptually absurd. From the standpoint of clock-measurable time there is no other temporal place in which one can be.

Even the term "present," thus, together with the experiences it adumbrates, is not amenable to exhaustive analysis in chronological terms. The experience of lived time, in short, is reflected in our living language. And an existential interpretation of various dimensions of time, both linguistic and extralinguistic, is unavoidable. To say that such dimensions are "metaphorical" gets us nowhere. It is to close one's mind to a set of important, transcendental philosophical problems. And time and space, of course, represent just two examples.

Clearly detailed descriptions and analyses of various praxis-oriented phenomena which are reflected everywhere in our ordinary language—and an examination of the manner in which ordinary language reflects these phenomena—is a significant and, if my intuitions are correct, transcendentally fruitful domain for investigation. The phenomenology of language, I believe, is uniquely equipped for this inquiry. Its results ought at the very least to be provocative.

Don Ihde

LANGUAGE AND EXPERIENCE

A problem for methods appears in a dialectic of phenomenology and linguistic analysis. This problem revolves around the *relation of experience to language*. I believe that in relation to this problem phenomenology and linguistic analysis display inverted models in which the countervalues of each method point to a naiveté area in its opposite.

In such a dialectic, however, a third consideration is presupposed, the working assumptions or hypotheses of the dialectic itself. I begin by stating these:

I am not sure that I know what language is. But I am relatively sure that proponents of linguistic analysis *think* that they know what language is and judge both phenomenology and the attempts to deal with experience upon this basis. I am not sure that I know what experience is either. But I am relatively sure that the proponents of phenomenology *think* that they know what experience is and judge language and analytic attempts to deal with language upon this basis.

Thesis #1: The methodological bases of phenomenology and linguistic analysis begin with inverse weightings of an essentially paired phenomenon, *language-experience*. The methodological drift of phenomenology is to begin with experience and attempt to deal with language from a description of experience in its movement toward expression. The methodological drift of linguistic analysis is, to begin with, a description of language and its structure from which experience is to be understood. These counterweightings are not neutral and lead to further consequences in relation to the paired experience-language phenomenon.

This thesis implies a further presupposition concerning the pairing of language and experience. Can one assume such a pairing? Although I shall not attempt to exhaustively justify this presupposition some support is called for. I find, when I am phenomenologically inclined (which is most of the time), that:

> Experientially I do not know what a prelinguistic experience is, since I already exist and am conscious in a world which is already immersed in language and one in which all my thinking is at least necessarily if not sufficiently linguistic in one of its forms. All my attempts to reach a total reduction to a prelinguistic world fail, and I cannot find such a "pure" experience.

And when I try to follow the analytic counter-method I find:

> Linguistically I do not know what a nonsubjective or nonexperienced expression is, since all speech acts occur in an experience-world which is a constant of my linguistic performances or is implied by all known linguistic formulations.

Thus the thesis which pairs experience and language may be stated both negatively and positively.

Thesis #2: There is no inexpressible experience. If there were, the implication would be an opting for *mysticism* in which the last word is silence but which is always belied by all forms of mysticism in the proliferous and indirect ways of describing silence. All silence may be described.

There is no expression without experience. If there were, the opposite of mysticism would be a crude *mechanism* in which the last word is the nonintentionality of a machine. Yet all machines are at least the indirect extensions of a very creative intentionality and experience, that of their inventors and programmers. If these persons prefer to model their minds upon their embodied contructs and ignore their prior "God role," they should not belie what comes first in the order of being both logically and chronologically. Positively: *Language and experience must be dealt with together as the paired foci of the single ellipse of subjectivity.*

Dialectics: The Inversion of Methods

The first moment of a dialectical movement toward the understanding of language and experience is one which locates limits to the theories which deal with the two foci of this paired phenomenon.

Phenomenology as a theory of experience: The phenomenological claim, "to the things themselves," is a theory of evidence in which the weighting of evidence finds its fulfillment in (immediate) experience and more particularly, in the late Husserl and much so-called existential phenomenology, in perception. Even if this immediacy is arrived at reflectively and thus indirectly rather than by simple introspection, the goal of phenomenology remains a pretheoretical and basically perceptual world. To secure this evidence the whole of the epoche and the phenomenological reductions are used to remove all factors which would obscure the richness of that experience.

The method is thus regressive in its direction, and attempts, layer by layer, to remove the secondary or tertiary series of presuppositions or beliefs which cover over or distort the original phenomena of pretheoretical experience. The suspension of the "natural attitude," the overcoming of abstractions and constructionist reifications, etc., all fall in this process of removal which successively reveals the naivetés and errors involved in taking theoretical constructs for experience itself. If experience is to be described in its richness, such a reduction of presuppositions, but not of experience, is necessary.

But such a method involves a circle which may be shown by an ambiguity which covers the idea of experience. In a broad sense, not only the basic perceptual life-world is experience, but the very presence of the theories, reified or not, constitutes part of experience. In this context phenomenology as a theory is itself the circle of experience within experience and its reductions are the arranging and valuing of how this global situation is to be understood. Within the circle of experience relative values are placed upon what is basic (the life-world or perception) and what is secondary (constructions).

This internal weighting of experience in relation to experience creates an effect in relation to language. With the primary weight upon a pretheoretical experience, language becomes secondary and is understood as a mediating function. In relation to language, the pretheoretical experience is termed prelinguistic, and phenomenology concentrates upon the movement from experience to expression. Language is understood to mediate experience.

The circularity of experience with experience within phenomenology is a recognition of a fate common to all theories and in itself is to be taken neither as a negative nor as a destructive criticism concerning the productivity of phenomenology. But by beginning from this internal circularity of experience with experience, the implication for language may be better understood. The implication is one which not only makes language secondary to experience but also tends to allow phenomenology to assume certain language functions. The way in which this effect occurs may be indicated in two examples:

a. Beginning students in phenomenology usually undergo what may be characterized as a sense of discovery. When they first begin to operate phenomenology as a philosophical method and attempt to describe their own experience phenomenologically, they are often struck by the complexity and richness of those experiences. But equally interesting are the linguistic effects of this operation in terms of what may be described as a *struggle with language*. Almost without exception the student reports variations of an "I-mean-more-than-I-can-say" phenomenon. And through the struggle with language the student begins to weave metaphorical statements, create neologisms, or even turn to quasi-poetic or literary forms to describe the newly discovered fullness of experience.

Nor is this discovery limited to students, since what they do is a repetition of what often occurred earlier in the work of the masters. Need I point to the predominance of newly coined terms and words which have emerged in phenomenological literature, which, save for their familiarity to us now, must appear clumsy: "being-in-the-world," "owned" or "lived" body, "incarnation," etc.? And the well-known turn of particularly existential phenomenologists to literary forms is not without reason.

I am implying that the very weight of (immediate) experience in phenomenological theory makes this a first operational outcome. But this outcome affects the phenomenological theory of language as well.

b. When one turns to the phenomenological literature on language, it turns out that most of it is a phenomenology of speech or of expressing. The emphasis is placed upon the genesis of an expression as it arises from the "prelinguistic" experiential basis (variously thought of as gesture, Merleau-Ponty; silence, Heidegger; or poetic symbol, Ricoeur). This emphasis is not accidental but a result of what the theory weights from the beginning. It is the intention to signify, the struggle with bringing experience to expression, the *vouloir-dire* of the speaking subject which seems to take precedence. The first move of a phenomenology of language is modeled upon its theory of experience.

Again, I do not wish to disparage this attempt—in fact, I praise it insofar as the phenomenological rediscovery of the richness of experience is a gain over the usually sparse or constructed notions of experience found in empiricist and most nonphenomenological accounts. But at the same time the selective weighting of experience over expression creates a naiveté area in phenomenological vision.

This limitation is most dramatically pointed up when the inverse method of linguistic analysis is placed dialectically up against a phenomenology of expression. (Note in passing that an inversion may indicate the opposite side of a single phenomenon so far as method is concerned.) This counterweighting in linguistic analysis may be displayed in reverse order by noticing that the phenomena which tend to take precedence in analysis belong to the class of "I-don't-know-what-I-mean-until-it's-said" phenomena.

First, examples: If I undertake to write a book or an article

I sometimes find something unusual going on. I make a decision about what is important and attempt to follow out the thought, only to find that the thought has a "life of its own," a "logic," which appears to me. This becomes more dramatic if, on the following day, I undertake to vary the decision even slightly and I find it necessary to almost totally revise what I had previously written. Experienced persons know very well that it is dangerous to attempt revisions and that to change a paragraph may mean to change a book. Need I point to the furious arguments which occur over differences in first as against second editions? It is a language phenomenon of this type which may be seen behind Wittgenstein's "Roughly, understanding a sentence means understanding a language." [1]

To get at these phenomena the linguistic analyst creates a different weighting of evidence. He suspends or suppresses immediate experience and plunges into a circle of language, the analysis of langue by means of a second use of language. This circle which weights first or ordinary uses as prior to analytic or secondary uses is a counter-reduction compared to phenomenology. Austin says, "Ordinary language is *not* the last word: in principle it can everywhere be supplemented and improved upon and superseded. Only remember, it is the *first* word." [2] From his point of view, experience, which becomes secondary, is structured via language. Through the increased sensitivity to the "logics" and complexities of language he better understands experience. Again Austin: "When we examine what we should say when, what words we should use in what situations, we are looking again not *merely* at words . . . but also at the realities we use words to talk about: we are using a sharpened awareness of words to sharpen our perception of, though not as the final arbiter of, the phenomena." [3]

Thus the struggle which emerges is a struggle with the complexities of language through which a sharpened awareness of the structuring of experience may be had. In the process the

1. L. Wittgenstein, *Bluebook in Philosophy in the Twentieth Century*, Vol. II, New York, 1962, 714.

2. J. Austin, "A Plea for Excuses" in *Classics of Analytic Philosophy*, New York, 1965, p. 386.

3. *Ibid.*, p. 384.

linguistic inversion finds the other side of the experience-language phenomenon to reveal the same investigatory excitement originally noted with students of phenomenology.

As the analyst looks at language he discovers a previously unnoted wealth and complexity. "But I owe it to the subject to say, that it has long afforded me what philosophy is so often thought, and made, barren of—the fun of discovery, the pleasures of co-operation, and the satisfaction of reaching agreement." [4] Language is discovered with an unexpected fullness which continues to point up the "I-don't-know-what-I-mean-until-it's-said" phenomenon.

The analyst is finally led to allow his own "bracketing" to remain in effect and to see the turn to language as the structuring of even the most complex experiences. Language, as experience, is rich so that, as Austin indicates,

> . . . the distinctions embodied in our vast and, for the most part, relatively ancient stock of ordinary words are neither few nor always very obvious, and almost never just arbitrary; that in any case, before indulging in any tampering on our own account, we need to find out what it is that we have to deal with; and that tampering with words in what we take to be one little corner of the field is always *liable* to have unforeseen repercussions in the adjoining territory.[5]

The second use of language in analysis finds the same difficulty which the phenomenologist finds. The struggle to describe language leads to "performatives," "behabitives," "illocutions," etc. As a field the world of language evidently displays parallel problems to what the phenomenologists call experience. In short, the analytic turn to the richness and strength of language, particularly in its directive or structuring power, is already a latent "phenomenology" of language as contrasted with a phenomenology of expressing. The linguistic-analytic reversed reading of the language-experience phenomenon allows this to stand out.

The choices of phenomenology and linguistic analysis remain inverted to the extent that different phenomena are developed in relation to the different weightings of the language-experience

4. *Ibid.*, p. 379.
5. J. Austin, *Sense and Sensibiliia,* New York, 1964, p. 63.

phenomenon. But both must be re-joined for a philosophical understanding of language and experience.

Where, then, does a dialectic of inverted methods lead? For me, back to the initial hypothesis concerning a need to maintain that language and experience are paired phenomena. I could suggest that even the minimal alternation of a phenomenology of expression with the analysis of ordinary language leads somewhere. The student of phenomenology who finds difficulty in his struggle to give birth to language would do well to take Austin's advice and turn to the dictionary, to legal distinctions, to psychology, and—I would add—to literature. There he would find an already extant wealth often unsuspected by the philosopher. Counter-wise I probably need not mention that the inverse side of this investigation is the analyst's need to look again to the experience of expressing and referring itself if he wishes to understand the why of linguistic wealth.

So my argument makes its own circle, and the end is the beginning which wants to presuppose that language and experience are paired. But it is a beginning in another sense, a beginning which is in keeping with a return to the early Husserl. If—as Paul Ricoeur points out, "In Husserl's first works . . . consciousness is defined not by perception, that is to say by its very presence to things, but rather by its distance and its absence. This distance and this absence are the power of signifying, of meaning. . . . Thus consciousness is doubly intentional, in the first instance by virtue of being a signification and in the second instance by virtue of being an intuitive fulfilling. In short, in the first works, consciousness is at once speech and perception" [6]—then in my terms, subjectivity is always at once language *and* experience.

6. P. Ricoeur, *Husserl: An Analysis of His Phenomenology*, Evanston, Illinois, 1967, p. 204.

Robert Goff

APHORISM AS *LEBENSFORM*
IN WITTGENSTEIN'S *PHILOSOPHICAL*
INVESTIGATIONS

I

This paper is about Wittgenstein's writing, but it is not about
Wittgenstein's style. It links the term "aphorism" to Wittgenstein's term *Lebensform*, form of life, but it does not maintain a
distinction between style and meaning. The distinction between
style and meaning, a distinction under which aphorism is regarded as a linguistic strategy aimed at the expression of certain
meanings, has been applied to Wittgenstein by several commentators. Single sentences of his, like "Whereof one cannot
speak, thereof one must be silent," or "Don't regard a hesitant
assertion as an assertion of hesitancy," or "To use a word without
justification does not mean to use it without right" have been
called aphorisms, and in acquiring this label they seem also to
have become isolated from the rest of their author's language.
Those commentators who have called these sentences "aphoristic"
hold that aphorism is a tool of style and that it may safely be
ignored by the philosophical interpreter. Such failure to attend
to Wittgenstein's *use* of language lies behind explanations which
assign the difficulty of his language to his "mystical" temperament, and it is by means of these explanations that anyone
who is accustomed to leaving matters of temperament to a

department of psychology is then free to substitute his own use of language for Wittgenstein's.

In what follows we allow a philosophical sense of aphorism to emerge instead of superimposing aphorism as a stylistic category. What we are doing has been begun, or at least suggested, by Erich Heller in "Wittgenstein and Nietzsche," [1] by Ingvar Horgby in "The Double Awareness in Heidegger and Wittgenstein," [2] and J. P. Stern in a chapter on the philosophical aphorism in his study of Lichtenberg.[3] Our work with Wittgenstein's use of language would bear comparison with an exhibition of the language of limits used by Franz Kafka and with an exhibition of the language of transformation employed in the philosophical parables of Jorge Luis Borgés. Also, what we are able to show about Wittgenstein's language may suggest comparison with metaphors which comprise the metalinguistic vocabularies of Heidegger and Merleau-Ponty.

Wittgenstein is widely known for statements to the effect that "the meaning is the use" (e.g., # 43). It may at least be gathered from such statements that he would have wanted his own meaning to be found embodied in his use. The sense of aphorism to be developed in this paper grows out of an exhibition and description of his use of language. Our approach recognizes, then, that Wittgenstein places upon himself the requirement that his statements about linguistic use must be borne out in his own uses of language or, negatively, the requirement that his language must not escape the direction and field which it establishes. His language is in some way "about itself."

Not only may certain of his uses of language be about themselves, but also all the reflections of the *Philosophical Investigations* taken together may be about themselves. The chief way that Wittgenstein's later work is reflexively about itself is by representing philosophy as an activity within a linguistic continuum. This may be shown with quotation and

1. *The Artist's Journey into the Interior and Other Essays*, New York, 1965.
2. *Inquiry*, II, No. 4 (1959).
3. *Lichtenberg: A Doctrine of Scattered Occasions*, Bloomington, Ind., 1959.

paraphrase of the language of the *Philosophical Investigations*. Wittgenstein says that his philosophy will "destroy houses of cards" (# 118) *and* that it will leave "everything as it is" (# 124). This expresses confidence in a natural relationship between the critical and the conserving role of philosophy. What it really is that is torn down and what really allowed to remain is not asserted, but other passages provide a clue. Philosophical problems, Wittgenstein says frequently, are like a disease, and philosophers are people who are most prone to it: the results of philosophy are malformations due to the excess of a one-sided diet (# 593), the terms of philosophy are thereby useless superlatives (# 192), and philosophers are users of a language that can bewitch (# 109), creating mindless compulsion (# 299) and regressive savagery (# 194). But in spite of all this, philosophy may be therapy, a way to health and freedom from compulsion (# 133, # 254, # 255), and Wittgenstein says that philosophical activity can give the philosopher rest from torment by yielding the capacity to stop doing philosophy (# 133). Philosophy is reflexive in that it finds itself to be its own raw material, its own intermediary, and its own cure. And the reflexiveness here is linguistic. The beginning point of philosophy is characterized by loss of engagement and direction in the use of language: "A philosophical problem has the form: 'I don't know my way about'" (# 123). Philosophers in this condition respond with a fascination for the fixed and the ideal, and they begin to act as though the city of language has only straight, regular streets and uniform houses (# 18). Wittgenstein maintains that the city of language has an old town with streets, houses, and squares in many styles as well as new boroughs with different sorts of regularity.

The idea here is that one finds oneself, one's direction, in the use of language. With his use of certain terms Wittgenstein claims the success of his philosophical therapy and his achievement of what he speaks of as the familiarity of the "everyday." The terms which signal the achievement include "language-game," "description," and "form of life." The famous term "language-game" is used against the requirement that any meaningful language must be an instance of a single use of language. Saying that we play games in language leaves open questions about the kinds of play and their relations. Wittgenstein's characteristic response to the regressive demand for the criterion for the rules of our language-games is that we often play games without knowing their rules and that there are many cases of play that do not exhibit what we could call "rules." In a similar way the term "description" satisfies Wittenstein as a resolution of doubts about criteria for meaning. He says that what "we" (as therapeutic philosophers) do is describe the use of language and not explain it (# 109). He links description to the restoration of the familiarity of language-in-use, and explanation to the fixing tendency of metaphysics. To demands for final standards for the accuracy of descriptions he replies that failure to establish final standards does not prevent the act of justification from ending somewhere: "What people accept as a justification—is shown by how they think and live" (# 325). Just as games are played without playing the game of rules, descriptions can portray without making use of justification. What remains when the search for rules, criteria, and justification loses its point is the form of life (e.g., # 19, # 23, # 211, # 217).

We are not trying to bring a final end to the numerous discussions and disagreements about what Wittgenstein means by terms like "language-game," "description," and "form of life." We simply note that his use of the terms throughout the *Philosophical Investigations* shows that he was able to use language as if his therapy were working, as if release from fixation and compulsion into freedom in the use of language were possible. Our understanding of the success of this acting-as-if depends upon our recovery of the linguistic uses which support Wittgenstein's use of "game," "description," and "form of life." Or, if we may do with these terms what we suggested for the term "use," and regard them as reflexive, what we are interested in is his game, his self-description, and his form of life.

II

We now turn to close scrutiny of Wittgenstein's use of language. Of particular interest is the way his language can be about the use of language, i.e., the way it can be reflexive and self-grounding. We have chosen only three examples, but each of them may be taken as paradigmatic of much of the *Philosophical Investigations*. With each of the examples we will find that reflexive meaning lies beneath the surface, beyond the literal and the commonplace. The first is language about the use of paradox. The second is language about the language of selfhood. The third is language in which forms of selfhood may be found embodied.

For our first example, here is Wittgenstein's use of language in a paradoxical recommendation: "Always get rid of the idea of the private object in this way: assume that it constantly changes, but that you do not notice the change because your memory constantly deceives you" (Part II, page 207). The idea of the private object serves the same need as the quest for a particular standard of meaning.[4] In the *Philosophical Investigations* someone's appeal to a unique and incomparable inner state, as in the statement "Only I can know 'my pain,'" defends a certain attitude toward language, an attitude in which uses of language are found to be determined by antecedent criteria such as states of mind, essences, or objects. The general approach followed in the *Philosophical Investigations* is an entertaining of the linguistic uses which employ states of mind, essences, or objects, and this of course dissolves into linguistic use what was thought to determine it from "outside." The function of dissolving and its means of attainment are important here: Wittgenstein often says that philosophical questions are not so much solved as dissolved (e.g., # 133). In terms of the present example this means that philosophical treatment of the idea of the private object should not amount to replacement of the idea with another one. The goal is to remove metaphysical compulsion, and not merely to

4. Note the use of "particular" in passages like # 173.

give it variety. Accordingly, the lines quoted must be taken to recommend a *procedure* for getting rid of the "idea of the private object" and not taken as requiring the necessary elimination or reform of a certain language. Wittgenstein says about his work: "In giving all these examples I am not aiming at some kind of completeness, some classification of psychological concepts. They are only meant to enable the reader to shift for himself when he encounters conceptual difficulties" (Part II, page 206). Let us examine the paradoxical use of language for a key to the method of enabling wherein one comes "to shift for himself."

The language quoted recommends the paradoxical stance of regarding oneself both as a speaker about an "object" which constantly changes and as a speaker about one's memory as constantly deceiving. The paradox works as follows: The user of the language of private objects, like most of us, is able to speak of an object which is changing. And he is also able to speak of his memory deceiving him. But putting these two ways of speaking together has a strange effect. It restores the status of the private object by saying that its changing is not noticed. But what change is it that is not noticed? A *constant* changing. And why is it not noticed? Because the memory *constantly* deceives. So the apparent restoration of the private object also shows it to be groundless because the means of the restoration, the constant changing which is not noticed because of a memory's constant deceiving, has no use in language. "Object" loses meaning (and use) when it is spoken of as constantly changing, and "memory" loses meaning (and use) when spoken of as constantly deceiving.

The route covered in the paradoxical use of language is from language that is "about" something—e.g., about states of mind or things of one kind or another—to language which is about the use of language. We may say that the route is from "mere" language to reflexive language. The "mere" language is that which is disengaged in a way that permits talk of objects changing and memories deceiving *alongside* talk of private (incomparable) objects. The reflexive language is the language which subjects language to itself, which subjects the speaker's language about the privacy of an object to the comparisons he makes in speaking that language. The language of privacy, which maintains the authority of an inner state as a criterion of meaning and which therefore requires an assumption of constancy and fixity, is subjected to the comparisons which support its use. In the present case, these comparisons are of objects that are fixed with objects that can change and of memories which deceive with those which do not. Wittgenstein's use of language suggests that the meaning of "constant" includes "comparability with 'changing'" and that "comparability" means "usable in relation to." The nonsense that the paradox issues in arises from the experience that the fixity of the private object has no use—in order to talk about it we must use language as if we were not using it, i.e., we must make comparisons which deny the possibility of comparison. In the example this means speaking of objects that are not objects —they constantly change—and memories that are not memories —they constantly deceive. The *use* of paradoxical language begins with a language that is only apparently in use. And it moves through a language that cannot be used because it maintains uses that cannot be significantly related. Finally, it yields a new use in which, through reflexive meaning, language comes to embody its oppositions, thereby exhibiting the philosophical comprehension of paradox.

Let us move to the second of Wittgenstein's uses of language that we shall consider. He reaches a point which he describes as "paradoxical": the attempt has been made to define consciousness, and in the course of the attempt a conflict emerges between the view which sees consciousness as an inner process in the brain and a view which does not see it that way. The "paradox" is expressed in the exclamation uttered while one clutches his forehead: "*This* is supposed to be produced by a process in the brain!" (# 412). Wittgenstein then notes William James's definition of the self as consisting "mainly of peculiar motions in the head and between the head and throat." He comments that James's introspection showed: "not the meaning of the word 'self' (so far as it means something like 'person,' 'human being,' 'he himself,' 'I myself'), nor any analysis of such a thing, but the state of a philosopher's attention when he says the word 'self' to himself and tries to analyze its meaning. (And a good deal could be learned from this.)" (# 413).

The significant thing about James's definition of "self," says Wittgenstein, is not the meaning it appears to assign but the state of a philosopher's attention when he considers matters of selfhood. The philosophical state of attention is not, therefore, an ordinary state of attention, but one which is revealed in the more or less extra-ordinary language about selfhood consisting of peculiar motions in the head. This difference between philosophical and ordinary states of attention is not the same as the difference between the form of attention which saw consciousness as a brain-process and the form which did not. Each of these latter forms of attention claims that consciousness, or selfhood, is subject to a single form of attention. The philosopher's state of attention, which is revealed when he says that the self consists of "peculiar motions," refuses to subject selfhood to a single form of attention. In his next paragraph Wittgenstein characterizes the nonphilosophical form of attention which insists upon the exclusiveness of a single form of attention: "You think that after all you must be weaving a piece of cloth: because you are sitting at a loom—even if it is empty—and going through the motions of weaving" (# 414).

Wittgenstein's language has brought "self" and "state of attention" into tension. In his linguistic use he has linked states of attention to the *expression* of selfhood by means of their effect on projects of defining "consciousness" or "self." The recognition of the ambiguity of selfhood is occasioned by the discovery in language of the ambiguity of one's own state of attention when it is philosophical. Wittgenstein says that James's definition *shows* the state of a philosopher's attention and that a good deal could be learned from this showing. It is the showing which is important. James's language shows Wittgenstein the ambiguity of the philosopher's stance when he defines selfhood, and Wittgenstein's language shows, on the basis of the insight that the activity of philosophical definition is carried on through the attention of a self, that the ambiguity of selfhood is represented in a philosophical state of attention. This

showing is the showing of the philosopher's use of language
about language. When a philosopher who is in the grip of com-
pulsions subjects consciousness or selfhood to a single form
of attention, then his language takes the form of paradox, as in
"*This* is supposed to be produced by a process in the brain!"
—said while clutching the forehead. But when a philosopher
uses language like that of James and recognizes in it the embodiment of his own philosophical state of attention in saying the
word "self" to himself, he is, we may say, showing himself
to himself.

Our third example of Wittgenstein's language refines what
it means to him for a self to appear in language. At one point
he says that " 'When one means something, it is oneself meaning'; so one is oneself in motion. One is rushing ahead and
so cannot observe oneself rushing ahead. Indeed not" (# 456).
"Yes: meaning something is like going up to someone" (# 457).
It is this directional understanding of meaning in the use of
language that we wish to look at. In the last two hundred or so
paragraphs of Part I of the *Philosophical Investigations* there
are some close discussions of "directional languages" such as
wishing, expecting, hoping, intending, and willing. These discussions move from the need for fixed criteria through linguistic
use to a kind of personal embodiment. Recognition of the
latter, of forms of life, is portrayed as the recognition of
gestures, tones of voice, and facial expressions.

A puzzle is noted: "A wish seems already to know what
will or would satisfy it; a proposition, a thought, what makes it
true—even when that thing is not there at all! Whence this
determining of what is not yet there? This despotic demand?"
(# 437). "It is a violation of common language to say that the
wish contains what would satisfy it. We speak of wishes which
remain unsatisfied, we speak of our wishes being satisfied when
we are not, and we speak of not really knowing what it is we
wish for" (# 441). If there is sense to the wish or expectation
containing its satisfaction, it is not the sense of identity or
inclusion. In the sentences, "I expect he is coming" and "He is
coming," the use of "he is coming" in one cannot be substituted
for the use of it in the other. How, then, can "he is coming"

be seen as the fulfillment somehow already contained in "I expect he is coming" (# 444)? The answer lies in tracing the way the language of expecting may be said to make possible the language of coming.

In what kind of linguistic surroundings does "I expect he is coming" occur? Presumably in those surroundings where I can talk of glancing at a clock, pacing the floor, doing something in a distracted manner, and so forth. And what are the linguistic surroundings of "he is coming"? Well, the door opens, he walks in, shows recognition, and so forth. Between these two linguistic fields Wittgenstein places an intermediate case. Suppose that *while speaking* the language of expectation—glancing, pacing, being distracted—I say, "I expect he'll come in." *Now* there is similarity to "He is coming." The language of expecting makes contact with the language of satisfied expectation (# 445). In this intermediate context, saying "He is coming" can carry along with it the language of having a place to come to and the language of an expected coming. Through Wittgenstein's mediation the two languages exhibit their common ground in the comparisons of expecting and being expected. In speaking toward someone and toward something, as in wishing and expecting, the fulfillment is embodied in the linguistic field which gives rise to such events as meeting and reception.[5]

The activity of therapeutic philosophy is restorative in its renewal of comparison (and therefore relationship) in language. Wittgenstein asks: ". . . how does he call *him* to mind?" (# 691) This is a perplexing question to the philosopher who has become caught in the welter of explanations designed to fix the meaning of calling a person to mind. But the answer given is simply: *"How does he call him?"* (# 691) The answer lies in recovering the linguistic acts by which we move from

5. In this context note the reflection: "We are—as it were—surprised, not at anyone's knowing the future, but at his being able to prophesy at all (right or wrong)" (# 461). Knowing the future, what happens in it, is found to be much less remarkable than being able to talk as if one knew the future. The talking-as-if expresses the intermediate cases by means of which one has been able to move from his own experience of linguistic use in the present to the field of use within which recognition can occur (whether it does or not) in the future.

the language of calling each other to the language of calling each other to mind. The language of this juxtaposition, of the question about calling a person to mind with the question about calling a person, is reflexively about the use of language because it recapitulates comparisons which compose likenesses and differences between calling to mind and calling. And with this recapitulation the language of the juxtaposition overcomes dichotomy and fixation of use by opening possibilities for new use. The same reflexivity appears with the case which effects contact between "I expect he is coming" and "He is coming."

III

Wittgenstein's form of life is to be seen in his use of language. This conclusion follows from his presentation of philosophy as a therapy conducted upon language and in language. Saying that aphorism is Wittgenstein's form of life may seem to go beyond the conclusion that his form of life lies in his use of language. However, the use of language exhibited in the three examples is reflexive, and this characteristic warrants our use of "aphorism." The reflexive use of language has been shown to go beyond literal meanings. In the situation of needing to get rid of the private object, the reflexivity of the paradox meant that it was not about objects, memories, or even about any ordinary sort of changing. The problem of defining "consciousness" and the puzzle about wishes fulfilling themselves also yielded nonliteral meaning.

The way that Wittgenstein's language yields nonliteral meanings lies in its aphoristic function. Aphoristic language brings about a shift from the commonplace to the extra-ordinary by cutting off fixed, ready-made meanings and by pointing reflexively to the context and direction of linguistic use. And the first step in such shifts is usually (in the *Philosophical Investigations*) showing that fixation and the appropriation of ready-made meaning (e.g., referential meaning, "pointing") are themselves linguistic uses. In our close scrutiny of the three examples of reflexive language the shifts were as follows: First, the shift was from a language about objects to a language, a form of life, in which it is possible to use, and accept the use of, paradox. Second, the shift was from language about two apparently separate subjects, philosophy and selfhood, to a language in which the two are encountered upon one field of comparison, namely the experiencing of oneself in the having of a form of attention. And third, the shift was from language about the state of expectation and the state of fulfillment to the use of a language within which states of expectation and fulfillment become embodied.

These shifts created in aphorism take the philosopher from compulsion and frustration to freedom and engagement. Metaphysicians, says Wittgenstein, can in the last analysis only repeat themselves (e.g., # 253, # 261). This aimless repetition is the using of language as if it had no use—it is language gone "on holiday" (#38), the wheel which we imagine works in the machine because it spins, although its spinning is idle and disengaged. The disengagement is shown in a statement characteristic of the metaphysician: "I can't imagine the opposite." We might say that this language is the opposite of the language of "understanding," a language which permits one to say, "I can go on" (# 150ff). To Wittgenstein, metaphysical statements signal closure in their denial of opposition, and arrest in their requirement of repetition. His answer to helpless inability to imagine the opposite is "Why do we say: 'I can't imagine the opposite'? Why not: 'I can't imagine the thing itself'?" (# 251) The "thing itself" is a creature like the private object or private language, whose privacy is its ultimacy as a standard of meaning, and therefore its removal from any possible comparison. Wittgenstein's treatment here is characteristically aphoristic. He acknowledges that we may be fixed upon an object and that we see no opposite, but he also reminds us that such a use of language, beginning with the statement "I can't imagine the opposite," allows for opposition. Giving reasons for talking one way rather than the other, for talking about inability to imagine opposites rather than inability to imagine the thing itself, leads out into the making of comparisons. A frequent comparison that appears in the *Philosophical Investigations* is of the language of metaphysical repetition to the condition

of being in pain. Both are exclusive and immobilizing. The
philosophical task is the use of language to lead pain out into
areas where it can stand comparison.

The linguistic tensions created in aphorism lead from opposition to likeness. It may even be said that aphoristic language
lets opposition be a form of likeness.[6] Aphorism turns idleness
into possibility, and fixity into motion, by placing the user of
language into his use, and by showing that description finally
amounts to self-description, that entities and states of being
rest on acts and ways of being.

"Meaning" is like "going up to someone," says Wittgenstein,
and "understanding" should be regarded as "can go on" (# 150).
The motion occurs in action which leads to embodiment.
When Wittgenstein uses the term "body" (# 559; Part II, page
178) he means the contours which become open to us in our
forms of life, in our using of language. He characterizes loss
of meaning with the term "sublime," which he uses in the
active sense as the occurrence which leaves nothing to touch
(# 38). And on the other hand he characterizes the person who
knows how to mean, how to use the "right" word, as one who
has experience in forms of life (Part II, page 227), and he
emphasizes that this experience includes "imponderable" elements such as subtleties of glance, gesture, and tone (Part II,
page 228). And it is his bodily understanding of meaning in
forms of life which leads him to recommend mime as a method
of philosophical representation (# 201, # 483; Part II, page
188). He asks, "What is the natural expression of an intention?"
and answers, "Look at a cat when it stalks a bird; or a beast
when it wants to escape" (# 647).

Using language to effect the transformations which lead to
embodiment is the enactment of aphorism, and it is Wittgenstein's form of life. It is not philosophically appropriate to
distinguish his style from his meaning, nor his use of language
from theories he is alleged to have about language. He regarded
theories as uses of language, and he dealt with his own theorizing
tendency by means of his use of language. These conclusions

6. Wittgenstein's remarks on negation (# 547–558) are especially
interesting.

about Wittgenstein's form of life lessen the temptation to isolate his uses of aphorism, and they find a unity of method in the diversity of his reflections. In the *Tractatus Logico-Philosophicus* he wrote, "Ethics and aesthetics are one and the same" (6.421). His achievement of a form of life in the *Philosophical Investigations* may be understood as an application of that description to himself.

Cyril Welch

SPEAKING AND BESPEAKING

The slightest philosophical reflection upon language proceeds on the assumption that the meaning of any given saying on our part lies in some sort of background more or less recalled by the saying. Moreover, it must be seen that the background providing the meaning for what is said is not immediately evident in what is said. In other words, reflection upon language is itself significant only because there is a puzzling difference between what in any given case is *said* and what is at bottom *meant*. And our part as speakers seems to remain just that: a part, a part of a background of meaning over which we have no immediate control and into which we have no immediate insight.

So it is often remarked that we have to put our minds upon the background of meanings as well as upon the foreground of sayings if we are to reflect meaningfully upon language. The question that has often been raised—and does indeed need to be raised—is: What and where is this background of meaning, this otherwise hidden spring from which our words flow? How do we begin thinking about the background and the ways in which it provides the foreground of saying with its meaning? —There seems to be some tacit if only very general agreement these days that the background of meaning is to be approached as the context of human labor, the context of our having to do with things, no matter how scientific or unscientific this context might be. Furthermore, since a context is already one of articulation, an articulation receiving its structure as well as its hue from a particular history, the background is that of some particular language. In other words, what we more obviously say at any given time and place is a product of a context of articulation, an articulation *of* the things that concern us *with* a historical language that is given to us.

Much can be said about this background itself. Much *needs* to be said about it. But after all is said and done in this regard, another kind of question remains outstanding: How does the background of our speaking move in to provide the foreground of our speaking with its meaning? This movement of the background of vocational and historical articulation up close to the foreground of our saying is truly an extra-ordinary event, even if it lurks as a conditioning possibility within the most ordinary of occurrences. In fact, I should like to say that philosophy and poetry are endeavors properly devoted in different ways to this same event. The event in question, then, is the event of extra-ordinary language as it might perchance be consummated in poetic and philosophic speech.

When we concern ourselves with the intricacies of ordinary language, we understand the ordinariness of the language not so much in terms of its currency or frequency in everyday use. The ordinariness of the language is understood more in terms of our ability to reduce its otherwise opaque elements to an origin which is for practical purposes (i.e., in postulated principle if not in experienced fact) determinate and established. The origin may be considered either as an interrelated mesh of historical meanings or as an empirical givenness of experiences. Thus reflection upon ordinary language dips below the surface waters of sayings, but only long enough to establish and determine a course for the saying; in effect, our concerns in and for ordinary language remain in the foreground of our speech. And according to this definition of the ordinariness of ordinary language, the contrived languages of technology as well as the so-called metalanguages of logic are paradigms of ordinary language: They are designed precisely so that their meaning lies entirely outside of them; they comprise pure foregrounds devoid of meaning, and they thereby facilitate the process of dipping back into the meaning of some ordinary endeavor or pursuit, whether scientific or casual. In other words, a constructed language is the formalization of ordinary experience, and so remains an ordinary language.

Meanwhile, the question is still outstanding: How does the background of our speaking move in to provide the foreground of our speaking with its meaning? Our speaking is indeed meaningful and relevant at times—times likely to be when we are doing what needs to be done, whether in the chemistry laboratory, in a shoe shop, or in the study: when we are sharing our labors with one another rather than trying to share our words. The question, then, is *how*, not whether, our speaking can bespeak its own origin, its proper background.

What I propose is not so much to say something about ordinary language as to suggest something about the way our speaking possibly and necessarily becomes meaningful, the way the background moves in close to the foreground, the way our speaking bespeaks its own origin. But the proposal of this line of reflection only makes sense on the condition that we recognize an impending and predominante danger hovering over everything we say: the danger that it may be or become meaningless and irrelevant, that it may fall flat as mere foreground without any background. After all, the issue is whether we have anything to say.

Stated more concretely, then, the question becomes: What are the *features* of human speaking that make speaking relevant, needed, meaningful? Or: What are the *conditions* according to which we might really have something to say? I myself would like to propose a fourfold reflection on this matter——.

One such feature or condition is the phenomenon of question. The individual who finds himself speaking or hearkening is one who finds that there is something questionable about or within his situation. What exactly it is that is questionable depends entirely on the context of articulation and what it offers as unsettled and yet to be determined. But one thing can be said: a genuine question is one that we knowingly pose only because the situation demands that we enter into its questionability. Thus a genuine question never pertains at bottom to something picked out capriciously or arbitrarily; the apparent exceptions are either ironical (designed to touch upon a hidden contingency of the situation) or pathological (designed to hide a contingency which one refuses to face).

Some sort of questionability about or within the articulate whole of the situation conditions the relevance and meaning of human speech. However, this suggestion is going to make sense only if we follow through a distinction between interrogating and being interrogated. In the case of interrogating, the individual appears to initiate the articulation and to pursue it in his own terms, while in the case of being interrogated, the individual becomes puzzled and perhaps even struck dumb, unable to initiate anything until such time as he at least meets, if not resolves, the puzzle. When one interrogates, one acts on the assumption that one knows the framework in which the question arises regarding some detail. When one is interrogated, the question becomes whether one knows the framework at all.

The act of interrogating need not be a condition for the act of speaking. But the event of being interrogated conditions both acts, since the posing of a question is an act of speech issuing from the assumption that the framework, the vocational and linguistic context, the articulate whole, is given or granted. Ordinarily we have no need to pause and consider the mode in which the articulate whole is given or granted. But from the extra-ordinary standpoint of reflection we can see that it is *not* given in the sense that we might just take it for granted or presume it while ignoring it. What characterizes the speaker's relationship with his vocational and linguistic context is its utter precariousness. The speaker must assume the context in the sense in which we speak of assuming responsibility for getting something done. One can experience this precariousness in the form of a paradox: to the extent that one insists on heeding only that which can be straightforwardly and securely handed over, one becomes oblivious to the context in and according to which such things can make sense—and then discovers that nothing at all makes sense, that nothing at all is given. The other side of the paradox is that attention to the needs and dictates of an entire context of action and thought can condition the utmost clarity about what indeed *is* given, about data and detail.

Since one's powers of initiation are conditioned by one's vocational and linguistic context, and since this context offers itself only precariously rather than straightforwardly, the articulate whole makes its appearance only as a total questionability. This questionability at least intimates, if it does not openly declare, to the individual that his contextual whole is tenuous, and the individual experiences this tenuousness as a being questioned, being interrogated. Thus if there is anything to initiate, anything to ask or say, it is because the individual is implicitly or explicitly heeding the event of his being interrogated, the event of the emergence of a contextual whole. Speaking more or less bespeaks this event.

A second feature conditioning the relevance of an act of speaking is the phenomenon of command. The individual who finds himself speaking or hearkening is one who finds that there is something imperative about or within his situation. Just what it is that is imperative is not always clear. In fact, one might deliberately ignore or avoid it, since it is more often than not rather disconcerting, owing either to its momentousness or to its triviality. But one thing can be said: a command is going to make sense only if it issues from the dictates of the situation and not from the chance whims of the individual. Apparently whimsical commands are, once again, either ironical or pathological, either calling for a more refined sense of imperative or retreating in the face of some foreboding imperative.

Commanding and being commanded are evidently not the same even though they might issue from the same root. The crux of the distinction is not easy to grasp, however. We might try to think of it as lying in the interaction of human beings, some commanding and some obeying. But this imagery only raises the question as to the ability of the one individual to hearken to the command of another—or to the question of another, as in the previous case. If we postulate that it is in the interest of the individual himself that he hearken to the expressions of others, then we have to ask what that interest is. If we try to convince ourselves that this interest is a matter of one's own drives, motives, and instincts, we are really convincing ourselves that one cannot make sense out of the expressions of others as others. But we occasionally do make sense out of the expressions of others. If we try to account for this occasion by arguing that the attunement of one's own drives, motives, and instincts with one's environment must for its own sake take subtle and somehow "symbolic" account of those forces in one's environment which are both more helpful and more detrimental—namely, human forces—then we are tacitly admitting once again that one does not make sense out of others at all, but only out of the requisite provisions for the satisfaction of such prereflective desires as the desire to survive.

The individual's recognition of his social nature, of his ability and commitment to hearken to the commands of others, suggests that the distinction between commanding and being commanded must lie in the character of individual experience taken as revealing a whole rather than as compounding parts. So conceived, the distinction might found the formation of a community of individuals. For the individual must discover himself being commanded before he can issue his own commands or obey those of others. The phenomenon of commanding and the imperative form of discourse, while not themselves prevalent conditions for the relevance of speaking, express an event which does condition there being anything to speak about or hearken to: the event of the imperativeness of the articulate whole in which it becomes relevant to speak and hearken. This event conditioning the meaningfulness of speech is not simply given, but it is more or less bespoken in any meaningful speech.

A third feature conditioning the relevance of discourse is expressed in the phenomenon of emotion or feeling. We have to ask ourselves whether it is possible to speak meaningfully without a "feel" for some larger context, a "feel" both for some vocational construct of endeavor and for a linguistic construct of expression. Such a "feel" takes on the character of feeling or emotion as the individual discovers that his own being is so bound up with this larger context that in some fashion he depends on it rather than it depending on him.

What makes us suspicious of the phenomenon of emotion is that it becomes conspicuous only at moments of relative failure within an enterprise: as when misjudgment issues from an attachment to particular elements within a situation or when violent outburst or pouting silence accompanies the confrontation of some obstacle. And yet it is also obvious that nothing gets done and nothing becomes clear except insofar as individuals find themselves passionately involved in what they are about.

The riddle of emotion is not going to be resolved until we distinguish between kinds of attachment. On the one hand, there is attachment to particular things within one's field of endeavor. One becomes attached to particular persons, particular objects, and particular constructs of one's own making (constructs such as one's pet theories, ideas, proposals, or self-images). Since the individual here tends to find his own being defined by the particular thing to which he is attached, such attachment gives rise to such hindering emotions as conceit and jealousy.

On the other hand, there is a kind of attachment which is defined and becomes clear in terms of one's whole field of experience. Here one discovers the need for a detachment from particular things within one's situation, a detachment conditioning their full manifestation and intelligibility as well as the distinction of one's own being. But this kind of detachment cannot be an indifference, a dearth of manifestation and distinction. It must be the result of another kind of attachment, an attachment to the articulate whole of one's having to do with things.

A sentimental attachment to, or feeling for, particular things may not condition the possibility of meaningful speech. But a recognition of being attached to, and motivated by, a vocational and linguistic context having to do with human and nonhuman beings conditions both the sentiment and the speech. Things in experience question and command, elicit affection and commitment. The recognition of things having this power deserves careful examination. The locus of the possibility of this recognition certainly does not lie isolated in things themselves, and the character of these experiences is decidedly vitiated if their locus is laid at the doorstep of the isolated subject. Attachment to, and detachment from, particular things makes sense only on the basis of a prior commitment to the context of endeavor forming an articulate whole. Since both the being of the self and the being of things become clear on this basis, the objective and the subjective facets of emotion are both metaphorical.

We often enough have mute tongues and deaf ears. To the extent that there is anything to say or hear, a vocational and linguistic context of concern moves in to define attachments and detachments. Thus the sense of a contingently given context conditions the meaning of factually given things. Speaking necessarily bespeaks the contingency and the emergence of this context and so occasionally embodies a high pitch of relevant feeling.

A fourth feature or condition of language is the phenomenon of performance. Spoken and written words can simply consummate an experience. Language of a ritual or legal nature is often of this type—witness the statements occurring at cocktail parties, in marriage ceremonies, the signing of a contract or the swearing of an oath. Perhaps, too, poetry and philosophy can shed a consummating light on certain experiences—at least momentarily. Language can also fulfill a performative function in many less conspicuous ways—as when the choice of words and the fervor of voice subtly reveal or precipitate the policy and nature of our actions.

The possibility of performative language must lie in the nature of performance. Here again we meet with two antithetical courses of investigation corresponding to two closely related aspects of performing. On the one hand, action or performance can be approached on the assumption that it is explicable in terms of the motion one goes through, in terms of its beginning, middle, and end, its motives, means, and products. On the other hand, it can be approached with a view to understanding what the behavioristic approach can never understand: the formative powers of performance. There is an activity of formation central to any performance or action worthy of the name. This activity of formation may indeed have a project, something formed such as an ordinary household artifact or an erudite historical fact. But formative power can hardly be understood by examining the finished product, namely, what comes after the power has ceased to function—and nothing is gained in this respect by appending after the fact an examination of the beginning and the middle.

The formative power of performance is grounded neither in objects nor in the subject. It is grounded in the emergence of a context of interest which elicits the attention of the self and defines the things which are to enter into the formative process. Performance is creative and not just manipulative. However, this comment gives rise to reflection upon a distinction between two senses of creativity. Most simply, to create means to come up with something new, something in some way different—quantitatively if not qualitatively; creativity here means as much as novelty. The question is, though, whether sustained novelty of production is possible apart from a sustaining formation and conservation of the articulate whole defining the beginning, middle, and end of an endeavor. It seems that all great and genuine productions, whether in art or in technology, have a way of recalling the context and the process which gave them their birth; and the humdrum of trivial productions lies in their failure to recall their generation. Creation of a whole is prior to innovation of products.

The formation of a product in action may not condition the possibility of meaningful and relevant speech. But a concern for forming and conserving a vocational and linguistic whole conditions both performance and speech, and allows them to coalesce into a concrete endeavor, the kind of endeavor in which action is coherent and speech is cogent. Speaking always bespeaks this vocational and linguistic whole—not, however, as something given or handed over to the speaker, but rather as it is precariously and variably emergent and as it is being graciously or frantically formed and conserved. It is no wonder, then, that the way we speak and write invariably sets the tone which our experiences have, are to have, and even had. We immediately make the conditioning context of our experience by our language, while we mediately make things within our experience by our hands.

——So what is the upshot of this fourfold reflection upon the conditions of relevant and meaningful speaking? ——We are once again at a critical crossroads of investigation: On the one hand, we could steer back into an analysis of informative speaking, a speaking which provides data relevant to an assumed context of interest. On the other hand, we can steer toward an understanding of fulfilled speaking, a speaking which comes to bespeak its own origin in a consummate manner.

The informative function of language is conditioned by the emergence of an articulate whole in which communicable facts can make sense. Information is what occurs within the whole and by virtue of it. The meaning of any item of information (a fact) is its integration into, its relation and contribution to, a vocational and linguistic context of endeavor. Thus information is a consequence and not a condition of speaking. We cannot understand language at all in terms of information and the communication of facts; on the contrary, we will always be understanding or misunderstanding information and communication in terms of our understanding of language.

Language can on occasion function informatively—but only because it first of all functions interrogatively, imperatively, emotionally, and performatively. After all, precisely the driest statement of fact becomes meaningful only in terms of some question which it answers, some need which it fulfills, some feel and feeling for a vocational and linguistic whole, and some performance incorporating and so verifying it. The statement loses its meaning to the extent that any one or more of these conditions fail to materialize. The analysis of information and communication can proceed beyond these conditions, but it constructs an oblivion if it loses touch with them.

The alternative course of investigation counteracts the oblivion by posing the question: What is it that speaking ultimately bespeaks? It first of all bespeaks a whole which is given as precarious: given only in the sense that it can be assumed (as one takes upon oneself a task, as one takes to oneself a gift) and not given in the sense that it can safely be presumed (as one takes something for granted, as one takes off without returning). But then speaking also bespeaks the way in which man the speaker and the things he works with and speaks about emerge and *become* what they are. Man the speaker emerges as the one who finds his being in terms of his particular and variable vocational and linguistic whole—in terms of how he assumes it. The

things with which he works and about which he speaks reveal
themselves and their being in terms of the speaker's mode of concern for, care of, and attention to them—a mode dictated *by*
the context *to* the speaker and so dependent upon the speaker
only in the sense that it is his response that materializes it. Thus
a vocational and linguistic whole has a subtle way of taking
revenge on the speaker to the extent that he presumes rather
than assumes it: to that same extent, the individual *has* no being
and *confronts* no being distinct from the context.

Language is grounded in being—if by being we mean the
emergence and submergence of man and the things with which
he has to do. But, if so, we will search in vain for a language
which can speak about the being of man and the being of things.
A language will always serve to speak about junctures and movements within a contextual whole. If philosophy and poetry convey
something of this whole and what might issue from the whole,
it is not so much because they speak *about* it as because they
bespeak it. In any event, though, we cannot rightly expect to
find in these realms any glaring and self-sufficient evidence to
the effect that there is anything distinctly bespoken or to be
bespoken. Patently speaking, a context of experience evidences
nothing but various forms of reference within itself. But not all
evidence need be patent and self-evident. There might be
evidence which manifests itself only if we are prepared to
witness it.

Albert Hofstadter

ON THE CONSCIOUSNESS AND LANGUAGE OF ART

Art is a language by which the human mind gives utterance to its own integrity. It holds the two main sides of mind, objective and subjective, in their appropriate unity, and it articulates that unity in an image for intuition.

One side of mind is theoretical, devoted to the formation of knowledge of reality. It attends primarily to the object of consciousness and concerns itself with ascertaining the being and content of that object. Its aim is truth, the agreement of the subject's intention with the reality. In the whole economy of life its function is the development of science, the illumination of reality. Within art, it gives rise to the tendencies known as realism and naturalism.

The second side of mind is practical, devoted to the exercise of freedom. It sets its attention on the subject's appetites and goals and concerns itself with realizing his desire and will in existence. Its aim is the goodness and rightness of things, actions, and persons, their agreement with the subject's chosen norms. Hence it aims at the agreement of the reality with the subject's intention. In the economy of life its function is the development of man's governance over things, including himself, in accordance with standards he determines as suitable for them—as in technology, law, morality, and politics. In art, this aim at freedom gives rise to counter-naturalistic, counter-realistic tendencies such as constructivism, surrealism, expressionism, and Dada.

Theoretical and practical mind are necessary factors in the integral unity of the psyche, just as the objective and the subjective are necessary factors in the unity of consciousness. What is the unity of consciousness, and what is the corresponding psychical unity of which art is the language? The nature of this unity is already indicated by the language we use to describe the ideals of its two indispensable sides, the theoretical and the practical. One is truth, the other freedom. In one, intention agrees with reality; in the other, reality agrees with intention. In both, the union is one of agreement. The ideal of mind in its integrity is agreement, the mutual agreement of intention and reality. But the intention has to be not merely the cognitive intention of theoretical mind and not merely the elective intention of practical mind, but the full intention of mind in its integrity—namely, the effective intention of the love that binds spirit to its affinity.

The third and unifying principle of mind is the spiritual one, whose aim is to reach the mutual agreement of intention and reality. It includes knowing, on the one hand, but is not mere science. It includes freedom, on the other hand, but is no longer merely freedom; for it yields itself completely to its other in devotion to it. Its essential aim is to exist in the mutual ownness of love, an ownness for which the classic formula is found in the words of the *Song of Songs:* "My beloved is mine, and I am his" (2:16).

This mutual ownness of love is the ultimate and true form of ownness. It transcends and includes the validity of all merely cognitive appropriation and all merely practical appropriation of reality, for in it is finally realized the basic underlying aim that gives rise to knowledge and practice, to consciousness of objects in their objectivity and consciousness of objects in their belonging to the self, their "mineness." The consciousness that belongs to this mutual ownness of love I call, by an obvious metaphor, *kin-consciousness*. It is the consciousness of self and other in their mutual belonging to one another, their mutual fitness, harmony, accord, kinship. The negative form of kin-consciousness is the consciousness of unbelonging, unfitness, discord, disharmony; and there are many modifications of it, complications of the positive and negative forms, among which are to be found notably the consciousness of the tragic and of the comic. Goethe celebrated it under the name of "elective affinity." Plotinus quite properly took it for the foundation of his interpretation of beauty:

> Our interpretation is that the Soul—by the very truth of its nature, by its affiliation to the noblest Existents in the hierarchy of Being—when it sees anything of that kin, or any trace of that kinship, thrills with an immediate delight, takes its own to itself, and thus stirs anew to the sense of its nature and of all its affinity. (*Enneads*, I, vi, 2, translated by Stephen Mackenna.)

This mutual ownness is the ultimate form of being, in which a person's being-toward-an-other is one in which the estrangement and alienation of otherness is completely—not merely partially—overcome. It is a reconciliation of self and other that consists not in a mere eradication of opposition or a mere quieting of otherness but in an affirmative and reciprocally enhancing appropriation of one another in, and through, and if need be despite, the reality of opposition. Love forgives the finite for what it is and takes it to itself precisely for what it is.

The language of art is the language of this mutual ownness, its negation, and its modifications. In art, man's spirit utters its meanings as unities of the subjective and objective which are not merely one-sided but reveal the essential bond between the two. The one-sided tendencies in art—namely, realism and naturalism on the one hand and the tendencies of abstract freedom on the other (constructivism, surrealism, etc.)—all nevertheless contain this unity of both sides, since they are art first and foremost. So, for example, expressionism, because of the tortured character of its love, must torture the object into a fitting distortion. Dada and surrealism, out of an indefeasible craving for the spontaneity of infantile being or of absolutely uninhibited freedom, must destroy every vestige of maturity or rational order in their object; only the nonsensical, absurd, and irrational shows itself to them as their very own. Still, neither the one side nor the other reveals in art the true wholeness and purity of spiritual unity. Only those art forms that do justice to both sides of consciousness and the spirit—the theoretical and practical, object-conscious-ness and own-consciousness, consciousness of the other in its objective being and consciousness of it in its essential relation to the self, truth and freedom—only such art forms give an ultimately true image of spiritual unity. These are the great classical forms of art that come into being and endure as long as a culture comes into the maturity of its conscious life and endures—normally, perhaps, only after the great mili-tary, political, and economic achievements are behind it. They are the arts that belong to periods like the Gupta in India, the T'ang and Sung in China, or the mature classical period in ancient Greece and the high renaissance and baroque in Europe. The greatest of artists and art works arise in these periods because they are periods in which the spiritual consciousness of the culture arrives at its natural fullness and demands utterance, and the material means are available in power and riches to give the artist scope for his task.

As an illustration of the language of art in its articulation of the unity of subjective and objective as a unity of mutual belonging, I choose a work that brings out clearly the character of this unity by a certain inner contrast. It is a poem written during a period of somewhat low key, written out of a mood of melancholy which realizes that it has lost the golden splendor of the great classical age, which knows it has to come to terms with an austerely real natural world, but which, in its very utterance of itself, in its own very moment of being, realizes for itself in its own way the essential unity whose loss it deplores. It is Matthew Arnold's "Dover Beach."

> The sea is calm to-night.
> The tide is full, the moon lies fair
> Upon the straits; —on the French coast the light
> Gleams and is gone; the cliffs of England stand
> Glimmering and vast, out in the tranquil bay.
>
> Come to the window, sweet is the night-air!
> Only, from the long line of spray
> Where the sea meets the moon-blanch'd land,

Listen! you hear the grating roar
Of pebbles which the waves draw back, and fling,
At their return, up the high strand,
Begin, and cease, and then again begin,
With tremulous cadence slow, and bring
The eternal note of sadness in.

Sophocles long ago
Heard it on the Aegean, and it brought
Into his mind the turbid ebb and flow
Of human misery; we
Find also in the sound a thought,
Hearing it by this distant northern sea.

The Sea of Faith
Was once, too, at the full, and round earth's shore
Lay like the folds of a bright girdle furl'd.
But now I only hear
Its melancholy, long, withdrawing roar,
Retreating, to the breath
Of the night-wind, down the vast edges drear
And naked shingles of the world.

Ah, love, let us be true
To one another! for the world, which seems
To lie before us like a land of dreams,
So various, so beautiful, so new,
Hath really neither joy, nor love, nor light,
Nor certitude, nor peace, nor help for pain;
And we are here as on a darkling plain
Swept with confused alarms of struggle and flight,
Where ignorant armies clash by night.

What is the form of outwardness here by which the kin-consciousness of art shows itself to the intuitive imagination? Let us begin by distinguishing between the particular dimensions of the showing and the essential connection between them. The particular dimensions are two: the presentation of objectivity and the expression of subjectivity.[1] The essential connection lies in the fitness, the kinship, by which they belong to one another.

1. Some discussion of these dimensions will be found in the author's *Truth and Art*, New York, 1965, Chapter 4, "Language as Articulation of Human Being."

In all art something has to be presented objectively as that to which the self in the work attends and with which it is concerned. Most familiar of the modes of objective presentation is the representation of objects. The work will be a painting of figures, animals, a landscape, a city scene; it will be the sculptured image of a god or man, the story of an event, the dramatic representation of a conflict, a lyrical representation of the self's world. But objective presentation also operates in modes other than literal representation. Art uses, as modes of presentation of objective matter, a symbol of an abstract concept, an allegory of a universal meaning, a metaphor, a simile, or other figure for an objectively thinkable content. It can present objectively that which transcends all finitely thinkable meaning—the mysterious, the infinite, the transcendent—by means of inscrutably suggestive images.

Even in the most subjective form of art, the lyrical, or the most subjective of the arts, music, there is present a strong and indelible objectivity. I do not merely mean that musical tones, fleeting as they may be, stand forth for themselves, insist upon themselves, and build the strongest structure out of the gossamer web of their relations in time—a Bach fugue, a Mozart sonata. That is the objectivity of the utterance itself. I mean rather to point to the fact that when music is at its most lyrical and subjective, as in the romantic melody of Schumann, Chopin, Brahms, and Wagner, it remains at the same time, however strangely and mysteriously, evocative of an unheard world, a world unnamed and undescribed, toward which nevertheless the subjectivity in the melody comports itself; and this merely adumbrated objectivity, the ghost of objectivity that remains with subjectivity when the latter retires into itself, is more truly representative of the function of objective presentation than the actual sounding of the tones! Lyrical art, generally, is the self pouring forth its utterance; but it utters its feelings in tones, words, verses, lines, colors, which are themselves powerful in the presentation of objectivity.

> Red lips are not so red
> As the stained stones kissed by the English dead.

Wilfred Owen (in "Greater Love") makes his speaker, in regarding the soldier's sacrifice, express the irony he feels by an image as objective as any image can be: the contrasting vision of the living, pulsating, warm red lips of the beloved kissed by the lover and the stone stained red with the blood of the slain lover of his fellow, his dead lips pressed against that cold, resisting, dead thing, his outpoured blood the actual kiss of death itself.

In a sense, abstract art shows this feature of objective presentation most clearly. In its most extreme form, so-called non-objective art, it is precisely the presentation of a pure objectivity. It abandons the representation of objects familiar in the world outside the work, and it concentrates on presenting only objects that are imagined purely through the medium of the work. The whole of the objectivity in the work is thus absorbed and exercised by the work itself, in its own purity of medium, freed from having to bring into itself objects from the external world. A pure design by Mondrian is stunning in its objectivity just because it disdains to copy trees, mountains, rivers, cows, men, buildings, and other such ordinary objects.

Objective presentation thus is essential to the constitution of the art work. But it is only a necessary condition, and it is not sufficient of itself to fulfill the artistic function of showing ownness and love. It is in itself indifferent to the artistic content of ownness—as is evident, for example, in mere photography and mere scientific illustration, from maps to electronic circuit diagrams. There is, however, one exception: namely, to present something objectively is to make it an image or an element in an image. This makes it present and accessible to the intuiting mind that apprehends it as an image. Hence it makes it the mind's own in an abstract and formal sense—it is the mind's in the sense that, whatever its content may be, it is appropriated by intuition in the form of an image. Objective presentation is a phase of theoretical activity and consequently partakes of the formal, abstract ownership practiced by the theoretical mind merely as such. Cognition, and *a fortiori* presentation of objects, is indifferent, not to the merely theoretical appropriation of the object but to what remains over and above its mere appropriation as an object. The indifference extends to everything in the object except the objectness of it. Once objective presentation has made the object intuitable, it is finished with it; whereas love has only then begun with it.

The second dimension of showing is subjective expression. This is as essential a function of art as is that of objective presentation. If objective presentation may be called the epical function in art, then subjective expression is art's lyrical function. A painting has to be made as something envisioned, a piece of music as something sounded, a poem as something spoken.

> The sea is calm to-night.
> The tide is full, the moon lies fair
> Upon the straits; —on the French coast the light
> Gleams and is gone; the cliffs of England stand
> Glimmering and vast, out in the tranquil bay.
>
> Come to the window, sweet is the night-air!

There is someone speaking here, from a personal point of view, bringing out in simple and strong imagery a visual scene from the window, speaking with a surface calm that, as the poem proceeds, proves to be a transparent medium for depths of disenchantment, and appealing in the end to his companion for the mutual trust of love. The poem is a short dramatic monologue; through the role it assigns to the speaker it lets him express a complex attitude, containing within it a vision of the present actuality, an understanding of the state of modern man's deliverance from religious illusion, the deep sadness that accompanies disillusion, and the hope for, and the will to find in finite human love, something of a finite answer to an infinite problem. The speaker expresses something of his own subjective experience and being—his perception, imagination, thought, feeling, aspiration, character, and temperament—while he is at the same time presenting an aspect of the world objectively in his language.

Everywhere in art something similar happens. Art articulates both the objective and the subjective components of human experience. It does this in such a way as to keep the objective objective and the subjective subjective. Objectivity is presented—pictured, symbolized, suggested, designated—and subjectivity is expressed in its role of viewing, thinking, feeling, willing. The visual arts construct not simply objects but visions of objects; music makes not just sounds but sounding expressions; in a poem, or other literary work, there is articulated an experience *of* something, a concrete consciousness that utters itself in words, both the objective aspect and the subjective aspect and, eventually, the unity of the two. In a drama, a mind broods over the struggles of men in their world; the audience, sitting with that world presented before it in immediate presence, is given the opportunity to participate in that silent contemplation, full of complexities of thought and feeling, as the pathos of *Romeo and Juliet,* the satirical contempt of *Tartuffe,* or the profound understanding of the human in Euripides' *Electra.*

As subjective lyrical art makes essential use of objective presentation, so objective epical art makes essential use of subjective expression. Every story has its narrator or narrators; every object seen has its seer, every thought its thinker, everything presented presupposes the emotion that feels it. The supposed pure objectivity of *Madame Bovary* is only the inverse side and reflection of an intensely passionate observation, insight, and moral judgment passed upon Emma, her husband Charles, the pharmacist Homais, and their bourgeois world and life, a complexity of attitude that is as much a phase of the composition of the novel as any objective situation represented therein.

Of the dimension of subjective expression we must say also that, taken by itself, it is a necessary but not sufficient condition for artistic revelation. It too is in itself indifferent to the artistic content of ownness—as is evident in forensic rhetoric, passionate argument, cursing and blessing, and what-not else. There is, to be sure, a formal element of appropriation in the very achievement of expression—for in it the subjective attitude has been made accessible to intuition and thereby appropriated by the mind as an intuitive content, part of an image. But the appropriation thus far is limited only to the formality of becoming an image; it has not yet extended to the substantiality of being an image of mutual ownness, of kin-consciousness.

We begin to approach the articulation of kin-consciousness itself only with the union of subjectivity and objectivity. For here, insofar as the artist is successful, the objective material presented and the subjective attitude expressed belong to one another, fit together into a unity of essential appropriateness. If, in Arnold's poem, the mood of disenchantment and muted consolation in human love is to be veritably expressed, the vision and thought of the world given to the speaker must work, be suitable to the attitude. The sea, with its ever-recurrent surf, has to actually work as an image, and, indeed, it does so powerfully in this poem. The calmness with which it is presented at the beginning will belong to the subjective attitude at the end. The slow, tremulous cadence with which the sounds of the waves make themselves heard—drawing back pebbles and flinging them at their return up the strand, beginning and ceasing, beginning and ceasing, again and again—is telling in its ability to

> bring
> The eternal note of sadness in,

without the slightest hint of a letdown into sentimentality. This sound that Sophocles heard long ago, that master of insight into suffering, brought into his mind, too,

> the turbid ebb and flow,
> Of human misery,

and we northerners, far in time and far in space from that golden age,

> Find also in the sound a thought.

The thought is of the vanishing of faith in the reality of beauty, joy, love, light, certitude, peace, help for pain in the world. That faith was once a Sea, like this, which

> at the full, and round earth's shore
> Lay like the folds of a bright girdle furl'd.
> But now I only hear its melancholy, long, withdrawing roar,
> Retreating, to the breath
> Of the night-wind, down the vast edges drear
> And naked shingles of the world.

The objectivity that is seen, thought about, and presented for feeling, acts to bring out with distinctness and vitality the

dominant mood, Dover Beach becomes an effective figure for
the world—that darkling plain

> Swept with confused alarms of struggle and flight,
> Where ignorant armies clash by night.

Here, then, where art does what it is able to do, the two
dimensions of its configurative action, the objectivity presented
and the subjectivity expressed, occur together in a relationship
of mutual belonging. The symbol of the sea, its tide, its surf,
the rhythm of its recurrence, the coast, the cliffs, the beach,
the vanished light, the whole content of the history of faith all
function to give a stand for the sad consolation, and the mood
itself functions to hold them all together in the unity of its
own meaning.

The poem articulates a certain truth. By this I refer not to
the thought that the world is no longer a habitation of the
divine, but rather to truth of a unique sort, an agreement
between subjective and objective of the kind that occurs here
between the expressed mood and the presented matter. There
is a rightness of each to the other, a reciprocal accord. They
belong together as do the tones of a harmonious chord. They
feed on one another, being true to each other. They are kin.
The mood lives, flashes up into a vibrant resonance, through
the shape of the objective matter; and the scene and world
that are imagined live, flashing up into an equally vibrant
resonance, through the inspiration of the mood.

Here, in this inner truth of presentation and expression to
each other, is our first glimpse of the ownness that is constitutive
for art. The objective matter is own to the mood, the mood is
own to the matter. The matter does not copy the mood; it
does not express the mood—it is the *words* of the poem that
both present the objective matter and express the subjective
mood. The matter and the mood stand in a special relationship
of own to own, mutual kinship. Here we encounter a relationship
of spiritual content to figural form, inside the work, which can
begin to show us how ownness finds its outward form.

The question is how the poem as words—the outward poetic
image or figure, the shape of the words as a poem—is able to

reveal the content of ownness, the mutual kinship or truth of presented objectivity and expressed subjectivity, the content of truthful being that is constituted by these two inner constituents that are true to one another. The words of the poem, shaped into the poem, are the poetic image in the most literal sense: the image that is the poem. The content which this image exists to figure forth, the poetic content as such, is the unity of the objective and subjective constituents within the poetic meaning, the unity of the objectivity presented and the subjectivity expressed. How does the linguistic shape do this?

It is not a copy of it. That is evident. The verbal structure does not look like a union of the two dimensions of consciousness.

It is not a physiognomic expression of it. The verbal structure is not like, say, a man's face as it expresses an inner feeling or character. It cannot be this, because the reciprocal truth, which is a union of the two dimensions of consciousness, is not a suitable content for physiognomic expression: it is not something merely subjective but a union of the subjective and the objective, a truth, a freedom.

The poem is not a symbol of the ultimate unity. A symbol represents its meaning as something different from itself, separate from itself, in place of which it stands here to point to the absent content there. The clearest example of the symbol comes not from art but from science, as when the physicist uses the letter G to stand for the force of gravitation. But the poem as shape does not stand for the truth, to remind us of it as G reminds us of gravitation. The poem *speaks* the truth. As the sentence "Burlap is made from jute'" *says* what it does, uttering this flat piece of information, so the poem more than merely says; it speaks in its own way, it poetizes, so to speak, its meaning, the truth it exists to utter. The sentence is not a symbol that stands for something else, even though it is made of symbols. It is a piece of language that speaks in its flat way of saying. The poem speaks in its full way—intoning, singing, weaving its rhythmical way through its utterance. As the truth which the sentence speaks is spoken *in* the sentence, so the truth which the poem speaks is spoken *in* the poem. It is spoken not by one or other of the words in the poem; it is not in the poem as a word or words.

(But is it not? Does not the poem speak the sentence:

> Ah, love, let us be true
> To one another!)

In the poem a man speaks. It is, I suppose, a man speaking to a woman. It is this man whose perceptions, memories, thoughts, wishes, moods receive expression and whose world comes to objective appearance in the poem. It is he who is doing the actual speaking, or through whose voice the poem speaks as it does. He begins:

> The sea is calm tonight.

Both the sea that he perceives and the mood in which he perceives it begin thereupon to come to utterance. He reaches out with his words and brings into picture the sea, calm, to-night. By his noun he begins to disclose to the imagination of the understander of the language a marine image; it is stilled by an adjective and brought to time by an adverb.

At the same time, by the same words, in the same sequence, he begins to disclose to the same imagination not an outward picture alone but also an inner consciousness, a disenchantment, a disconsolate consolation, which now just begins to be felt but will grow and gain definiteness as the reading of the poem continues. The understander of the language is able to imagine this subjective phase in the manner in which subjectivity is understood. That happens not by looking at the mood, as though one were turned toward it as an object, but by an empathic participation in it. As we are conscious of our own mood, not by looking at it objectively but by being in it and being inwardly and nonreflectively conscious of it, so we are aware in imagination of the mood of the poetic speaker. Our own mood is conscious of itself not as an object but precisely as itself, in itself, by means of itself. It knows itself along-with itself, con-scius.

At the same time, by the same words, the speaker brings to imagination the unity of the objective and subjective components. The disenchantment intends the calm sea. This is an essential constituent both of the disenchantment and the sea. The disenchantment is of and about the sea—among other things, naturally—and it permeates both the seeing of the sea and the sea as seen. So, later, we hear the tremulous cadence of the grating roar of the pebbles, which brings in the eternal note of sadness—the sadness is out there in the moaning of the surf as well as in here in the breast of the man. The words of the speaker make us understand; they give to our intelligent imagination this essential unity by which the sea belongs to the mood and the mood to the sea.

Why does the disenchantment choose the sea? Why not something else, somewhere else? Why do you choose the city in which you live? Why not a village, in another country? In and through the sea that the disenchantment chooses, or by which it is itself chosen, it lives its own being, comes to articulated shape in its intentional congruence with it, as you come to be what you are in your living dwelling within your city. The sea is own to the disenchantment because the sea is precisely the object of which the disenchantment is the subject; the sea is the disenchantment's other, which the disenchantment has been able to make its own, in the way in which disenchantment can own things. The sea has captured the disenchantment, perhaps through capturing the disenchantment's imagination, fascinating it, casting a spell over it. Is it through the power of this spell that the disenchantment perhaps comes to spell the name of the sea, to tell its own story through telling the story of the sea? Is it this spell, permeating the sea and the disenchantment, that reaches out into the man's language and seizes upon the words that spell its own name and story?

What makes sea and disenchantment own to each other makes the language of sea and disenchantment own to itself.

But this is only half the story. It tells only how the mutual ownness of the disenchantment of this poem and the sea of this poem finds the verbal form of this poem to be its very own utterance. It is therefore the story only of a particular poem, but not of poetry; and only of a poem, but not of the work of art as such. The question is, What happens not just with this poem and not just with poetry but with art and with every art work?

Wherever there is a work of art there is an utterance of some particular union of the subjective and objective in their concrete being own to each other, as the disenchantment and the sea are to each other. The way in which objective matter is presented and subjective matter expressed varies from art to art, genre to genre, and work to work. Dancing is in some respects a more objective art than music and in some respects a more subjective art than architecture. Lyric poetry is more subjective than dramatic or epical, and poetry in general is more subjective than drama or epic or novel. Chopin is more subjective than Haydn, Keats than Dryden. Architecture makes an external world, painting represents it, music adumbrates it, poetry imagines it through meaning, drama presents it in a semblance. The self in lyrical poetry utters itself, in drama it silently looks on, in the novel it narrates. Music does not make use of the sentences of the intellect's language; literature is full of them. Music is auditory, painting visual, literature imaginative. And so forth. The changes can be rung on all the different ways in which subjectivity and objectivity occur in the arts; but throughout the arts and in all the works, one essential universal prevails—the reciprocal ownness, the kinship, of the subjective and objective components to one another, the inner truth to each other by which, together, they form a true unity. As with "Dover Beach" so with every other work: one could, given the means of investigating and understanding, discriminate the objective and subjective components in the intention-structure of the work, and in the same process bring out for awareness the way in which the two belong to each other and to the whole, and the way in which that whole finds its utterance in the external shape, the existence of the work in the world.

El Greco's *View of Toledo* (Metropolitan Museum of Art, New York City) transforms hills, buildings, river, clouds, and sky into an image full of mystery and foreboding, as though some awful miracle is about to happen; it is seen with an intensely passionate concern that transcends everything merely earthly, looking beyond to the infinite for the meaning of what happens in time and space. We learn to live our way into an understanding of the transcending concern by learning to see the tremendous image, and conversely; and as we accomplish both at the same time, we rise to a concrete intelligence of the interior truth by which the two belong to each other, which we are able to partake of in imagination. This painting, like the poem, is able to stand for all works; each stands for all and all for each.

What makes the work a work of art is the interior truth that takes the outward shape as its vehicle of utterance and articulation. Art is the uttering and articulating of just the interior belonging to one another of subject and object, an uttering which itself belongs to that belonging, is true to that truth. The artist is the locus in which this process takes place, in and through whom the poetic content finds its language and the language articulates the content.

Art is a way of being possessed by ownness itself, or, as we may say, by love itself. The artist is the creature of love and art is love's way of uttering itself, by finding the language that belongs to it. Deeper than the disenchantment and the sea, deeper than the truth that unites them in the poem, is another kind of attitude, and object, and unity. For the poet, the disenchantment is not the final mood—not so long as he is and remains a poet. The disenchantment is a constituent in a poem—other poems, other attitudes, enchantment perhaps, gaiety, terror, or what not. For the poet, again, the sea is not the final image—other poems, other images, eagle, shipwreck, bridge, west wind, or what not. These too are constituents in poems. The unity of disenchantment and sea, elation and eagle, transcending piety and miraculous mystery—these, too, are constituents of poems, unities of content that have, belonging to them, the unity of the outward shape of the poem, the painting, the work. It is this ultimate unity of inner content and outer shape, of total meaning and external vehicle, that casts its spell over the artist, making him an artist.

Here is where art becomes something real, something that exists in the world, and where the artist is at work in the world as an artist. The meaningful totality that consists in the unity of the subjective and objective—the concreteness of full consciousness—needs to be given utterance; indeed, it needs to find utterance in order to articulate itself. The spirit needs the world to give shape to itself by finding and shaping something in the world that is kin to it, of which it can truly say, "That is mine and I am its." It needs the world as it needs its own kin. Art is the spirit's attaining to its kinship with the world. The artist is seized by the spirit of ownness—that is, of truth and freedom and love—in search of its own utterance. Every poem he makes, or every painting, or dance, or building is one sound in the grand utterance. In each of them the ultimate subjectivity, the love of truth, freedom, and love, reveals itself, not by casting itself forth into the world but by speaking its own language. The concealment by which the speaker says what belongs to him is the revelation by which he gives himself to us to have as our own. As we receive this gift, we come to our own self, giving it to him, and in that gift coming at the same time to possess it for ourselves.

Edward S. Casey

MEANING IN ART

In approaching the theme of aesthetic meaning, at least three questions arise immediately: Does art mean anything at all? What is the meaning *of* art? What is the nature of meaning *in* art? I would like to consider the first two questions only briefly in order to concentrate on the third. First, there can be no doubt that art does mean, even in its most anarchic excesses; the more difficult problem is to see *how* it means. Nihilism and ontologism are allied in denying meaning to art—the one attempting to destroy art, the other to assert its sheer being. But Dada, the high point of nihilism in modern art, failed in its self-contradictory effort to *create* works of anti-art: what were meant to be meaningless ready-mades or *objets trouvés* turned out to be so charged with meaning that painting and sculpture today are still exploring their ramified significance. Similarly it could be shown that the most sustained and penetrating ontological interpretation of art in this century, Heidegger's essay "The Origin of the Work of Art," cannot avoid attributing meaning to art under the guise of "truth." For Heidegger, art is the establishment of truth in the work: "art lets truth originate." [1] But the art-work is not a meaningless thing; although Heidegger self-consciously avoids the term "meaning" as metaphysical, it is clear that one major effect of establishing truth in art is to

1. Martin Heidegger, "The Origin of the Work of Art" in *Philosophies of Art and Beauty,* ed. Albert Hofstadter and Richard Kuhns, New York, 1964, p. 698.

render art meaningful; truth could not be "illuminating" or art "institutive" if both were not inherently capable of meaning. Thus, no more than a Dadaist disdain for meaning, can an ontological emphasis on truth in art effectively deny that art means. Art has meaning as well as being—in fact possesses being only insofar as it *is* meaningful.

In asking the second question—What is the meaning of art? —we move directly to metaphysical terrain, for we are seeking the general essence of art. It is this kind of question which has dominated Western aesthetics in its repeated attempts to define the nature of the art object. In this venture, an isolatable essence is sought which specifies what art is generally. In Husserlian terms, such a generic essence would belong to regional ontology, functioning as an *a priori* for the material region of "art objects." Valuable as this inquiry is, I do not see how it can be completed, or even undertaken, until a more basic and detailed investigation is made into what has been called, in the third question, "meaning *in* art." Rather than a formal or generic essence, meaning in art is more like a singular essence, a unique time-bound structure that informs a particular aesthetic object.

But two preliminary distinctions are in order at this point. The first is between meaning and essence. For a phenomenologist, an essence must be given with "originary," "live" evidence [2] and be the object of a special intuition or insight. I believe that meaning in art is indeed self-given—as are essences in *Wesensschau*—but this meaning is given wholly in perception and feeling; it possesses no special cognitive evidence and requires no act of theoretical intuition. Moreover, the meaning, unlike the essence, is not detachable from the work of art in which it is ingredient. In Husserl's or Scheler's view, essences are systematically related and may even fit into an ascending hierarchy; this is made possible by their generality and by their putative "omnitemporality." [3] By contrast, meaning in art

2. Edmund Husserl, *L'Origine de la géométrie,* trans. J. Derrida, Paris, 1962, p. 184.
3. Cf. Edmund Husserl, *Erfahrung und Urteil,* Hamburg, 1964, par. 64, p. 309 f.

is wholly specific to the art-work; its being is temporal and is
exhausted in its presentation. This brings us to the second
distinction: that between the work of art and the aesthetic
object. Following Roman Ingarden, we can say that the work
of art is the "schematic structure" underlying all of its possible
"concretizations" in perception.[4] The aesthetic object is what
is phenomenally experienced in a given concretization; it is the
work of art made actual in aesthetic experience. Thus the
work of art is not the material, existent entity but a schematic
scaffold, riddled with lacunae, indeterminacies, and potentialities.
It achieves completeness—"distinctness" and "self-presence"[5]—
only as an aesthetic object; that is, through incarnation in a
perfomance and in contact with a public. In this paper I shall
be talking mostly about the work of art, for meaning in art
forms the skeletal structure of the work. But this meaning is
not objective in the sense of ideal; it does not possess what
Husserl calls "the perduring presence of 'ideal objects.'"[6] Instead
it inheres in the sensuous matter of the work as presented concretely to the spectator in the form of the aesthetic object.
Hence this object, and especially its formal element, cannot be
wholly neglected while focusing on the work of art.

I

Until recently, phenomenologists have taken a quite different
view of meaning in art. Husserl subsumed this meaning under
the objective signification intended by the logos of language.
Such "logical" signification is considered an "ideal unity";[7]
itself objective, it serves as the basis for referring to all objectivities, whether these be real or ideal. What Husserl calls
the fundamental "meaning-intention" in language aims at an

4. Roman Ingarden, *Das Literarische Kunstwerk*, Tübingen, 1965,
Chapters 1, 2, 13.

5. Ingarden uses the former term (*Ausprägung*) throughout *Das Literarische Kunstwerk*, especially pp. 370 ff.; the latter (*Selbstgegenwart*)
is found in his *Untersuchungen zur Ontologie der Kunst*, Tübingen, 1962,
p. 165.

6. *L'Origine de la géométrie*, pp. 185–186.

7. Cf. Husserl, *Logische Untersuchungen*, Halle, 1913, II, 1, par. 29.

ideal para-grammatical object transcendent to language itself. Husserl believed that something like this also happens in art, as he hints in a statement from *Formal and Transcendental Logic:*

> Language primarily interests the logician simply in its ideality —as an identical grammatical word or proposition . . . the situation of the aesthetician (*Ästhetiker*) is wholly similar; his theme is the specific work of art, the sonata, the painting, etc.—not as a physical complex of sounds (which is ephemeral) or as a physical painting, but precisely as the painting itself, the sonata itself—the aesthetic object properly speaking, as in the parallel case of the proper grammatical object.[8]

The "proper grammatical object" is an ideal meaning which is infinitely repeatable in varying subjective acts of consciousness. In Husserl's analogy, the "aesthetic object properly speaking" would have a similarly objective signification. Thus, if Husserl does not specifically make meaning in art into an essence, he does give it essentialistic overtones; and he assumes that a theory of logical meaning would include the case of aesthetic meaning. Salutary as his emphasis on the objectivity of the work itself is, his implicit thesis as to the objectivity of aesthetic meaning is, I believe, quite dubious. It cannot be assumed that *all* kinds of meaning are objective, hence transcendent both to their vehicle and to the intention that aims at them. And it is precisely meaning in art—as I hope to show —that forms the outstanding exception to Husserl's rule.

Ingarden, in his classic *Das Literarische Kunstwerk,* tries to effect a compromise between the rigid Husserlian position and a more exact account of meaning in art. He discerns "meaning-unities" in literature as forming a special stratum inherent in the literary work; these unities are not in themselves conceptual but serve rather to "project" the objects and states of affairs forming the next higher stratum, that of "depicted objectivities." [9] In spite of their indispensable role, however, the meaning-

8. *Formale und Transzendentale Logik,* Halle, 1929, par. 2.
9. *Das Literarische Kunstwerk,* Chapter 7.

unities are not wholly immanent in the work; they depend on, and derive from, "ideal concepts" [10] transcending the work of art altogether. In this sense, Ingarden's account remains under the guiding hand of Husserl; by finding the source of aesthetic meaning in ideal concepts surpassing the work, Ingarden fails to show how meaning can be indigenous in art. His related view of the "heteronomy" of the work of art as a whole also tends to undermine the autonomy of aesthetic meaning. Only the transcendent ideal concepts, along with the "subjective operations of consciousness," are allowed autonomy; no basis is provided for the immanency of meaning in art.

The first systematic attempt to liberalize former phenomenological descriptions of meaning in art is found in Mikel Dufrenne's masterful *Phénoménologie de l'expérience esthétique*. This encompassing work can be read as a defense of the idea that meaning in art is specific and ingredient. In a sentence that is a touchstone for the entire book, Dufrenne writes that in art "meaning is immanent in the perceptible [matter of the work]." [11] In this view, any search for objective significations in art is misguided, for the only meaning that counts is that which is effective in the work itself, structuring its sensuous base. If objective significations are sought in logic and metaphysics, in art we are enmeshed in a self-sufficing and self-enclosing experience which presents to us a plenum of immanent meaning: "What the aesthetic object says to me is said by its presence in the very heart of the perceived." [12] This insight puts a phenomenology of art on the right track; only if meaning is interpreted along this line can the phenomenologist rejoin the artist and the spectator in the very presence and experience of art. Matisse said that "a work of art must carry its complete meaning within itself." [13] The concreteness and plenitude of this meaning is precisely what distinguishes it from the hollow objectivity of logical meaning or the ideality of metaphysical meaning. The presence sought by an ontology of art can be

10. *Ibid.*, p. 386 f.
11. *Phénoménologie de l'expérience esthétique,* Paris, 1953, I, p. 41.
12. *Ibid.*, p. 44.
13. From *Notes of a Painter*.

secured phenomenologically by an adequate apprehension of meaning in art as immanent.

II

Insofar as we follow in the direction of Dufrenne, we may be able to avoid the danger of overemphasizing the objectivity of meaning in art—a danger that reappears in Albert Hofstadter's concern with art's "objectively thinkable content." [14] It is true that Hofstadter does not link the objective with the logical in Husserlian fashion, but he makes a parallel move by speaking of the "merely adumbrated objectivity" in art; such objectivity, bordering on the metaphysical, is no more innate to the work of art than a logical signification. But to establish more fully the case for the immanency of aesthetic meaning I would like to examine in succession two of its most prominent aspects: its *expressive* and its *iconic* character.

The problem of expressivity in art has obsessed artists and aestheticians of the modern period. The most frequent interpretation of expression in our time has consisted in claiming that art expresses emotions and that in this respect it is like a language. Both Collingwood and Hofstadter adopt versions of this view, though they sophisticate considerably the crude theories of emotivism. For Collingwood, "psychic feeling" is transformed by imagination into the language of art; the content of the work of art becomes an expressive and transfigured emotion.[15] Similarly Hofstadter contends that "everything presented [in art] presupposes the emotion that feels it." [16] This thesis is expanded to include the expression of mood and "ultimate subjectivity"; art is said to articulate, utter, or "speak" the subjectivity that is thus expressed. While I think this approach offers a welcome extension of the possible expressive content of art beyond Collingwood's arbitrary restriction to emotion, it is open to a critique parallel to that which has just been leveled

14. See Hofstadter's article in this book.
15. R. G. Collingwood, *The Principles of Art,* Oxford, 1958, Chapters 6, 7, 10.
16. Cf. article in this book.

against the pretended objectivity of meaning in art. For if art is held to be the expression of subjectivity or "human being," [17] then its content and implicit reference become external to its appearance. What Husserl called a "transcendent intentionality" [18] would be required to go beneath or beyond the presented work to its "real meaning" embedded in an underlying mood or human self. The final focus would be diverted from the work itself to some facet of subjectivity expressed by it.

What, then, is the nature of expressive meaning? In my view, it has three main characteristics: potential universality, nonconceptuality, and felt quality. Expressive meaning is universal in the sense that it is universally comprehensible; this is one reason why the ready intelligibility of art has often—and perhaps too hastily—been compared to the language of gesture. The expressivity of art is open-ended; it is not the private possession of its creator, portraying his inner emotions or even his subjectivity. If these emotions *are* expressed, they are made accessible to all; the expressed emotion and subjectivity itself become the property of the work, open to apprehension by anyone who achieves a correct aesthetic perception of them. In aesthetic experience they are expressed in the aesthetic object and embodied in its meaning. But many things other than emotion or self are expressed in art: historical or political events, imaginary objects, formal relationships. These too are all possible "subjects" of expression in art, and they transgress the limits of subjectivity.

Yet if the expressive meaning in art is thus potentially universal—open to perception by all and unbounded in possible subject matter—it is not conceptual in character. Even when a concept seems to be expressed in art—say, in de Chirico's "metaphysical" paintings—it is expressed not as a concept but as the equivalent in *feeling* of a concept: how the concept might look and feel when fully embodied in the artistic medium. As fully infused in what is presented, expressive content or mean-

17. This is Hofstadter's term in *Truth and Art*, New York, 1965, Chapter 4.
18. Cf. E. Husserl, *The Phenomenology of Internal Time Consciousness*, Bloomington, Ind., 1964, par. 43.

ing is not conceptual. A conceptual content involves a meaning that is detached or detachable from the vehicle in which it is expressed. Thus in conceptual signification, there is a relation of indication between content and vehicle. The movement of meaning is here irrevocably centrifugal, away from the center that is the vehicle or work itself. This movement is what we ordinarily call "denotation," but it may include nonmetaphoric types of connotation as well. In expressive meaning, however, the relation between vehicle and meaning is intrinsic. Metaphor is a prime example of this relation; the literal and figurative meanings of the same term coalesce in the felt unity of the presented matter. *Expression* can occur only when the resulting single meaning is ingredient in the sensuous matter itself, instead of being merely referred to by this matter.

The mention of metaphor should not mislead us into thinking that art is in fact a form of language. It is all too easy to conceive of art as itself a language in analogy with verbal language. Usually the comparison with verbal language is qualified by a critical nuance: Collingwood sees the language of art as that of expressive bodily gesture, Heidegger makes the language of art into the language of Being, Hofstadter envisions art as the language of spirit. Art speaks in many tongues—or better, it speaks "with tongues"—but none of them, I think, is comparable to verbal language. For one thing, forms in art do not allow of codification into anything like a vocabulary or a syntax. Further, there is no "immotivated" or arbitrary relation between sign and meaning in art; art proceeds in terms of natural affinities and kinships: the intelligibility of art is immediate and not a matter of convention. Most important, art (including literary art) does not possess the distance from vehicle to meaning that characterizes nonpoetic verbal language. It is the very immanency of content to vehicle that makes art an expressive, not a discursive, phenomenon. When we claim that art "speaks" or "says something," we are in fact contending that art expresses or means something inherent in itself. This meaning is not patterned from the meaning of verbal discourse, and it need not be explicit; in fact, it is most often indirect and allusive.

The muteness of expression in art, so eloquently underscored by Merleau-Ponty,[19] partially results from its nondiscursive character. But it also comes from the third characteristic of expressive meaning: its felt quality. That meaning can be felt is a thesis that has been solidly established by thinkers as diverse as John Dewey and Erwin Straus. Susanne Langer has drawn the consequence for aesthetics: in art, "the factor of significance is not logically discriminated, but is felt as a quality." [20] But for Langer this significance or "vital import" is contained in a symbol—an expressive symbol of feeling. Thus the source and model of meaning is distinguished from its expression, and Langer's attempt to parallel feeling and meaning becomes perilously dichotomous. The problem comes to a head in the very notion of symbol, which is admitted to involve an element of "abstraction." [21] If so, it is then difficult to see how felt meaning can be *presented* in a symbol. Moreover, the essential articulateness of the symbol seems to be inappropriate to the expression of feeling. We must discover a vehicle fit for the presentation of felt meaning which does not depend on factors like abstraction and articulateness—notions surreptitiously borrowed from verbal language. This vehicle cannot be a concept, for then meaning in art would be something thought, not felt or perceived. Expressive meaning must be sensuously presented; this is what the process of *aesthesis* is all about. Yet the vehicle cannot be an emotion or mood either; nor is it a product of will or even of spirit. In fact, I do not believe that the vehicle suitable for the felt expressive meaning of art can be specified in terms of any of the traditional metaphysical categories of cognition, volition, emotion, or spirit.[22]

III

It is at this point that I would like to turn briefly to the notion of the iconic sign as Peirce conceived it. This notion provides a

19. Cf. "Indirect Language and the Voices of Silence," in *Signs*, trans. Richard C. McCleary, Evanston, Ill., 1965.
20. Susanne K. Langer, *Feeling and Form*, New York, 1953, p. 32.
21. *Ibid.*, p. xi.
22. These categories continue to tempt Hofstadter throughout *Truth and Art*.

useful model for the way in which expressive meaning is embodied in art. As it may involve self-reference, the iconic sign
also contributes to an understanding of the immanency of
aesthetic meaning. Yet it does so without, on the one hand,
consigning art to a formless, senseless chaos or, on the other,
inflating it into an overly explicit symbol. Contrary to appearances, to use this model is not to intellectualize aesthetic
experience, for the icon—the core of the iconic sign—is itself
a felt quality: an instance of Firstness. Thus, in becoming
iconic, expressive meaning does not lose its affective character.
Indeed, only an iconic sign is an adequate model for showing
how expressive meaning *signifies* in art. An indexical sign turns
expressive into literal, referential meaning, and a symbol tends
to transform expression into communication. Of course, all signs
signify—that is, they "mean"—but iconic signs alone signify in
terms of likeness or resemblance. This unique characteristic
allows them to be self-designative, since there is no limit to what
the iconic sign can resemble. (Perhaps because of the indexical
overtones of "designation," Peirce himself preferred the more
neutral term "representation" to indicate what all signs have in
common; iconic signs represent by similarity—a function which
Peirce sometimes called "exhibition." [23] We shall return to this
point in a moment.)

First, it should be made clear that in considering the work
of art as an iconic sign, I do not mean to imply that it is subject
to what art historians call an "iconographic" or "iconological"
analysis. For it is not a question here of viewing certain forms
in the aesthetic object as "carriers" of "conventional meanings" [24]
or as revelatory of underlying historical or even metaphysical
significations. However valid this kind of analysis is for certain
isolated works of art, it cannot be applied indiscriminately to
art without denying the immanent character of genuine aesthetic
meaning. This meaning is found at the level which Erwin

23. Cf. C. S. Peirce, *Collected Papers,* ed. C. Hartshorne and P. Weiss,
Cambridge, Mass., 1960, 2.282, 3.556, 4.448. C. W. Morris insists on
using "designation"—see his "Esthetics and the Theory of Signs," in
Journal of Unified Science, 8 (1939), 132.
24. Erwin Panofsky, *Meaning in the Visual Arts,* New York, 1955,
p. 29.

Panofsky terms the "primary or natural subject matter": [25] that of colors, lines, masses, movements. The meaning is ingredient in these very sensuous elements, which are thus not "pure forms" as Panofsky claims, but already significant or meaningful forms. The semantic cannot be separated from the formal dimension in art, however necessary this move may be in reflective analysis.

Iconic likeness is not to be confused with mere proportional similitude; thus the work of art as iconic is not a mere simulacrum of some pre-existing object. If it were, it would become a secondary thing whose being and meaning are exhausted in its reference to an external model, and thus we would confound iconic with indexical representation. Even in the most extreme pictorial realism, indexical representation is not aesthetically paramount; and in any case, the reference of the aesthetic object to perceptual or historical reality is at best marginal; of course, there may be reference by or through this reality but not primarily *to* it. This is only another way of stating the earlier point that transcendent meanings *per se* have no place in art. Now we see exactly why: their content bears no essential resemblance or affinity to the content that is already incorporated in the form of the work. Transcendent content or meaning can only be indicated or pointed to; it cannot be *shown* in art. Yet the nature of the aesthetic icon or image is precisely to exhibit or show; the spectacle of art *means* by showing— which is not to point out or reveal but to put forth and display.

The work of art shows by a special kind of iconic representation: self-representation. This is not the same thing as self-*re*-presentation. The work does not have to reproduce its literal appearance (though this is possible and has been done effectively in certain recent examples of "light art" constructed with self-reflecting mirrors).[26] I construe the term "iconic self-representation" quite broadly; it does not contradict Leonardo da Vinci's dictum that "the most praiseworthy painting is most

25. *Ibid.*, p. 28.
26. See Robert Doty, *Light: Object and Image*, New York, 1968.

like the thing represented." [27] But "the thing represented" is ultimately the work of art itself, which, instead of literally reproducing itself, is both like itself and identical to itself. More precisely, it is like itself in being itself. This peculiar combination of resemblance and identity is not confined to the aesthetic realm, though it is seen most conspicuously there. Peirce has shown that iconic resemblance is normally qualitative and that the icon serving as a common form or *quale* is self-identical in the terms it relates: "A pure icon does not draw any distinction between itself and its object . . . whatever it is like, it insofar *is*." [28] There is a process of assimilation—not unlike, but more radical than, Husserl's notion of "pairing" [29]—by which the resemblance of the terms of a relation draws them toward an ontological identity. Something quite similar occurs in the case of art; what the work of art "means" is so like the forms that it presents that the meaning becomes in-formed and the forms meaningful. Reciprocal approximation leads to a total presentation that is felt as a continuous self-identical phenomenon in which meaning and form no longer have separate, assigned domains. In aesthetic perception, there is an experience of merging, of absolute self-likeness. This complete self-resemblance is felt as a qualitative self-identity, where by "qualitative" is meant formal in a sense sufficiently broad to include not only configuration but also expression. The work of art is a total expressive form which *means* (in both senses of this word) *itself*. As experienced—that is, as an aesthetic object—it is perceived as an icon signifying itself—which is not to signify nothing, since inseparable from itself is its meaning: but a meaning unique to the work and thus not objectively specifiable and comparable to other meanings. Open and indeterminate as it is, this meaning forms the schematic structure of the work of art; its actualizations in the aesthetic object are always only partial, time-bound, and idiosyncratic.

27. Quoted in *Artists on Art,* ed. R. Goldwater and M. Treves, New York, 1945, p. 54.
28. *Collected Papers,* 5.74. Emphasis mine.
29. See *Cartesian Meditations,* trans. Dorion Cairns, The Hague, 1960, pars. 50–51.

IV

It is not surprising that a discussion of meaning in art should end with a consideration of form. For this meaning, the skeleton of the work, needs form as the flesh of its presentation. It also needs form for a self-limitation that is at once a stabilization and a sedimentation. Form secures meaning, making it immanent to the presented matter of the work. Aesthetic meaning becomes apprehensible by being drawn into an intimate embrace with form. In this embrace, meaning is often called "content," and it is frequently observed that in art content and form vary reciprocally: "complexity of form is sophistication of content." [30] Collingwood says that form and content "exist together or not at all." [31] In a similar vein, Professor Hofstadter speaks of the "ultimate unity of inner content and outer shape, of total meaning and external vehicle." [32] But I believe that we have to do with more than unity here. As an instance of iconic likeness, the relation between form and content involves an element of identification. Form and content become so like each other in full expressivity that they merge and become indistinguishable. In Ben Shahn's words, form becomes "the very shape of content." [33] We are not limited to Greek sculpture for the perfect fusion of form and content, as Hegel thought; it occurs whenever full expression or what we normally call "style" is evident. (Style is not so much "constant form" [34] as a constant congeries of resembling patterns which qualitatively and iconically link various expressive meanings in the works of a given artist or period of art.)

Form is also the way in which the work of art is presented

30. W. K. Wimsatt, Jr., and Monroe C. Beardsley, *The Verbal Icon*, Lexington, Ky., 1954, p. 82.

31. "Form and Content in Art," reprinted in *Essays in the Philosophy of Art*, ed. Alan Donagan, Bloomington, Ind., 1964, p. 231.

32. Hofstadter, article in this book.

33. Ben Shahn, *The Shape of Content*, New York, 1957, p. 62.

34. Meyer Schapiro, "Style," reprinted in *Aesthetics Today*, ed. Morris Philipson, New York, 1961, p. 81.

to us. It is the mode of its presence as an aesthetic object. There is not only a metaphysical link between form and presence, as Heidegger and Derrida have shown; [35] there is also a phenomenological connection. The full form or style, which includes the content, is what we feel in the presence of the work of art: the Firstness that presents itself to us iconically. Regarded as an iconic sign, the work of art exhibits or exposes what it is *like*—that is, *itself*. This exhibition is a form of self-presentation; or rather, the form that exhibits the work of art presents the work itself. Representation in art is perforce *presentation*. In concluding, I would like to focus on presentation in art.

Aesthetic presentation is undeniably a kinaesthetic affair. Expressive form is dynamic: a species of "directed tension," in Arnheim's term; [36] "the graph of an activity," as Focillon said.[37] As such, form in art appeals not to a pure intuition, but to a kinaesthesis of the body. Collingwood and Merleau-Ponty have both underlined this process of "re-enactment," [38] of "vibration or radiation" [39] from the work to the corporeal perceiver. Yet in spite of the kinaesthetic presence of the work—its sensuous givenness—we must observe that the aesthetic object is not felt as an *existent* object. The "carnal essence" [40] of art involves no necessary relation to existence. As Husserl saw, the aesthetic attitude is paradigmatically "non-positional" or "neutral" [41] with respect to the existential status of its object. Again this accords with the nature of art as iconic. Peirce once wrote of the iconic sign that "Its object may be a pure fiction, as to its existence." [42] Meaning in art in no way depends on a *reference* to existence,

35. See Martin Heidegger, *Platons Lehre von der Wahrheit,* Berne, 1947; and Jacques Derrida, "La forme et le vouloir-dire" in *Revue Internationale de Philosophie* (1967), Fasc. 3, pp. 277–299.

36. Rudolf Arnheim, *Art and Visual Perception,* Berkeley, 1965, p. 363.

37. Henri Focillon, *The Life of Forms in Art,* trans. C. B. Hogan and G. Kubler, Yale, 1942, p. 2.

38. Cf. Collingwood, *Principles of Art,* p. 311 f.

39. Maurice Merleau-Ponty, "Eye and Mind," trans. C. Dallery, in *The Primacy of Perception,* ed. James M. Edie, Evanston, Ill., 1964, p. 184.

40. *Ibid.,* p. 169.

41. Cf. Husserl, *Logische Untersuchungen,* II, 2, pars. 39–40; III, par. 45; *Ideen I,* pars. 111–112.

42. *Collected Papers,* 4.531. Peirce capitalizes "object."

even though the materials of the work are fully existent. These materials, however, function only as the support of the pure image that is presented in the actualized aesthetic object.[43]

For we should not forget that the work of art fulfills itself in presenting the "visible," understood in its broadest extension. The visible is presented in the form of an icon, or image, whose meaning is given enmeshed in an expressive form. Meaning in art is brought to visibility in and with this form—brought from a state of inchoate invisibility to luminous appearance. Paul Klee spoke of the artist as making "secret visions visible"; the paradigm of aesthetic presentation is to bring "the antecedents of the visible" into the sheer visibility of the image.[44] One of these antecedents is meaning, which the artist struggles to formulate in a maximally expressive form. If successful, the artist makes the meaning so immanent to the form that the two coalesce. What is thus created is a presentation, not an essence; the artist presents no evidence, only an image.

It is true that aesthetic perception may often require something like a spontaneous reduction of distractions in order to grasp this image; and we may even say that under optimal conditions the aesthetic image is given "in person" (i.e., self-given) and "corporeally"—terms used by Husserl to describe the intuition of essences. But the clarity, cogency, and adequation of essential insight are not typically found in aesthetic perception. Instead of "coincidence" (*Deckung*),[45] there is in art a certain distantiation of perceiving subject from aesthetic object, resulting in an ineradicable translucency and latency of meaning in the presented object. This distantiation is not, however, measurable in objective terms; in place of a metric and static distance, there is a kinetic and qualitative proximity that continually changes, yet always falls short of sheer coincidence. In this rich realm of oscillating propinquity—and especially in the presence of great works of art—there takes place what

43. For the concept of "support" or *Träger*, cf. E. Fink, *Studien zur Phänomenologie*, The Hague, 1966, pp. 72–77.
44. Paul Klee, *On Modern Art*, trans. P. Findlay, London, 1962, p. 51.
45. Cf. Husserl, *Logische Untersuchungen*, VI, 1, par. 8.

Merleau-Ponty called "the conceptless presentation of universal Being." [46] But Being, like meaning, is intrinsic to the work. An ontology of art, no less than a phenomenology of art, must remain at the autochthonous ground-level of presentation in immanence: the elemental and dense soil in which meaning in art lies rooted.

46. "Eye and Mind," p. 182.

John J. McDermott

DEPRIVATION AND CELEBRATION:
SUGGESTIONS FOR AN AESTHETIC ECOLOGY

> This isolated line and the isolated fish alike are living beings
> with forces peculiar to them, though latent . . . But the voice
> of these latent forces is faint and limited. It is the environment
> of the line and the fish that brings about a miracle: the latent
> forces have become dynamic. The environment is the composition.
> profound. Instead of a low voice, one hears a choir. The latent
> forces have become dynamic. The environment is the compositino.
>
> WASSILY KANDINSKY [1]

I

Perhaps we may be allowed to sound an introductory positive
note as accompaniment to the extensive turbulence which
characterizes contemporary American culture. At this time we
are witnessing an extraordinary intensification of the experience

1. Cited in Robert Goldwater and Marco Treves, eds., *Artists on Art*,
New York, 1947, p. 451. Cf. also Lee Nordness, ed., *Art U.S.A. Now*,
New York, 1962, p. 12, for a statement by Allen S. Weller: "In a sense,
the physical facts of nature become less and less important to us in themselves; we have gone beyond a stage in which recognition and identification of material forms is of primary significance. It is the tension between
forms, the effects of movements on shapes and qualities, the active
spaces which surround solid masses, which seem to be the most tangible
things with which many artists need to work. There are of course
striking parallels to the social and economic situation of our times. The
great problems of our period are not material ones; they are problems
of basic relationships."

of self-consciousness along with a parallel growth in our sensitivity to environmental problems. Dissatisfaction in our culture proceeds not only from the traditional critique of inadequate surroundings but also from the escalating awareness of the complex needs of the human person. Contemporary man suffers more, or at least complains more, in part because he has come to believe and feel that his needs are infinitely more complex. While such a development has obvious political and social roots, the thrust of this presentation will be to show that in large measure the revolution in our time is aesthetic—that is, a revolution in feeling. And we contend that one of the meanings of contemporary art is the light it casts on this transformation of human needs and possibilities.

The all too characteristic attempt to deal with this revolution by a mere shift in the external functions of our institutions is now proving to be abortive. In his book *Symbolism*, Whitehead spells out the implications of an insensitive approach to institutional transformation.

> It is the first step in sociological wisdom, to recognize that the major advances in civilization are processes which all but wreck the societies in which they occur: —like unto an arrow in the hand of a child. The art of free society consists first in the maintenance of the symbolic code; and secondly in fearlessness of revision, to secure that the code serves those purposes which satisfy an enlightened reason. Those societies which cannot combine reverence to their symbols with freedom of revision, must ultimately decay either from anarchy, or from the slow atrophy of a life stifled by useless shadows.[2]

Whereas Whitehead refers to the "symbolic code," we speak here of man's "affectivity." The important question confronting proponents of social change has to do with how men actually feel about their situation. Efforts to ameliorate the human condition must be sensitized in a very specific way as to what those persons in question "care for"—in a word, that toward which they are affectionate. The failure to achieve this sensitivity looms large as a factor in generating the savage contemporary critique of the "do-gooder," the "liberal," and the Establishment-sponsored

2. Alfred North Whitehead, *Symbolism*, New York, 1955, p. 88.

programs for social welfare. Too often our programs attempt to help people become what we *assume* they should become. Too often we impose our own social style on others, even in some instances our own social trap. We claim that such programs are liberating although we rarely have any understanding of the strength of the variant life-styles with which we tamper.[3]

We look back, for example, on the recent efforts at urban renewal. The diagnosis seemed obvious: a ramshackle environment complete with all the attendant physical and social evils. The solution seemed equally obvious: destruction of the environment and either relocation to a new context or a subsequent return to the rebuilt neighborhood. Now quite aside from the fact that the hard-core poor were rarely provided opportunity to return, another, more subtle problem existed. For even when the original occupants were returned to public housing, they seemed not to take care of these new dwellings. The first reason offered was typically insensitive: "What can you expect of such people? They are incorrigible." A later reason was more humane but nonetheless paternalistic and wide of the mark: "Such people have had no experience in caring for a new environment. They have to be taught."

It is only in our time and only when we listen to the people involved, in their own language, that we come close to understanding this problem. A neighborhood, a block, a tenement is not simply an external setting. Rather it is a complex field of relationships that form an ecological network, the strength of which is often beneath the surface. The human organism struggles for salvation, no matter how impoverished his context. He does this by building himself into his environment by means of establishing confidence in a number of relational ties. They may involve "landmarks"—a candy store, a playground, a house of worship, a merchant tradition, or perhaps vicarious participation in the passing scene. Such relations become internalized, that is, taken for granted. Their full power, their function as

3. Contemporary social science and literature abound in material on the complexity of cultural styles. Cf., e.g., the work of Oscar Lewis, especially *La Vida: A Puerto Rican Family in the Culture of Poverty— San Juan and New York,* New York, 1966.

lifelines become manifest only when they are uprooted. The problem thus becomes obvious. With the cutting of these inexplicit yet deeply felt ties, people become estranged, and while thrashing about in search of a recognizable hold, they tend to reject a new and comparatively alien environment.[4] It is imperative, therefore, that our diagnosis of social ills include a recognition of the positive factors at work in the situation under evaluation. The more serious our affliction, the deeper the affection we have for those aspects of it which are humanizing. Little if any growth is achieved if by our social changes we truncate these relations, especially in view of the failure of contemporary pedagogy to develop in many of our people the ability to make new ones from scratch.

John Dewey has told us that "order is not imposed from without but is made out of the relations of harmonious interactions that energies bear to one another."[5] Why, then, do we fail to recognize that personal growth does not usually proceed from an imposition of values, however noble in intent, but must rather be continuous with the experienced situation in which a person finds himself? Such growth, particularly when found in the midst of social and economic impoverishment, often does not appear to be impressive when judged by standards external to the undergoing of the experience, as, for example, long-standing sociological sanctions primarily related to the problems and aspirations of another time. Many of us still assume that the mere shift from one environment to another is equivalent to a personal breakthrough, as though mobility guaranteed depth of participation. In fact, the external character of the environment is not a necessary guarantee of the quality of involvement. The personal growth of which we speak, no matter what the setting, signalizes an integration of the needs and possibilities of the person, taken, in Dewey's phrase, as a "live creature." That an environment should generate and sustain such a development in the person is obvious. That it should not

4. Cf. Theo Crosby, *Architecture: City Sense,* New York, 1965, pp. 76–83. For the importance of local landmarks, cf. Kevin Lynch, *The Image of the City,* Cambridge, Mass., 1960, p. 48.
5. John Dewey, *Art as Experience,* New York, 1958, p. 14.

systematically prevent such growth is equally obvious. Where we seem to be in the dark is in the evaluation of specific environments. We seem quite incapable of recognizing and sustaining the redeeming factors in what has come to be known as a deprived environment, just as we ignore the lethal factors in those considered to be more acceptable. A contrast of the worlds of Henry Roth and James Agee with those of John Updike and John Cheever gives aesthetic intensity to the long-standing questions about the relationship of affluence and personal growth. One of the reasons for failure to recognize and strengthen the humanizing dimensions of impoverished environments is that, on methodological if not psychological grounds, contemporary efforts to engender social change often fall victim to a colossal instance of "vicious intellectualism," as phrased by William James. "The treating of a name as excluding from the fact named what the name's definition fails positively to include, is what I call vicious intellectualism." [6]

James warns us that the consistent use of certain "names" is not a necessary indication that the experiences so named have maintained an equal consistency in meaning and import. Names of large and complex experiences such as "city," "poverty," and "black" have developed an illegitimate clarity over the years. Upon deeper analysis, particularly when sustained by the articulation of persons actually involved, we find that many of our assumptions are seriously out of touch with the nature of the situation as experienced. It is instructive in this regard to acknowledge the new use of the term "visibility" when applied to "black people" and the "poor," for it refers to the upending of the mass stereotypes which have resulted from structuring our definitions in such a way as to preclude new data. Assessing the "failures" of black Americans in the context of immigrant success and the attribution of the circularity of hard-core poverty to lack of initiative are glaring instances of such stereotypes. In each case, when challenged, these assumptions have been shown to misdirect our attention and keep us from confronting even the most obvious causal factors in these massive social problems.

6. William James, *A Pluralistic Universe,* New York, 1909, p. 60.

More subtle dimensions of our lives—the nature of the learning process, for example—have shown themselves to be sur-
prisingly opaque, when analyzed by traditional concepts. Many
of our people are profoundly alert to their situation and are
responsive in an original and creative way to their environment,
yet judged by most of the criteria we have enshrined, they
would be found bereft of insight. Again, it is instructive to
remember that the previous extensive revolution in our educational system also involved a break with a massive stereotype—
namely, the contention that interest and social relevance were
inversely related to the importance of what was to be learned.
Symbolized by the new psychology of William James and the
pedagogy of John Dewey, the breakthrough in educational
practice at the turn of the century involved a radical relocating
of the question. The experience of the child as a child rather
than as a small adult became the focal point, and from this
proceeded extensive changes in what we call the aesthetic
setting: the design of the classroom, its furniture, and the
overall provision for continuity between the school as environment and the needs and interests of the child. Unfortunately the
results of this breakthrough have themselves now become stereo-
typical and often function to prevent articulation of the considerably new needs and style of more recent generations. As then, a
new aesthetic setting for inquiry is necessary. The phrase "Tell it
like it is" has roots not only in the anguish of the black
revolution and in the hippie critique of the middle class, but
is rooted also in a more generalized attack on the bifurcation
between our experience directly expressed in aesthetic terms
and statements about experience. These latter statements are
accused of becoming a world unto themselves, complete with
seductive metaphorical changes intended to indicate contact
with reality.

In this last regard, our capacity for self-deception seems unlimited. Too often we credit ourselves with an awareness of
others' experience simply on the basis of a mere shift in our
language. We domesticate or legitimize the most radical protest
by borrowing its phrasing and thereby claim institutional awareness and accommodation. On a more profound and integral level,

however, such language as "black argot" or "poverty speak" is
rooted in a very different version of the world and cannot be
absorbed. As a way of preventing such a shallow response,
the disenfranchised have taken to expressing themselves in
obviously aesthetic terms, peculiar to their own sense of experience. Gatherings of the poor, blacks, and now students tell
a remarkably similar story in pointing to this gap between
radically different styles of articulation. The present revolution,
therefore, addresses itself not so much to the values in question,
on which there is considerable agreement, but rather to our
way of interacting or, in Dewey's phrase, to our way of "having
an experience." What is being sought, then, can be phrased as
a new cultural pedagogy in which the "affective" dimension
moves from the periphery to the center, as a resource for evalu-
ating the quality of our environment. I offer here that contemporary art, taken in the broad sense, is incisive about this
need and yields significant philosophical and methodological
approaches, which would prove liberating if we were to adopt
them in our attempt to bring about basic institutional changes.
Further, again on methodological grounds, it would be salutary
if our efforts to bring about social change were influenced as
much by the arts as by developments in the natural and social
sciences. Let us now attempt to offer some sustenance for
these contentions.

II

The fundamental question has to do with our basic understanding of human activity. Although seldom put so crudely,
the fact is that a common attitude is reflected in the statement
that man is a thing among things, manipulable from the outside.
Other images are only slightly below the surface, holding that
man is a box, a container, a chessman externally moved upon
a world board with a finite number of places to occupy. Perhaps
we should call this a Euclidean geometric anthropology, in
which man "fits in" and the angles "prove out" in the end. For
those of us who credit a life of reflection, for the supposed
avoidance of this attitude, we are now warned by the fact

that the very institutions created to sustain such insight have recently been among those accused of gross personal manipulation.

Now, if there is any generalization we can make about contemporary art, it has to do precisely with this approach to human activity. To bathe ourselves in the variant art styles of our time is to come away with the conviction that man is an energizer and a maker of worlds,[7] rather than a derivation from worlds already made. In an effort to stress the novel aspects of creative experience, contemporary art has introduced the performing of "happenings." While it has to be admitted that, despite the claims of increased flexibility, such "happenings" are stylized and even planned, the full implication, however, of such a direction is that man himself is a "happening" and that at any given time, he can "aesthetize" his living. Coupled with recent experiments in the theater, we find here a concretization, from the side of art, of Dewey's insight into the rhythm and activity of the "live creature." Dewey even anticipated the contemporary artistic commitment to immediacy and its denial of the tendency to store up for another generation.[8] He tells us that "the time of consummation is also one of beginning anew.

7. The work of Edward Keinholz and Louise Nevelson is especially pertinent in this context. Cf. also Allan Kaprow, *Assemblage, Environments, and Happenings,* New York, 1965.

8. The most perceptive comment on the sense of immediacy which characterizes recent art is to be found in an essay by Leo Steinberg. After reading Exodus 16, he comments: "When I had read this much, I stopped and thought how like contemporary art this manna was; not only in that it was a God-send, or in that it was a desert food, or in that no one could quite understand it—for 'they wist not what it was.' Nor even because some of it was immediately put in a museum—'to be kept for your generations'; nor yet because the taste of it has remained a mystery, since the phrase here translated as 'wafers made with honey' is in fact a blind guess; the Hebrew word is one that occurs nowhere else in ancient literature, and no one knows what it really means. Whence the legend that manna tasted to every man as he wished; though it came from without, its taste in the mouth was his own making.

"But what struck me most as an analogy was this Command—that you were to gather of it every day, according to your eating, and not to lay it up as insurance or investment for the future, making each day's gathering an act of faith." "Contemporary Art and the Plight of Its Public," in *The New Art,* Gregory Battcock, ed., (New York, 1966, pp. 46–47.

Any attempt to perpetuate beyond its term the enjoyment attending the time of fulfillment and harmony constitutes *withdrawal from the world.*" [9] Out of a different context, Robert
Jay Lifton describes this development in the assessment of
human activity, as the creation of "a new kind of man—a 'protean man'." He continues:

> As my stress is upon change and flux, I shall not speak much
> of "character" and "personality," both of which suggest fixity
> and permanence. Erikson's concept of identity has been, among
> other things, an effort to get away from this principle of fixity;
> and I have been using the term self-process to convey still more
> specifically the idea of flow. For it is quite possible that even
> the image of personal identity, in so far as it suggests inner
> stability and sameness, is derived from a vision of a traditional
> culture in which man's relationships to his institutions and symbols
> are still relatively intact—which is hardly the case today. If we
> understand the self to be the person's symbol of his organism,
> then self-process refers to the continuous psychic recreation of
> that symbol.[10]

Lifton's understanding of the self as the "person's symbol
of his organism," contrary to the use of the term "self-identity,"
enables us to avoid blocking off the necessary awareness of the
novel qualities in our experiencing. Rather than taking the
creative artistic process as a departure from life ordinarily lived,
we should see it as an articulation of possibilities inherent in the
flow of each person's experience. In this vein, with contemporary
art as the focus, we gain access to a new set of metaphors,
considerably more viable in any consideration of human
activity.

Contemporary art presents us with an open system. Order is
maintained, but at the service of novelty. The future is anticipated not as a codification of our intention, rather as a har-
binger of surprise. Indeed, intention itself emerges with clarity
only when we are far into the creative process, and is often
retrospectively reconstructed when our work takes a surprising
turn. More specifically, the work of contemporary art is largely

9. Dewey, *op. cit.*, p. 17. Italics added.
10. Robert Jay Lifton, "Protean Man" in *Partisan Review*, Vol. 35, No. 1
(Winter 1968), 13.

themed by a tension between the pressure for improvisation and the need to maintain some structural continuity, at least to the satisfaction of the artist. So demanding is the burden of improvisation that the beginning artist of our time often feels compelled to start from scratch and create an entirely new environment. Thus we have a dizzying array of new approaches in which the artist, by his work, not only avoids even the broadest imitation but, in deeply personal terms, challenges the assumptions about the nature of art prior to his contribution. Consequently, what is striking about this art is the variety of technique and, above all, the materials used, for both are decisive factors in the creating of a new environment. Also it is rare that works by different artists now reveal enough in common for us to utilize the comparative method to evaluate them. Generic terms like "pop art," "combine paintings," "mixed media," and "assemblage" are merely catch-holders and lack clear criteria of distinction and evaluation. We come closer to the quality of this art if, upon confrontation, we do our best to participate in the artist's "managing process," with an eye to our own experience. Contemporary art does not tend to create objects of honor. Rather, it honors the act of creating, and it celebrates the personal as an aesthetic dimension. In some instances of electronic sculpture, the observer becomes a direct participant, a co-creator, as his body scent or sounds are taken as factors in the activity of the sculpture. The contemporary artist, at his best, is pressing us to aesthetically reconstruct our own environments rather than to have us participate vicariously in idealized versions of a world distant from our own experience. We should pay heed here to John Dewey, who wrote that works of art are "celebrations, recognized as such, of the things of ordinary experience. Even a crude experience, if authentically an experience, is more fit to give a clue to the intrinsic nature of esthetic experience than is an object already set apart from any other mode of experience." [11]

The element which binds Dewey's metaphysics to the contemporary "art of the ordinary" is to be found in the dimension of affection. It is necessary to have a genuine care for common

11. Dewey, *op. cit.*, p. 11.

experience, if celebration is to take place. By virtue of an emphasis on improvisation, the affirmation of the potential majesty of the ordinary, and the denial of rationalistic criteria for aesthetic evaluation, contemporary art has shown itself to be of relevance for certain attempts to revitalize personal life now under the press of vast institutional bureaucracies. If we truly seek a new cultural pedagogy, the task before us is to bring about a decisive movement from the pervasive experience of deprivation to one of celebration. If we think in terms of human ecology, such a shift would involve two major approaches. First, we hold that the nature and worth of our interactions, biological and sociological, should not be evaluated apart from their "affective" quality, as self-consciously experienced and articulated by the participants. Second, we should rejuvenate the aesthetic dimension of common experience inclusive of the technological, both industrial and electronic.[12] Both of these approaches cannot be limited to personal belief, as a sort of therapy, but the community has to indicate some sanction for these attitudes by building them into our institutions, the school for example. With the generalized attitudes of contemporary art as a backdrop, let us open the question of an aesthetic ecology.

III

The basic difficulties in an aesthetic ecology emerge when we move from rural to urban experience. It has not been enough noticed that such a development really means a change from nature as the resource to artifact as the resource, for the purpose of building a personal evironment. There is a profound and unsettling paradox at work in American culture which has given rise to considerable difficulty in our attempt to face the now dominant urban experience. In an almost mythic sense, we are tied to the land, although in increasing numbers our experience of it is either vicarious or in an artifactual

12. The electronic analysis of organismic experience is given some structural treatment in Lucien Gérardin, *Bionics,* New York, 1968.

context, as in a park. Yet we have failed to mythologize the urban environment so as to provide experiences necessary to human growth—namely, among others, nesting, creative participation in daily ritual, and celebration of odds and ends— recognized to be worthy by the larger community.[13]

We have, perhaps, taken too much for granted in man's adaptation to an urban context. What is involved in the young man being a "sitter on curbs" rather than a "swinger of birches"? Does "concrete" blunt affection? Can man truly achieve a sense of continuity with his setting when he works through technological intermediaries? The fact that modern man dwells in the city does not of itself indicate that he is affective toward it. Some say that we have repressed our sense of space and our enjoyment of a more organic setting. In this view, we merely tolerate the urban setting as necessary to other goals.

I suggest that the increasing acceptance of such a view spells disaster for city life. While it is unquestionable that certain offensive characteristics of urban experience, such as congestion, air pollution, and social afflictions, have to be drastically reduced, a corresponding positive task also awaits response. We have failed to articulate, for purposes of common experience, the aesthetic quality of a technological environment. Our nostalgia for the things of nature, however repressed, has kept us from the marvels of sound, design, texture, and light which constitute modern urban life.[14] I do not believe that the aesthetic dimension of the city is to be found primarily in its museums or resources for the performing arts. Indeed, a too heavy dependence on such institutions has perhaps warped our sense of the aesthetic and caused us to think of much of our surroundings as paltry and trivial, and, worse, to treat them in that vein.

For Dewey, the basic problem was "that of recovering the

13. Cf. John Kouwenhoven, "To Make All Things New" in *The Arts in Modern American Civilization*, New York, 1967, pp. 103–136.

14. Cf. the *Vision and Value Series* edited by Gyorgy Kepes, particularly the volumes entitled *Education of Vision, The Man-Made Object,* and *Sign, Image and Symbol,* New York, 1965, 1966, 1966. Cf. also Kouwenhoven, *op. cit., passim,* and David Pye, *The Nature of Design,* New York, 1964.

continuity of aesthetic experience with normal processes of living." [15] To anaesthetize these processes is to set the stage for deprivation, which not only results from the absence of conditions necessary to basic human life but proceeds as well from an inability to draw nourishment from a person's immediate situation. Whatever the paucity of our environment, if we enter into it as an active, engaging self, making relationships and building a personal style, this will constitute some growth. In this way, our basic attitude would be characterized by a reaching, a cresting—that is, by being open to new possibilities. Deprivation is the loss of this ability and can be found even in environmental settings rich in detail. Now, one of the causes of this situation is that too many of our experiences are proscribed, so that our responses are external and perfunctory. This is particularly true of the myriad of artifacts which we encounter in our everyday experience, many of them fascinating in vernacular design but unsanctioned by traditional artistic judgment. In still other instances a cultural hierarchy of values is at work, ascribing the worth of situations apart from the person's potential relationship to them. Paraphrasing John Cage, we hear the "names" of sounds and see the "names" of things, often ranked in importance by an objective order and rarely touched by us in a personal way.[16]

We might strike a parallel here by a reference to the development of modern art since impressionism.[17] Speaking in broad terms, modern art has attempted to upend the fixed character of aesthetic values and of late has contended that any material and any technique, given a relational context, can bring forth a work of art. This sense of the new, of beginning again in personal terms, is given statement by Thomas Hess, writing on the painter Willem de Kooning. "The crisis of modern art presupposes that each shape, even a plain oval, be re-invented

15. Dewey, *op. cit.*, p. 10.

16. Cf. John Cage, *Silence*, Cambridge, Mass., 1966.

17. For a discussion of this development from the side of a metaphysics of relation, cf. John J. McDermott, "To Be Human Is to Humanize: A Radically Empirical Aesthetic" in Michael Novak, ed., *American Philosophy and the Future*, New York, 1968. pp. 21–59.

—or, rather, given an autochthonous existence in paint. Nothing could be accepted or received on faith as a welcomed heritage." [18] Perhaps the most revealing style of this concern of modern art is found in that of assemblage, which has considerable symbolic meaning for our discusison of ecology. Assemblage is historically rooted in futurism, with its concern for a "completely renovated sensitiveness," [19] and in Dada, which, in the words of Tristan Tzara, held that art would be created by "materials noble or looked down upon, verbal clichés or clichés of old magazines, bromides, publicity slogans, refuse, etc. —these incongruous elements are transformed into an unexpected, homogeneous cohesion as soon as they take place in a newly created ensemble." [20] In assemblage the context is the source of meaning. The materials shed their prior meanings and regather along different, even drastically different, lines of intelligibility. Nothing belongs anywhere until it is present. And with every new entry to the assemblage, all the other entries are reconstructed in their meanings. One of the intriguing factors here is that the masters of assemblage are very young children, for they are the least dominated by definitions of materials and, in the pejorative sense, by "proper" space, color, and texture relationships.

Now, if we phrase the other side of our parallel, the attempt to forge a viable aesthetic ecology involves us in issues very similar to those found in the development of modern art. Celebration cannot take place if it is a response to experiences whose worth and meaning are predetermined by criteria alien to our own experience—to our having and undergoing. Deprivation cannot be ameliorated if we assign worth to activities as proportionate to their place in a hierarchy of values, independent of our experiencing and unreconstructed by our participation. Learning is not going to be a rich experience if it is tied solely to the economic ladder or if competition becomes its dominant

18. Thomas Hess, *Willem de Kooning*, New York, 1959, pp. 15–16.
19. Cited in William C. Seitz, *The Art of Assemblage*, New York, 1961, p. 30.
20. Seitz, *op. cit.*, p. 39.

theme. We are not going to have affection for our environments if their worth is determined by a comparison with a fixed and largely unobtainable standard.

Assemblage has much to teach us here. Out of bits and pieces, some old, some new, some thrown away, some kept out of nostalgia, we assemble a new environment and return life and meaning to these fragments. As an application of this approach, we can look at the city as a great pyramid with clear delineation as to top and bottom. Depending on our personal position in this arrangement, experience is exhilarating, trying, or simply oppressive. At its best, however, the city yields to another vantage point, as a masterpiece of assemblage. In this instance the technological has aesthetic quality, and the unity achieved is not hierarchical but is rather built up out of a coalescence of relational wholes, each giving to its participants a sense of control, of management, of enjoyment, and, above all, continuity with their most immediate needs. The question is not how far we go but how rich is the journey. At the conclusion of *Human Nature and Conduct*, John Dewey says it better.

> Within the flickering inconsequential acts of separate selves dwells a sense of the whole which claims and dignifies them. In its presence we put off mortality and live in the universal. The life of the community in which we live and have our being is the fit symbol of this relationship. The acts in which we express our perception of the ties which bind us to others are its only rites and ceremonies.[21]

21. John Dewey, *Human Nature and Conduct*, New York, 1930, pp. 331–332.

José Ferrater-Mora

REALITY AS MEANING

I. *Ontological Dispositions*

This paper is part of a larger philosophical exploration in the realm of ontology.[1] It is assumed that all realities can be conceived from two contrasting and complementary viewpoints called "Being" and "Meaning." These terms do not aim at designating any kind of reality, whether ordinary or extraordinary; there are no such things as beings or meanings. "Being" and "Meaning" are, to begin with, names of tendential ontological modes, or, as I shall call them, "dispositions," in a sense of "disposition" which it would be too tedious to elucidate here. Let it suffice to say that such dispositions are not to be construed as properties, essential or otherwise, of realities. To say that "Being" and "Meaning" are names of ontological dispositions is only to say that any reality whatsoever is and behaves as if it tended, in varying degrees, toward both "Being" and "Meaning," which are understood as ontological poles, or limiting-concepts, of all realities.[2] Furthermore, any reality can be conceived both as a "being-reality" (when it is seen as tending toward Being) and as a "meaning-reality" (when it is seen as tending toward Meaning). The expressions "being-reality" and

1. Cf. my book, *El Ser y el Sentido,* Madrid, 1967.
2. See my book, *Being and Death: An Outline of Integrationist Philosophy,* Berkeley, 1965, particularly the Introduction and Chapter I.

"meaning-reality" can be equated with the expressions "reality as being" and "reality as meaning," respectively.

I will confine myself here to clarifying the notion of reality as meaning against the (for the moment merely implicit) background of the notion of reality as being. I will emphasize the ontological features of the concept of meaning (or, as it might also be called, "sense") and hence will not discuss its semantical aspects. The semantical and nonsemantical notions of meaning may not be as completely extraneous to each other as has often been contended, but there is little doubt that to speak of a reality as meaning and to elucidate the function of "means" in "'....' means '...'" are not the same thing.

Realities can be said to exhibit the ontological disposition called "meaning" in various ways, or modes, of which "intention" and "nexus" seem to be particularly noteworthy.

II. *Meaning as Intention*

Every reality can be meant, and thus can be the object or "terminus" of the so-called "intentions." This is the same as saying that it is an intentional object in one or a number of modes: as thinkable, knowable, etc. Now, to assert that every reality is intentional, or better, "intentionable," is not to claim that there is, on the one hand, a reality and, on the other, its "being intentional" (or "intentionable"). Any reality is intentional or intentionable insofar as it is a reality.

It may be argued that intentionality can never be ascribed to any *reality*, because intentional acts bracket the reality of the intended object, so that to say that an object is intentional is tantamount to saying that it is only the terminus of an act. Such an argument is faultless if by "being intentional" we mean some real property similar to such properties as being blue, being broken, and so on. It is less acceptable, however, if we conceive of intentionality as an ontological *tendency* exhibited by all realities, so that the latter would not become termini of intentional acts unless they were themselves "intentionable." The intentions here referred to are, therefore, the realities themselves *as* meanings, or, as they have already been called, the "meaning-realities."

Let us now probe into the manner in which the intentional dispositions of realities are manifested. This happens through acts which may also be called "intentional" but which are at the same time real acts of thinking, meaning, knowing, etc. These acts are real insofar as they are actual acts of subjects, and specifically of persons. As real acts of real subjects, or persons, they permeate the meanings with a "halo" of reality. Nevertheless, since it is desirable not to confuse the contents of the acts with the meanings which they apprehend, the question arises as to whether we do not posit, at this point, a world of meanings independent of the real world or constituting the (epistemological or, as the case may be, ontological) foundation of the latter.

The answer is as follows: real acts aim at real objects, and actually produce meanings—thoughts, significations, etc.—which can be expressed by languages and, in general, symbol-systems. Now, two things must be taken into account: First, the meanings are actualizations of the disposition "meaning" in the realities themselves; if the latter lacked meaning, the corresponding acts would cease to be intentional. Intentional acts are, in sum, real acts of intentions, capable of actualizing what is intentional, or "intentionable," in the realities. Second, actualization of the disposition "meaning" does not consist simply in discovering or disclosing what is "lurking down there." Actualization is not a passive reflection of realities; it is a seeing, understanding, meaning, or conceiving of them. The realities appear then as seen, understood, meant, conceived, etc. In some way, therefore, meanings are produced. But they are not to be separated from the realities—not only because they ultimately refer to realities but also, and mainly, because the very same meanings in turn can be constituted as realities. Meanings can be "objectified" and thus can be turned into intentional, or "intentionable," objects. Thus, for instance, thoughts about realities may in turn be objects of further thoughts and, in general, of further "intentions."

The process just described may lead to an "enrichment" of reality of which the best (perhaps the only) example is the human cultural process. What is so "enriched" is not, of course, the reality which was originally "intended" but the very same reality insofar as it has already been "intended." Let us consider a scientific theory. We may conceive it, *grosso modo,* as the result of real intentional acts of many kinds (observations, comparisons, inferences, conceptualizations, systematizations, etc.). The theory actualizes meanings; that is to say, it makes explicit by means of descriptions, explanations, etc., that which is "intendible"—knowable, intelligible, etc.—in physical reality.

In turn, the theory itself becomes an objectification, an object of further intentional acts. Reflection about the theory —for example, about its conceptual structure—is never completely extraneous to the reality which the theory attempts to describe or explain, for the theory is *about* some reality or set of realities. As a consequence, reflection about the theory is in turn reflection about the way in which the theory "intends" ("understands") the reality. At the same time, reflection about the theory is reflection about an objectification, or a system of objectifications which were originally an actualization of a cluster of meanings.

Such actualization may be viewed as an infinite task. Meaning produces meaning. To be sure, the knowledge of a reality does not add anything to the being of the latter; the reality remains the same in its *being,* whether it is known or not. However, the knowledge does add something to the reality in its *meaning;* at any rate, it makes explicit an implicit meaning, and by so doing it enlarges its meaning. Meanings are given neither in nor outside of reality once and for all. They result from a relation to the reality which makes it increasingly better known and, in consequence, increasingly "significant."

There would still be meaning in the world even if there were no acts of "intention," for the latter presuppose that realities are "intendible." Nevertheless there would be, so to speak, "less meaning" if there were no intentional acts. It goes without saying that such acts are not necessarily limited to the cognitive grasp of realities: all human activities usually summarized under the name "culture" are at the same time meaning-possessing and meaning-producing. Let us consider a tree. It can be "apprehended" by means of a painting. The painting is of the tree, whatever its degree of resemblance to a "real tree." The tree can thus be said to be "paintable," yet the (actual) painting of the tree gives it a meaning which was not originally "contained" in the tree. A tree does not include all its possible paintings; it simply has the possibility of being painted. Nevertheless every painting of the tree makes it more "significant," and more "meaningful." One could say the same thing, *mutatis mutandis,* about various other modes of "intending" the tree: it may be "intended" as a symbol of strength, the dwelling of a god, the rallying point of a political movement, a place from which justice is dealt with, a plant on whose bark lovers inscribe their names as a reminder of their eternal troth, etc. With all this we are coming out from the realm of meaning as intention and are moving toward other fields of meaning. The latter, however, are not to be separated from the former, since all forms of meaning are given within the frame of meaning-reality. Once again, there is no reality plus meaning, but reality as meaning.

In the notion of meaning as intention the role played by language is of paramount importance. Language is, in fact, one of the basic modes in which intentions are manifested, i.e., in which realities as meanings are actualized. Language is not a part of the world in the sense that the world can speak about itself, but it is a part of the world insofar as it arises from activities carried out by real subjects in intentional attitudes.

It has been repeatedly pointed out that the features of language are not features of the world. The expression "It is raining pitchforks" is neither wet nor forky. The expression "The earth is round" is not itself round (or it need not be). Even allowing for the possibility of a certain degree of isomorphism between certain expressions and certain realities (or between some forms or structures of both), we need not conclude that the world described by these expressions is linguistic in character. Yet certain expressions are capable of describing the

world, or parts thereof, because of the "intendible" character of
the latter. Language actualizes the describability of the world
in a way similar to that in which knowing acts actualize the
knowability of realities. On the other hand, language does not
limit itself to reflecting reality; it turns it into into a cluster
of meanings. When linguistically expressed, these meanings become objectified, and are thus the object of further intentions
and possibly of further descriptions. One speaks about language
in language. In this case, the difference between the features
of language and the features of what language describes weakens
considerably. "It is raining pitchforks" and "The earth is round"
are written in English, and so is "It is written in English." To
be sure, one language does not necessarily merge into another,
since it is *about* another. But in any case the meaning-reality
which we call "language" is actualized by means of another,
higher level, language.

I noted earlier that semantical and nonsemantical notions of
meaning should not be confused, so that whenever we use the
term "meaning" we should keep in mind the context in which
the word is uttered. Yet semantic meanings as objectifications
fall within the scope of some of the meaning-realities I have
alluded to in the preceding paragraph. The objectifications produced by some intentional acts yield languages which are not
worlds of meanings totally alien to the "world" but which are
nonetheless clusters of realities, as such "intendible" and worthy
of being scrutinized from an ontological point of view.

It is obvious that languages are not composed only of descriptive expressions. The ordinary language we use abounds
in expressions which utter commands, desires, imprecations, beliefs, opinions, etc. Nevertheless all expressions can be said to actualize meanings. These are the meanings intended by human
beings in their interpersonal and social relations, in their attempts
to understand the world, and, in general, in their cultural and
historical settings. In many cases meanings are not to be confined to intentions, though the latter may provide the ground,
or the general framework, for all meanings, There is always
something "intended" in intentional acts; yet what is intended
is never pure meaning independent of facts or of realities:

it is always facts, realities, situations, acts, etc., within the ten-dential disposition called "meaning." I have emphasized here meanings which are exhibited in knowledge, etc., but this does not exclude the possibility of scrutinizing those meanings manifested in actions, productions, creations, and so on.

III. *Meaning as Nexus*

It should be noted that the disposition called "meaning" is not only "tendential," but it is so in various ways and degrees, Let me confine myself for the moment to the question of de-grees. The lowest degree (where "lowest" is not to be construed as a result of a value judgment) amounts simply to being "in-tendible." Such a degree of intentionality is so slight that it is sometimes extremely arduous to distinguish it from the disposi-tion called "being"; the fact that something is what it is and the fact that it is "intendible" seem to coalesce. On the other hand, actually being "intended" evinces a higher degree of meaning. Being intended may still be grounded in "being in-tendible," but it extends and increases the latter, thereby gener-ating not an independent and irreducible universe of meanings but a greater meaningfulness in realities.

I am not dealing in any case with meanings or with beings themselves. As I hope to be able to show, no degree of meaning or of being is ever independent. What I dub "degree of mean-ing" is such only in relation to being. Conversely, any "degree of being" is such only in relation to meaning. Therefore, we are allowed to speak of the passage from meaning-*reality* to reality-*meaning* only within the frame of the aforementioned correlation and interdependence. "Meaning-*reality*" is the name of a maximum degree of being and a minimum degree of mean-ing; "reality-*meaning*" is the name of a maximum degree of meaning and a minimum degree of being. In either case, neither being nor meaning is left out of the picture.

Let us go back to our tree. It is seen both as an example of "being-reality" and as an example of "meaning-reality." To be sure, the tree is "intendible"—it can be drawn, painted, de-scribed, etc. As an actual object of intentions, it is, in fact, "intended"; its meaning is thus extended and increased *insofar as* it is compared and contrasted with its being. No intentional act ever brackets the being of the tree, but such a being becomes, as it were, drowned in the increasing amount of meaning, or meanings. On the other hand, the meaning, or meanings, of the tree, as resulting from real intentional acts, are in their turn beings; it only happens that we are moving forward from meaning-*reality* to reality-*meaning*.

The tendency toward meaning is thus exhibited primarily through the actualization of intentions. It is, *a fortiori*, exhibited through the intentional acts themselves—real acts which not only receive but also give meaning. Such acts are, as stated above, acts of subjects called "persons," who, of course, "have being" or, in accordance with the vocabulary proposed here, are realities possessing or exhibiting (as all realities do) the ontological disposition "being." This includes their physical structure—in a rather broad sense of "physical"—and specifically their bodily structure. From this point of view, persons are bodies, but they are bodies in an "intentional attitude." Hence the person as "personal body" may be described, *grosso modo*, as a unitary cluster of intentions.

Thus every reality is intentional *qua* meaning-reality, but its intentionality can be manifested in many ways. In the last analysis, a reality such as a tree—and natural realities generally —is not only "intendible," i.e., a possible object of intentions, but it is also in some degree intentional. I am not claiming, of course, that a tree can perform intentional acts such as describing or understanding. But the tree does share in the basic condition of every intentional structure—that of pointing beyond itself, namely, being related to some other reality. Its own "being intendible" is intentional in an "active" way: if something lends itself to being an object of intentions (of acts of knowledge, of description, etc.), then it does not consist only of what it is, but it is also, *sit venia verbo* a "being-for. . . ." Much as I dislike the term "transcend," I see no harm in its being used to indicate simply that a reality may be variously related to others. Now, transcending in *this* sense is an outstanding feature of a level of meaning which, though related to intentionality, is clearly distinct from it. I call this level "meaning as nexus."

The term "nexus" is employed here in a "neutral" sense or, at any rate, in a sense sufficiently broad to leave unspecified any particular kind of nexus. For lexical convenience, I also call a nexus a "relation." There are many modes in which realities may be reciprocally related: by juxtaposition and, in general, co-presence, by causal links, functional dependence, and so on. If one also keeps in mind the multiple kinds and forms of reality, one will realize the extent to which the connection (or type of connection) between and among realities varies.

At this point we face an embarrassing problem. A number of connections seem to pertain to the disposition "being," while others seem more appropriate to the disposition "meaning." It has been held, for example, that while the causal connection (whether deterministic or probabilistic) characterizes those realities usually called "natural," a connection like the one Dilthey called "meaning-relation" (*Sinnzusammenhang*) characterizes realities which are not supposed to be, strictly speaking, natural but rather "cultural," "spiritual," etc. This assumption has often been held through other distinctions; there is, some have maintained, a basic difference between causal and functional relations, real and ideal relations, etc. If the assumption proved true, we should subscribe to the view that underlying basic differences in types of relation are fundamentally different types of realities. Now, although I think that realities exhibit many ways and modes of being (not to say of behaving), I also believe that all of them are located on the continuum of "what there is" and that only within such a continuum may one properly speak of realities in their dispositions called "being" and "meaning."

It thus appears that I must either give up a substantial portion of the ontology underlying this paper or else reinterpret the concept "nexus" in such a way that it may comprise all possible connections, not excluding those pertaining to reality as being. In such a case, however, one would not be allowed to speak of meaning as nexus.

A way out may be discerned in the following principles: (1)

There are in fact nexūs among realities to the extent that a reality is always connected with *some* other. I have spoken elsewhere of the possibility of conceiving what there is as organized in many different "groups"; now the possibility of "grouping realities" is the same as the possibility of nexūs. (2) Certain nexūs are, or tend to be, entitative in character, and others are, or tend to be, "significative" in character. Examples of the former are coexistence, causality, reciprocal influence; of the latter, being in a situation, proceeding toward a goal. (3) Some nexūs appear to be (ontologically speaking) "located" at a point midway between the tendency toward entitative character and the tendency toward "significative" character. Examples include functional dependence, the part-whole relation, the means-end relation. (4) Despite the differences noted between types of nexūs, there is no such thing as a double universe of nexūs corresponding to a similarly double real universe. Just as every reality is, in varying degrees, reality as being and reality as meaning, so every nexus is a nexus as being and a nexus as meaning. We are dealing, however, with a single nexus exhibiting both directions. A nexus considered to be primarily entitative may also be viewed in its meaning-tendency, and one considered primarily as "significative" may also be viewed in its entitative tendency. This explains why the causal relation is not entirely purged of meaning and why relations like that of being-in-a-situation, or carrying out a certain purpose, are not completely lacking in entitative connections. In sum: just as with every reality, every nexus can be said at the same time "to be" and "to mean."

The above does not enable us to conclude that there are, on the one hand, realities and on the other, nexūs between or among them. Nor can we conclude that it is altogether wasteful to distinguish conceptually between realities and nexūs. Nexūs are realities insofar as they are connected or connectable.

Thus any nexus—where "nexus" is an abbreviation for "connected realities"—can be looked at in the two directions just referred to. A nexus maximally approximates to the disposition "being" when it is as external as it can possibly be with respect to the corresponding realities—even to the point where it seems to do nothing but express the fact of their connectedness. When this situation is pushed to the limit, it issues in the idea of relations as (purely) external. On the other hand, a nexus maximally approximates to the disposition "meaning" when it is as internal as it can possibly be with respect to the corresponding realities—even to the point where the fact of connectedness almost disappears and is replaced by pure internal coherence or even fusion. This situation, too, if pushed to the extreme, issues in the idea of relations as (purely) internal. For reasons which I cannot go into here, but which are implicit in the ontological explorations of which this paper is a part, I reject the view that relations and nexus are ever absolutely or exclusively either external or internal. Every relation, like every nexūs, is more or less external (or internal), which means that realities *qua* connected are more or less external (or internal) to each other.

Let us now consider nexūs under the species "meaning." It follows from what has already been said that no nexus is either purely "significative" or purely "entitative." Any nexus may be viewed in its significative or in its entitative aspect, depending on the direction which is emphasized in a given case. Granted that at present I am calling attention to the nexus as meaning— or, what comes to the same thing, the meaning as nexus—we will have to admit that even a nexus in which the disposition "being" prevails is not wholly lacking in meaning. Such is the case, as I noted earlier, with causality, which probably exemplifies the minimum degree of meaning in the nexus but is not wholly "meaningless." In terms of its "direction" toward being, we evince a causal relation when we raise, and try to answer, the question "Why?" The very same relation becomes "significative"—however minimal its meaning—when we supplement or complement the question "Why?" with questions like "For what?" "What does it come to?" "What is the point of?", etc. In all these cases we bring in an antecedent or a consequent or both. In each case, however, the answer has a particularly distinctive function. The "direction" toward meaning is emphasized when, instead of limiting ourselves to an exploration of the nature and structure of a given causal relation, we try to fit the latter into a much larger context, including a sufficiently complex causal chain. When the causal relation is (or is supposed to be) tied up to "whatever there is" we are dealing with a highly "significative" nexus. If, for example, we ask "Why is it raining?" we may answer by pointing to a series of factors which have produced the rain—stopping more or less arbitrarily at some point. But if we continue to ask questions in causal terms, the phenomenon called "rain" becomes part of a broader context which in the end might include (although in fact it never does) the entire universe. Every causal relation, or type of causal relation, may appear as a phenomenon, or chain of phenomena, which acquires some meaning within the cosmic context. This explains why, although a deterministic doctrine limited to a relatively well-circumscribed conjunction of natural phenomena and processes is maximally neutral with respect to meaning, a completely deterministic doctrine is an answer not, or not only, to the question of the mode of being of reality as a whole but also and mainly to the question of the meaning which the latter may exhibit. The meaning of (natural) reality, we may then conclude, consists in being fully determined.

Nevertheless, meaning as nexus is made most evident when we come to relations which are not, or not merely, causal. Such is the case when we consider whether a reality—entity, fact, event, process—"counts" or "matters," whether or not it "means" anything; whether or not it is pertinent or appropriate; whether or not it is, as is sometimes said, "going somewhere"; whether it "has a point," etc. In these cases we are clearly dealing with some kind of "end" or "purpose"; the question "What does it amount to?" is closely linked to the question "What is it for?"

If we enter a theater after the play has begun, we may be bewildered by what we see happening on the stage—by the actors' utterances and gestures, the stage settings, etc. Even if we believe that it is a "happening," we are at a loss to know what is, in fact, happening. None of it seems to "add up" or be to the point, so we begin to suspect that the whole thing is meaningless. However, gradually or, as the case may be, suddenly, we see the point; particular words and gestures are understood in relation to others, and these in turn to others. We may have a glimpse of what had happened on the stage before our arrival; and when the play is over we may grasp the meaning of the various nexūs of which it was composed. These meaning-nexūs produce a total meaning which *prima facie* appears not to go beyond itself. The stage play is a reality which, in addition to its disposition "being" also has the disposition "meaning." The same thing may happen with a human life and with a historical process: both constitute a framework within which we can say that such-and-such a fact or event has (or lacks) meaning or seems to have more or less meaning. To be sure, no meaning is ever complete because no particular reality is ever exhausted —and no complete totality is ever reached.

Meaning as nexus is also apparent in purposes. These are not expressible simply by such words as "in order that"—for example, in order for the gun to fire it is necessary that the powder explode, and this requires that the trigger strike the cap. But the trigger could strike the cap to no avail if the gun should fall to the floor and thus upset the firing mechanism. For a purpose to be manifest it seems necessary that an agent fire the gun for some reason—to make a noise, to check his aim, to shoot a bird, to kill his neighbor. Whether there is an initial agent and a final purpose is controversial, but to the extent that there are purposes, there are also meaning-nexūs. It is possible for the meaning as nexus to manifest itself *eminenter* in a certain relation between realities, a relation which, in contrast to co-presence, causality, interaction, functional dependence, internal articulation, purpose, etc., may be called "attending to"—in its various modes of "being concerned with," "caring for," "interesting oneself in," etc.

"Attending to" is also a mode of intentionality, but here we treat it as foundation of a nexus whose most striking example, and perhaps the only one, is the way in which man is in the world. In my opinion, being in the world is not the foundation or even the "horizon" of "what there is," for the reason, among others, that being in the world is a mode of what there is. This does not prevent us from recognizing it as a supremely important mode. Of course, being in the world, as a mode of being real, has, like every reality, the disposition "being." At the same time, being in the world entails the existence of real—psychophysically real—human beings in a real world having physical, cultural, and other features. Thus, being in the world in the disposition "being" is describable and characterizable as a conjunction of "facts"—such-and-such a man, born in such-and-such a place, weighing so-and-so much, with such-and-such abilities, is in a world which is a fragment of the earth: he inhabits it, moves about in it, learning, teaching, tilling the soil, making and selling things, playing ball, commanding, obeying, rebelling. All these "facts" also have more or less of the disposition "meaning." But the maximum of this disposition—at the level of "nexus"—is possessed by the reality called "being in the world," provided that it is understood as a basic situation. For man is "in" the world in the way a physicist is "in" his science, a revolutionary "in" his cause, or a lover "in" his love.

IV. *Being and Meaning*

If realities were oriented exclusively either toward being or toward meaning—if they were totally and exclusively being-realities or meaning-realities—we could not say that one given reality "is" more or less than another, or "means" more or less than another. When realities are looked at from only one of the previously discussed ontological dispositions, we can only assume that they are what they are and mean what they mean. An atom "is" no more and no less than a cell; a stone "is" no more and no less than a galaxy. These entities, or types of entities, differ among themselves in their features, their structure, the function which they serve, or may serve, within the context of other realities, etc. But they do not differ in being, in the sense of "degree of being." We cannot say of realities *qua* beings that some of them "are" more than others. Neither can we say such a thing about the various types of realities belonging to a given ontological group (physical things, persons, "cultural objects"); a palm tree "is" no more and no less than a person or a political institution. *Mutatis mutandis*, a person "means" no more and no less than a political institution or a palm tree, if we consider these realities from the exclusive point of view of the disposition "meaning." The palm tree, the political institution, and the person mean what they mean, and each of them in each case has the meaning which it has. Clearly they can "mean" in various ways and even change their mode of meaning, but that is no basis for concluding that any one of them has a greater or lesser degree of meaning than another.

It should be remembered here that, within our ontological framework, no reality has only the disposition "being" or only the disposition "meaning." In fact, the very notion of "disposition" excludes such a one-sided "posession," since, as stated earlier, dispositions are "tendential" ontological modes. Thus it cannot be admitted that realities could be exclusively oriented either toward being or toward meaning. "Being oriented," ontologically speaking, toward one ontological pole presupposes being oriented toward the opposite and complementary pole and thus always being "situated" between the two. We can now proceed to make the following assertion: if a reality can "be" more or less than another or "mean" more or less than another, it is only because it is ontologically oriented. And if it is so oriented, it must be so not in one direction but in two, or in the mode of a confluence of the two. Moreover, the "orientation" here referred to involves a double direction, which in turn involves an "orientation."

Only under these conditions may we claim that a reality, or type of reality, "is" more or less than another. Its situation in this regard depends in large measure on the interrelation of the corresponding ontological dispositions. Such a situation is not necessarily established once and for all—as though in the continuum of reality where the ontological dispositions of being and meaning intersect there were something like fixed reality-species, resembling those which were once thought to constitute living species. Realities change and perhaps even evolve. Thus it is understandable that their ontological positions at the confluence of being and meaning should change and evolve as well. On this basis one could also assert that the whole of reality is tending toward meaning after a supposedly "initial" moment when it tended mainly toward being; or that after having tended maximally toward meaning it should once more tend mainly toward being, etc. Nevertheless we shall not make any such assertion, which may have some sense within the frame of an axiological metaphysics but which has none in ontology. We shall not speak of degrees of reality but simply of degrees of being or of meaning —of being as related to meaning and of meaning as related to being.

To say that a reality, *a*, "is" more than another reality, *b*, is not, again, to say that *a* is more real than *b*, but only that *a*'s orientation toward the disposition "being" is more pronounced than *b*'s—which in turn entails that *b*'s orientation toward the disposition "meaning" is more pronounced than *a*'s. Thus a marble block has more being and less meaning than a marble statue, and the statue has more meaning and less being than the block. That the marble block has more being than the statue is due only to the fact that the latter has more meaning than the former, and the fact that the statue has more meaning than the block is due to the fact that the latter has more being than the former. A shift in ontological position in the confluence of being and meaning, of course, occurs in one and the same entity, merely by its becoming differently "disposed." A stone lying at the side of the road has more being and less meaning than the same stone used as a landmark, and the latter has correspondingly more meaning and less being than the former. It is not always easy to specify the "ontological position" of a reality—whether it is an entity, an event, a fact, or a process. One may even raise the question whether the marble block has or does not have more meaning than the statue when, for example, the block is the object of various intentions—is examined, analyzed, known, used as an example of something obeying scientific laws, etc. On the other hand, the fact that one reality has more meaning than another does not necessarily imply that it is better (or worse) than the latter. We are dealing here with what is and not with what ought to be or ought not to be. An earthquake in a desert region has less meaning than one in an area heavily populated and rich in cultural treasures, the latter may result in victims and ravages, while the former merely agitates the earth. This indicates, we may note in passing, that meaning is not necessarily desirable in itself. Although every "good" or "evil" operates upon realities *qua* oriented toward meaning, and thus upon all realities, meaning itself is, in principle, ontologically neutral. As a matter of fact, there is no such thing as meaning, there is only an ontological orientation toward meaning which is measured in terms of the contrasting orientation toward being.

PART TWO

NIHILISM AND THE ABSURD

Stanley Rosen

NIHILISM

In the early decades of the nineteenth century, intelligent Europeans, stimulated by reflection upon the French Revolution and the career of Napoleon, were already commenting upon the decline of the West. The characteristic form taken by these comments was a comparison between Western Europe in, let us say, 1830, and at the close of the pagan Roman empire. The Roman civilization was destroyed by the combined pressures of internal decadence and external barbarism. Nineteenth-century Western Europe, with Russia (or perhaps even America) cast in the role of the barbarian, seemed to be undergoing the same destiny. Very generally we may say that belief in the decline of the West was at the same time an accusation of the failure of the Enlightenment. By freeing man from "superstition," the Enlightenment had also dissolved the religious and political doctrines which rendered society stable and gave meaning to individual existence. By freeing man from nature, scientific technology had also forged the chains of a new bondage to the desire for acquisition, the debasement of spiritual and aesthetic standards, and the accelerating rule, in all spheres of life, of reification, quantification, or, as men were now called in imitation of Newtonian physics, the *masses*. Just as the Enlightenment was synonymous with "the age of reason," so a repudiation of the Enlightenment tended to be a repudiation of reason or rationalism—that is, of the view that man is, and ought to be, primarily a rational animal.

So, too, the criticism of reason tended to be a praise of the animal, of the "positive" force of life as opposed to the "negative"
force of reason. Not even the defenders of the Enlightenment, or
of reason, escaped the consequences of the conception of reason
that emerged from the dialectic of mathematical physics and the
philosophy of history during the seventeenth, eighteenth, and
nineteenth centuries. Marxism, positivism, behaviorism, to mention the most important, combined the mechanism of mathematical physics, or the virtual identification of "mathematical" and
"rational," with a consequently irrational, "vitalistic" belief in
the necessity of historical progress and human creativity. Friend
and foe of reason alike accepted a conception of reason as at
best an instrument of irrational forces and at worst an obstacle
to the achievement of animal, i.e., existential, integrity. Both accepted the essentially irrational or, more euphemistically, the
"pre-rational" nature of the sense or significance of human existence. It is therefore irrelevant whether, as a result of this "new
Enlightenment," speech about the sense or significance of existence was suppressed as irrational or exalted as pre-rational. In
both cases, the possibility of rational speech about the sense or
significance of life was excluded from the outset. But this excluded the possibility of assigning a rational sense or significance
to speech altogether, whether rational or pre-rational. The "rationalists" responded to this recognition with manifestos that it
not be spoken about; more precisely, that rational speech be
restricted to mathematics or identified with quasi-mathematical
analyses of what those who do not speak about speech normally,
commonly, or ordinarily say. The "pre-rationalists," after an abortive experiment with descriptive, scientific or phenomenological
positivism, in which they sought to combine the purity of mathematical speech with the spiritual edification to be derived from
speech about the spirit, admitted their failure by repudiating the
old ways and attempting to found a new speech or thinking in
which the sense or significance of speech emerges not from
speech but from presence before, or communion with, the silent
source of speech. So far as historical influence is concerned,
"phenomenology" survives not as the scientific or quasi-mathematical description of essences but as the exploration of the

radically historical life-world. The problem of the subjectivity
of the transcendental ego as itself radically historical has thus
been replaced by the problem of the disjunction between the
abstract structure of the life-world, itself expressed in terms derived from Galilean science, and the historical content of the
life-world. It would therefore seem that the desedimentation of
the life-world, were it to succeed, would result in resedimenta-
tion, or the establishment of essentially mathematical categories
for the classification of purely historical content.

In all these cases—logical, phenomenological, and ontological
—the net result, when we strip away what Napoleon and Marx
both call the "ideology," is a longing for silence. No logical,
phenomenological, or ontological incantations can obscure the
fact that speech both is and ought to be governed by reason.
Granted the incapacity of speech to speak rationally about itself,
i.e., about its sense or significance, whether this be called logical
consistency or existential authenticity—granted the inability of
speech to speak about the significance of consistency or authenticity in terms of a reason which is not reducible to arbitrary
choice or postulation—then mans' instinct of self-preservation,
whether it be called a belief in scientific progress or a transcendence of the ontic, leads him to silence in the deepest sense of
the term. Speech maims and destroys (it is now held); it reifies
and alienates. Silence, the knowledge of the blood, the wisdom
of the body, the reasons of the heart, *heals*. Medicinal or (in the
literal sense of the word) "psychiatric" silence also seems to have
the godlike power to allow man to continue to speak, provided
that he does not attempt to speak, i.e., to speak rationally, about
the sense or significance of his speech and therefore of himself as
a speaking animal. Psychiatric silence, then, is altogether compatible with logical or ontological speech. Logical speech is
about the mathematical structure of speech; metalogical speech
defines the mathematical or quasi-mathematical "rules of the
game"—i.e., the boundaries beyond which our medicinal draught
of silence prevents us from peeking. Provided that we are silent
about the synoptic (as distinct from the "metalogical") sense or
significance of speech, we may speak indefinitely or infinitely.
The "substance" of speech is thus the senseless buzzing of his-

tory, sometimes politely referred to as "local use." Essentially the same situation holds good in ontological speech. The goal of ontological speech is not discourse about beings, but the revelation of Being. Since speech is itself an emanation of, rather than (as in the case of contemporary linguistic analysis) identical with, Being—i.e., since speech, as discursive, necessarily "runs through" or is bound to the disjunctive multiplicity of *things*—speech necessarily separates us from Being. (And so, parenthetically, the lot of the linguistic analyst is more desperate, a more extreme form of alienation, than that of the ontologist. The ontologist discerns more or less that it is silence he yearns for. The linguistic analyst struggles to keep talking.) Speech differentiates or articulates. The wholeness, coherence, unity, and transcendence of the non-thingly Being is accessible only via the integral nonarticulation of silence. If silence is the source of the significance of speech, speech signifies silently; i.e., it cannot bespeak its significance but can negatively "incarnate" it by lapsing into silence, the *corpus mysticum* of fundamental ontology. The word "ontology" is thus, in the Napoleonic and Marxist senses, an *ideological* term. It is much sound and fury, signifying nothing— or should I say nothingness?

But the two versions of logistics are, philosophically speaking (and there is no other way to speak), in the same situation. The reduction of the "structure" of the world to a universal logical calculus would lead, if successful, to the same elimination of human significance, and even existence, as was accomplished in the seventeenth and eighteenth centuries by the elevation of Newtonian physics to the role of the sense-giving or royal component of philosophy. A mathematical formula, as a collection of symbols, has no significance apart from the speech by which it is interpreted, but becomes a mere heap of marks. If the interpretive speech must derive *its* significance from the formula, the result is silence. If the significance comes from local use ("ordinary language"), the result is to equate sense with the factual, or with "what's happening," which is to say that it is senseless to criticize the significance of what happens (and hence, too, the cultural or rhetorical vulgarity of those who are eager to show themselves as up to date or as orifices for the silence of the *Zeitgeist*). What happens, or what is said, is silent about the goodness or badness, the nobility or baseness, the significance or insignificance of what happens or is said. More accurately, one cannot say "what" happens, since the "what" transcends the local or historical, but only *that it happens* (like the old "red here now" chant). The "what" must itself be reduced to a symbolic structure of "thats." But the symbolic structure, as other than its "thats," or identical to itself, is (we are told) an ideological phantom, an illusion of bad logic or bad ontology. Now the phrases "bad logic" and "bad ontology" are themselves significant only by contrast with "good logic" and "good ontology." Since the logician and ontologist are beyond good and evil, they employ the term "good" and its opposites in purely technical or instrumental senses. The phrases "good logic" or "good ontology" cannot derive their significance from speech about the significance of logic or ontology. But neither can they derive their significance from *within* logic or ontology, since both are beyond the "good," which smacks of subjectivism, perspectivism, and pharisaism. To say that a logic is "good" if it obeys the rules of the game is in fact to say that "one ought to obey the rules of the game"; but this is not a sentence in logic, or, if one refers to modal logic, it does not derive its justification as a rational speech from extralogical sources. It is the voice of desire and, as such *illogical* or indistinguishable from other such utterances, or a meaningless internal articulation of silence. To say that an ontology is "good" if it uncovers or manifests Being is to say that the goodness of speech lies in its cancellation by silence. To summarize: In all these cases nothing can be said (rationally) about good speech. Reason and "good" (even when "good" is defined technically or instrumentally) are mutually exclusive. This being so, it is mere ideology (i.e., hypocrisy) to say that one speech is better than another. No speech is better than another because "better" is unspeakable, since obviously the same dilemmas would face an instrumental definition of "better" or "good"—e.g., why is this instrument better than that? Speech is then factic happenstance. It makes no difference what we say, because "difference" is internal to speech and speech cannot speak about its own sense or significance. If it makes no difference what we say, then everything is sayable: *Alles ist erlaubt,* and this is nihilism.

The line of development (or deterioration) from the French to the Russian Revolution, from Napoleon to Hitler and Stalin, has brought with it an intensification, but not a genuine change, of predominant historical characteristics. Intelligent observers of the period between the two world wars were making essentially the same predictions concerning the decline of the West as were their predecessors in the nineteenth century. The same arguments transpired in both centuries concerning the positive and negative aspects of the impending (or already present) nihilism. It is true that we are now in imminent rather than future danger of global destruction or enslavement, thanks to contemporary scientific technology. But this difference is neither logical nor ontological; the contemporary horrors which are the shadow of the Enlightenment were already obscuring the sunlight of the nineteenth-century belief in progress. I rather suspect that the anxiety and pessimism of contemporary philosophers and intellectuals are by now less intense than the anxiety and pessimism of the nineteenth-century prophets. Having settled down in the promised land of nihilism, we have become used to or negated by it, and lost the existential integrity that characterizes the homelessness of the prophet. I do not wish to minimize the importance of imminent global destruction, but I must state candidly that the real contemporary problem is to my mind how to speak rationally about the importance of destruction. If Being is indeed Nothingness, or if silence is the sense of speech, I fail to see why destruction is not logically and ontologically superior to vulgar ontic existence. Differently stated, the intensification of the historical characteristics of the nineteenth century has terminated in flaccidity or spiritual slackness, in the discursive incoherence of our own parlous time. The energy and articulateness with which nineteenth-century thinkers prophesied impending silence have now been replaced by the consequences of the fulfillment of their prophecies. Ours is an age of the debasement of *Logos,* or of indiscriminate chatter, or of ideological infections upon the body politic of silence. Communication has been replaced by communication theory, the message by the medium, the celebration of order by the celebration of the absurd. No doubt disoriented by the accelerating decay of the old linear civilization, Marxists are now existentialist humanists; ordinary language analysts indulge in ontology and even, *horribile dictu*, in metaphysics; scientific linguists are being assaulted by the scholastic occultism of neo-Cartesians; still more radically, as our sociologists and psychologists inform us, men are turning into women and women into men. In the age of the corporeal hermaphrodite, the masculine and feminine dimensions of the psyche negate each other. The invocation to "make love, not war," although initially a democratic corrruption of the older, aristocratic doctrine of the will to power, now known as "flower power," nevertheless depends for its fulfillment upon the discrimination between two modes of conduct by distinct, i.e., diversified, individuals. But the discrimination between modes of conduct, like the identification of individuals, depends upon standards of discrimination, or the discursivity of speech. In our age, with all its cant about individuality, uniqueness, creativity, autonomy, spontaneity, and the like, the "individual" is rapidly being transformed, not even into the corporeal hermaphrodite but into the mathematical monad.

"What," as that well-known existentialist Lenin asked, "is to be done?" If "to do" is "to do well" and "well" means both reasonable and good, then there can be only one answer to this question. We have to rethink the prevailing conceptions of "reason" and "good," and this means to place in brackets the whole course of modern philosophy by which the two were sundered, or to return to the fundamental philosophical stratum of the quarrel between the ancients and the moderns. In order to do this, it is necessary to "reappropriate" the history of philosophy, or to rediscover the philosophical psyche within the historical corpus. The ancient thinkers taught that there is a rational link between reason and the good; the decisive founders of modernity deny this link. But the modern denial, having lost the impetus of seventeenth-century pride and egoism, has decayed into nihilism. One cannot overcome nihilism by a return to the past, and let me emphasize that I am not advocating the nonsensical effort to reverse the direction of history.

All talk of a "return to the past" is as much a mark of enslavement to history as is the desire to be projected into the future. It is precisely the nihilistic consequence of historicism that the temporal present is necessarily obscured by the temporal past and future. But life is lived in the present, by which I do not mean the *hic et nunc*. The quarrel between the ancients and the moderns, or the fundamental reflection upon the relation between reason and the good, is accessible to those who know how to think, or who are not slaves of history. The transformation in any sense of history itself depends upon the rational reapportionment of the extrahistorical present, and this in turn depends upon the accurate and detailed knowledge of history. History destroys those who are unable to speak rationally about it. The first step in the war against nihilism is therefore itself necessarily negative. One must show how contemporary speech, in its various historicist disguises, is self-negating or self-silencing. Differently stated, one must show how contemporary speech, although passing for logical and ontological manifestations of Being, is rather a historical sedimentation which conceals Being from man. In an older terminology, one must show that nature, not history, is the link between, or the source of the significance of, reason and the good. If this cannot be done, then nothing is to be done; for indeed, *das Nichts selbst nichtet*. The negative will of the negative God of the present epoch of historicity is in full command of events, nor will a thousand volumes, each of a thousand pages, on the meaning of historicist-bound hermeneutics stay his hand or cause him to cancel half a line of the silence he has already "written" onto the *tabula rasa* of the spirit of contemporary man.

Arthur C. Danto

SEMANTICAL THEORY AND THE LOGICAL LIMITS OF NIHILISM

Nihilism, as I shall understand it here, asserts that the maximal state of cognitive entropy is our very state. It claims that, in the most ultimate respect, reality is absolutely indifferent to the content of all our beliefs, which, from the point of view of truth and falsity, are maximally disordered. By the criterion of being true or false, it does not matter what we believe—however it may matter by some other kind of criterion—not because we cannot attain the truth but because there is no truth to attain.

Such a theory can be profoundly unsettling, as we may see if we think for a moment of some of the experiences men have had or described through which the cognitive vacuity abstractly propounded by nihilism was brought home emotionally. Think, for example, of the Marabar Caves in *A Passage to India*, in which every statement made elicits, like any nondescript noise, always the same unvarying echo: a prayer, a declaration, a song, a searching question, an eructation, all come back as the unindividuated *bou-oum*, which reduces to a common denominator of cosmic static whatever is said, however structured. And the echo has no real existence of its own, for when there is no noise there is no echo, only the glassy dark silent inner surface of the undifferentiated Marabar Caves, each like the next. There are other examples. Surely one of the shattering consequences of the doctrine of Eternal Recurrence was the thought that nothing I believe or do can have the meaning or point I should want it to have, for each thing is exactly iterated infinitely through the future and through the past, so that the *same* thing *has* to happen and to have happened end-lessly (and we know that repetition beyond a certain very finite point destroys meaning), so that, as Nietzsche puts it, *es fielt die Ziel; es fielt die Antwort auf das Warum.* And there is, again, the description of total boredom in Heidegger's *Was ist Metaphysik?* where the whole of existence flattens out and nothingness is felt virtually as an active force, swamping the distinctions and distractions that articulated and relieved the surfaces of life. These perceptions of a totally vacated reality, as seeming revelations of an objective nullity, have the quality of mystical experiences, and as such we are obliged to respect them. They are not exalting ones, to be sure, and if Nietzsche affirmed the pointlessness superinduced by inane repetition, Mrs. Moore's soul cracked in the Marabar Caves, and she emerged an irascible, dotty old woman.

I cannot be concerned in the present paper with these vision-ary matters, unfortunately, for nihilism as a philosophical teach-ing cannot invoke in support of itself such reports of experience, however vivid, and must stand or fall by rather more exacting criteria. Yet I am sufficiently sensitive to the import of these experiences of negativity that I should want to acknowledge their force to this extent: any analysis of nihilism must at least be consistent with the poetry of their dark, unsettling revelation.

I

I shall begin by considering Nietzsche's strident *Wort,* "Every-thing is false," which expresses nihilism succinctly, inasmuch as Nietzsche was speaking as a metaphysician when he uttered it and not, as it would be most natural to interpret him, as a denunciatory prophet railing at his contemporaries' institutions and values. Our values may indeed be false, but only in a philosophically uninteresting and metaphysically irrelevant sense of *false*. There is a lethal ambiguity in the latter word which in fact infects many words in the crucial category to which it belongs, and we may see this by marking two distinct ways in which we might read the sentence "S is a false sentence." It can mean either but not both (i) that which is denoted by S seems to be but is not really a sentence, or (ii) that which is denoted by S is a sentence but a false one—i.e., if one is a correspondentialist, fails to correspond to the world. In (i), "is false" is a *descriptive predicate*, which has only incidental application to bits of language. Thus it is used univocally in (i) and in (i'), "M is a false friend," despite whatever differences may exist between words which fall short of sentencehood and acquaintances who seem to be but are not friends. But (ii) uses it as a *semantical* predicate, which has (logically) unique application to bits of language. If "is false" is used semantically in (i'), the latter degenerates into nonsense. I am not saying that the discovery that something is descriptively false is always philosophically irrelevant, but only that the *concept* of descriptive, in contrast with the concept of semantical falsity is philosophically irrelevant. Or, more guardedly, they have radically different relevancies. If we take descriptivity as criterial for predicative status, then "is false" is a false predicate—i.e., as in the famous case of "exists," seems to be but is not a predicate. But of course this is extreme: it is not that "exists" seems to be but is not a predicate but that it seems to be predicated, say, of wasps in the sentence "Wasps exist," when in fact it is predicated, but not *descriptively*, of the *term* "wasp," of which it says that it has instances, viz., wasps. "Exists" thus is a semantical predicate, like "false" (and "true"), which may have descriptive uses; but these are largely irrelevant philosophically, at least as regards those contexts in which the predicative status of "exists" has been mooted.

The descriptive-semantical ambiguity in such crucial words as "false" and "exists" has caused no end of philosophical chaos, but once alerted to the danger, it can easily be evaded. Thus a man is not inconsistent who happens to be at once a noncognitivist in ethics and a jeremiah in morals, holding that no value-assertions are true and that all our values are false.

There is indeed reason to believe that this complex stance was almost exactly the one Nietzsche took in his writings, as at once a ferociously iconoclastic critic of his society and a cool noncognitivist in metaethics. Since there have been those known as nihilists who sought to destroy the institutions they detested because they were "false," they have to be distinguished from what I might term semantical nihilists, who in saying "Everything is false" were using "false" as a semantical predicate. It is a striking fact about Nietzsche as a philosopher that he proposed through semantical nihilism to achieve the destructive ends of nihilism as a moral critique: semantical nihilism was by and large the hammer he philosophized with.

II

I shall now proceed toward the true threshold of our subject by the device of working through some plausible objections to "Everything is false."

1. It seems savagely to turn against itself in the suicidal manner of semiparadoxy. Suppose "Everything is false" is true. Then all sentences, it included, must be false. So nihilism is false if true. But if not true, what philosophical interest can there be in nihilism?

Minimum semantical prophylaxis readily deflects this sophistry. Consider the set Z of sentences which are about the world. Nihilism holds that every sentence which is a member of Z is false. Call this sentence N. N is about the members of the set Z but is not *itself* a member of Z. And now the falsity of N is not entailed by its own truth. It is not even an exception to its own claim; it only could be that if it applied to itself which it does not, since it is not about the world but about *sentences* which are about the world.

2. Surely this will not do. For after all, language is part of the world, and N is about language. So N is a member of Z, and so self-destructively false.

I regard this as a deep but essentially misguided objection, which cannot be fully dealt with here. Language indeed is in the world. Sentences are uttered at times and places by creatures of flesh and blood. They exist in the air and on the surfaces of graphic media. They have determinate structures and conform to law. They cohere in systems which are subjects of genuine scientific investigation. They are in the world in absolutely every respect except, unfortunately, the relevant one —namely, that it is the world which makes them true or false. It is just here that our semantical-descriptive ambiguity is particularly treacherous. A false sentence, recall, is something which either fails to be a sentence or which is a sentence but fails to be true. The members of Z purport to describe the world. According to N they fail in this. But this does not entail that they are false descriptions—that is, seem to be but are not descriptions. They are descriptions, only false. It is just the same description, whether it is true or false. There is a deep internal difference between a piece of false gold and a piece of true gold; but no internal difference exists between a description when it is true and when it is false. A description is true when the world makes it so, and in this respect there exists an essential contrast *between* the world *and* the members of Z taken as a class. When taken *as descriptions* the members of Z are about the world. Descriptions are, to be sure, things in the world. But they are in a crucial respect outside the world. Language is within the world and without the world at once. And in the relevant sense, there is supposed a space between language and the world: when there is language, it is as though a space were opened within the world, between it as a whole and a bit of itself which is also a portion of the world as a whole.

N is thus not about the world but about the connection between language and the world, which it declares never to hold as we should like when we are concerned to describe the world truly. So N is not about the world as such nor about language as such. Any sentence, indeed, which is about language just as such is a sentence about the world, for language as such is part of the world. But the way in which N is about language is that in which language is one term in a relation, the other term of which is the world. So N is not a member of Z and so does not entail its own falsehood, for it does not fall within its own range. This is why I speak of it as semantical nihilism. It is not *just* a theory about the world. It is about us and the world, when we set out to describe the world as it really is.

3. The strategy of the reply to (2) is shifty, but let us grant it. Let us also disregard the perplexing question of how N can be true, granting it is not self-defeatingly false: for since it is not made true by the *world*—that being ruled out by the strategy it used to preserve itself from self-defeat— the way in which it could be true is dark. But at any rate it has to be false, since it is now plainly incompatible with widely acknowledged truths of logic. To say *these* are false is not nihilism but just chaos. But now let T be a member of Z, i.e., about the world, i.e., a description. Its being a description, by the defense of (2), is not affected by its being either true or false; viz. it is the very same description whether it is true or false. It is plausible, therefore, to assume that if T is a member of Z, not-T is a member of Z. But T and not-T are contradictories. If T is false, then not-T has to be true. But N would hold them *both* false. But this is incoherent. So N is false.

Now nihilism is prohibited from preempting one sly strategy which philosophical analysis affords. Consider the traditionally opposed A and O categoricals. These cannot both be true and both be false, so they cannot both be false. But of course it does not follow from their being contradictories that either of them *is* true, granted that if one of them is, the other is false. They can remain contradictories in a counterfactual way, but neither of them needs, taken singly, either to be true or to be false. Suppose the question of truth or falsity did not arise. There are theories of language which might hold that sentences are not descriptions of the world but instruments for getting about in it, that truth and falsity simply have no application to sentences. So sentences are not true. Nietzsche, in fact, held such a theory of language, being a precocious instrumentalist who dramatized his view that sentences are not true by stating that they are false, when what he meant was that they are neither true nor false. This is unfortunately as bad a move for nihilism as the objection it sought to find shelter from in making it. For instead of T and not-T being members of Z, neither T *nor* not-T are members; and Z in effect is empty. So let us say that nihilism is either false or empty. And now what can the nihilist do to make his theory non-empty and true, and true in such a way as to be compatible with the principles of logic which nihilism, like any philosophical position, must regard itself as bound by? There is an answer, I think. But we have reached the threshold of the topic, and our reply takes us across it.

III

Let us turn from "Everything is false" to its philosophical near-of-kin, "Nothing exists," a shift licensed by the semantical status of "exists." As "true" applies to sentences, so "exists" applies to names and terms. "Charles exists" is not, recall, about Charles at all, but about the proper name "Charles" of which it says that it has a referendum, Charles *même,* as it happens, due to the logical nonanonymity of proper names. "Nothing exists" is of course not about nothing and, treacherously, not even about "Nothing"; it is about the class of semantical vehicles to which "exists" has proper semantical application, viz., names, terms, and the like. "Nothing exists" thus holds that no name succeeds in referring and that all predicates are empty or, in the idiom of classes, that classes and their complements alike are void, for every class.

It may seem at first glance that "Nothing exists" admits a trivial refutation somewhat along the lines of the sophistry of objection (1) against N. Thus, suppose "Nothing exists" is true. Then there have to be semantical vehicles which fail to have referenda, or which are empty, or whatever. So there has to be *something,* or otherwise the thesis is false. So the thesis is false. This argument has about it something of the ill-starred enterprise of Henry of Ghent's logically insane quest for the *esse essentia* or, more recently, of Prichard's silly effort to demonstrate against Descartes that a generalized doubt is untenable. Prichard held this because he believed we have to know what knowledge is in order sensibly to deny that there are instances of it; so there is this one instance, and so generalized doubt cannot be expressed. But once unfolded, Prichard's argument traffics on that deep confusion between truth and meaning which infests, if it does not generate, the entirety of philosophical literature. It does not follow from the fact that we *understand* the concept of knowledge that the concept is *instantiated*, since the concept does not instantiate itself. And similarly "Nothing exists" could leave us the full array of names and terms and predicates and classes, the paraphernalia and the vehicles of human understanding—all of them unfortunately empty—so that understanding fails (as always) to provide us with knowledge, just as meaning fails to yield truth. "Nothing exists" then has to mean: there is no world for any of this language to connect with. Against this it is correct but irrelevant to point out that, as in Objection (2) against N, language is part of the world.

Now "Nothing exists" entails N, since the subjects of all sentences lack referenda and every sentence's predicate is empty, when (i) the sentence is a member of Z and (ii) one accepts the view that every sentence of the form *x is F* is true when and only when *x* refers and the referendum of *x* lies within the extension of F and where, finally, (iii) no sentence which is a member of Z can be true if every subject of sentences of the form *x* is F lacks reference, i.e., if "Nothing exists" is true.

One way in which all subjects of all sentences which are members of Z could lack referenda, and "Nothing exists" could be true, would be if there were *no world at all:* no reality beyond the secondary reality of our semantical vehicles. I shall call this existential nihilism (=idealism, on certain interpretations), and while not without some interest, I do not believe existential nihilism is the position we are seeking. It misses somehow the spirit of those profound and poetic visions I began by citing. There cannot be an encounter with nothingness if there is nothing to encounter. The question, then, is whether N can be true in a way which is compatible with existential nihilism being false.

One suggestion is this: We allow that we can succeed in referring to the world. But further than that it *is*, we can say nothing about the world which is at all true. All that we can say about the world is that it is *there*. But nothing further. Relative to the descriptive resources of language, it might as well be a *mundus rasus:* a bare thereness which corresponds, supposing it referential, to the *tabula rasa* of our alleged original endowment, before it is sullied by experience. There have been great philosophers who find such a view incomprehensible, who wonder to what idea this "thereness" could possibly correspond and, finding no idea, dismiss it as a superstition. Such, notoriously, was the teaching of Berkeley. But it rests, as an objection, upon the fundamental confusion of meaning and reference. The reference of a semantical vehicle is not part of its meaning: *that* a sentence, say, succeeds in describing is not something further which it describes; the truth of a sentence is never part of its meaning. Berkeley sought to assimilate the referential dimension of language to its descriptive dimension, a notable failure which explains why, by his own confession, he could frame no *idea* of existence, and had to conclude that the idea of *x* existing collapsed into just the idea of *x*. The logical distinctness of meaning from reference guarantees Berkeley's failure, and, his criticism now rendered inapplicable, we may suppose our new nihilism at least tenable, which consists in reference without description. So let us suppose that T and not-T equally and indifferently refer but equally and indifferently are false. And since sentences of the form *x is F* are so crucial for the non-emptiness of Z, let it be that *x is F* and its denial are equally false. This is our new nihilism.

The justification, let us suppose, is one which we find to some degree in Nietzsche. If the form of sentence *x is F* were somehow true to the way the world is, then indeed, if *x is F* is false, its denial must be true. But suppose the whole form of *subject-predicate discourse* is wrong, and so *x is F* is wrong through its form. Then if its denial should be regarded *true,* this is not because we are predicating not-F successfully but because we are rejecting the predication of F: and in the sense of rejecting predication, *x is F* and *x is not-F* equally are rejected, equally are false. The rejection in question is essentially a rejection of a *form of language,* every sentence in which is rendered false through its structural inadequacy for descriptive purposes. So mere referential success counts for little; as with the system of logically proper names, which Russell once proposed as constituting the vocabulary of an ideal language, pure reference is achieved at the price of saying nothing, unless we smuggle into the referential acts some illicit characterization of referenda as, say, individuals. But in doing this the descriptive nihilist, as I henceforth shall designate him, would say we are falsifying reality. His posture is *neti neti,* which is not a negative description but a negation of descriptions as such. Let us gloss this curious posture.

IV

Philosophers who have taken the world as one term in a relationship, the other term of which is language, have tended to characterize the world in terms dictated by the structure of language: as though, if the world did not answer to such terms, it must be precluded from entering the relationship at all, and language then is a floating, undescriptive veil, logically opaque where it appeared transparent. I think it is correct that to understand a sentence S, which is a member of Z, one must know how the world would have to be if S were true: but it does not follow that the only way in which this could be guaranteed, and hence the intelligibility of S secured, would be if there were some antecedent structural isomorphism between the world and S. But assuming that there must be this, philosophers have tended to articulate the world into portions which exactly fit the units of meaningful discourse, and emerge with a theory roughly to the effect that in its deep structure the world just *is* language, crassly embodied. Consider, thus, facts. Facts were to have been that in the world which corresponded to propositions when the latter were true. Facts and propositions would be conjugate entities, held in tandem by the primitive theory of correspondences to which I have just referred. As Strawson proposed, facts and propositions were made for one another: eliminate propositions and the facts leave with them, the world being none the poorer, the world being (in his arch paraphrase of Wittgenstein) the sum total of things, not facts.

Now we might ask how much we could prize off the surface of the world, leaving it as little poorer as the falling away of facts seems to have left it. Imagine, for example, that someone said the world was made of individual things distinguished from one another by their properties, obeying thus a famous principle of Leibniz. And suppose someone responded: individual things were made to answer to the subjects of singular propositions; properties were made to answer to predicates; Leibniz's principle is only a guarantee of nonsynonymy for sentences, not a law of nature. To *say* the world is constituted of things and properties is to fall blindly into correspondentialism. So prize the properties off the individuals and the individuals off the world, and the world will be none the poorer. Nietzsche proposed that there are no things, that things are *our* fictions, by which he was not denying that there was a world but only that the world is constellated out of individual things: organizing the world *into* things is just—*our* way. Now there may be an element of convention in our particular articulations. Why should not the birds in a tree be *part* of the tree, as much so as the branches, so that a tree is an individual with a relatively stable core and highly vagarious boundaries, its topography shifting from moment to moment? Nietzsche's view goes further: it is not that what is and what is not to count as an individual thing (and a part of an individual thing) is conventional, but that the *whole idiom of things,* which Nietzsche saw as projections of the adventitious grammatical class of nouns, is distorting. *Remove* this grammatical class, and the world loses its seeming reticulate character, fusing into a glutinous mass what once was misleadingly thought discrete.

Nietzsche took his theory very seriously indeed. He thought it possible to work out another language, different entirely from all of ours, worked out upon a radically different grammatical armature. It is a hard question whether there could be a different depth-grammar which could generate anything we might recognize as languages at all—that is, whether they would be intelligible as languages to creatures such as we, or for the world we live in, which includes us, since the structure of language we impose upon the world we also impose upon ourselves, the inner and outer worlds sharing a common grammatical structure (and perhaps even the distinction between *inner* and *outer* answers to a grammatical distinction). In effect, to change our language is at once to change ourselves and to change the world, all three being structural reflections of one another, so that everything must be changed at once if there is to be any serious change at all. Otherwise we move in a foreclosed meander of unbreachable categories. And so remain members of the herd, to which we are linguistically forever condemned.

But suppose a new breed of men should, through some wild mutation, acquire a wholly new grammar and enter then a fresh new world, whose character *we* could not logically hope to describe, since the mechanisms of description available to us would exactly distort it. We could not translate their language into *any* of ours, for their language stands to ours in a relation utterly different from that in which our languages stand to one another. The question only is whether their language is any the less immune to a Nietzschean critique than ours, since their world would have to be the image of their language and they surely could have no better argument that the two were not made for one another than we have. How, without begging every question in issue, could they demonstrate that the world really *is* like their language if we are precluded from demonstrating that the world is made of *things?* And why, after all, should it be necessary? For what argument have we to begin with except the antecedent persuasiveness of the doctrine of correspondences that unless our language *does* reflect in its grammatical structure the structure of the world, it is inadequate or "false?" And what argument have we for *that?*

Let us think for a moment of what it means to say: remove the things and the world is none the poorer. Should a man think, perhaps, that latitudes and longitudes were scorings on the globe which it bothers him he cannot see, we say no: they are not there; the world is none the poorer for their removal, for they never were there to begin with. But I could not say:

remove the wasps and the world would be none the poorer;
or I could only if I meant to say something bitter about wasps.
A waspless world would be impoverished, and a factless world
would be impoverished as well, only if facts were there, alongside the wasps. And here we touch the crux. Asked what the
world contains, plain men will say, *inter alia,* wasps. Scientists
will add entities the plain man knows nothing of. The philosopher as such is interested in neither of these lists. To the
same question he will answer: facts; constituents and components of facts; intentions; essences; classes; things and properties and relations. The two sorts of lists are nonoverlapping.
The philosophical list does not enrich the other; the discovery
of negative facts does not reveal in the world something we
never knew of, like the discovery of coelacanths, or antimatter.
But surely it should be obvious that the philosophical list is
only due to solidifying and constituting as real the categories
of language? Surely the philosopher only is, in the idiom of
Shankara Charya, *imposing* on reality? Like the man who looks
for the equator?

When this is recognized, then along with the things and
facts and the rest goes the Nihilism, which celebrated their
absence only by supposing the same theory of correspondences
which led to their imposition to begin with. For when we prize
them off the world, it is not as though nothing remained. It
only is that nothing of the same order as they remained. The
world is a blank only relative to a description of it which
had no application initially. But when, finally, we surrender
the doctrine of correspondences which makes nihilism a metaphysical possibility, we surrender the need to revise language
in such a way as to bring it more into conformity with the
world; for sharing the world structure is no longer a necessary
condition a language must satisfy in order for sentences expressed in it to be true.

I think that we can say something slightly more constructive
than this, however. Language is articulated into sentences, terms,
names, predicates, and the like. And the lines of references by
which language reaches the world across the space which stands
between it and the world will be different for different parts of

language. Referential relations do not belong to the world, since the world is one of their terms. They belong instead to the space, one limit of which is the world. If we rotate these relations onto the world, we are indeed imposing something onto it which is not its own. But when we prize language off the world, and set it at the proper semantical distance, then the structure of the interspace remains to be charted. This is the province of philosophy, which has no proper concern with the world and whose task is primarily to provide a theory of reference, which in a clumsily misconcretized way it has always been doing anyway.

V

When we release ourselves from the grip in which the doctrine of correspondences holds us, the *structure* of descriptions can no longer be regarded as descriptive in its own right, and the basic vision of nihilism evaporates with the bad semantics, of which it is the disguise. "Everything is false," which is taken as the inverse of "Nothing is true," fails to survive objection (3) against N because "Nothing is true" is only the doctrine of correspondences' failure mischaracterized. So the cognitive entropy of nihilism may be counted false: if we can succeed in referring, we can succeed in describing, structural variations from language to language notwithstanding. The question of how the world *is* is then not to be deduced from the *structure* of language, but is in the end just the scientific question of which sentences are true. But before closing the discussion, we might think for a moment of an area where, rather than in metaphysics, nihilism would seem to make its natural first appearance: moral theory.

Nietzsche's noncognitivist metaethics was combined with an interesting theory about moral systems, which he regarded as the imposition of a form and order upon a group by the group itself's will-to-power. Let us consider these separately for a moment. The proposal that no moral statement is true has at times been taken to mean that there is no objective restraint upon moral judgments and that accordingly anything goes—

"Everything is permitted," in the celebrated phrase of Dostoevsky. To be sure, this is apt to be unsettling only in relation to the sorts of beliefs we have about what men in fact *will* do if everything is permitted: whether they will behave like the sunny Thelemites or like Stavrogin, as hedonists or sadists, is essentially a matter of empirical psychology, in the light of which we will attack or praise morality as inhibiting innocent pleasure taking, or as preserving us from one another's darkest appetites, or something else. It was not Nietzsche's teaching that everything is permitted, but only that there are no external or objective restraints on which moral *system* we are to live under. He never suggested that it was either desirable or possible to live under *no* moral system, but only that there is an abstract permissiveness about the kind of moral system we might choose. No moral system can permit everything, as no deductive system can permit every inference; and as the latter may be regarded as guiding us inferentially, so the former may be regarded as guiding us in life. Once within a system, we cannot do whatever we wish. But in some measure, Nietzsche thought, and this in consequence of his noncognitivism (overdramatized as nihilism), there is no objective basis for choosing among moral systems; any moral *system* is permitted, in the sense at least that no moral system is, as such, *true*. In actual fact, of course, the will-to-power of the group we are in pretty much holds us within a given form of life.

It is this extrasystematic stance which is beyond good and evil, good and evil being, according to Nietzsche, values which arise *within* a system rather than properties which attach to systems as such. And one of Nietzsche's most audacious philosophical moves was to generalize the noncognitivism from moral theory to theory as such, producing what we might call a noncognitivist theory of cognition. This is to take a stand beyond truth and falsity, truth or falsity attaching, according to this view, only to elements within a cognitive system, not to systems as such, which can, like moral systems, be regarded as an imposition of a form and order onto the universe through the spontaneous exercise of will-to-power. So again, everything is cognitively permissible, not in the respect that, once we have a system we can believe whatever we wish, but in the sense that there is no external restraint on which system we choose, granting again that we are likely to see the world in terms imposed upon us as members of a given group. We now have sufficient insight into the parallel logics of beliefs and of moral choices to find the analogy persuasive. And thus restated, perhaps, nihilism finds a philosophical reprieve. My point so far in this paper only has been that the arguments from the structure of language cannot be enlisted in support of the view that the world has just the structure we give it, and *none* of its own. In the twilight of this paper I cannot hope to do justice to this further view. But perhaps I can say a very few words.

It seems at least plausible to say that we may after all regard systems as true or false, and perhaps even as a function of the truth or falsity of the sentences which are their elements. But this is a sensible proposal only if we have some extrasystemic way of determining the truth or falsity of single sentences. To be sure, a sentence may be said to derive its meaning from its location in a given system. And so it may be that we cannot understand a given sentence without understanding the entire system of which it is a part. But it will not follow from this that its *truth* is a function of its location in the system: a sentence may derive its meaning from a system which in turn derives its *truth* from its sentential components. So if a sentence *s* is false, so is the system it is part of. It will be argued, of course, that this notwithstanding, it is possible to imagine systems incompatible with one another, whose sentences nevertheless are true. But this cannot happen. Systems are incompatible only if the sentences which compose them are, and they can be opposed only if they have the same meaning, and they can have the same meaning only if they derive it from just one system. So whereas we may, antecedently to questions of truth or falsity, have some choice over systems, this choice is aborted when actual questions of truth or falsity arise. Only antecedently to questions of truth and falsity can we take a stand *beyond* truth and falsity. This will be a stand taken with regard to the possible array of systems, before we worry which of them is true. So I do not believe cognitive Nihilism tenable, since semantical predication over systems is plausible.

I do *not* believe questions of truth or falsity ever arise for moral systems, however, since they do not arise for moral *sentences*. If noncognitivism goes for moral sentences, it goes as well for moral systems as such. This does not mean, of course, that everything is permitted. For this would follow only if truth were a *relevant* criterion to begin with for questions of permissiveness and impermissiveness to arise upon. But if it is merely a metaethical error to regard moral propositions as descriptive, and so as legitimately admitting of semantical predication, then questions of what is permitted remain unaffected by the discovery that the propositions of morals are "not true." Everything remains just as it was, only patterns of justification requiring alteration. Meanwhile, if moral propositions are not descriptive, *systems* of these are not either. But in neither case does it altogether follow that everything is permitted. And here I must be programmatic.

Just to be *moral* systems at all presupposes, as true, certain beliefs regarding the sort of creature who is required to live under them, for without implicit reference to men, it is difficult to see how something might be regarded as a moral system at all. Beliefs about men, however, are true or false, and hence our beliefs about ourselves are relevant to questions of adjudicating between moral systems, inasmuch as the differences between such systems may in the end just turn on differences in beliefs about human beings. Such differences, admittedly, are not always easily settled, not least of all because our beliefs about ourselves *can* contribute to their own validation, so that often we are what we are because we believe ourselves to be the way we are. But this is not always so, especially when our beliefs about ourselves logically presuppose other factual beliefs. Our belief, for instance, that we are the chosen or the despised of God cannot survive the truth of the proposition that God does not exist; if God does not exist, certain beliefs about ourselves are no longer rationally permissible, and certain moral propositions no longer have application. Such a view backs us cautiously toward a kind of Natural Law theory, not in the sense that we can deduce a moral system from facts of human nature but in the sense that increasing our factual knowledge of human nature provides us with the basis for serious *criticism* of prevailing or projected moral systems. But it would be irresponsible to go beyond this point in the present paper.

The characterization of Nietzsche's nihilism is based upon my study, *Nietzsche as Philosopher*, New York, 1968. The semantical theory implicit here I attempt to develop in my *Analytical Philosophy of Knowledge*, Cambridge, England, 1968, Chapters VII and XI.

George L. Kline

THE VARIETIES OF INSTRUMENTAL NIHILISM

Nihilisms may not be as "plentiful as blackberries," to paraphrase Peirce, but they do come in several distinct ideological
shades. There is, on the one hand, what might be called "instrumental" or "propaedeutic" nihilism and, on the other, "noninstrumental," i.e., "self-contained" or "terminal," nihilism. It is the
second kind, *le nihilisme pour le nihilisme,* which has been
the principal—though not exclusive—preoccupation of the two
previous symposiasts. Mr. Danto has focused on cognitive or
semantic nihilism, Mr. Rosen on both linguistic and ontological
—that is, *fundamentalontologische*—nihilism.

To redress the balance, I shall concentrate on instrumental
nihilism in two of its Russian varieties. Instrumental nihilists
advocate negation and destruction as means to sociopolitical
or cultural ends; they thus view destruction as, in a perverse
sense, constructive and creative. They do not say, "Everything
is permitted" (Dostoyevski's *vsyo dozvoleno*) but rather,
"Everything is permitted which serves the new order."

Mr. Rosen has noted that nihilism entails both historical pessimism and a rejection or critique of rationality. This is clearly
true of noninstrumental nihilism; it is also true of *one* of the
forms of Russian instrumental nihilism. But it is not true of the
majority of instrumental nihilists in Russia, who have been
optimistic about the movement of history and enamored of

reason and "science" to the point of "epistemolatry"—if I may coin an awkward but reasonably accurate term.

The most influential and celebrated form of Russian instrumental nihilism was that of the capital-N Nihilists, the *Nigilisty* of the 1860's—Chernyshevski, Dobrolyubov, Nechayev, Pisarev, and, to a degree, Bakunin. All these "men of the '60's" were historical optimists and champions of reason.[1] (Pisarev, the cleverest of them, was also a precocious noncognitivist in ethics.) All of them proposed to negate or "annihilate" without mercy whatever they saw as obstructing the path of rational and "scientific" historical progress.

Nietzsche's thought, too, includes a strand of instrumental nihilism, interwoven with his more characteristic "terminal" nihilism. In an early work Nietzsche proclaimed the propaedeutic power of forgetting as a mode of negating or annihilating the dead weight of the past, thus freeing men for vital cultural creativity aimed at the future. In later works he contrasted active nihilism to passive, "tired" nihilism, insisting that creation involves preliminary destruction, that "life lives at the expense of other life."

A quite different kind of instrumental nihilism appeared in early twentieth-century Russian thought with the religious existentialism of Leon Shestov. Shestov negated or "revolted against" reason and "epistemolatry." He was a historical pessimist but a "transhistorical" optimist. His aim was to negate whatever he took to be obstructive or repressive of human values and of trans-historical salvation. He saw a sharp collision between reason and value, or "the good." Like Nietzsche, whom he greatly admired, Shestov moved beyond noncognitivism in ethics to a non- or anticognitivism *überhaupt*.

I

The first clear statement of Russian instrumental nihilism appeared (in 1842) in German (in Arnold Ruge's *Deutsch-Französische Jahrbücher*) over a French signature ("Jules Elysard"). The author, of course, was Bakunin; his title: "Die

---

1. However, during the 1860's Bakunin sharply criticized the "rule of science," i.e., scientifically based technocracy.

Reaktion in Deutschland"; his central theme: "the negation of what exists . . . for the benefit of the future which does not yet exist."

In 1840 Bakunin had waxed lyrical over the "incessant self-immolation of the positive in the pure flame of the negative." By 1842 he was speaking of the "pure flame of the negative" as a necessary ingredient in revolutionary political action. The latter is possible only where "real contradiction" exists. Political reaction is doomed to impotence because it attempts to block the movement and deny the historic right of negation. What exists exists necessarily, but its negation is no less necessary. Resistance—hence struggle and destruction—is a necessary condition of individual and social progress. Reconciliation or compromise of any kind—any "liberal" attempt to find a "modest and harmless place" for the negative within the positive—will fail; the whole meaning of the negative lies in the annihilation of the positive. "The Positive and the Negative get along no more than fire and water." [2]

"The Negative," Bakunin continues, "as determining the life of the Positive itself, alone includes within itself the totality of the contradiction, and so it alone also has absolute justification." [3]

"Let us therefore," Baukunin concludes, "trust the eternal Spirit [Geist] which destroys and annihilates only because it is the unfathomable and eternally creative source of all life." [4] The men of the '60's were less exuberantly romantic in expression, but, like Bakunin, they glorified destruction and at the same time celebrated creation, for they conceived destruction and creation as complementary aspects or dimensions of the same process. "The passion for destruction," as Bakunin had put it in the climactic last line of his article, "is a creative passion too." [5]

The dialectical paradox lies on the surface of Bakunin's mind,

2. "The Reaction in Germany," trans., Mary-Barbara Zeldin, in *Russian Philosophy*, James M. Edie, James P. Scanlan, Mary-Barbara Zeldin, and George L. Kline, eds., Chicago, 1965, Vol. I, 389.

3. *Ibid.*, p. 397.

4. *Ibid.*, p. 406.

5. *Loc. cit.* The German word here translated "passion" is *Lust*, which carries the double meaning of (a) "joy" or "pleasure" and (b) "passion" or "desire." Bakunin clearly meant to exploit this ambiguity.

although he never stated it in a straightforward way. Destruction is the only truly creative activity. Wholeness lies in contradiction—in the negation of the positive—for this negation "includes" the positive value which it negates. Such is the earliest "dialectical" form of Russian instrumental nihilism.

II

Alexander Herzen in his own way also anticipated the men of the '6o's, defending a mild form of instrumental nihilism and sketching the outlines of a noncognitivism in ethics during the 1840's and '50's. I begin with the second point:

Herzen was a moral relativist; he denied that moral rules or principles have objective validity. "What was admirable behavior yesterday," he declared, "may be abominable today. . . ." [6] He considered moral valuations simply statements of taste or preference on the model of the assertion, "I like lobster"—some people do and some do not, and that's an end of the matter. Such statements, being "subjective" and arbitrary, are not binding on anyone else.

Herzen endorsed the Stoic rejection of moral rules and maxims, adding "the truly free man *creates* his own morality." [7] "There are no general rules," he wrote in 1867, "but [only] an improvisation of conduct, a comprehension, a tact, an aesthetics of human actions, to which the developed human being brings himself, and which comprises the moral orbit, and forms, of his actions." [8] Herzen's position anticipates the "aesthetic amoralism" developed by Konstantin Leontyev, and later by Nietzsche, as well as Pisarev's noncognitivism.

Herzen often called his own position a "nihilism"; but he

6. *From the Other Shore,* Isaiah Berlin, ed., New York, 1956, p. 141. The title of this chapter, characteristically, is "Omnia mea mecrum porto." The original Russian text is to be found in *Sochineniya,* III, 360. (References are to the convenient nine-volume edition of Herzen's works published in Moscow during the late 1950's. One passage from a late letter—quoted in footnote 8—does not appear in this edition and is quoted from the thirty-volume Soviet edition of the 1960's.)

7. *From the Other Shore,* p. 141; *Soch.,* III, 360.

8. Letter to his son Alexandre, Nice, July 17, 1867: *Sochineniya,* Moscow, 1963, XXIX [1], 148.

used the term in a very broad sense, as roughly equivalent to "ironical and disillusioned skepticism." "Nihilism" in this sense is "science without dogmas, unconditional submission to experience and unmurmuring acceptance of the consequences, whatever they may be, so long as they spring from observation and are required by reason." It does not reduce "something to nothing; rather, it reveals that the nothing which had been taken for a something is an optical illusion. . . ." [9]

Herzen rejected as "illusory" not only the *referenda* of traditional religious beliefs but also the *referenda* of metaphysical and ethical statements. He spoke with nostalgic bitterness of his lost, and of course illusory, beliefs—his Hegelianism, his Christianity, his faith in the Revolution of 1848.

> Often in moments of despair . . . when I doubted myself, and the ultimate, and all else—these words came to my mind; "Why did I not take a gun from some workman and mount the barricade [in Paris in 1848]?" Struck down by a random bullet, I should have taken to the grave with me at least two or three beliefs. . . .[10]

In this mood—and it was a recurrent one—Herzen found Leopardi and the Byron of *Don Juan, Manfred,* and *Cain* his most congenial authors.

> Neither Cain, nor Manfred, nor Don Juan, nor Byron himself has . . . any "moral." . . . Byron's . . . last word . . . is "The Darkness" . . . This is why I now value [his] courageous thinking so highly. He saw that there is no way out, and proudly proclaimed this truth.[11]

Such "nihilism" is noninstrumental, "terminal," and of a distinctly Nietzschean cast. Nietzsche's own reflections on "European nihilism" may in fact have been partly inspired by Herzen's work, which had appeared in German and French translations during the 1860's and to which Nietzsche occasionally referred in his early letters.[12]

9. From an 1869 text entitled "Yeshcho raz Bazarov ("Bazarov Once Again"), *Soch.*, VIII, 393.
10. *Byloye i dumy (My Past and Thoughts), Soch.,* V, 491.
11. *Ibid., Soch.,* V, 378.
12. Nietzsche was personally acquainted with Herzen's daughter Olga (later Mme. Gabriel Monod) and with Malwida von Meysenbug, German translator of Herzen's memoirs. In a number of letters written from

Herzen's first kind of "nihilism" ("unmurmuring accept-ance . . .") is essentially epistemological or methodological. The second kind ("darkness" and "no way out") is cultural or "spiritual." A third kind of nihilism—political and "dialectical" —came to the surface of Herzen's thought during the years immediately following the Revolution of 1848. It was this kind of nihilism which brought him briefly within ideological hailing distance of Bakunin, Chernyshevski, and Pisarev.

The central slogan of "dialectical nihilism" was forged by Herzen himself: "Hegel's philosophy is the *algebra of revolution:* it liberates man in an extraordinary way, and does not leave one stone upon another in the Christian world, the world of legends, which has outlived its time." [13] Herzen had read and approved Bakunin's manifesto of dialectical nihilism when it was first published in 1842. But his own statements date from the period just after 1848:

> Negation derives all of its force from that which it negates, from the past. . . . Like a flame, it consumes the stronghold of what exists, but it is itself conditioned by the existence of what is consumed . . . the past is not wasted . . . ; it is made other, conscious.[14]

Sounding very much like Bakunin, who had called the *Lust der Zerstörung* a *schaffende Lust,* Herzen declared: "Of course, destruction creates: it clears a space, and this is already creation; it banishes a host of lies—and this is already truth." [15]

Basel during the second half of 1872 Nietzsche spoke admiringly of Herzen and warmly recommended *My Past and Thoughts* (in German translation) to several of his correspondents. Cf. Nietzsche, *Historisch-Kritische Gesamt-Ausgabe,* Briefe, Bd. 3, Munich, 1940.

13. *Byloye i dumy, Soch.,* V, 20.

14. Quoted in D. Chizhevski, *Gegel v Rossii* (*Hegel in Russia*), Paris, 1939, p. 205.

15. Quoted in *loc. cit.* However, in 1869 Herzen broke with Bakunin on just this point, challenging him to specify "the process (apart from sheer destruction) which will accomplish the transformation of old forms into new ones. . . . By denial alone, however intelligent it may be, one cannot possibly combat false dogmas. . . , however crazy they may be." Herzen concludes: "You rush ahead as before with a passion to destroy, which you take for a creative passion, breaking down obstacles and respecting only the history of the future. I no longer believe in the former revolutionary paths. . . . " ("K staromu tovarishchu" ["To an Old Comrade"], *Soch.,* VIII, 402, 403, 410.)

Insisting that it was "impossible to move in the ancient forms without breaking them," Herzen added, in a strikingly Nietzschean image: "We do not build, we destroy; we do not proclaim a new revelation, we eliminate the old lie. Modern man . . . only builds a bridge—it will be for the unknown man of the future to pass over it." [16] From this metaphor it is only a short step to the Nietzschean "man as a bridge to the *Übermensch.*" Nietzsche may well have read Herzen's text before he formulated his own position.

"Everything which has been touched by the hot stream of winnowing thought," Herzen writes, "is revealed as unstable and lacking in independence. Thought, joyous and exultant like a spirit of death, an angel of destruction, wreaks havoc among the ruins, giving itself no time to think about what should replace them." [17]

Herzen's own idea of what would replace the existing European order was apocalyptic, yet somehow optimistic. "Europe," he asserted in 1850, "will live out her miserable days in the twilight of imbecility, in sluggish feelings without conviction, without fine arts, without powerful poetry." But ultimately, "spring will come, life will play on their tombstones; the barbarism of infancy, full of chaotic but healthy forces, will replace senile barbarism," and the "third [socialist] volume of universal history" will begin.[18]

III

We have distinguished three forms, or levels, of nihilism in Herzen: (1) a methodological nihilism, which is close to skepticism; (2) a future-oriented cultural nihilism, which merges into an apocalyptic vision of European history; (3) a political or "dialectical" nihilism, which is formulated in the "algebra of revolution." We have also seen that the latter two forms of nihilism were of passing rather than permanent significance in Herzen's own intellectual development, although he remained to the end something of a skeptic, or "methodological nihilist."

16. *From the Other Shore*, p. 3; *Soch.*, III, 233.
17. "Letters on the Study of Nature" (1845), *Soch.*, II, 170.
18. *From the Other Shore* (Epilogue, 1849), pp. 146 f.; *Soch.*, III, 339.

In these terms, Russian Nihilism, as a generalized social and intellectual phenomenon of the late 1850's and '60's, was primarily political and dialectical—though not without tinges of methodological and cultural nihilism.

The announced goal of the Nihilists was the annihilation of the existing order—social, political, economic, cultural; the means which they advocated were radical, often violent. All of them were enormously impressed by the success of the natural sciences and convinced that the development of physics, chemistry, and experimental zoology would ultimately provide answers to all social and moral, not merely scientific or technological, problems. "It is precisely in the frog," Pisarev proclaimed, "that the salvation and renewal of the Russian people is to be found." Opposed to the (laboratory) "frog" as the symbol of applied science and exact useful knowledge *überhaupt*, stands "Pushkin" as a symbol of overrefined and socially useless aestheticism.

The Nihilists were antiromanticists in general culture; they were anti-idealists in philosophy. They distrusted "airy speculation" and admired "brass tacks." Pisarev expressed their "'realism" (in all three senses) in his manifesto: *Slova i illyuzii gibnut; fakty ostayutsya* ("Words and illusions perish; facts remain").[19]

In writings centered around 1861 Pisarev went on to develop an extreme moral relativism, sketching a noncognitivist position in ethics and hinting at a more general "cognitive nihilism."

"A common ideal," he declared, "has just as little *raison d'être* as common eyeglasses or common boots, made on the same last and to the same measure." Eyes differ, feet differ, individuals differ; hence glasses, boots, and ideals should be individually fitted.

Morality is a matter of individual taste, like the preference for port or sherry. Such preferences cannot be rationally grounded. However,

> . . . when it is a matter of judging port or sherry, we remain calm and cool, we reason simply and soundly . . . , but when

19. D. I. Pisarev, "Protsess zhizni" ("The Life-Process"), 1861, *Sochineniya* (St. Petersburg, 1897), I, 321.

it is a question of lofty matters, we immediately put on a Lenten countenance, get up on our stilts, and start to pontificate. . . .[20]

Pisarev formulated his instrumental nihilism in terms of what he called "criticism" and "skepticism":

The touch of criticism is feared only by what is rotten, by what, like an Egyptian mummy, crumbles into dust from a draft of air. A living idea, like a fresh flower drenched by rain, grows stronger and more vigorous under the test of skepticism. Only phantoms disappear before the tempering force of sober analysis. . . .[21]

This is reminiscent of Herzen on the "illusory something," as is the Nihilist sequel:

What can be broken should be broken; what will stand the blow is fit to live; what breaks into smithereens is rubbish; in any case, strike right and left, it will not and cannot do any harm.[22]

IV

Shestov's position is usually considered a (theistic) existentialism rather than an (instrumental) nihilism. In fact it is both: his nihilist "destruction of reason"—parallel in many respects to Pisarev's "destruction of aesthetics"—is a propaedeutic, intended to clear the way for an assertion and defense of the "values of human existence." Like Nietzsche and the Nihilists, Shestov was, in Berdyaev's words, a thinker who "philosophized with his whole being, for whom philosophy was not an academic specialty but a matter of life and death." [23]

20. "Idealizm Platona" ("Plato's Idealism"), Soch., Moscow, 1955, I, 83. Pisarev not only denies the absoluteness of truth; he asserts that "views (vozzreniya) can be neither true nor false; there is my view, your view, a third, a fourth. Which it true? For each—his own." (Skholastika XIX veka" [Nineteenth-Century Scholasticism"], Soch., Moscow, 1955, I, 135.)

21. "Nineteenth-Century Scholasticism," Soch., I, 133.

22. Ibid., p. 135.

23. N. A. Berdyaev, "Osnovnaya ideya filosofii Lva Shestova" ("The Fundamental Idea of Leon Shestov's Philosophy"), Put, No. 58 (1938–39), p. 44.

Shestov was what the Russians call an *odnodum*—a man with a "single thought," i.e., an obsession, or *idée fixe*. What he attacked, what he struggled mightily to reduce to a *nihil,* was the "rule of reason" or, as he preferred to call it, the "tyranny of rational necessity."

Shestov's "revolt against reason" reached its climax in the claim that God (for whom "all things are possible") can undo what has been done and, in particular, can make the horrors of the past "not to have been." Shestov's examples of such horrors include Job's loss of his children, Socrates' drinking of the hemlock, Nietzsche's decline into madness, Kierkegaard's giving up of Regina Olsen. It is in God's power, Shestov insists, to make the dead not to have died, as when Job's children—the *same* children, not a new brood—were restored to him at the end of the biblical story. God can cancel the "eternal truth" that Socrates was poisoned—that is, he can make it be the case that Socrates, retroactively, so to speak, was *not* poisoned after all.

The heart of philosophic rationalism—for Shestov—lies in the unquestioning acceptance of necessary objective laws, as formulated in the "truths of pure reason."

Shestov distinguishes sharply between *laws* and *decrees:* Necessary objective *laws* say, in effect, "thou shalt" and "thou shalt not"; they demand obedience. Nonnecessary subjective *decrees* say, in effect, "let it be so" or "it need not be so." On Shestov's view, both species of nonnecessity—namely, (natural) contingency and (human or divine) arbitrariness—make possible free choice, decision, and creativity.

In contrast, universal, necessary norms limit and repress free creativity. For Shestov, as for Nietzsche, "all life is creative *tolma* ["daring," or "audacity"] and therefore an eternal mystery, irreducible to anything . . . intelligible." We "rationally" fear chaos as a loss or deficiency of order. In fact, Shestov insists, "chaos is not a limited possibility, but the direct opposite, an unlimited opportunity." [24] Earlier he had written that "the first

24. *In Job's Balances,* trans. C. Coventry and C. A. Macartney, London and New York, 1932, pp. 158, 226.

and essential condition of life is lawlessness. Laws are a refreshing sleep—lawlessness is creative activity." [25]

In Part I of Dostoyevski's *Notes from Underground*, which Shestov found both congenial and deep, rational necessity is symbolized by the "stone wall" and "twice two is four." Against both of these "truths of reason" the man from the underground "absurdly" rebels. Not to rebel against such "necessities" is to acquiesce in the "horrors of existence." [26] Men regularly accept theoretical truth even when it encroaches upon "what is most precious to them, upon what they consider sacred." Truths are truths, Shestov complains, "whether or not men need them, whether men (and even gods) are gladdened or saddened by them, filled with hope or with despair." [27]

In the terms of Genesis, the serpent lied to Adam: theoretical truth does not make men like God or the gods; rather it makes God or the gods like men, equally subject to necessary and universal truth. Reason commands; man must obey. *Roma locuta, causa finita.*

However, for Shestov, when reason speaks, the case is far from closed. Theoretical reason, being destructive of human values, must itself be destroyed. ". . . The tree of knowledge shall no longer deaden the tree of life."

According to Shestov, men can live with and by faith, but they cannot live with or by reason, because the absolutization of theoretical truth is inevitably a relativization and, in a sense, destruction, of life—of human existence. Shestov was fully prepared to move in the opposite direction—to relativize, and even destroy, theoretical truth in order to absolutize moral and religious values and thus "redeem" the existing individual.

The point may be expressed in terms of the rich and ambiguous Russian term *pravda*, which means both theoretical truth

25. *All Things Are Possible*, trans. S. S. Koteliansky, London and New York, 1920, p. 127.
26. In this connection Shestov refers to Nietzsche's early insight into the "horrors and atrocities of existence" (*Schrecken und Entsetzlichkeiten des Daseins*). Cf. *The Birth of Tragedy*, 1872; Golffing trans. p. 29.
27. "In Memory of a Great Philosopher: Edmund Husserl," trans., G. L. Kline, in *Russian Philosophy*, III, 264, 276.

(*istina*) and practical justice (*spravedlivost*), or "truth-justice." Rationalists such as Chernyshevski and Pisarev assume that theoretical truth (*pravda-istina*) can and should serve as a support for practical justice (*pravda-spravedlivost*) in individual and social life. The antirationalist Shestov insists that moral values, or the humanly valued (here expressed by *pravda-spravedlivost*) must take, or rather retake, priority, displacing or denying the claims of theoretical truth (*pravda-istina*) in all cases of conflict. And it was Shestov's special insight—or obsession—that the cases of conflict are frequent and total, since the "moral world-order" postulated by rationalists who assume that *pravda-istina* offers a support for *pravda-spravedlivost* is a pernicious illusion.

Shestov claims that his own "either/or"—*either* "rational necessity" and the horrors of existence which it "legitimates," *or* a faith that promises salvation from those horrors—is not a choice, as rationalists would claim, between reason and unreason, between sanity and insanity. It is an "absurd" existential choice between two kinds of madness—the madness of theoretical reason, which accepts as necessary and inevitable those "self-evident" truths which "rationalize" and legitimate man's finitude, suffering and mortality, and the madness of the "leap of faith" —the desperate struggle against such truths in the name of the values of human existence.[28]

V

Bakunin, Herzen, and the Nihilists of the 1860's diagnosed the ills of the nineteenth-century world as springing from a deficiency of reason; they sought to purge away the pathologies of that world in order to usher in the joint reign of healing reason and saving good. That "reason in history" could and would support the humanly good was for them an article of (implicit) faith.

Shestov diagnosed the ills of the human world as springing

28. I have given a fuller account of Shestov's position—contrasted with that of Berdyaev—in *Religious and Anti-Religious Thought in Russia*, Chicago, 1968, Chapter 3.

from an excessive submissiveness to reason; he sought to purge away the pathologies of human existence in order to restore man's irrational, trans-historical, and "salvific" good. That an all-powerful God could and would support what is good for man was for Shestov an article of (explicit) faith.

As between the opposed faiths of the two Russian variants of instrumental nihilism and the non- or anti-faith of Western European "terminal" nihilism, the difference is wide and the choice—within those nihilist limits—relatively clear. But is there are any compelling reason for staying within the nihilist limits? Should we not rather take up an intellectual position "beyond both instrumental and noninstrumental nihilism"?

EXISTENCE AND THE ABSURD

It is not only true that existential thinkers are interested in the paradoxical in their world; they are frequently paradoxical in the use which they make of many of their key terms. It is paradoxical, for example, that when men postulate a word such as "nothing," they also seem to be quite capable of saying something about it. Similarly it is disconcerting to see how much hopefulness accompanies the use of the word "despair" —so much so that we are led to believe that our only hope is to lose hope. This is again a paradoxical procedure. It is paradoxical as well to encounter writers who deal with "meaninglessness" in such a way that the topic seems anything *but* meaningless; indeed in such a way that the meaningless appears as the category for a whole new universe of human meaningfulness.

This is equally the case with the curious word "absurdity." What is paradoxical here is that a term which indicates a cul-de-sac and an absolute termination of thought should be in fact the absolute beginning of an entire suite of philosophical discourse. There is something wrong with the use that has been made of this curious term, and the few remarks that are contained here are designed to suggest what has gone wrong and to indicate as well the broader context in which we may think about this term—"the absurd."

Because of the brevity of these remarks I wish to forgo any

effort to justify my understanding of the absurd, either ety-
mologically or traditionally; I wish only to state the way in
which I have come to understand and use this term in my
own thought and how I see many others use it.

The first thing I must mention is that I do not attach to
this word the significance which Kierkegaard attached to it.
The fact that Kierkegaard, an existential thinker, used the term
a century ago, and the fact that certain French existential
thinkers used the term a century later, need not lure us into
the futile effort to find some meaning which is common to both.
The word is the same, but the usage is quite different. For
Kierkegaard, the absurd is a situation of utter paradox which
an individual is invited to accept as an intellectual and moral
reality. Kierkegaard's interest was in effecting a subjective transformation within man, and thus he presented men with a
radical paradox, the acceptance of which would, he felt, entail
a radical transformation of the individual. This is precisely
what the twentieth-century use of the term is not designed to
express. In the twentieth-century usage, the absurd is not an
invitation to be responded to; rather it is a problem to be
struggled with and solved. Kierkegaard went seeking the absurd;
contemporary philosophers of the absurd do not seek it but
instead are unwillingly stuck with it. From our present point
of view, Kierkegaard's invitation to embrace the absurd à la
Abraham or à la God-man is an invitation to sickness and insanity. The mid-twentieth-century understanding of the absurd
is, contrarily, that it is a given situation which one must lucidly
recognize and struggle against if one is to be able to retain
one's health and sanity.

Secondly, in declaring my own understanding of the term
"absurd," I want to insist that it not be taken as some exclusive
philosophical concept which stands sovereignly aloof from certain obviously similar terms in the existentialist's vocabulary.
With only slight qualifications in each case, I would be quite
content to use Nietzsche's "pathos of distance," Sartre's "nausea,"
Camus' "revolt," Heidegger's "dread," and even the journalistically
popular word "meaninglessness" as just as useful as the word
"absurd." Taken in this sense, the word in Kierkegaard's vocab-

ulary which happens to more nearly fit this same meaning is his term "despair."

So, then, the term "absurd" is a useful and important term for existential thought, but the task is not to fight for the word but to interest ourselves in the situation to which it points. If we do so, not only may we clarify some of the muddied issues in existential philosophy, but we may quite possibly gain the interest and sympathy of those who are antagonized by the paradoxes of existential thought.

What I and many others understand by the absurd is your or my experience of ourselves in an irreducible situation of difference from our environing world. This is not to say that one experiences separation, estrangement, or alienation from one's actual environment—this is nonsense, inasmuch as none of us are separate and cut off from actuality. What we are speaking of is our experience not of separation but of difference, a difference which may be spoken of metaphysically or morally but which is fundamentally ontic: this is to say that the absurd is an individual's experience that the structure and needs of his own existence are not commensurate with the structure of his actual environing world. Heidegger and Sartre are interested in this difference at an ontic level; this is also my own interest. But Camus is interested in it in terms of its moral import. Others, such as Jaspers and Marcel, are interested in this difference between individual and world from a metaphysical viewpoint. The levels of interest vary, but the structural situation does not vary, for in every case it indicates an individual's experience of being a centrum of existence which is structurally different from the given structure of one's environing world. This experience is a datum from which philosophical discourse can operate, and I would insist that it is the primary datum from which existential and phenomenological thought works and is the primary datum against which it justifies its thought. Because it is the primary existential datum, one can communicate one's philosophic concerns about it only to those who are in possession of the same datum—which is to say that existential discourse takes place effectively only among those who have shared this same experience of ontic difference. Those who have not shared this experience of ontic difference will not be able to penetrate beyond the words to the experience which they express: instead, they will hear the words, see the paradoxes, and, quite rightly, pounce upon what they see to be words without signification and discourse without logical consistency.

In this respect it should be remarked that the bulk of what finds its way into print concerning existential philosophy seems to be written by those who are fascinated with the curious words and paradoxes of existential thought but are not in possession of this primary datum; consequently, it is those who call themselves existential philosophers who frequently supply the occasion for antiexistentialists to pounce quite justifiably upon statements which do not bear close scrutiny. A typical and basic example of this is the custom of referring to the absurd or the experience of meaninglessness as an experience of that which is irreducibly irrational. This is a crucial error, inasmuch as it not only betrays a fundamental misunderstanding of the primary datum of existential thought but, by staking everything upon the term "rational," it opens the door to the kind of scrutiny for which the Anglo-American mind has great expertise.

It should be sufficient to say that the assertion that the world is "meaningless" is not to indicate that it is irrational but just the contrary: it is to indicate our awareness in the mid-twentieth century that our environing world has never before displayed so much rationality; it is to indicate that the rationality of our actual environment is now for the first time a flat, working presumption of our scientific-technological civilization and that now for the first time individuals experience a flat, working presumption of their own given structural difference from that known environment. What has happened during the twentieth century is that our observable world has been drawn closely about us into tight, practical patterns of rationality which, for the first time in the history of the human race, is not a metaphysical or theological hope but is a day-to-day technological fact for every individual in the Western world and is increasingly so among the awakening nations of the Orient and the southern hemisphere.

So if the prime assertion of existential philosophy is held to be that the world has been discovered to be irrational, then existential philosophy has declared itself to be puerile rubbish. And when those of an analytical temperament view such assertions and conclude that existentialism is tripe, their only fault is that of understatement.

But the accusation of the universe as being irrational is not what the primary datum of existential thought has the least thought of suggesting; rather, the assertion is that the actual environing world is now clearly seen to be what it is in its undeniable rational structure but that this rational structure is not the structure which one experiences within one's individual existence.

A simple illustration of the authentic existentialist assertion is the following. Let us take the very common contemporary statement: "I find that life is meaningless because the world is absurd." When a thoughtful, rationally minded person hears this typical collegiate statement, he properly replies: "But this is nonsense to say that life is meaningless and pointless; everything is utterly meaningful and rational. In fact, life has never before been so meaningful. Every individual now has a meaningful chance in life: he has his youth so that he may become thoroughly educated and trained for his role in society and his professional vocation; then he is able to get a job, so that he can fulfill himself in marriage; and through marriage, he can know the joys of sexual bliss and the pleasures of his own children; and he works at his job and aids his children so that they too may have these same experiences. So, then, I ask you, what could be more meaningful and rational in life? And, beyond this, let me point out that this is not simply a vague hope, it is, in the twentieth century, a practical possibility which we have placed within the grasp of all men. Therefore, contrary to what you say, this is the most happy and rational and meaningful and successful of all previous periods in the history of the human race." This would be a proper and forceful rational-minded reply to the assertion that "life is meaningless."

If, however, one is in possession of the primary existential datum, one's correct response to this typical rational-minded position would be this: "You are unquestionably right about your understanding of the utter rationality of human life. You are quite right when you say that we are born so that we can be properly nourished and reared, and that we have sound bodies and minds so that we can be educated and that we are educated so that we may have jobs that will support society and allow us to marry, and that we marry so that we may have children, and that we have children so that they may be properly nourished and reared, and so that they may have sound bodies and minds and can be educated, and that they are educated so that they may have jobs that will support society and allow them to marry, and that they too will marry so that they may have children, and they have children so that these children too can be properly nourished and reared, so that they too can be educated, so that they too can have jobs, so that, etc., etc. It is true that this interlocking series of reasons for existence is utterly rational as it moves ineluctably and smoothly from generation to generation, but the question is, 'What is the point of it? Why should I do any of these things when all I can see is that they are ultimately meaningless to me as an individual?' "

This is a rather exact expression of the experience of the absurd which gives utter recognition to the given rationality of one's environing world, not only on its physical level but even on its social level, but still raises the ultimate question as to the relation of this rational structure of things to what one feels to be the given structure of one's own life. This is the primary experiential datum which we must keep in mind if we are to think in terms of the unique focal point of existential thought and if we are to refer to that which can justify this kind of thought.

So, then, whether we are to refer to this experience as that of the absurd, or of meaninglessness, or of despair, or nausea, or revolt is indifferent; what is crucial is the given reality of the experience itself, and once this reality has been given to an individual philosopher, he has no option but to think honestly in terms of it, even though there will be others who are unable to understand or sympathize with his philosophical concerns, inasmuch as they do not share the same primary datum.

I think that if existential as well as phenomenological philosophy is to develop further as a strong and consistent movement in contemporary philosophy, we must keep resolutely in mind this primary datum. I say that we must do so resolutely, because one risks being seriously bothered by the implication which this has—that existential philosophers represent an élite who, because they have had a certain experience of themselves and their world, are set apart from those who have not had this experience. A philosophical élite who share a certain experience smacks too much of private experience, unverified fantasy, antiscience, antiobjectivity, and antidemocracy to sit well with many Western philosophers. The temptation of the existential and phenomenological movements is precisely this temptation to deny the primary experiential datum and justify the movement in terms of more public, verifiable, and democratic procedures. To accede to this temptation—which is a prime temptation among American philosophers—is to abandon at its fundament the seminal impulse of existential thought, which is the impulse to resolutely explore the uniquely given structures and needs of living individual existence. This is to say that to attempt to justify existential and phenomenological philosophy in terms of traditional Western categories of thought is to falsify and destroy the movement itself. Even so, this is exactly the risk which this philosophy currently runs.

The reason one need not fear that a resolute philosophizing from the primary datum of absurd experience is the philosophizing of an isolated élite is that this experience is far more common than academic philosophers realize and is becoming the increasingly common experience of successive generations within the twentieth century. Already, among those of college age now, the so-called absurd experience provides the cutting edge of unrest and of disaffection with our technologically oriented society; and this is an experience which has not been learned thanks to the efforts of existential philosophers, but which has come about as a flat and workaday discovery of what it means to grow up in an efficient, technologically oriented society. The importance of this discovery is such that if many young people cannot have this experience early in life, they feel quite justified in resorting to antiinhibitory drugs so as to allow them to share this common experience of their chosen peer groups.

What I am suggesting is that the experience of the absurd is not uncommon, abnormal, and élitist but is becoming a common, normal, and utterly healthy human response and adjustment to an actual environment which is one of successful theoretical and technological organization.

What I am suggesting as well is that the negativistic terms of "absurdity," "despair," "meaninglessness," "alienation," "dread," "revolt," "fragmentation," et al., are already futile and misleading terms, inasmuch as they describe only the original negative side of the primary experiential datum of existential thought. To attempt at the present time to characterize existentialism in terms of these negative expressions is to misunderstand what existentialism takes as its fundamental datum. These negative expressions are all descriptive of the twentieth-century disappointment in an actual environment which does not correspond to the structure and needs of the human individual. This much is well taken, but the immediate philosophical task is not to dwell upon the initial negative experience of disappointment with one's environment but to resolutely explore the positive implications which this experience has for an understanding of the unique and indigenous structures and needs which human existence presents to its environment.

This is a task which is at once philosophical and psychological. It is a task which, as a positive movement, will erase the earlier distinctions between what we call existentialism and phenomenology and develop a more clearly constructive posture. What we call the experience of the absurd is two things: It is a unique twentieth-century discovery of disappointment with the actual world in which we now live, and it is at the same time a unique twentieth-century discovery of the peculiar structures and needs of human existence which must be understood and heeded if we are to thrive and remain whole within a technological environment never before experienced in the lineage of the human race. Whatever name we may eventually give to it, the task I refer to is that of positive existential thought, a type of philosophy which is only now beginning to see the light of day.

Paul G. Kuntz

MAKING SENSE OF THE ABSURD

What philosophic category—if it is a category—is at present more controversial than the absurd? Rather than take the experience of the absurd to be the key to understanding existence, or condemning talk of the absurd as the product of madmen, I have undertaken a preface to other studies: to sort out meanings of "absurd." Is it controversial that the term has many senses? The growing literature, both of the friends of the absurd and its enemies, has, I believe, neglected definition. The history of "absurd" is not mere etymology; it can help us toward a more adequate philosophy by illustrating some meanings which we must reject and others which we may accept. My own position is that of a dialectician in the present controversy, considering, as Aristotle urged, difficulties on both sides, with the intention of detecting truth and error. Few topics are more fitting for a symposium (except perhaps dialectic itself) because no one person can see the many aspects as a whole.

I am grateful for criticism to José Huertas-Jourda, now of Pennsylvania State University, and other members of the philosophy department; to the graduate students who endured an earlier version; and to the secretary, Mrs. Susan Livingston, who did, as usual, more than her share of the drudgery. But for them, this essay would be even more erroneous.

I. *The Category of the Absurd: An Important Contemporary Problem*

A noted authority on English language and literature recently expressed alarm at the number of clichés that are taking the place of critical reflection. Among them, held up for ridicule, are "Experience is absurd," "Life is absurd," "Destiny is absurd." In essay after essay Professor Robert Heilman reads this sort of thing "as if it were an unarguable truth." This is a challenge we should endeavor to meet. Are we encouraging loose thinking that shows up in bad writing? In the critic's view "the problem [arises from] the quasi-critical taking over of a fashionable word, the begging of the philosophical issue, being in the swim, and seeming to have an up-to-date key for virtually all literary locks—not to mention helping spread a rigid unilateral view of reality." [1]

Similarly the noted director and translator of plays, Mordecai Gorelik, damned "the absurd absurdists." The plays are formless, the content negation of human aspirations. Such expressions of futility were appropriate to the defeated French under the Nazis but continuation of the mood is inappropriate now.[2] Gorelik argues that philosophers must share responsibility for nihilism, both the denial that knowledge is possible and the denial that any ends are worth pursuing.

The topic is of far wider than literary significance because the absurd is used now by critics of society in characterizing alienated youth.

The philosophic discussion will not remain merely parochial for another reason. Theological thought has continued to use the absurd in its apologetics: not only the familiar way of Tertullian, Pascal, and Kierkegaard but that of Camus. There are

1. Robert Heilman, "The Critic and the Academy," *Literature and the Academy* (April 16, 1966), Grinnell, Iowa, pp. 20–21.
2. Mordecai Gorelik, "The Absurd Absurdists," *The New York Times*, Section 2, August 8, 1965, pp. 1, 3; a reply by Martin Esslin "The Theater of the Absurd Isn't Absurd," *ibid.*, August 29, 1965, pp. 1, 3.

several essays on the Christian as Camus' absurd man or man in revolt. Therefore the sharp rejection of the category of the absurd will stir religious interest. Recently we witnessed the sharpest polemical attack in philosophy since the positivists attempted to destroy metaphysics. Brand Blanshard went after nonsense and perversity with relentless zeal. English and American philosophers, especially of the analytic types, have been indifferent to, or contemptuous of, any continental philosophy, especially existentialism. Now we have evidence of a depth of hostility that does not bode well for reunion in philosophy.

However hostile and unsympathetic this context of discussion, many of the questions are excellent. The most valuable of all these is that of Blanshard: is not "absurd" a wildly ambiguous term? Later I shall discuss the five meanings of "absurd" Blanshard finds in Kierkegaard. Here I should like to make clear that even if there are ten or fifteen meanings of "absurd," this itself is damning only if each philosophic term is properly to have one and only one meaning. The criterion of strict univocity does not seem appropriate to philosophy, even if it is proposed under the apparently altogether unquestionable label "clarity."

Particularly if "absurd" is a categorical term, should we not expect it to be somewhat ambiguous? It has been known since Aristotle that "being has many senses," and this has been a bright page in symbolic logic to find ways of substituting for "is" in "$2 + 2$ is 4," "There are ivory-billed woodpeckers in Texas," and "God cannot not be," etc. If "absurd" is predicated universally, and it is now applied to things, persons, acts, ideas, statements, situations, how does the meaning vary?

This kind of inquiry will at least give us a wider perspective on a problem which we may have seen too narrowly. The great alternatives are that the absurd is the great truth about man in the world, even a saving truth, or that it is the most harmful kind of cynicism, a madman's perversion of legitimate human purpose. But if there are many senses of absurd, and the term was once, like *hyle*, a literal term, now extended metaphorically, as is matter, should we not be cautious? We may want, on reflection, to affirm one sense and deny another. Sometimes when we say "*x* is absurd" we may be saying something true and important. At other times we may be saying something false and trivial. We need to ask ourselves which is which?

II. "*Vox Absona et Absurda*": The History of a Term

We are far more sure of what Cicero meant by the Latin "absurdus" than we are of anyone using the term in English or any other modern language. This is but a common paradox of once literal terms like *spiritus* (or *hyle*) that before extension designated a specific kind of thing. "Absurdus" designated sounds that were heard to be "*out of tune, hence giving a disagreeable sound, harsh, rough.*" No one disagrees that *absurdus* is from *surdus,* deaf, the *ab-* an intensive preposition. Cicero refers to a "*vox absona et absurda.*" The word is extended from the musical to the rhetorical, thence to the logical. The general meaning in our dictionaries is what is offensive to "common sense or sound judgment." Hence absurd things are not sounds only but things said, things done, and even persons who say and do absurd things.

Implicit in judging something to be absurd is always some criterion. I should surmise that our meanings of "absurd" are less clear than Cicero's because, as absurd gets extended, the criteria become ever less empirical. Typical instances from the *Oxford English Dictionary,* where the criteria are relatively easy to state, are the beliefs "that the whole is less than the sum of the parts," or that "8 minus 12 is an Absurde number, For it betokeneth less than nought by 4," or that the absurd people who do absurd things are "a dozen travelers in one party [who] light a dozen separate fires, and cook a dozen separate meals."

"Absurd" is philosophically interesting when in "*x* is absurd" we can replace *x* by almost anything: things, persons, acts, ideas, statements, situations. How did predication of a certain subset of sounds get extended beyond the narrow confines of the class of things heard? I believe the crucial turn here is due to the kind of Christian, like St. Paul, who gloried in aspects of the Gospel that were to "the Jews a stumbling block and to the Greeks a scandal." Whereas the above examples of absurd beliefs are rejected as contrary to a received axiom of geometry, or contrary to the arithmetic of 1557, or contrary to the economic good sense of Jevons in 1878 (to get the maximum result from the minimum effort), the Pauline Christian has no fear of shocking official reason: he delights in being outrageous. Shall we listen, as Cicero said, to the voice (a *vox absona et absurda*, like the croaking of frogs), of Tertullian?

> Which is more unworthy of God, more shameful, to be born or to die? . . . Answer me this, you butcher of the truth. Was not God really crucified? And if he was really crucified, did he not really die? And if he really died, did he not really rise from the dead? . . . Is our whole faith false? . . . Spare what is the one hope of the whole world. Why do you destroy an indignity that is necessary to our faith? What is unworthy of God will do for me . . . the Son of God was born; because it is shameful, I am not ashamed; and the Son of God died; just because it is absurd, it is to be believed; and He was buried and rose again; it is certain, because it is impossible.[3]

Can we make sense of *credo quia absurdum?* I believe so. Tertullian knows how the events of the Gospel sound to the common sense of Stoic lawyers of the empire, men trained in the tradition of Roman history. A virgin brings forth a son, he is believed the son of God, he performs miracles, is crucified and rises on the third day from the dead, descends into hell, ascends to heaven, and reigns at the right hand of God the Father Almighty. Absurd.

The importance philosophically of *credo quia absurdum* is that what is utter nonsense when read as ordinary history makes sense when read as *Heilsgeschichte.* The story of salvation is very different from the story of kingdoms, republics, and empires, and we have different standards of credibility by which we judge events in these different realms. What is then incredible by one set of standards is credible by another. It is not at all my point to defend the content of Tertullian's faith—only to say that one can make sense of someone's saying what Tertullian said. For there are indeed different realms or orders of discourse

3. Tertullian, *De Carne Christi*, V, from Bernard Williams, "Tertullian's Paradox" in A. Flew and A. MacIntyre, *New Essays in Philosophical Theology*, New York, 1955, pp. 189–190.

and being. What is orderly in one realm appears disorderly in another. Of course Tertullian, on this account, should have said *"credo quamquam absurdum,"* but the *quia* is a delightful snort of defiance, a snapping of his fingers, and the whole modern use of the absurd by Pascal, Kierkegaard, Camus, and Sartre seems to have a tone of revolt against excessive rationalism. Must there be one system, everything following logically from one set of absolute principles? Just as Dostoevsky in *Notes from Underground* pictures a revolt against the perfect mathematical and mechanical order of the crystal palace, so the common element of the absurd seems to be a protest of spontaneity, freedom of choice, brute unrationalized matter of fact, chance events—at least one of these, if not all four.

As long as there is the belief in one right method to study anything, we shall need the doctrine of *l'esprit de finesse* against *l'esprit géométrique*. John Wild's case for the *Lebenswelt* seems to me in this tradition. Not only can we defend the peculiar perspective of man seeking salvation over against universal deductive mechanism; we can see the one from the perspective of the other. "For in fact what is man in nature? A Nothing in comparison with the Infinite; an All in comparison with the Nothing, a mean between nothing and everything." [4]

To be both nothing and everything is now a familiar Pascalian paradox, a seeming contradiction. The importance for our study of the absurd is that it applies not to some beliefs, some situations, some acts but to man himself, man in relation to nature. I believe another constant point running through Pascal, Kierkegaard, Camus, and perhaps Sartre is the stress on discontinuity of orders. I use Pascal's formulation because it seems the clearest doctrine that no deduction in the order of nature ever gets to the history of man and no knowledge of the order of human events gets to such spiritual problems as belief in God. Put historically, Hegel was in the Cartesian tradition of putting all in a *single order,* treated by a *single method,* and Kierkegaard was a Pascal protesting in the name of *plurality* of orders and methods. There is an order of existence over against an order of essence. We can operate logically with propositions of the

4. Pascal, *Pensées,* New York, 1958, p. 17.

form "All A's are B's" and deduce "Some B's are A's," and a logician's convention has it that the latter is existential, not merely hypothetical, but do we know from logic alone that there is a B? Never, from logical manipulations of class membership. Is this too far from the point of Kierkegaard that the absurd is that which "nobody, trusting reason alone, could understand"? Kierkegaard stresses the gulf between different orders. He despises those who try "to make the absurd less absurd"— that is, to formulate degrees by which we might get from one to the other, bridging the gap.

Kierkegaard's point can be stated independently of the Christian faith he was selling his readers. He was selling Christianity the ironic Tertullian way: this is utter nonsense, self-contradictory, scandalously immoral, a crucifixion of common sense, but still worth trusting. "The absurd is not one of the factors which can be discriminated within the proper compass of the understanding: it is not identical with the improbable, the unexpected, the unforeseen." [5]

Surely Camus belongs to this tradition; he sets over against each other man and the world: "The absurd arises from the opposition between man who asks, and the world that remains silent." There is a gulf, a lack of the anticipated relationship.

If, then, the absurd is a lack of an anticipated relationship, we must know what sorts of relationships there are between things, how different sorts are made intelligible, and which sorts we need and desire. To be related in some definite way is for things to be in a certain order. The problem of the absurd, in these terms, is not, then, any utter lack of relation and order but that the orders we know are each limited and cut off logically from others. The world as such may be a spatial-temporal-causal mechanical order mathematically intelligible. And man as such may have constant and almost universal needs. Some of our questions, such as those put by Galileo, Kepler, Pascal, Newton, are answered beautifully. Some others, like those put by Job and Augustine about evil, are not answered at all.

So I complete my meditation on my historical sketch of the term "absurd." The world gives "a disagreeable sound, harsh,

5. Robert Bretall, *A Kierkegaard Anthology*, New York, 1959, p. 126.

rough." Do we expect answers to our questions about character-istically human concerns: "Why do the righteous suffer?" The world does not tell us.

Yes, we may reasonably say, "The world is absurd" and "Life is absurd."

III. *The Absurd Has Many Meanings*

In his brilliant attack on Kierkegaard, Brand Blanshard dis-tinguished five meanings of "absurd," all of them to be rejected, the last two even less acceptable than the first three. Although I shall cite these five meanings—and I admire Blanshard's sharp-ness, far exceeding that of sympathetic interpreters—I do so only as a prelude to a more general account. This is required because Kierkegaard made a special apologetic use of the cate-gory, which we might reject while yet making sense of the category in its more general meanings.

Blanshard's meanings, culled from Kierkegaard, which I have numbered, are:

Absurd$_1$, *believing* a contradiction.
Absurd$_2$ *doing* an evil deed because God commands it.
Absurd$_3$, *holding* the improbable or paradoxical passionately.
Absurd$_4$, *suspending* a principle one continues to use.
Absurd$_5$, *feeling* the world absurdly.

Absurd$_1$ is believing "the contradiction that God has existed in human form."

Absurd$_2$ is Abraham's taking Isaac, his only son, to offer him as a burnt offering to God because, for no reason, God requires it.

Absurd$_3$ is faith, holding the paradox with "the passion of inwardness."

Absurd$_4$ is suspending such a principle as contradiction (a proposition cannot be both true and false at the same time, in the same sense, for the same believer). Blanshard takes this to be an example of the "crucifixion of the understanding."

Absurd$_5$, feeling the world absurdly, is expressed by Kierke-gaard: "The whole of existence frightens me; from the smallest fly to the mystery of the incarnation everything is unintelligible to me, most of all myself; the whole of existence is poisoned in my sight, particularly myself."

In the end, the last meaning suggests to Blanshard that we are dealing, in this knight of the absurd, with a madman.[6]

Before reading Blanshard, I had known only those who read Kierkegaard as an ironic writer. The dictum "the absurd . . . [is] the only object that can be believed," where absurd has meaning$_1$ or meaning$_4$, is self-contradictory. It contradicts "only the nonabsurd can be believed," and one would have to believe that too—in other words, suspend the principle while acting on it—and then is there anything further that can be believed? I had thought, before reading Blanshard, that Kierkegaard was playing the game of trying to shock the rational reader and that the game was to be played, on the reader's part, by not allowing that he had expected anything else from him. Is this meeting bad faith with bad faith? But perhaps Kierkegaard really was himself convinced of what he said. . . .

Blanshard has given us five ways in which the absurd doesn't make sense. I find five ways in which it does make sense:

Absurd$_6$, *experiencing* what doesn't fit the common expectations of men individually and socially.

Absurd$_7$, *communicating* significantly by use of paradox.

Absurd$_8$, *recognizing* that logic deals only with the abstract and cannot exhaust the concrete, and cannot (with perhaps a single exception) prove existence.

Absurd$_9$, *choosing* values for ourselves because we do not find them prescribed by nature objectively.

Absurd$_{10}$, *respecting* real chance in events and making place for such in our ontology and metaphysics.

Absurd$_6$ is Camus' example of war. "When a war breaks out people say: This is not going to last long. It is too absurd. Without doubt a war is certainly too absurd. But that does not prevent it from continuing; . . . Reason can neither understand nor prevent its opposite, the absurd."

There are also individual experiences, such as groundless fear

6. Brand Blanshard, "Kierkegaard on Religious Knowledge," mimeographed version read at December meetings of the American Philosophical Association, Eastern Division, Philadelphia, 1966, pp. 16, 18–23, 23–24, 25–27, 27–35.

or, better, anxiety, such as Tillich's example of the threat of meaninglessness. William James wrote of a "sick soul," supposedly himself, aged twenty-eight, entering his dressing room at twilight "when suddenly there fell upon me without warning, just as if it came out of the darkness, a horrible fear of the darkness, a horrible fear of my own existence. . . . I became a mass of quivering fear." [7]

Doubtless death is called absurd because men live as though they could continue forever.

Absurd[7] is best illustrated by Pascal's paradoxes about man. When analytic philosophers talk of absurdities they come up with such examples as "Friday (the fifth day of the week) is in bed," etc.[8] "Men are so necessarily mad, that not to be mad would amount to another form of madness." And similarly on the greatness and wretchedness of man: "The greatness of man is so evident, that it is even proved by his wretchedness." Why, asks Pascal, do philosophers contradict one another? Because "the nature of man may be viewed in two ways: the one according to his end, and then he is great and incomparable; the other according to the multitude, just as we judge the nature of the horse and the dog . . . ; then man is abject and vile. These are the two ways which make us judge him differently. . . ."

Absurd[8] is respecting the limits of logic. If to exist is to be an individual and concrete, and logic deals only with classes in the abstract, then we can never from logical assumptions prove the existence of anything. To recognize existence is, then, to encounter the nonlogical or nondemonstrated or nondeduced which we may call "absurd."

Absurd[9] is the stress on choosing values. Whereas classical philosophies were ways of discovering hierarchies of values in nature or God, this is now claimed to have been mistaken. What is of value depends upon our choosing. If so, then we cannot provide objective evidence for value. Either we esteem, praise,

---

7. R. W. B. Lewis, "The Varieties of Jamesian Experience," review of G. W. Allen, *William James*, in *New York Times Book, Review*, May 14, 1967, p. 1. See William James, *The Varieties of Religious Experience*, New York, 1902, etc., pp. 159–162.

8. Haig Katchadourian, "Vagueness, Meaning, and Absurdity," *American Philosophical Quarterly*, Vol. 2, No. 2 (April 1965), 5 ff.

cherish, or we do not. Otherwise, say defenders of this new way of thinking, we fail to respect human freedom and man's power to confer meaning.

Absurd$_{10}$, respecting real chance in events, is of course the denial that chance means only our ignorance of what is in principle knowable and predictable from necessary regularities of events. Another name for this ontological absurd is "the irrational," which Morris R. Cohen built into his metaphysics, following C. S. Peirce's tychism. This is the best brief exposition of this position:

> Such brute fact . . . is not something utterly inexplicable, nor does it reveal its true or full character to unreasoned observation. . . . Nevertheless, though the existent is the locus of all abstractions which define it, it is not exhausted by any number of these universals and to this extent it constitutes an unattainable limit of analysis. Always there remains the beyond, the unexplained, the contingent.
>
> Any explanation only pushes back the contingency of our fundamental assumptions. Ultimately the universe is just what it is and contingency is uneliminable.
>
> When the irreducible diversity of existence is viewed in its temporal aspect, it appears as the novelty which makes the future unpredictable and the historicity which makes the past irretrievable. . . . To the extent that we are creatures in time and must add fact to fact, we can never logically exhaust the totality of nature. There is thus something which will always be for us beyond rational form or system, and in that sense appropriately called irrational.
>
> We must grant, then, the contention of modern empiricism that existence in the actual world is more than rational connectedness and that it cannot be entirely grasped by mere reasoning.[9]

Absurd$_{6-10}$ all seem to be truths about man's experiencing, communicating, reasoning, choosing values, thinking metaphysically. I have not supposed that I could exhaust the meanings and complete the list of discriminable meanings of "absurd." We owe much to Blanshard for picking out striking weaknesses in Kierkegaard's apologetic use of "the absurd." But something needs saying for the general category of the absurd.

9. Morris R. Cohen, *Reason and Nature: An Essay on the Meaning of Scientific Method,* Glencoe, Ill., 1951, pp. 135–137.

What might absurd$_{11-15}$ be? One of these surely would be the comical absurd, the incongruity at which we laugh. Perhaps one of the benefits gained by freeing the topic from its rather lugubrious theological upbringing will be to pay more attention to the fun we have from the absurd. I wonder why there are so many recent essays on the absurd (I have read about forty). I suspect some of the fascination is sheer fun.

Conclusion

What is commonly said about the absurd is very inadequate because some accounts are purely logical, other accounts purely psychological, other accounts purely theological—even narrowly Christian, other accounts purely ontological, other accounts purely ethical. To give an account of the category of the absurd involves showing how the absurd applies to all the realms or orders of being. I have striven for adequacy, but the inclusiveness of a list is not the integrity of a system. If one follows Pascal, as I do, in discriminating the orders, how do the orders belong together in a world? The orders are logically distinguishable, but we live in many orders at the same time. Is this recognition of togetherness the experience of the nonabsurd?

Accounts of the experience of the absurd fail to include a reference to what it is to experience the nonabsurd. Sometimes we are not told what the nonabsurd is even abstractly. Usually the criterion that the world fails to meet is left implicit. Hence we need to analyze what Kierkegaard, Camus, and Sartre had expected of the world that made them state their disappointment in the absurd, revolt, or nausea. This task is worthwhile, and I have not the learning to perform it. Perhaps when we have a full account of both absurd and nonabsurd, it will appear that the apparently positive is negative and the apparently negative is positive. If they are polar categorical terms, and all categories are polar pairs, like order-chaos, relative-absolute, subject-object, the category is absurd-nonabsurd, not either one alone.

I have not concentrated on specific experiences of the absurd, and if philosophy should go back to experience as its *fons et origo,* my account is excessively verbal and secondhand. My only excuse is that I cannot see, in those who stress specific experiences, how this gives rise to a category applied to anything and everything—in some sense of "absurd." At the other extreme from one literal meaning I have stressed the ambiguity of the meanings. But is there between them a family resemblance? This might seem to the traditional philosopher a doctrine of the analogical meaning of the transcendental term "absurd." This aspect has been left unclear.

Philosophers of the absurd seem to me to have many valid points against rationalism, particularly order-monism. In siding with the order-pluralism of Pascal, I will not have made sense to the rationalists. What I have advocated as truths will appear to them as falsehoods. And by espousing Blanshard's critique of Kierkegaard, I will have alienated the Kierkegaardians and half the theologians. I cannot hope, because my exposition is metaphysical, to have made much sense to the logical empiricists or the linguistic analysts. Not only can I be certain that I could not have made sense to everyone; I cannot be sure that I have made sense to anyone.

Perhaps my whole account is wrongheaded. Insofar as the category of the absurd is the mark of an existentialist and the existentialist deals with individual existences, part by part, I have in the end admitted that I would wish philosophy to exhibit "the totality of the parts." Therefore I must hold that exclusive existentialism is a defective philosophy, at best a corrective. And therefore I must appear to have erred, not only by ignorance of its tenets in detail but by a basically different allegiance.[10]

In many aspects this essay on the absurd is itself absurd. The essential meaning of "absurd" is not to be related in some definite way. And in the end my account is absurd because the orders I have discriminated have not been related to each other in a definite way. But in the end, if my metaphysics fails, I may succeed by failure in having given an account of the category of the absurd.

10. Cf. Paul Weiss, *Philosophy in Process,* Vol. I, Carbondale, Illinois, 1966, 299.

Carl R. Hausman

INTELLIGIBILITY AND THE
EXISTENTIALLY ABSURD

If recent literature serves as a standard, a study of existence and the absurd should be concerned with the human condition in its most fundamental sense. When considered in this way, there are reasons for saying that reality for the human being is profoundly absurd. In the context of such an absolute limit, reality is what I should like to call the "existentially absurd."

In this paper I shall be concerned primarily with the notion of "the absurd" in the light of what I believe it means prior to its association with specific conditions of human life. I want to consider what general conditions disclose the absurd in whatever form it may appear. However, toward the end, consideration of the way these general conditions affect human existence will be brought into focus as a suggestion for future study.

My plan is to begin by discussing ways in which the absurd is a condition of the inevitable eluding of rationality or intelligibility as intelligibility traditionally has been interpreted. At the same time I shall suggest that the absurd is intimately assocated with intelligibility in a positive way, because it occurs with its own peculiar structure and because it is evoked by the requirements of intelligibility itself. The absurd will be considered as having its foundation in two sources: in the relation of novelty to its past and in the relation of finite consciousness to intelligibility. In connection with the latter source, I shall suggest that on a model of intelligibility different from that given us in the tradition, the absurd is intelligible. Finally, I shall indicate how this second model leads to a fundamental paradox which serves as the condition of what I shall call the "existentially absurd."

It should be pointed out that although I do not intend to develop the thought of any single writer within a tradition that might be identified as "existentialism," I have obviously been influenced, in particular, by Camus, Heidegger, Plato, and Sartre. In addition, it should be emphasized that I do not claim that the following discussion provides any startling or novel conclusions. I only hope that it is a defensible development of the topic through a close look at what I believe is the basis for other, and perhaps all, notions of absurdity.

I. *The Absurd and Intelligibility*

In its most general and loosest meaning, the term "absurd" may be applied to that which fails to make sense. The failure to make sense occurs under a variety of conditions. For instance, it may occur as an event that seems impossible, such as meeting a person thought to be miles away. It may occur as something unexpected, such as if a man were to laugh at the loss of his most valued possession. It may occur as what is contrary to reason, such as if rain were to fall from a cloudless sky. Occurrences of absurdity may provoke a range of responses. For instance, absurdity may appear to be foolish, thus provoking laughter. It may provoke terror, as in cases in which incongruity in experience is threatening. Or it may be the condition for an insight into man's relation to the world.

However, whatever our responses to the absurd and whatever the various forms the incongruity or inconsistency may take, there seems to be a common ground for all these. In every case that which is absurd is something out of place. There is an incongruity, an inconsistency, a conflict with lawful, orderly experience. As Camus points out, absurdity "springs from a comparison," a comparison between two aspects of reality which do not appear to be in harmony.[1]

Even though this characterization of absurdity is, I think, accurate as far as it goes, it does not reveal a distinction that needs to be made. This distinction lies in what appears to be temporarily absurd and what persists in being absurd, between what I shall call "apparent absurdity" and "fundamental absurdity." That which is only surprising or temporarily incongruous ceases to be an absurdity once it is made congruous. By contrast, that which is fundamentally absurd resists being made coherent. It defies characterization by means of consistently applied categories. The distinction between apparent and fundamental absurdity is important for a point to be made later.

Of course, there is a sense in which every instance of incongruity can be subjected to order. Incongruities can be conceptualized or related to categories, even if only by contrast. Thus it might be claimed that there are only instances of temporary or apparent absurdity. All occurrences of what fails to make sense are, in principle, amenable to some sort of order. The world is, after all, rational. In response, I would admit that all occasions of absurdity can be related to rationality in one way or another, but I do not believe that this makes all incongruities only temporary or apparent. For there are, I think, some inconsistencies that are not resolvable within themselves. There are some occurrences or conditions of occurrences that cannot be understood as self-consistent. It is this kind of absurdity, I think, which is the basis for the meaning generally given the term "the absurd." And it is this fundamental absurdity which is coincident with unintelligibility. In order to emphasize and clarify this point, it will be helpful to look more closely at what is meant by intelligibility.

If we follow a model which I believe is suggested by Plato and an important strand in the tradition of thought after him, we can say that to discover something which is intelligible is, most generally, to apprehend the determinateness of that thing. Determinateness is what makes the thing identifiable in the

1. Albert Camus, *The Myth of Sisyphus and Other Essays,* New York, 1955, p. 22.

midst of differences. Determinateness is the unity that is identified and recognized and thus shows the thing for what it is. And in order to be so identifiable, the determinateness of a thing must be consistent with itself and invariant throughout variation. It must remain steadfast, as an identity which is stable in the midst of variation and change. Thus, to be determinate is to be distinct and fixed. Intelligibility in this general sense is, I take it, something like what Heidegger, in his essay "Plato's Doctrine of Truth," refers to as the unhiddenness of truth.[2] But in addition to being disclosed and manifest, on the model I am suggesting, intelligibility requires the presentation of immutable determination, or what can be called "essence" or "form," in the sense of a Platonic Form or Idea.

In characterizing intelligibility in terms of form, I risk being charged with limiting the model of intelligibility to the way it is given in the rationalist tradition and, for that matter, perhaps in only one strand of this tradition. However, the requirements of intelligibility thus emphasized are also present, I think, in other traditions. Surely consistency, repeatability, and identity are required of data which serve as evidence in even the most tough-minded empiricism. And a narrowly defined nominalism presupposes that intelligibility depends in some way on identity in difference—on something invariant in variation, if only because nominalism requires the consistent use of names. In any case I shall assume that intelligibility depends upon the recognition of an unchanging factor in what is intelligible, and this unchanging factor will be called form.

However, I do not want to assert that intelligibility is identical with form. Intelligibility is distinct from, and more fundamental than, form. Thus form reveals the presence of intelligibility, which in turn is a condition or the ground of form. This, I believe, is consistent with what Plato considered crucial in the relation of the form to the Good. The forms lead dialectically to the Good, which in turn is the intelligible source of forms. This suggestion deserves much more attention than

2. Martin Heidegger, *Plato's Doctrine of Truth*, trans. John Barlow, in *Philosophy in the Twentieth Century*, William Barrett and Henry D. Aiken, eds., New York, 1962, pp. 251–270.

can be given to it here. However, what is essential to the present topic is that, on the model of the tradition, immutability is the mark of intelligibility. On the model of the tradition, intelligibility is not present unless form is present, unless there is a manifestation of self-consistent, unchanging determination.

The suggestion that a form in itself is not identical with intelligibility points to another requirement which is insisted upon by a dominant part of the tradition. That which is intelligible depends upon mediation. Thus a form taken in itself, in isolation, not only would not be the same as intelligibility, but it would not, in itself, reveal intelligibility. For a form requires a condition or set of conditions in order to be understood and thus to be intelligible. Thus, on this model, forms must be determined as having a place in a system. They must interlace and connect in such a way that some are more basic than others and in such a way that each of them depends upon its relation to a whole. This model is not only the kind which is required by various versions of idealism; it also is present in one side of Plato's thought. For Plato, forms are to be understood through the mediation of other forms, all of which are discerned in a dialectic which exhibits a hierarchical organization crowned by the Good, or by that which, ideally, would bring them together in a whole.

The demand for mediation and for being grounded in a whole is important for what has been said about the relation of the absurd to intelligibility. For the absurd has been characterized as the violation of the consistency required by systematic order; and surely the violation of system, conceived as wholeness, would be a prime example of absurdity. However, I think intelligibility is more fundamental than this ideal of mediation through a system at first suggests. Indeed, the requirement of system as the basis for the intelligibility of a part of the system cannot dispense with the assumption of intelligibility in immediacy; for the system or whole must itself be evidenced in the immediately intelligible. It is intelligible by virtue of its being based on a determinate unity—that is, a complex form. The reason this point needs be made is that the fundamentally absurd has been described as a violation of immediate intelligibility. Thus what contradicts wholeness and system is a violation of intelligibility in its immediacy and is a manifestation of the fundamentally absurd.

Against this model of intelligibility, it is possible to sharpen the view of the absurd under discussion. As the incongruous, the inconsistent, or that which is without reason, the absurd is manifest unintelligibility, which is to say that it is what is opposed to form. However, this unintelligibility is not simply the occurrence of the unexpected, surprising, or puzzling. It is not simply an appearing of the unknown. The unexpected and the unknown may be only apparently absurd. To equate the absurd with the eluding of intelligibility in the sense of what is puzzling is to give priority to the knower and to interpret the absence of order as provisional, i.e., as a problem awaiting the power of intellect to overcome it and thus to reestablish intelligibility. But the absurd in its fundamental sense is not merely the absence of rationality. Nor is it the unknown remainder of an incomplete construction of forms in a system. The fundamentally absurd is the unintelligible in principle. It is that which persists in being an incongruity. It is the necessarily and radically unintelligible in that it denies reason, negates the requirements of intelligibility, and defies being transformed into form.

Translated in the terms of the model of intelligibility described above, to be radically unintelligible is to be unstable, impermanent, indeterminate, inconsistent. It is to be the enemy of form. But, as radical, the fundamentally absurd is also permanent impermanence; it is the consistent manifestation of inconsistency. Another way of putting this is to say that the fundamentally absurd shows itself as the formless in essence, which is to say that unlike apparent absurdity, which is simply the absence of form, the fundamentally absurd is disclosed in the presentation of a form, the form of inevitable formlessness. The paradox involved in this point will be seen to recur later in connection with what will be said about the existentially absurd.

It will be helpful next to consider evidence or data which disclose the absurd in the radical sense I have suggested.

II. *Two Conditions of the Absurd*

Evidence of fundamental absurdity might be found in a review of the data appealed to by writers who have been most explicit in speaking about absurdity in connection with human existence.

Sartre's writing, for instance, contains much that is richly suggestive. In his novel *Nausea* there are vivid presentations of the awareness of absurdity: for instance, in Roquentin's dizzying realization of the elusiveness of self-awareness and in his recognition of the contingency of the reality to which he ascribes meanings. Passages in Sartre's philosophical works are, of course, also relevant. in *Being and Nothingness,* when he speaks of the absolute contingency of human reality, he refers to the absurd in the sense of the radically unintelligible or fundamentally absurd. However, rather than explore illustrations of this sort, let us, for the purpose of this paper, concentrate on the absurd in its most pervasive aspects, as a structure or condition of various kinds of occasions.

In what contexts, then, can such radical unintelligibility occur? It occurs, I think, under two primary conditions: in occurrences of spontaneity in both nature and human activity and in the relation of the spontaneous functioning of consciousness to form. Let us first consider spontaneity.

The claim that spontaneity is a condition of the absurd depends upon a view of spontaneity that must be presented here only in outline. Spontaneity is activity which issues in the exemplification of novel form. And an instance of spontaneity is an instance in which there is intelligibility that is not included in what had been intelligible before its occurrence. It should be noted that the novelty that issues from spontaneity—a kind of novelty which, I think, should be called "novelty proper"— is distinct from the novelty that may be attributed to every particular by virtue of its uniqueness as an individual. Thus each particular, insofar as it is individual, is in some sense novel. But it does not therefore exhibit novelty proper. Novelty proper only occurs where the outcome of spontaneous activity is constituted by a structure which is intelligible by virtue of a form different from all preceding forms. Spontaneity is a kind of activity that yields intelligibility which is without precedent.

This characterization of spontaneity depends, of course, upon the assumption that there are occasions of irreducible novelty in the world and that there are first occurrences of structures which are first exemplifications of forms. The basis for this assumption must lie in arguments which I cannot repeat here.[3] In any case, I should think that anyone who has come this far in the discussion is at least willing to entertain the claim that spontaneity yields novelty which, in terms of the traditional model, must be intelligible by virtue of unprecedented form.

In what way, then, does the absurd appear in instances of spontaneity? It might seem, at first blush, that absurdity appears at the moment of the first occurrence of the novel structure. For the novel structure is a break with the formal intelligibility in the world up to the moment at which the novelty occurs. But this initial unintelligibility is temporary and reveals only the apparently absurd; for the novel structure takes on intelligibiilty as its exemplified form is "recognized," and as it is seen to contribute to the intelligible world which hitherto excluded it. Thus this initial appearance of the absurd is not fundamental.

However, a second aspect of spontaneity presents absurdity which is not merely apparent but which endures and is fundamental. The new structure is a manifestation of intelligibility which transforms the intelligibility of the world. This transformation is effected because the form of the new structure negates the intelligibility in its past. It negates the strands of identity that lead to the convergence of antecedents which precede but only partially condition the occurrence of spontaneity. Continuities which held in the past are broken. Unintelligibility, then, is necessarily present in the discontinuity between that which was intelligible prior to an instance of spontaneity and the new structure. Spontaneity is precisely the occurrence of this discontinuity. And there is necessarily incongruity in each activity which leads to an instance of the radically novel. Though

3. See, for instance, my "Spontaneity: Its Arationality and Its Reality," *International Philosophical Quarterly*, IV, No. 1 (February 1964), 20–47.

the new structure takes on intelligibility by virtue of manifesting form, still it is *ex nihilo*, without cause and in defiance of reason. Thus the fundamentally absurd appears in the gap between the old and the new. It appears as the foundation of novelty.

The second kind of occasion or evidence of the absurd arises out of the criteria traditionally associated with intelligibility. It has been claimed that, on the traditional model, intelligibility depends upon the manifestation of immutable, self-consistent determination. Intelligibility must be presented in what has permanence, in what abides and sustains identity in the face of variations. But the traditional account of intelligibility (at least since Plato) also demands that the knower be oriented correctly toward the known. And if this is so, I do not see how such an orientation can be realized other than in a relation that stabilizes the act of knowing in accordance with the intelligible object. Thus the consistency and permanence that are necessary to the presence of intelligibility is an ideal that could only be met by an intellect or a consciousness which is as stable as the object to which it should be adequate. The knower must endure as an identity in difference which is equal to the permanence of its object. Thus not only does form serve as the model for intelligibility, but it also serves as the model for a consciousness which is adequate to its ideal object. Consciousness must be established in an unchanging determination that is dominated by an unchanging determinate object.

However, human consciousness is finite and, in having a beginning and a terminus, it is temporal. How, then, can a finite consciousness existing in time achieve the ideal required for the presentation of form? Only a consciousness transcendent of its temporal and finite existence could meet this requirement. Only a divine consciousness could fully measure up to the ideal demands of intelligibility. Surely this was implied by Plato and Aristotle as well as a host of others who followed them. The philosopher is a lover of wisdom. But if he were to reach his goal, he would have died as a human being in love with form; he would have attained perfect vision and union with a permanence that terminates all transition.

There is a sense in which Plato's allegory of the cave suggests the point that human consciousness does not, after all, fulfill this ideal. Not only is the prisoner who is chained dazzled by intelligibility, but after the journey into the sunlight is complete, the soul cannot rest. It returns to the shadows. Even if one accepts the argument that this return is the result of force or that it is done against the will of the wise man, it should be noted that if the wise man were not finite and human he would not succumb. Human consciousness is not, after all, divine. It is human and finite, and its vision cannot abide with ultimate intelligibility.

Finite consciousness, then, cannot endure this demand of perfection. It is in a perpetually unstable relationship with form. Form is too dazzling for human attention. And to the extent that the goal of intelligibility draws near, intelligibility becomes excessive.

The transition from excess intelligibility to unintelligibility is, I think, illustrated when we encounter frequently repeated exemplifications of a form. The continued repetition of a word, for instance, leads to a loss of intelligible meaning. What is understood is perpetuated with such emphasis that it loses its power to stand as an identity before consciousness. Or, from the other side of the cognitive situation, consciousness loses its strength to endure the persistence of the meaning. Only the sound remains; and that, too, falls into the ludicrous, unless in some way it is captured for aesthetic purposes and thereby given a different status. The repetition of a figure or a part of a melody on a broken record also passes into the ridiculous. What is at first musically intelligible loses its intelligibility for us as it is repeated. I do not think this happens because the repeated sounds make up a fragment whose whole is lost by virtue of undue emphasis on the fragment. For there is no reason why the complete melody or composition need be lost to sight. Indeed, if an entire composition were repeated over and over, it too would strain toward the unintelligible.

Someone might object that these examples do not illustrate loss of intelligibility but rather boredom and loss of attentiveness on the part of the hearer. There is no doubt that in such cases attention wanes. But this does not show one way or the other whether intelligibility remains. What is shown is that finite consciousness fails to remain steadfast and loses adequate contact with intelligibility. This objection, however, raises a more basic issue of the relation of consciousness to form, and this issue will be considered further, in a moment.

The occasion for the absurd in the relation of consciousness to form also may be realized in situations in which forms are given independently of sense perception. For example, unqualified attention to a form such as triangularity, or to the determinations expressed by the words "number" or "ratio," is also an ideal which reveals loss of intelligibility. Only if all such determinations were given stability in a whole could they be perfectly understood and recognized in full intelligibility. Moreover, the whole itself would need to be stable and undisturbed by intrusion. But then either finite consciousness is an intrusion which is distinct from the whole, or it must vanish by being absorbed as an element within the whole. And this latter alternative would mean that human consciousness must transcend itself and become one with what it is not.

Consciousness seldom recognizes the absurd as revealed in the relation of itself to form. Most of us do not normally encounter the absurd in this fundamental manifestation. Rather, we are more comfortable in perpetually passing from one determination to another familiar determination—from one known form to another known form. Thus consciousness refuses to admit its restlessness. It refuses to admit its fundamental finitude and inevitable inability to attain full intellectual satisfaction. On rare occasions, however, consciousness does apprehend this source of the absurd. There are moments when the knower is pervaded with the incongruity of form and consciousness.

At this point it is necessary to consider the peculiarity of the special relation of form to consciousness. For it might be interjected that this source of the absurd is possible only in a view that makes intelligibility dependent upon consciousness. Thus it is consciousness which is responsible for the model of intelligibility presented here, and the relation of consciousness to form gives rise to apparent rather than fundamental absurdity.

It must be admitted that what has been called the second source of the absurd does depend upon consciousness as it is related to its object. However, this is a special, primordial relation. It does not necessitate a view of intelligibility as subjective or as dependent upon the whims of consciousness. But it does necessitate a view which asserts that the ideal conformance of finite temporal being with atemporal being is unintelligible and is fundamentally absurd. Thus intelligibility and fundamental absurdity do not depend upon consciousness alone. But the absurd does have a dependence upon the primordially incongruous relation of finitude to the ideal of immutability. For the unintelligibility of this relationship is ineradicable and primordial. It is at the foundation of all unintelligibility.

Consciousness, then, does not create the incongruity between itself and immutable form. Nor is the absurdity dependent simply on the incapacity of consciousness to achieve the ideal. For both consciousness and form are given. Consciousness discovers itself *within* the relation of itself to form. It is given as one mode of unstable being in the face of another mode of stable being—a mode of being which, as intelligible, is required to be stable form. Thus the model that comes from the tradition is not an arbitrary construction. It is given, just as the instability of finite consciousness is given. It cannot be abandoned. The identity of that which confronts consciousness and of consciousness itself depends upon intelligibility appearing as form. And it is the inescapability of this model as well as the finitude of consciousness which is the basis for the claim that intelligibility turns into the fundamentally absurd.

Although the absurd has been described in the light of the model of the manifestation of consistent determinateness or form, it is possible, I think, to view fundamental absurdity on a different model which construes it as intelligible. This model would not replace the first but would supplement it. Development of this claim, of course, is a topic in its own right. However, I should like to sketch very quickly the alternative I have in mind.

The second model would emphasize one side of the requirements called for in the first—namely, the requirement of being
manifest. But instead of insisting upon consistency of determinateness realized in form, the manifestation would consist in the
presentation of change, of passage in duration. The intelligibility
of a musical composition apprehended as a concrete object
may serve as an illustration of such a model. The patterns of
sound that constitute the composition, to be sure, may be
conceived on the traditional ideal which would call for understanding in terms of an apprehension of a fixed structure that
can be exemplified in time, in the way a form is exemplified in
its particulars. But if the piece of music is apprehended as
heard music, as the musical object in its concreteness—that is,
if the structure is given relevance in time—it defies intelligibility
in terms of immutable form. For, paradoxically, its form must
be transcendent, so as to govern the musical components, and
at the same time its form must be immanent, so as to maintain
the concreteness required of the unity of form and matter in the
musical composition.[4] Nevertheless, music in its concreteness is
in some sense intelligible. And this intelligibility must lie in
patterns that undergo passage, in patterns that move in and
through discontinuities within continuities. Its musical sense is
inseparable from such transitions which constitute and fulfill
the overall structure.

This suggestion for a second model of intelligibility needs
much more attention. However, there is good reason, I think,
for considering what is absurd on the traditional model as
intelligible in terms of the second model. And the reason is
that a notion of intelligibility is needed to accommodate that
to which the traditional model cannot do justice: finitude and
discontinuities in temporal alteration. This point will be taken
up again in the last section of this discussion.

The above consideration of temporal finitude points to the
last aspect of the topic to be considered: the "existentially
absurd." For if we see that absurdity is disclosed in the relation

4. The paradoxical character of form in art is discussed in my "Intra-
diction: An Interpretation of Aesthetic Understanding," *Journal of Aesthetics
and Art Criticism,* XXII, No. 3 (Spring 1964), 249–261.

of intelligibility to finite consciousness, we have associated absurdity with something that has being in some way other than the being of form. That is to say, absurdity has been associated with the existence of consciousness.

III. *Intelligibility and Existence*

A consideration of existence is faced with a well-known difficulty. For to treat existence as a topic is to suggest that we can discuss a concept of existence. But if it is appropriate to speak of such a concept, it must be emphasized that the concept is a peculiar one. It is not like concepts which refer to definite terms brought into relation, or to sets of properties, or to classes of particulars. Nor is existence itself a property or attitude such that it can be conceptualized as a predicate in a proposition. Nevertheless I shall adopt the view that assertions of existence are neither redundant nor empty. To assert that a thing exists is to make a claim which adds to the thing something distinct from the character or intelligibility of it.

There is, for example, a difference between 1,000 imaginary and 1,000 existing dollars. To be sure, the concept of "dollar," "1,000," etc., remains the same. We do not add to the form or intelligibility of 1,000 dollars in thinking about the existence of these. Nor is the intelligibility of what is thought about necessarily changed by virtue of the existence of the form of 1,000 dollars. The difference added by existence does not lie in the properties or meanings of what is thought about. Rather it lies in their function. Existent dollars bear effective relations with sense-experience and with practical, concrete consequences.

Most generally, I should like to say that whatever exists is in a certain mode of being in which that thing can function temporally. The point that existence has to do with temporal functioning suggests a notion which, I think, is closely associated with the meaning given to the term "existence" in one strand of common-sense thought. In the broad sense I have in mind, existence is a way in which a form is related to functioning. Thus, in this very general sense, an existent is something whose determinant form makes a difference for other forms by virtue of functioning in process. To exist is to be in process. An existent, then, is an object which temporally exemplifies a form. It is that whose form seems to endure in a continually altering duration.

The claim that an existent has a form that seems to endure, however, is not adequate. It would be more accurate to say that an existent is an object consisting of a core of a complex of properties. Insofar as this complex is intelligible, it is a totality which has sufficient identity and unity to be a confluence of properties identifiable as a form.

There are many distinctions that should be made among the ways existents function in processes. And it is necessary to observe a few of these in order to see the relation of existence to the absurd. There are certain complexes which are not only in process but which also undergo modification by virtue of their roles within process. This modification consists in a reconstitution of the complex so that the form of the complex changes. Moreover, some existents are complexes of properties that are modified not passively but by virtue of cores that are sources for the reconstitution of the complex. This source of power is what is ordinarily ascribed to living existence. Finally, in addition to being participating sources of the processes in whch they are as existents, some cores of properties are spontaneous. These existents effect novelty and, as instances of spontaneity, they violate the identity in which their properties reside.

Now, if a living existent is a power of reconstituting itself as a complex of properties, it may be a human existent. And if such a power is both spontaneous and human, it is what is ordinarily called a creative person. However, being a source of change and being creative is not a guarantee that the source is a human existent. The guarantee for being human lies in there being not only a radical breaking of continuity but also a break brought about through reflective consciousness. Every instance of reflecting on the form of process is to effect a break. Thus every reflective act requires that consciousness effect a negation of itself by regarding itself as its reflected object, thus treating its original existence as a complex of properties and thus constituting itself as a reflecting existent which is independent of its object. And this is to exist as absurd. For it is to constitute the essentially formless in the face of form, to introduce a negation of formed, patterned existence. It is to bring about the realization of the difference between human existence and intelligible being.

On the model of the tradition, and in the view of human existence just presented, to be guaranteed as human is to be intelligible. To be a human existent is necessarily to be without reason, without identity in determinate essence. To exist not only as a living existent but also as a human existent is necessarily to exist as absurd.

On the other hand, an existent that falls short of the spontaneity of reflective consciousness, and thus falls short of a realization of human existence, may also tend toward the absurd. It does this by tending toward a stability proper to immutable form rather than finite existence, though it would not be aware of this relation to the absurd. Thus to live a life that falls into routine pattern is to sink into a situation that points to the absurd. To fall into a repetition that mirrors stability is to violate the human condition at its fullest. This is to disclose the absurd through effecting an incongruity of human existence with what a human existent is not. The disclosure appears for others, however, rather than for the one who falls into repetition. If one were himself aware of the absurd in this condition, he would have reflected on himself. Yet in so reflecting, consciousness once again would live the absurd, but would live it by existing in accordance with human finitude. Thus man is "condemned" to the absurd. His existence is absurd if he lives up to his reflecting, spontaneous possibilities. But he is also absurd if he drifts into unreflective, routine patterns.

It should be clear that to be compelled to exist as absurd is the result of the paradoxical condition of human existence. Being human is to be in denial of intelligibility, to be what determinate being is not, and at the same time to be intelligible only by being what a human being is not as a finite, reflective source of incongruity. However, there is another way in which the paradox appears. And this appearance of the paradox is

important because it arises when we turn to a different model
of intelligibility—the one in which the absurd is intelligible.
I should like to conclude with a suggestion about this version
of the paradox.

It has been said that the model of intelligibility in the tradition demands more of human consciousness than it can accomplish, short of transcending its existence as human and being
in perfectly stable adequation of itself to a permanent whole.
Is it possible that the absurd would not be present in human
existence if the ideal of intelligibility provided by the tradition
were replaced by another model?

In answering this question, it should be emphasized, first, that
even on the traditional model there is a sense in which the
human existent and the disruption of form is meaningful, even
though not intelligible. Although an occurrence of the absurd
exhibits indeterminateness and incoherence, it is nevertheless
a manifestation. This is to say that the occurrence of the absurd
is a presentation recognized by consciousness. Granted, what is
presented lacks determination. It cannot be identified and it
negates form; yet it nevertheless is there before consciousness,
recognizable as that which is fundamentally without reason.
But the point here is not to assert simply that the absurd
is meaningful because it shares its character of unintelligibility
with other such instances. The point is that each occurrence of
the absurd is also recognized in its own terms, as an occurrence
which violates form in a specific context of forms. This contextual meaning is, I think, illustrated in literary presentations
of absurdity. For example, the absurd in the life of Joseph K.
in Kafka's *The Trial* is distinguishable from the absurd in the
life of Roquentin in Sartre's *Nausea*. This is due to the difference
in the forms of the different lives. Thus the absurd numbs
and finally kills Joseph K. It dizzies and in a sense redeems
Roquentin.

The point that the absurd is thus contextually meaningful
serves to highlight the fact that the absurd viewed from the
standard model of intelligibility may be relevant even to one
who denies its intelligibility. Moreover, as a meaningful or
relevant occurrence it calls forth a demand to find in it some-

thing that is intelligible. Now, the absurd might be considered intelligible on the second model suggested earlier—that is, on an ideal more closely accommodating the limitations of consciousness. If intelligibility were to require the consistent manifestation of discontinuous alteration and passage rather than the presentation of consistent determinateness, the existence of consciousness may be considered intelligible insofar as its being is to function in process.

However, there are two reasons why we do not avoid the absurd as the fundamentally unintelligible by proposing this second model of intelligibility. First, the model of the tradition cannot be abandoned. As already suggested, the second does not replace but rather supplements the first. Finite consciousness needs two models of intelligibility: that of the tradition, requiring immutable form, and a second, requiring the manifestation of transition. The first is needed as a basis for giving consciousness identity and the security of stable determination; the second is needed to do justice to the undeniable and meaningful presence of change and finitude. But the need for both models again reveals the paradox of human existence. In its own way the appropriateness of the two models reveals the absurd, the necessity of form and formlessness, of eternality and change—in one determinate being. The point I am trying to make is that both ideals are appropriate to human consciousness. And because human consciousness needs both, the absurd cannot be avoided.

Moreover, there is a peculiarity about consciousness in its demand for these two different criteria of intelligibility; and it is in this peculiarity that the paradox of human existence reappears. In order to recognize both ideals, finite consciousness must transcend them. It must exist in such a way as to compare them and be aware of its own reflective activity in doing this. But short of some third ideal of intelligibility, this transcendence is unintelligible for both models. This is to say that, short of being in some way that is beyond both being and becoming, consciousness is unintelligible in a more radical way than in its spontaneity and negating of form. It must be unintelligible in negating both form and process. And the only way I can see that this kind of being is possible for finite consciousness is for it to vacillate between form and process. Its transcendence is carried out in a vacillation, in a "passage" back and forth between process and permanence. But it is carried out in a way that must appear as paradoxical. For this vacilllation *itself* is neither form nor sheer change. If it were sheer change, it would be without determinateness. If it were form, it would be without finitude and process. Hence it must appear inevitably as at once the unintelligible and the intelligible absurd.

PART THREE

THE SELF, SOCIETY, ACTION, AND HISTORY

James M. Edie

NECESSARY TRUTH AND PERCEPTION:
WILLIAM JAMES ON
THE STRUCTURE OF EXPERIENCE

Recent research has begun to uncover a large number of themes in contemporary phenomenological thought which find parallels in the thought of William James.[1] Some of these can be traced to the direct influence of James on Husserl, but for the most part they transcend such direct historical interaction and rather show a common spirit and temper, developing independently but convergently toward the same goal—namely, the establishment of the bases for a method of *radical empiricism* in philosophy. This unattained goal, a radical philosophy of experience, has been the dream of many philosophers and philosophical schools, but it has remained up to the present time a largely unfulfilled hope. Empirio-criticists, positivists, pragmatists, and phenome-

1. Apart from the papers at the present symposium, "William James and the Structure of the Self," by Robert R. Ehman, and "William James and the Phenomenology of Belief," by John Wild, one could recall "William James and Existential Authenticity," by John Wild, in *The Journal of Existentialism*, Spring 1965, pp. 243–256; "Notes on the Philosophical Anthropology of William James," by James M. Edie, in *An Invitation to Phenomenology*, Chicago, 1965, pp. 110–132; and above all, Johannes Linschoten, *Auf dem Weg zu einer phänomenologischen Psychologie, Die Psychologie von William James*, Berlin, 1961. Bruce Wilshire read a further contribution, entitled "The Phenomenological Breakthrough in the Psychology of William James," at the meeting of the American Philosophical Association held in December 1967.

nologists have all announced the program, but few have been able to flatter themselves at having accomplished more than a "beginning." One of the major philosophical problems which has always halted the initial empiricist thrust is the problem of accounting for our experience of "the kingdom of truth," as Husserl expressed it.

The question of the origin of categorial truth in experience is unsolved. Forbidden by the exigencies of its method from introducing any "metaphysical entities" into its explanations which cannot be justified within the texture of experience itself, phenomenology in particular is confronted with this problem. It preoccupied Husserl throughout his life from the *Prolegomena* to *Erfahrung und Urteil;* Merleau-Ponty, who announced his program in the *Primacy of Perception* to examine "the relation between intellectual consciousness and perceptual consciousness" and to show how "ideal truth" is related to "perceived truth," [2] died without writing the work which was to be entitled *L'Origine de la vérité.*[3]

Given the methodological similarities which have already been established between James on the one hand and such phenomenologists as Husserl and Merleau-Ponty on the other,[4] I believe it would be interesting and fruitful to examine how James approaches this particular question. I will, for the purposes of this discussion, postpone any elaborate treatment of his later "pragmatic theory of truth," which has so preoccupied his commentators, and instead go to the original sources of his later theories as they are given in the *Principles of Psychology,* his most important systematic treatise. We will find a striking similarity in the early Jamesian and the later phenomenological approach.

2. Maurice Merleau-Ponty, *The Primacy of Perception and Other Essays,* James M. Edie, ed., Evanston, Ill., 1964, pp. 19–20.

3. Merleau-Ponty, *ibid.,* p. 8.

4. I am here taking for granted the methodological conclusions of "Notes on the Philosophical Anthropology of William James," *op. cit.,* and of an article entitled "William James and the Phenomenology of Religious Experience" which will appear shortly in a volume edited by Michael Novak, *American Philosophy and the Future.*

I. *The Orders of Reality and the Primacy of the Perceptual World*

It is a commonplace of phenomenology that any given act of consciousness is a highly complex and highly structured *synthesis* of elements and "forms" which, though they can be isolated for purposes of analysis, are given together inseparably in the unified whole which is an actual act of consciousness. Elements of "the imaginary," of "the fictive," of "the past," of the "historical," of the "cultural," of "the ideal" surround and are inextricably *given with* any complete act of perception, not to mention the qualities of feeling, mood, volition, or emotion such an act may contain as well. One of the chief tasks of phenomenology is precisely to *analyze* the complex intentional acts which are our experience of reality, to distinguish qualities, characters, and levels of such experience as they are inextricably given together. To say that such qualities, characters, and levels of consciousness have their own specificity, that they can be isolated from one another by analysis, that they can be distinguished within the pulsating flux of our conscious life is not to deny that, in actual experience, they are all inextricably given together and mutually implicate each other in our objectification of the world. The world as given to human consciousness, the world of "objects," is the world we experience *because* it is the correlate of a consciousness which can simultaneously and successively live in "different orders of reality," in the perceptual, the imaginary, the ideal, etc. On the level of the prereflexive constitution of reality, of our experience of the real world, our perceptual consciousness is a consciousness which anticipates (in operating imaginative and fictive intentions) and retains (in operating memory intentions) its world, which structures it in accord with past and anticipated experience, which "understands" it and "values" it by finding in it and conferring on it a coefficient of ideality.

From the *Prolegomena* onward one of Husserl's constant doctrines is that meaning and value are strictly correlative to factual experience, that the meaning (or "essence") of an experience is that in terms of which a given experience is structured by and for consciousness, that meaning and fact are never separate in experience, since any essential structure (i.e., that which is understood when one understands something in the flux of experience) is the meaning of the factual situation *of which* it is the essence. The realm of prereflexive, prejudgmental perceptual experience is "alive" with the "ideal" and with meaning. The emergence of sense and meaning is not, thus, something reserved for the higher, fully reflexive acts of judging consciousness but is immediately experienced prior to any theoretical reflection about it. Meaning, he says, is "immanent" to experience on all its various levels, and there is a thread of intentional unity which binds the meanings given in perception to their correlates in imagination, memory, and even in categorial thought.

Moreover, the most fundamental realm of meaning in which we live is precisely the level of perceptual experience, of prethematic, operating intentions which form the foundation for later categorial acts of reflection and imaginary reconstruction, etc. (the "active syntheses" of consciousness as opposed to the passive" or "automatic syntheses" of prethematic perceptual awareness).

"It is *we* who are the genuine positivists," [5] claims Husserl, and Merleau-Ponty calls this thesis of the "primacy of perception" in the orders of experience a "phenomenological positivism." [6] A large number of thinkers, beginning with William James, have asserted this thesis and attempted to outline its import and its consequences. James speaks of the "paramount reality" [7] of the world of sensations and of the "many worlds" or "sub-universes" built upon and surrounding it. Straus speaks of "the primary world of the senses" as the source of all "sense." [8] Schutz speaks of the "finite provinces of meaning" of "multiple realities" centered around the "world of practical

5. Edmund Husserl, *Ideas,* trans. W. R. Boyce Gibson, New York, 1931, p. 86.

6. Merleau-Ponty, *The Primacy of Perception, op. cit.,* p. 50.

7. William James, *The Principles of Psychology,* II, New York, 1950, 299.

8. Erwin Straus, *The Primary World of Senses: A Vindication of Sensory Experience,* New York, 1963.

life" with its dominant "pragmatic motive," [9] whereas Gurwitsch prefers the expression "orders of existence," which he conceives as meaning-contextures which analogously implicate each other on the fundamental basis of the contextures of perceptual experience.[10]

These differing terminologies ought not to confuse us, since all these thinkers recognize the intentional structure of experience and that the order of reality or existence with which we are dealing in perception, or in imagination, or in categorial thinking is strictly correlative to conscious acts. Thus whether we begin primarily with an intentional analysis of acts of consciousness (such as perceiving or imagining or thinking) or whether we turn our attention to the noematic correlates of such acts (the orders of reality or existence experienced as such), the one approach necessarily and correlatively implicates the other.

We can begin with James. Like Husserl, he distinguishes the world of "real existence" or "practical reality" from the other orders of "reality" whose distinctions are determined by the degree and kind of ego-involvement they express.

> *The fons et origo of all reality . . . is ourselves. . . .* The world of living realities as contrasted with unrealities is thus anchored in the Ego, considered as an active and emotional term. That is the hook from which the rest dangles, the absolute support.

9. Alfred Schutz, "On Multiple Realities" in *Collected Papers,* I, The Hague, 1962, 207 ff.

10. Aron Gurwitsch, *The Field of Consciousness,* Pittsburgh, 1964, pp. 410 ff. At this place Gurwitsch recalls Aristotle's doctrine of the analogy of "being" (without adopting its metaphysical implications) to indicate the kind of *metabasis eis allo genos* involved in speaking of the various "orders of existence" correlative to the perceptual, imaginative, fictive, and idealizing intentions of consciousness respectively. If one wanted to pursue historical parallels, it would be interesting to note that Husserl also spoke of "truth" and "being" as being both "categories" in the same sense and as being correlative. *Logische Untersuchungen,* Erster Band, "Prolegomena," Halle, 1928, 228 (cf. Marvin Farber, *The Foundation of Phenomenology,* New York, 1962, p. 124). This sounds a little like the Aristotle of the Ninth Book of the *Metaphysics,* for whom "being" or "existence" was not a univocal category. *To on polachos legetai,* the term "being" is predicated in many different senses, and the primary sense belongs to the *ousiai* of perceptual experience within the real world.

And as from a painted hook . . . one can only hang a painted chain, so conversely, from a real hook only a real chain can properly be hung. *Whatever things have intimate and continuous connection with my life are things of whose reality I cannot doubt.*[11]

The "paramount reality" is given to us through our perceptual insertion among other beings and objects in whom we have a practical and emotional involvement through our "tangible" relationships with them. It can be defined as the world within the reach of our senses, the world we can grasp immediately, upon which we can act and which can act upon us. Only a real dagger hurts when it is thrust into our flesh; only real poison can be taken into our mouths.[12] Within this world we are always situated in a *place* which is located by our bodily presence and from which all other objects and situations recede as from the zero point of a system of coordinates; our apprehension of the objects of our perceptual world is always perspectival, subject to further clarification and exploration. All together they constitute the indefinite horizon within which any present object emerges from a background of mutually implicating horizons which, at the limit, involve all other contemporaneously co-existing bodies in time and space. This world has a special temporal and spatial structure which is rooted in our own experience of temporality and spatiality. The experience of phenomenal time and phenomenal space gives us the primary conscious syntheses on the basis of which we can then construct the idea of "standard time" and the notion of "objective space." This is the world which we can never wholly escape; at every moment of our conscious lives we are subject to the laws of phenomenal time (the irreversible and temporally synthetic stream of consciousness), to the embodiment of consciousness in a perceptual space perspectivally related to other real beings.[13] While the perceptual world can never be experienced as a whole, and thus can never be given *as such*, it is nevertheless always *given with* any perceptual object whatsoever as its

11. William James, *Principles,* II, 296–298.
12. *Ibid.,* 306.
13. Cf. Gurwitsch, *op cit.,* p. 418.

ground, as the invariant structure of perceptual coherence which
could be explored *ad infinitum*.

It is thus evident that, though perception gives us the
"primary reality," the perceptual world is not the whole of
reality for us. It gives me, together with my immediate sense
experience, a ground of possibilities, a virtual space which is
indefinitely explorable. In this most fundamental sense the
world of perception cannot be separated from the world of
imagination, since to perceive a world as a *human world* is to
perceive it as constituted of possibilities, absences, potentialities,
of an indefinite number of other aspects—*implied* in the aspect
given to me here and now—which *could* become the objects
and themes of future perceptions. There is a "subjunctive" aspect
of perceptual experience, and this is the reason why Husserl
and Merleau-Ponty say that consciousness, on this primary
level of experience, is more of an "I can do" than an "I think
that," an invitation to exploration rather than to contemplation.

But over and above the primary prethematic operations of
imagination, memory, feeling, etc., which are involved in *any*
complete perceptual experience, there are more explicit and
deliberate types of imagining and remembering which give us
access to regions of reality which have their own consistency,
their own temporal and spatial structures, their own "logic,"
independent of perception. Take, for example, the realms of
aesthetic imagination, which we owe chiefly to the work of
artists. The world of the Karamazovs created by Dostoevsky
could serve as an example, but so could the worlds created
by a Proust, a Faulkner, a Kafka, a Cézanne, a Beethoven, or a
Brahms. We come to live in the world of the Karamazovs only
with some difficulty and little by little. It has an ontological
status different from that of this mundane world of perceptual
consciousness, which we can never really leave while reading
Dostoevsky or while living in his imaginary world. But as we
become acquainted with the characters and temperaments of the
sensualist old Fyodor and his atheist son Ivan, as we savor the
innocence of Alyosha, as we begin to see and smell the streets
of a nineteenth-century provincial Russian village, and as we
penetrate the troubled thoughts of the dying monk Zosima,

we gradually enter a different time, a different place, a different moral, social, and spiritual atmosphere from that of our own existence. We may live through the development of a whole generation of Karamazovs in a few hours of our own time. And once we have entered such a world, once we have grasped its distinctive style, its own inner logic, its own necessary laws of development, its own ontological consistency (thanks to which we could never confuse the world of Dostoevsky with that of Faulkner, for instance, or either one of them with our own mundane existence), we discover that it, too, is an incomplete world, in which many things could happen in the future or could have happened in the past which we recognize as the specific but unfulfilled possibilities of this story. These possibilities are perfectly determined in the sense that they must be fully consistent with the inner psychology and the inner logic of what has been recorded, but they remain indeterminate invitations to our imagination to complete and fill in the vague and obscure regions whose details have only been sketched.

When we relate such a world of the imagination to the primary world of perception we find that our mode of access to it is determined by very strict laws. Strictly speaking, we cannot *really enter* such a world.[14] We can interrupt it, leave it at will, ignore it, and it is there to be imaginatively re-created and rediscovered *just as we left it*, but without our being able to alter it. It has an ontological consistency, a time and temporal development, a place in history wholly independent of our own mundane existence. There is a sense in which such a world can reveal to us values of truth from which we are cut off in our ordinary real existence. Sometimes such a world appears as *more true* and *more real* than the real world of our perceptual experience. It can be *more true* because it can give us at a glance, so to speak, an essential insight into some aspect of human experience which we ourselves will never experience,

14. Cf. Maurice Natanson, "Man as an Actor," a paper read at the Second Lexington Conference on "Phenomenology of Will and Action," held at Lexington, Kentucky, May 15, 1964, to be published by Duquesne University Press. In these remarks I am here repeating some observations I made originally in reply to Natanson's paper.

never *could* experience, except in imagination. At the same time such a world is wholly built up of the materials of perception, and it is because we can transpose perception into the realm of the imaginary that it can be invented at all. The world of the Karamazovs is perceptually real for the Karamazovs, and while we live in their lives vicariously we are perceiving their world, the rooms of the family villa, the icons on the walls, the borscht and kvass on the table, the socialistic effusions of the journals Ivan has brought with him on the stage from Moscow, etc. Through a fictive manipulation of the perceptual experiences of this, our own ordinary, nondramatic, mundane, perceptual world, we (either of ourselves or following the creative imagination of an artist) are able to transpose the possibilities they offer us to another level of experience and thereby create another world which is nevertheless fully and irrevocably *founded* on this one, though it is not in any sense reducible to it. In this sense the realms of imagination (particularly but not exclusively aesthetic imagination) are higher-order syntheses of thought founded on the primary synthetic activity of perceptual consciousness.

Another example of an order of reality which is founded on perceptual experience but which follows laws different from those which obtain in the real world and which has its own ontological modality is that of memory. There is here, as with imagination, a fundamental prethematic operating activity of memory which is inseparable from perceptual consciousness itself—namely, the primary retentions of consciousness in its ever-flowing temporal stream, thanks to which we experience ourselves to be occupied with stable objects through a given pulse of phenomenal time. It is thanks to this fundamental operating memory that we are able to entertain the *same* thought or the *same* object through a series of psychological processes which are temporally successive to one another. But there is the more explicit and active sense of remembering in which, either deliberately or by some accidental association, we re-live segments of our past. Some persons are more practiced in this than others, and there are occasions, as for instance the psychiatric interview, when such attempts to "live in the past" are more sustained than they are in everyday life. For instance, if I am now confronted with the task of making some sense of my life which will go beyond the immediate conscious projects of my present situation, I am likely to reflect on patterns of behavior which have recurred at various times in my past experience. At such a time I may "re-live," and even become absorbed over a period of time in, a past experience or series of experiences which now take on a very special typicality, a special emotive and personal meaning. What I have done, what I have made of myself, what I have become, the sense I have given to my life through disparate past decisions and bifurcations, taken at the time independently of one another and often without any apparent connection with one another, suddenly emerge as having a sense and meaning I could not have foreseen but which I now recognize as the sense and direction of my past existence. The re-creation of the past in this way, and my present experience of it, clearly confronts us with a level of experience essentially different from, and yet necessarily founded on, perceptual experience. When I remember past events or when they intrude upon my consciousness as significant, I do not repeat moment for moment what actually happened during some segment of my past life. I am, in fact, largely incapable of doing this with any accuracy. Certain salient features of past events are organized into patterns, time is telescoped, new typifications and emotional qualities emerge —none of which can claim to have been those I actually experienced at that more or less distant time I am now evoking. And yet it is clear that this is a reordering of "impressions" which at one time were perceptually real for me and that their interest for me lies in their being a restructurization of my *real* perceptual and historical consciousness.

From such orders of reality we could naturally move to the orders of cultural and historical objects, to the order of religious experience, to the objects (constructs, hypotheses, concepts) of the theoretical attitude which is operative in scientific or philosophical research, etc., and ultimately to the level of the most purified idealities (formal or material) of categorial thought. Take, for instance, the cultural institution which is the English language. This is a historical and cultural reality and force of which I am a part and which has formed me and my intellectual processes. It is mine in a very personal sense, since I could not even "think" without it. Yet it is above all a means of intersubjective and historical communication. There was a time, before the fifth century, when it did not exist; moreover, in its diachronic development the morphological, syntactical, lexicographical systems which constitute it have evolved and are at the present moment undergoing changes. These changes depended and now depend on the effective "usage" of this cultural instrument by all those who in actual fact have spoken and are speaking it, thanks to which its syntax and morphology are at any one time sufficiently fixed (even though they have never been perfectly codified) and its vocabulary sufficiently delimited to distinguish it from other worlds of linguistic expression. We recognize it in the most ungrammatical efforts of children and illiterates and in the harshest accents of foreigners. In what sense can it be said to exist or be experienced by me? Certainly nobody will deny that it is real. It is "wholly" at my disposition when I need to use it, just as it is wholly and entirely at the disposition of all the members of this linguistic community; my peculiar use of it does not inhibit its distinctive use by others. It belongs completely to each and all of us. Yet no one author has exhausted its possibilities, and no one speaker at any given moment can be said to have fully utilized its resources for expression.

The mode of existence of a cultural reality of this kind, dependent on the historical and present linguistic behavior of those who use it, is clearly not the mode of existence of a perceptual object in the primary sense. It exists rather as a kind of cultural space within which I think and speak and write. Its mode of existence is at any given moment more virtual than actual; it offers me an indefinite number of linguistic possibilities among which I choose, without reflection, those I need just now. I perceive it on the lips of others and in the writings of those who have left us books from the past. Clearly it is tied to, and founded on, perception in that its whole reality can be actualized only to the extent that it is an instrument to be

used in the real, historical, perceptual world. But it is no less
clear that its mode of existence, like that of other intersubjective
cultural institutions, is of another order than that of perceptual
reality as such, that, though it is tied to time and history, it is
endowed in my experience with an atemporal and a nonspatial
quality.

Or we could turn to such historical and cultural realities as
"feudalism," "capitalism," "Calvinism," "the proletariat," "class
warfare," "common law," etc. These are at once historical forces
which owe their existence and reality to human action and
human intentionality, as well as explanatory hypotheses and
concepts. Their mode of reality greatly transcends the real experiences which they thematize and signify, and yet they are
clearly founded in the primary mode of consciousness which we
call the perceptual world.

It is impossible in this short space to give a complete delineation of the various "orders of reality" and trace out the precise
lines of their dependence on the primary structures of perception. At most we can enunciate a thesis to be argued, and it
will be convenient to do this in terms of the relationship of
categorial thought in general to perception. That such orders
of experience as the imaginary, the past, culture, history, etc.,
are founded in the primary structures of perceptual experience
seems evidently less questionable than that the structures of
categorial thinking in general are so founded. Moreover, we
cannot here do more than allude to the well-known position
of Husserl and of Merleau-Ponty and their attempt to avoid
the extremes either of "logicism" on the one hand or of "psychologism" on the other in their statements of this thesis.[15] My
purpose, thus, is not to present a final demonstration of this
thesis but only to investigate its meaning and its claim as it

---

15. Husserl discusses the founding of categorial acts primarily in the
Sixth Investigation and in *Erfahrung und Urteil,* though this theme is a
constant throughout his writings, as in the first chapter of *Ideas,* which
would be unintelligible without it. Merleau-Ponty comes back to this
theme very frequently in his writings, but perhaps the most explicit
texts are to be found in "The Primacy of Perception" and in "Phenomenology and the Sciences of Man," both included in *The Primacy of
Perception, op. cit.*

was first stated by William James. This is, therefore, a partial and preparatory study, a restatement of the thesis in Jamesian terms rather than an attempt to establish a definite conclusion.

II. *James's Refutation of Psychologism*

The thesis of the "primacy of perception" in experience can have two senses, and William James anticipated phenomenology in his contribution to the development of each of these. First of all, it can designate the "inescapable" character of the perceptual world and our embodiment within it. On whatever level of conscious awareness we may be operating, our bodily presence to the world continues to be felt and experienced. Even when lost in the worlds of fiction, phenomenal time (i.e., the actual order of our successive acts of imagining) remains the basis of all such other levels of experience, and we continue to grow older even while we advance our scientific and philosophical theories. Even in the most purified realms of theoretical thought, when our physical existence is deliberately bracketed from our consideration, it nevertheless continues to be present in marginal awareness as the inescapable *place* and time in which our thinking takes place. So long as consciousness lives, the perceptual world remains for it its most constant and pervasive realm.

But this is not the most important sense of the thesis of the primacy of perception. There is a stronger sense according to which it is asserted and argued that the perceptual world is not only the necessary (though often more or less marginal) accompaniment of other orders of experience but that the "higher orders" of experience, and more particularly categorial thought, i.e., the realm of (formal and material) ideal meanings, are *founded* on the structures of perception. It is this latter and stronger form of the thesis which we wish to examine with reference to William James.

There is one form of the thesis which must be immediately rejected, and that is *psychologism*, or the belief that the structures of reasoning are to be identified with psychological processes (whether of the individual or of the human historical community as a whole). Husserl's treatment of psychologism is well known, but it is worthwhile reminding ourselves that Husserl himself acknowledged his debt to James's "brilliant observations" in descriptive psychology and credited James's "genius" with helping him learn to avoid the pitfalls of psychologism in his own investigations.[16]

The first level of James's rejection of psychologism is found in his criticism of the "mind-stuff theory" of the British empiricists, particularly Locke and Hume, and his uncovering of the "psychologist's fallacy." [17] As Aron Gurwitsch has claimed of the Gestaltist rejections of "the constancy hypothesis" (i.e., the exclusive and isomorphic dependency of "sense-data" on physical stimuli), James's rejection of the "mind-stuff theory" can be considered to be an implicit phenomenological reduction.[18] James clearly anticipates both Gestalt psychology and the phenomenology of perception in his rejection of atomism or "elementism," i.e., the view that experience is made up of finite, discrete, "substantial" bits of color, hardness, softness, thermal qualities, etc. Against such a view, he shows that no psychological act of consciousness and no given sensation ever recurs twice, that consciousness is "cumulative" and is never twice in identically the same state, and that we cannot construct perception out of the materials of "the perceived." [19] What remains the "same" in a perceptual experience, for instance, are the transcendent "objects" of conscious acts and their meanings, which are fixed by consciousness and stabilized through temporal and synthetic acts which themselves have none of the qualities or characters of their objects.

Against such "empiricism" he writes:

> If the thing is composed of parts, then we suppose that the thought of the thing must be composed of the thoughts of the parts. If one part of the thing have appeared in the same thing or in other things on former occasions, why then we must be having even now the very same "idea" of that part which was there on those occasions. If the thing is simple, its thought is

16. *Logische Untersuchungen*, Zweiter Band, I. Teil, Halle, 1928, 208.
17. James, *Principles*, I, 145 ff., 196, 235–236 ff.
18. Gurwitsch, *op. cit.*, p. 168.
19. James, *Principles*, I, 230–231.

simple. If it is multitudinous, it must require a multitude of thoughts to think it. If a succession, only a succession of thoughts can know it. If permanent, its thought is permanent. And so on *ad libitum*. . .

No doubt it is often *convenient* to formulate the mental facts in an atomistic sort of way, and to treat the higher states of consciousness as if they were all built out of unchanging simple ideas . . .

But . . . A permanently existing "idea" or "Vorstellung" which makes its appearance before the footlights of consciousness at periodical intervals, is as mythological an entity as the Jack of Spades.[20]

James's contributions to the phenomenological theory of consciousness which stem from this criticism of "psychologism" have already been well studied, and it is unnecessary for our purposes to recapitulate them here.[21]

There is a second level of James's critique of psychologism which he developed at the end of the *Principles* in the chapter entitled "Necessary Truths and the Effects of Experience" in particular reference to John Stuart Mill and Herbert Spencer, who had argued that even the formal structures of categorial thinking could be *reduced* to psychological processes. Like Husserl in the *Logische Untersuchungen* which he partially inspired, James utterly rejects this kind of psychologism. James discusses three "ideal" worlds: those of aesthetic, of ethical, and of scientific experience. In all these realms, he says, we experience "ideal and inward relations amongst our objects of thought which can in no intelligible sense whatever be interpreted as reproductions of the order of outer experiences." [22] And it is in the realm of the "forms of judgment" [23] which govern logical necessity that we find the clearest examples of laws of thought

20. *Ibid.,* 236, transposed.
21. Gurwitsch, *op. cit.,* has analyzed James's contributions to the phenomenological theory of consciousness in considerable detail, treating of his doctrines of "sensible totals," pp. 25 ff.; his concept of the "object of thought," pp. 184 ff.; his theory of the "fringes" of consciousness, pp. 309 ff.; etc.
22. James, *Principles, op. cit.,* II, 639.
23. *Ibid.,* 633.

which can in no sense be reduced to empirical experience or associative connections. Spencer had argued that even the laws governing logical relationships are the result of "accumulated . . . experiences continued for numberless generations," and can thus be accounted for by the "frequency" with which certain connections have been experienced in the psychological development of the race.[24] Factual investigations of a psychological, anthropological, and physiological character, in short an "evolutionary" epistemology, will uncover the nature of these laws.

In answer to this hypothesis James proposes a purely mental (one might say an "eidetic") experiment:

> Suppose a hundred beings created by God and gifted with the faculties of memory and comparison. Suppose that upon each of them the same lot of sensations are imprinted, but in different orders. Let some of them have no single sensation more than once. Let some have this one and others that one repeated. Let every conceivable permutation prevail. And then let the magic-lantern show die out, and keep the creatures in a void eternity, with naught but their memories to muse upon. Inevitably in their long leisure they will begin to play with the items of their experience and rearrange them, make classificatory series of them, place gray between white and black, orange between red and yellow, and trace all other degrees of resemblance and difference. And this new construction will be absolutely identical in all the hundred creatures, the diversity of the sequence of the original experiences having no effect as regards this rearrangement.

> . . . Black will differ from white just as much in a world in which they always come close together as in one in which they always come far apart; just as much in one in which they appear rarely as in one in which they appear all the time.
> . . . .
> To learn whether black and white differ I need not consult the world of experience at all; the mere ideas suffice. *What I mean* by black differs from *what I mean* by white, whether such colors exist *extra mentem meam* or not.[25]

What James discovers in this "free imaginary variation" is the "ideal law" which governs judgments of comparison, and

24. *Ibid.*, 620–621 ff.
25. *Ibid.*, pp. 641–642, 643–644.

he sees that it functions independently of associative experience on the perceptual level. If we could, *per impossibile,* be restricted to the phenomenal materials which spontaneously offer themselves in temporal continuity and succession to perceptual consciousness, it would be utterly impossible for consciousness to conceive of any general law at all. "From the point of view of strict empiricism nothing exists but the sum of particular perceptions with their coincidences on the one hand, their contradictions on the other." [26] The "sense" or "meaning" of sameness and difference is experienced in another way than the temporally ordered objects of perceptual experience. There is a realm of experience, to which judgments of comparison belong, which is not subject to the conditions of perception. Such judgments of categorial thought have an a-temporal and a-spatial quality of a very special kind, which we can call "ideal." James goes on, then, to examine this "large body of *a priori*, or intuitively necessary truths" [27] which are implied in systematic classification, logical inference, subsumption, etc. Such "truths" are experienced as endowed with a universal validity for which no "mere outgrowth of habit and association" could account.[28] They are "necessary and eternal relations" which "form a determinate system, independent of the order of frequency in which experience may have associated their originals in time and space." [29]

III. *The Ideal and the Perceptual*

Thus James vindicates the distinction between categorial thought and perceptual consciousness and asserts that the structure of relationships which he call "laws of logic" or the "forms of judgment" have a mode of reality independent of psychological processes (whether of the individual or of the race as a whole). He has, therefore, escaped *psychologism*. It is also certain that nobody has ever accused him of logicism or Plato-

26. *Ibid.,* 637, note.
27. *Ibid.,* 677.
28. *Ibid.,* 649.
29. *Ibid.,* 661.

nism on the other side. St. Augustine had argued that in such purely conceptual realms as those of logic, mathematics, ethics, etc., the experience of eternal truth proves that there is a kind of knowing which gives us an object *superior* to our perceptual faculties and our embodied intellects, and he went on to prove, on this basis, that God is the necessary foundation of such superior truths. In short, according to Augustine and the Platonists, we have two radically distinct faculties directed toward radically distinct kinds of objects (and there is only an indirect, ontological connection between them). The traditional affirmation of the superiority of pure intellectual intuition over sense intuition, and of the "separateness" of its object from the data of sense, remained intact through Leibniz and the early Kant. With his elaboration of the *a priori* forms of space and time, Kant discovered a kind of object of knowledge intermediary between intellectual intuition and sense intuition—namely, the universal and necessary forms under which sensibility synthesizes everything presented to it. Husserl continued this development by arguing that there are not two radically different kinds of objects of knowledge but rather that intellectual (or categorial) intuition and perceptual intuition are two different ways of having the *same object*, that these two levels of intuition are inseparable and coordinate means of objectifying the world. It is easy to situate James in this historical development, even though he himself is unaware of it. He does not at any point recognize a superior "intellectual intuition" as a function of the mind utterly separate from its other powers of cognition, which could commune with "necessary truth" outside the whole tissue of factual, empirical experience. Like Husserl, he would argue that necessary truths are "of perception," that they are inseparably given together with primary, perceptual reality. He argues always that we experience "feelings" of *and,* of *if,* of *but,* and of *by* as surely as we do feelings of *blue* or *cold.* When he says, for instance, that "the inmost nature of reality is congenial to our powers," he is making a statement on reality and a statement on knowing; the world which we perceive and the world which we think are the same world, and logic and perception play into one another's hands. He would agree with Albert Einstein that "the eternal mystery of the world is its comprehensibility." His problem is to unite what is given in experience as inseparably conjoined (both in the subject and in the object) and yet distinct: perception and thought.[30]

Our final question here, then, will be to ask how James conceives the interrelations which obtain within experience between the ideal order of categorial thought and the real order of perceptual reality. Should we say, as we would of Husserl and Merleau-Ponty, that the categorial order is *founded on*, though certainly irreducible to, the perceptual?

That the ideal orders of number systems, of mathematics, of logical laws (whether formal or "transcendental") constitute an autonomous order of experience, distinct from the perspectivity, the phenomenal time and phenomenal space which characterize perception, is clear.[31] But this is also the case for any eidetically distinct domain of consciousness, of the imaginary, of memory, of cultural objects, of the theoretical constructs of science, etc. The question is, rather, how we should view these peculiarly ideal operations of consciousness which we encounter in categorial thought. The empiricist tradition, in its psychologistic form, has attempted to reduce them to perception; the idealistic and logicist tradition has attempted to locate them in the spiritual realm and to postulate a special spiritual power in man, distinct from his ordinary powers of consciousness, to account for our experience of them. The phenomenologists have attempted to show that, though consciousness can live in different orders of reality, all these realms are interrelated and ultimately grounded in perception, that reasoning and judgment

30. James, *Essays in Radical Empiricism,* New York, 1942, p. 42; *The Will to Believe,* New York, 1956, p. 86. We are not here concerned with James's physiological studies or with his account of how the possibility of categorial thought might be accounted for on the basis of "mutations" in brain structures, since this part of the work is logically independent of his "phenomenological" reflections—as he himself recognizes.

31. Note that we are not here posing the question of the ontological status of such "entities." We are considering them only phenomenologically, i.e., as noematic orders of experience.

are implied in the prereflexive experiences of perceptual consciousness, and that the ideal of "truth" is given implicitly in the least perception.

As Merleau-Ponty has stated it:

> By these words, the "primacy of perception," we mean that the experience of perception is our presence at the moment when things, truths, values are constituted for us; that perception is a nascent *logos;* that it teaches us . . . the true conditions of objectivity itself; that it summons us to the tasks of knowledge and action. It is not a question of reducing human knowledge to sensation, but of assisting at the birth of this knowledge, to make it as sensible as the sensible, to recover the consciousness of rationality.[32]

Like Merleau-Ponty, James centers his studies on the phenomenon of "rationality" rather than on a hypostatized and static *reason.* In his study of thinking and reasoning James particularly insists on the teleological and "practical" character of the structures of classification, analogy, and definition which we employ. He calls them "teleological weapons of the mind." [33] Meaning and essence, as they emerge in thought, are determined by my active interest in the objects with which I am dealing.

> All ways of conceiving a concrete fact, if they are true ways at all, are equally true ways. *There is no property absolutely essential to any one thing.* The same property which figures as the essence of a thing on one occasion becomes a very inessential feature upon another. Now that I am writing, it is essential that I conceive my paper as a surface for inscription. If I failed to do that, I should have to stop my work. But if I wished to light a fire . . . the essential way of conceiving the paper would be as combustible material. . . . It is really *all* that it is: a combustible, a writing surface, a thin thing, a hydrocarbonaceous thing, a thing eight inches one way and ten another, a thing just one furlong east of a certain stone in my neighbor's field, an American thing, etc. etc., *ad infinitum.* Whichever one of these aspects of its being I temporarily class it under, makes me unjust to the other aspects. But as I am always classing it under one aspect or another, I am always unjust, always partial, always exclusive. My excuse is necessity—the necessity which my finite and practical nature lays upon me. My thinking is first and last

32. Merleau-Ponty, *The Primacy of Perception, op. cit.,* p. 25.
33. James, *Principles,* II, 335.

and always for the sake of my doing, and I can only do one thing at a time.[34]

But, someone may urge, this may be all very well and good for the empirical and practical meanings (or essences) by means of which we constitute and order the immediate chaos of perceptual experience, but what of the more formal aspects of categorial thought? How do these relate to such practical experience? While it is true that James does not advance any explicit theory on this subject, he was throughout his life interested in the interrelations between "theoretical" and "practical" thinking. James recognized two kinds of truth: *a priori* truths (which are "of thinking") and *a posteriori* truths (which are "of experience"). He attempted to coordinate and interrelate these two kinds of truth by giving the primacy to truths "of experience." Thinking and perceiving are two hierarchically ordered and coordinated ways of dealing with the same reality.[35]

Reality, as it exists, is a *plenum*. "All its parts are contemporaneous, each is as real as any other, and each as essential for making the whole just what it is and nothing else." [36] But *as we experience and think* reality, this *plenum* (which is itself neither experienceable nor thinkable as such) takes on the diverse qualities of perceptual organization, of invitations to our imagination and our affections, of objects of our theoretical and scientific interest.

> The world as it is given at this moment is the sum total of all its beings and events now. But can we think of such a sum? . . . we break it: we break it into histories, and we break it into arts, and we break it into sciences; and then we begin to feel at home. We make ten thousand separate serial orders of it. On any one of these, we may react as if the rest did not exist. We discover among its parts relations that were never given to sense at all—mathematical relations, tangents, squares, and roots and logarithmic functions—and out of an infinite number of these we call certain ones essential and lawgiving, and ignore the rest. Essential these relations are, but only *for our purpose,*

34. *Ibid.,* 333.
35. Cf. Ralph Barton Perry, *In the Spirit of William James,* Bloomington, Ind., 1958, p. 49.
36. James, *Principles,* II, 634.

the other relations being just as real and present as they; and our purpose is to *conceive simply* and to *foresee*.[37]

James likes to show that the theoretical constructions of categorial thought—far from being eternal and nonhistorical ideas in the mind of God or the impersonal order which only a universal thinker, who could view the whole of reality in all its interrelated aspects from every point of view and from no point of view in particular, as he says, "without emphasis," could conceive—are rather progressively elaborated and precarious "instruments" or "weapons" men have forged in order to think the real.

There are many possible constructions of purely theoretical reason, in which logical relations might obtain, and be recognized as valid, but which could be of no conceivable use to human thought. We must, therefore, attempt to understand, says James, why it is that our very peculiar world, the life-world of immediate experience, "plays right into logic's hands." [38] We are able, in fact to think the world of objects within which we live according to abstract formal laws of relationships, which constitute, in themselves, a "fixed system," particularly congenial to our intellects but without apparent and immediate justification within the empirical order of phenomenal time and space. In his studies on rationality and belief James shows that it is a "postulate of rationality" itself that the world *be* rationally intelligible on the pattern of *some* ideal system.

> The whole war of the philosophies is over that point of faith. Some say they can see their way already to the rationality; others that it is hopeless. . . . One philosopher at least says that the relatedness of things to each other is irrational . . . and that a world of relations can never be made intelligible.[39]

James is not such a philosopher. He argues for a view which would render justice to the "truths of reason," to the formal laws of thought, while at the same time believing that the manifold structures of consciousness are a unified, overlapping, and interconnecting texture. The unity of thought and percep-

37. *Ibid.*, 635, note.
38. *Ibid.*, 652.
39. *Ibid.*, 677.

tion is ultimately founded on our experience that the world which we think is the same world as that in which we are immersed by perception and which is the correlate of our active and practical interests. The laws of logical relationships are in fact discovered again in the internal and external "relations'" of perceptual experience, and it is for this reason that they are "applicable" to it. Perceptual consciousness and categorial thought are not totally separate "faculties," without interconnections, but in our experience itself they play continually into one another's hands. Ultimately, we would have to ask the question of whether the world we perceive would be the same world it is if it were not constituted by a consciousness capable of thinking it as well as imagining it and, conversely, whether the structures of categorial thought could exist for us at all except as instruments implied by the world of perception for use within that world. If we state the question in this way, there is no doubt where James stands in "the war of the philosophies."

But, in conclusion, can we give a clear and final assessment of James's contribution to this problem? In a symposium dedicated to William James *and* phenomenology there is a double danger: of minimizing his contributions as accidental stumblings onto "truths" which only the full-fledged phenomenology of Husserl can justify or, conversely, of maximizing James into a phenomenologist in the contemporary sense of the term. With the Yankee honesty which should characterize any treatment of James's texts, I think it is necessary to conclude that, on this problem at least, James remains a precursor—but a *genuine* precursor. As is frequently the case in James, his problematic is more interesting than his systematic conclusions. He gives a clear, provocative, and contemporary statement of the problem. There is no doubt as to the thesis he holds or as to the direction in which research must be initiated to discover the solution. But he left it to his progeny to work out the arguments and the demonstrations. It is at once in the unfinished nature of his reflections and in what we see to be their continuation and completion in Husserl and Merleau-Ponty, that we find our right and our duty to continue the discussions we have begun here.

Robert R. Ehman

WILLIAM JAMES AND THE STRUCTURE OF THE SELF

I

For James no structure of experience is more fundamental than the self: in his own words, "Every thought is part of a personal consciousness." (*Principles*, I, 225.) In my contribution to this symposium, I shall turn my attention to James's analysis of the self. In the first part of my discussion, I shall deal with his analysis of self-relatedness, or mineness, and his analysis of the central core of the self; and in the second part, I shall consider his account of our sense of personal identity. In raising the issue of self-relatedness, of what makes something our own, I shall consider whether James's analysis in terms of our feeling of emotional involvement and interest does justice to the full range of our sense of self-relatedness and to the full scope of objects that we feel to be our own. I shall suggest that we must analyze self-relatedness in a wide variety of modes in order to do full justice to it. The description of self-relatedness carries us directly to the second of our issues, that of the central self. In my account of James's view on this point, I shall attempt to guard him against some of the more common misunderstandings to which he has been subject, but at the same time I shall focus on an inadequacy in his understanding of self-consciousness, an inadequacy with disastrous consequences for his whole account. In turning, thirdly, to the issue of our sense of personal identity, I shall point out the central place of memory in James's account and try to show that he ought also to have brought in other modes by which we feel our identity. I shall attempt to indicate something of these other modes and attempt in addition to bring in the future dimension of identity, which James strangely ignores. The main point of my remarks as a whole will be to show that James's empirical account of the self leads to a wider and richer concept of the self than the traditional alternative views.

II

In his descriptions of conscious life, James stresses the character of flux and flow; and as an introduction to our account of James's analysis of the self, it might be well to dwell for a moment on this feature of his view. For those who approach James from a classical perspective, it is puzzling that James never raises the issue of the permanence or stable background against which we experience the stream of our conscious life. In his detailed criticism of the classical concept of a substantial self, James fails to deal with the essential function of providing a permanent substratum of change. The classical thinker might argue that James's whole analysis presupposes substance as the substratum of the very flow that he describes. However, for James the problem is not that of understanding the possibility of flow. The sense of flow is primordial and ultimate, and the problem is to understand the possibility of some identity and stability in the ceaseless change of consciousness. The whole of James's description of our temporal identity, to which we will return in the second part of our discussion, is an attempt to show how identity can be constituted in and with the flux. The important point to see is that identity for James is not to be regarded as a postulated condition of the flux above or behind it but rather found in an immediate felt continuity and resemblance of the phases of the flux themselves. The present living pulse of experience appropriates past pulses that appear with similar emotional qualities of warmth and intimacy. For James, the flux of experience does not rule out an immanent, constant self-relatedness within experience itself. The identity is a matter of constant accumulative appropriation of earlier by subsequent phases of experience, not of inherence in a permanent *thing*.

In opposition to James, it might be argued that we must have a stable background in order to measure and determine the flux. Mere felt flux cannot be dated or correlated with other things; it is only lived through. However, this simply emphasizes the orientation of James's analysis. He is not concerned with the self or with conscious life primarily as a measurable and objectifiable entity; and he does not take the measured locomotion of physical objects in space as the model for the understanding of the flow of conscious life. More basic than its measurable and objective character is its flowing, streaming, felt bodily life. James penetrates beneath the level of an objective science of the self, beneath our objective conceptual and experimental knowledge about the self, to the flowing life which we directly feel and which we can never exhaust from the perspective of objective science; as James puts it, "It is the re-instatement of the vague to its proper place in our mental life which I am so anxious to press on the attention." (*Op. cit.*, 254.)

In putting James's interpretation of the self to the test, it is necessary to bear in mind that he is suspending consideration of those dimensions of the self that are accessible through inference or through the observation of a third-person witness. He appeals to our own first-person experience and describes the self as it appears prior to theoretical elaboration. While this might not include the whole range of the self, it lays the groundwork for all further investigation, and it is to the evidence of the self as we directly experience it that we must appeal in putting theories of the self to the test. For James, our direct acquaintance with an object is in every case our most primordial and fundamental mode of cognition of it; and while bare acquaintance might be brute and dumb and have only a minimal conceptual component, it is only by operating upon the data of acquaintance that we can attain genuine knowledge. "Feelings are the germ and starting point of cognition, thoughts the developed tree." (*Op. cit.*, 222.) One might go beyond mere lived experience, but one must always refer back to it.

Bearing in mind the methodological limits of James's inquiry, let us turn to James's interpretation of self-relatedness. For James, a man's empirical self in the widest sense includes the "sum total of all that he *can* call his," "his body and psychic powers, his clothes and his house, his wife and his children, his lands and horses, and his yacht and bank-account." He calls these his own because, in the words of James, "all these things give him the same emotions. If they wax and prosper, he feels triumphant; if they dwindle and die away, he feels cast down, —not necessarily in the same degree for each but in much the same way for all." (*Op. cit.*, 291.) While for James there are various degrees of intimacy with which a person feels that something is a part of his self, and much fluctuation in what he feels as his own at different times, a thing is his own in the measure that, and so long as, he is interested in and emotionally involved with it. The immediate interest is, in James's own terms, "really the meaning of the word *my*. Whatever has it is *eo ipso* a part of me. My child, my friend dies, and where he goes I feel that part of myself now is and evermore shall be." (*Op. cit.*, 324; italics in text.)

In this manner of regarding self-relatedness, James is putting into question the supposition that we must antecedently and conceptually recognize something as our own in order to emotionally respond to it and take an interest in it. He is rightly pointing out that self-love and self-feeling are instinctive modes of behavior and emotional response that presuppose no conceptual awareness of a pure ego. The welfare of our body and family, the opinions that others hold of us, and our mental powers and moral dispositions immediately excite our interest without our subsuming them under a principle of selfhood. We do not take an interest in these because we judge them to be our own; rather we judge them to be our own because we take an interest in them. Their relation to self is direct and prereflective, not a result of an inferential or explicitly reflective act. For James, a pure principle of selfhood is useless in accounting for self-love and our immediate interest in things, since we cannot take an interest in a pure ego; we can take an interest only in the empirical realities which affect our welfare and standing in the eyes of others: "the words *me* and *self*, so far as they arouse feeling and connote emotional worth, are *objective* designations meaning all *of the things* which have the power to produce in a stream of consciousness excitement of a peculiar sort." (*Op. cit.*, 319; italics in text.)

While we might admit this, there nevertheless remains a serious question as to how far James means this to be an exhaustive interpretation of self-relatedness even at the immediate and prereflective level. There are two crucial issues here. The one concerns the analysis of the excitement and interest that constitute an object as a part of the empirical self, and the other concerns possible felt dimensions of the self in which we fail to take an interest. In his analysis of our instinctive interest and self-feeling and self-love, James tends to treat these as purely reflex reactions and fails to recognize the felt reflexivity, the felt reference back to self, that is present in all self-feeling and self-love on the adult human level. (*Op. cit.*, 320–321.) Feeling is not *self*-feeling simply because we feel it and live through it; in order to be a feeling of self, it must disclose its object as bearing on our living existence. The reference to self must not exist only from the standpoint of an outside observer, as James suggests it does, but must also exist for the subject himself. (*Op. cit.*, 323.) In taking the reactions of the infant as a paradigm of selfishness and self-love, James fails to appreciate the distinction between mere insensibility to all but immediate needs and the preoccupation with self that involves in addition a sense of a distinction between self and other and an exclusive concern for the bearing of objects on our own self as opposed to their bearing on others. The infant fails to appreciate this distinction. He does not feel objects in their bearing on him; he simply grasps or neglects them in reflex reactions.

In regard to the second issue, James fails to account for our feeling of the relevance to our self of certain items in which we may have no interest and to which we may fail to respond emotionally. While interest is a basic mode of self-appropriation, it is not the only mode. To be sure, James is not at this point dealing with the relation to self of experiences and movements that we live through in the center of our lived bodies; he is concerned only with peripheral dimensions of the self. However, it does not appear to be the case, as he suggests, that the opinions held of us by others are felt as pertaining to us by virtue of our instinctive emotional response to them (*op. cit.*, 322); we feel that they belong to us by recognizing their reference to us apart from, and prior to, an emotional response. Moreover, the mere fact that objects in our environment are oriented around our living bodies makes them in some sense *our own* objects and instruments, even when we have no interest in them and hardly attend to them. There is a need for a fuller analysis of mindness than James provides. However, we can nevertheless agree with the central place that James gives to our emotional involvement with things and agree with him that mineness is empirical, something experienced at the level of our immediate bodily existence and not something that needs to be added by a reference to a pure ego or nonempirical principle of selfhood.

For James, our emotions and interests themselves are not our own because we take an interest in them. They are rather the content of our central self and constitute in James's terms the *I* which serves as the center for the empirical self in a wider sense. The central self for James is "the home of interest, the source of effort and attention, and the place from which appear to emanate the fiats of the will." (*Op. cit.*, 298.) There is no need for a principle to make our emotions and feelings our own; they are there in the heart of our central self, and it is in relation to them that all else becomes our own. They are in each case our very self because we exist as living through them. They are "warm and intimate" in a manner in which nothing else is.

In order to see the full significance of this, it is necessary to indicate the connection between the central self and the body. When James attends to his own thinking and feeling as he lives through them, he puts into radical question the traditional idea that there is a pure spiritual activity, a pure thinking, that is not infected with the body. For James, even our thinking acts appear as felt bodily movements. "The acts of attending, assenting, negating, making an effort are felt as movements of something in the head; . . . in attending to either an idea or a sensation, the movement is the adjustment of the sense organ felt as it occurs." (*Op. cit.*, 301.) In the same vein, James's famous account of emotions as feelings of bodily motions puts into question a pure spiritual activity. (*Principles*, II, 449.) There is perhaps nothing in James that has been more radically misinterpreted than his account at this point, and he has often been taken as a mere materialist. However, there is in fact no materialism here, no denial of thought or emotion, but simply the observation that we are unable to grasp these as purely psychical, as nonbodily. For James, the acts of thought and feeling are felt as bodily acts; and the body is felt as a vehicle of consciousness. When James asserts that the "acts of attending, assenting, negating are felt as movements in the head," the term *as* ought to be taken literally. From the point of view of the most radical self-reflection, there is no evidence of traditional dualism. The purely psychical and the purely physical both appear as conceptual constructs rather than as data of living experience. However, James opens the door to misunderstanding by failing to distinguish clearly between the body as a mere physical object as studied by physiology and the body as we feel and live through its movements in our actual conscious experience. The body as a physiological entity containing the central nervous system and brain is an object for the detached attitude of science; it is not our localized, felt subjective life.

While James finds no pure spiritual activity at the heart of the self, he is too imbued with the dualist tradition to rule it out of court. In his descriptions of the central self, James struggles to put long-standing theories to the test and to remain open to the impartial deliverances of our direct experience, and in this respect he presents a model of empiricist method in philosophy. He recognizes how difficult self-observation is in this case and is sensitive to the presence, beyond his descriptions of bodily feeling and adjustments, of an "obscurer feeling of

something more" (*Principles,* I, 305), which might be either a
pure psychic activity or simply a dimmer feeling of further
bodily movements. While we might sympathize with James's
hesitation on this point, we must nevertheless put into question
one feature of his analysis which fails in any case to hold up;
and this brings us to a crucial critical point with regard to the
very nature of self-consciousness. When James considers the
possibility of a pure psychic activity, he always assumes that it
feels its existence in its very activity; on the other hand, when
he considers the possibility that our central self might be
bodily, he admits that the bodily movements might be mere
objects to a nonreflexive consciousness. (*Vide op. cit.,* 304.)
For James, on this hypothesis, the reference to self would be
simply the reference of peripheral objects to the warm and
intimate central body, and the central as well as the peripheral
self would be objects in an anonymous stream of consciousness.
In the measure that James takes the central self to be bodily,
he takes the self to be an object to a stream of consciousness;
he does not take the further step of taking the stream of
conscious life itself as a self-conscious feeling of bodily life,
as the self-feeling of the living body. In any case, for James
"its appropriations are less to itself than to the most intimately
felt part of its present object, the body, and the central adjustments which accompany the act of thinking in the head. They
are the kernel to which the represented parts of the Self are
assimilated, accreted, and knit on; and even were Thought
entirely unconscious of itself in the act of thinking, these 'warm'
parts of its present object would be a firm basis on which the
consciousness of personal identity would rest." (*Op. cit.,* 341;
cf. footnote, same page.)

While James is right in recognizing that the present pulse
of our conscious life is in some sense the "darkest in the whole
series" and that nothing can be known *about* it in its concrete
particularity until it has begun to recede into the past and become an object, it does not follow that our present pulse cannot
feel prereflectively its own existence in its very act. The present
pulse must itself feel itself as the central self; it cannot have
the central self as a mere object before it. For in this case it

could not in a radical sense feel bodily motions, sensations, attitudes, and locations as its own; and in appropriating peripheral objects to its bodily center, it would not appropriate them to *itself*. In order for the present pulse to feel the warmth and intimacy of the body and bodily life, it must feel that this is close to itself. There is a moment of self-relation in the very experience of intimacy: intimacy is intimacy *to;* and for an anonymous, nonreflective consciousness everything would simply appear as present, as objective; nothing would appear warm and intimate. The body would always in this case appear as an external object, never as its own body, as the location of its own life. In maintaining that our present pulse of conscious life might be selfless, James opens himself to the criticism that his interpretation of the central self as felt bodily movements is indeed reductive. The interpretation is viable only in the measure that he admits self-relatedness in and with our immediate bodily consciousness and regards the body as being aware of itself.

Unless he admits reflexivity in the present pulse of bodily awareness, James not only gives a distorted account of the central self but also contradicts his own descriptions of our sense of reality or belief. For James, as Professor Wild in his paper for this symposium has pointed out, "that sense of our life which we at every moment possess is the ultimate for belief" (*Principles,* II, 297); and the "stepping outside" of the object which constitutes it a reality as distinct from a mere idea consists in "the establishment either of immediate practical relations between it and ourselves, or of relations between it and other objects with which we have immediate practical relations." (*Op. cit.,* 296.) From the standpoint of a "bare logical thinker," "without emotional reaction," we give reality to whatever objects we think of; and we can only distinguish reality from fiction by turning to them with our emotional and volitional consciousness and thereby relating them back to our living bodies. The world of sense is primary for James because it is here that we bodily live and act. When we emotionally react to something or turn to it with a will, we in this very act reveal it as belonging to the world of our emotional and active life. When we are emotionally neutral, we can regard the object as real only so far as we perceive its connection with something with which we are emotionally and volitionally involved. The objects of will are real as something to which we attend and consent with our bodily activity; mere objects of imagination are unreal in that they merely float in a realm of their own on the horizon of the practical world. Our belief in the objects of will is our consent to their future reality; our lack of belief in objects of mere imagination is our indifference to them and our failure to connect them with what we do believe already. For James, belief reveals reality by revealing the object as belonging in past, present, or future to the same spatial-temporal field as our active bodily life, and in this sense belief is reflexive.

In the end, for James the distinction between the sense of reality or belief and self-awareness appears to be simply that the sense of reality is the wider, embracing all that is continuously related to the self in a spatial, temporal, or causal manner and not merely what belongs to the self itself. The self is the "anchor" of reality but not the whole of reality, and in this respect James's view of reality is not subjective. However, the "sting of interest" is fundamental to both belief and self-awareness, and the sting of interest is a feeling of emotional involvement and interest. In some passages James speaks of belief as a mere feeling without disclosive power, a mere feeling of acquiescence or consent, but this goes against his deeper view that belief is a sense or perception of reality, a mode in which reality is cognized. The distinctive cognitive moment is the sense that the objects are bound up with, and a part of, the same world as our felt existence.

The prereflective reference to self to which we are pointing in feeling and belief does not require us to abandon James's critique of a transcendental principle of selfhood. While the relation to self is irreducible, it is not something apart from, or distinct from, the feeling of the flux of our immediate bodily life. In opposition to the prereflective feeling of self in our bodily life, a transcendental principle of selfhood is an object of reflection, something that must be able to be involved in order to bring an originally selfless manifold of empirical data into relation to a unified self, but not something experienced in and with the flux at the primordial level. The transcendental ego is radically distinct from an immanent prereflective mineness or sense of self in being nonbodily and in being experientially present only from the standpoint of explicit reflection. There is no need for a nonempirical principle of selfhood to account for the self unless we have already reduced the immediate stream of bodily consciousness to a mere natural stream without an intrinsic self-relatedness. For James, the stream of conscious life is in itself a self; it does not need to be made one by an appeal to a higher principle. The self is a genuinely empirical reality.

III

When we turn to James's interpretation of our sense of personal identity, we find the same need for reflexivity in the present pulse of conscious life that we found when considering the nontemporal relation to self. For James, we appropriate and regard as our own those phases of past experience that share the warmth and intimacy of our present bodily existence. The warmth and intimacy of our present bodily life serves as the point of reference by which we recognize past phases as parts of our self. Unless the present pulse of conscious life were aware of itself, it could not appropriate past phases to itself and could not recognize them as warm and intimate. The bare feeling of warmth and intimacy already includes an element of self-relatedness, and James can analyze self-relation in these terms only because they already connote self-relation.

In maintaining that we appropriate past phases of our experience on the basis of their warmth and intimacy resembling that of the living present, James might appear to be saying that we re-live our past experiences and that we feel them with the immediacy of our present experiences. However, for James, no experience simply recurs, and if it did, it would not appear as past. The distinctive character of James's account at this point is that we can now feel phases of experience that we recognize as past with an immediacy and warmth similar to that with which we feel our present experience; one might almost say that we now live through them again as past. For James, both primary memory, the receding dimension of the specious present, and memory proper, the recall of something that has once been distinguished from the living present, involve us in some measure in their objects; in both we immediately feel that they are a part of the stream of our experience. The warmth and intimacy of the remembered experience might be regarded as our sense of its reality, our primordial and underivative belief that it is a part of the same self as our present living experience. Our immediate sense of our own identity, for James, extends as far as the warmth and intimacy of represented past experiences. When we no longer feel a phase of experience from our past with a warmth and intimacy similar to our present life, we no longer feel that it is our own, even though, to be sure, we might know that it is our own in some other manner.

There is a question as to whether this does full justice to our immediate sense of our personal identity. When describing our experience of searching for the right word, James points out that even though we do not know the word we are searching for, the feeling of the act by which we search is distinctive of that word; in an analogous manner, one might argue that when we forget a fragment of our past or our childhood, we still feel that past as our own even though we have only a vague sense of its content. The past does not appear to us only in memory, as James comes near to affirming. When we recall our earliest memory, we feel that this was not the beginning of our existence; we feel that we were already there and that something has been forgotten. The experience of having forgotten is as important in our sense of identity as our experience of remembering. Moreover, even in the case of memory there is a wide variation as to the warmth and intimacy with which we feel the remembered events. James himself is aware that we might remember something only in a "cold and abstract" manner. (*Op. cit.*, 336.) In these cases we feel that our remembered past is cold and alien but do not feel for that reason that it is not our own. The sense of being remote and estranged from our past is as primordial a manner of feeling it to be our own as is the sense of its intimacy and warmth. The feeling that our past is alien and that we have a "new self" does not reduce our sense of continuity with our past to a mere matter of intellectual knowledge.

There is still another mode by which we feel our personal identity which James fails to bring to the fore. The nature of our past experience now affects the meaning that objects have for us; and unless we had already learned certain concepts, acquired certain interests, and had certain emotional reactions to things, we would not now experience them in the manner that we do. In speaking in this manner, it might appear that we are making a mere remark about casual influence, but such is not in fact the case. The reference to the past is not merely causal; in recognizing a familiar object, we see it and feel it as familiar, as something that we have seen before; in encountering a strange object, we see it and feel it as something strange, something that we have not seen before. In neither case need we have an explicit memory of the former experience. In the absence of memory, there is still a feeling of familiarity or strangeness, and the feeling points back to the past in its own meaning. There is hardly a single emotional reaction that does not implicitly in this manner refer back to previous experiences. When I become angry with someone for a second time, the anger is qualitatively different from the first; it is quicker, more intense, and less easily calmed because I feel that the "person has done it again." I am not only angry in this case in the face of a single act but in the face of a past series of faults to which the present fault belongs. For this reference to past experiences to be present in our present experience of objects and persons, we need not in every case recognize its presence explicitly. There is in any case more present in our experience than we recognize in it. The sediments of historical meaning in our present experience penetrate back to our earliest experiences.

In the whole of his discussion of our sense of personal identity, James says nothing about the identity of the present with the future self. James brings in the future self only when considering the question of the ethical value of the diverse dimensions of the peripheral self. "In each kind of self, material, social, and spiritual, men distinguish between the immediate and actual and the remote and the potential, between the narrower and the wider view." (*Op. cit.*, 315.) For James the future self appears to be simply an aspect of the peripheral self and to be our own for the same reason as the present peripheral regions, viz., because of our interest in, and concern for, it. It is real for us because we are concerned for it and turn to it with a will. There is a need to ask at this point why James finds no further problem in relation to personal identity in the future dimension whereas he does find a further problem in relation to personal identity in the past dimension. In the measure that he regards warmth and intimacy as feelings of personal identity and regards these in terms of emotional involvement and interest, there is nothing more to our appropriation of past experiences than the emotional involvement and interest that James recognizes in regard to our future self. There are good grounds, on James's view, for taking our sense of identity in the past as well as in the future as consisting simply in our feeling of personal involvement with it. However, this does nothing to account for the disparity in the attention that James gives to them. The sole explanation for James's failure to deal with the future self in the same manner as the past self appears to be that he believes that there is only a question of a peripheral self in the case of the future dimension, whereas in the case of the past self there is in addition a question of a central self. In the case of the past, it might be argued, we feel that we have lived through a given experience; in the case of the future, we merely hope for, or strive for, certain objects or events. However, in fact, in the case of the future as well as the past, there is a reference to a central self, a central vital core. In anticipation, we look forward to living through a certain experience or performing a certain action just as in memory we recall having lived through it or having performed it. There is a central self in the picture in both cases, and we feel as much identical with the anticipated vital core of the self of tomorrow as we do with the core of the self of yesterday. The future projected bodily experience is now felt with warmth and intimacy in anticipation and fear just as the past bodily experience is felt with warmth and intimacy in memory or regret. The felt presence of our bodily life has not only a backward but a future dimension; we feel not only that we have lived through a chain of previous experiences and actions but that we are about to live through a chain of future experiences and actions. The appropriation of temporally distant phases of our own existence is rooted in the same underivative reference of our present bodily life beyond its temporal present in the case of both the past and future.

When we reflect back, in conclusion, on the outcome of our assessment of James's view of the self, it becomes apparent that James points the way toward a full account of self-relatedness, the central core of the self, and personal identity by a description of our living immediate experience without a need for nonempirical principles or postulates. He reveals the self to be a genuine empirical reality present in the flux of our living experience. In order for his account to stand, he need only to have further analyzed the modes by which we feel that things are our own, recognized the need for a reflexive awareness in our present bodily feeling, opened himself to further modes of the disclosure of our temporal identity, and appreciated that we sense our identity with the future in a manner parallel to that with which we sense our identity with the past. In this paper it has been impossible for me to develop the analysis of self-relatedness or temporal identity as far as it ought to be developed. There is much more to be said. However, in spite of the need for further development, I hope that I have shown that in his attempt to describe the living depths of our experience without reduction and with a full recognition of its inescapable vagueness and ambiguity, James has not only cut beneath traditional rationalist and Kantian views but has also accounted for self-relatedness and the center of the self far more faithfully than do traditional empiricist views, and in this manner made a vital contribution to the contemporary phenomenological study of the self and the structure of experience.

John Wild

WILLIAM JAMES AND THE PHENOMENOLOGY OF BELIEF

By *structure* here is meant any eidetic pattern that can be found in examples of lived experience and can be phenomenologically described and contrasted with other patterns. Belief is such a pattern. Most men realize that they believe in certain things and persons and disbelieve in others. So they are at least directly familiar with this phenomenon. Plato did not sharply distinguish it from unstable opinion (*doksa*), and in the whole classical tradition it was disparaged as against scientific theory (*episteme*), where alone stable and well-grounded knowledge is to be found. This influence is still active in our time, where we find a widespread tendency to merge belief with opinion and to think of them both as inferior expressions of subjective interests, which should be replaced as soon as possible by scientific theory or objective analysis.

Many of us now, both in Europe and the United States, are beginning to see that William James was, in fact, a phenomenologically oriented thinker with a primary interest in describing empirical structures as we live them through. It was in the light of this interest that he was able to question traditional assumptions and to work out a descriptive account of belief, or conviction, which in my opinion is largely accurate, highly suggestive, and very widely misunderstood. In this paper I shall, therefore, first of all give a statement of James's theory and try to correct certain misunderstandings. Second, I shall point out certain respects in which it is inaccurate and incomplete. And finally, I shall suggest certain further descriptions and analyses that might bring it further toward that adequate phenomenology of belief which has not as yet been written and which we so badly need.

James explains the foundations of his theory of belief in the important Chapter XXI of his *Principles of Psychology,* published in 1890. The first section (II, pp. 283–287) is devoted specifically to the nature of belief, but in order to get a sound understanding of James's theory it is essential to read the whole chapter. At the very beginning he makes it clear that belief and reality are essentially correlated. To believe in something is to accept it as real. Thus he defends Brentano's distinction between merely thinking of an object, bringing it before the mind, and holding it to be real (*Principles of Psychology,* II, p. 287). He quotes the words of Brentano (*Psychologie,* p. 266), "it is then twice present in consciousness, as thought of, and as held to be real or denied," accepts it, and emphasizes it throughout the whole of the chapter. There are degrees of belief which are correlated with degrees of reality for the believer. Thus the more intensely I believe in some object, the more real it is for me, and the more real an object—perceived, imagined, or thought about—is, the more I believe in it.

Without claiming to give an exhaustive list, James then considers seven subregions or subworlds which we find in the structure of our lived experience. First there is "the world of sense," as James here calls it. This includes physical things, primary and tertiary qualities, real forces like gravity, storm, and electricity, and the living human body as we directly or "instinctively apprehend them" (p. 292). Second comes the world of science—in James's time, as in our own, the chief competitor with the life-world for the position of supremacy. There is no room here for the secondary qualities, since, as James points out, "the molecules and ether waves of the scientific world simply kick the object's warmth and color out" and "refuse to have any relations with them" (p. 293) except as their causes. But in this way they are "reduced to relative unreality when their causes come to view" and may be dismissed as subjective appearances in the mind. "Strange mutual dependence this," he says (*ibid.*), "in which the appearance needs the reality in order to exist, but the reality needs the appearance in order to be known."

With other subworlds we must be more brief. Third comes the "world of ideal relations or abstract truths believed or believable by all" as objects before the mind. Some of these systems have been found to apply to the sense world, where realities become present to us in the flesh. But in any case, there is a world of conceptual norms and systems—mathematical, logical, aesthetic, and moral—with many regions and subregions of its own. Fourth, there is the "world of idols of the tribe," by which he probably means the public worlds of different tribes and peoples, each containing distortions, prejudices, and superstitions peculiar to itself. Fifth come the worlds of religious mythology and other types of fiction, like the world of Ivanhoe on which James comments at some length. In the sixth place, we find the "various worlds of individual opinion, as numerous as men are" (p. 293), and finally, seventh, "the worlds of sheer madness and vagary, also indefinitely numerous."

Now, according to James, all these manifold regions and objects possess the minimum reality which belongs to objects brought before the mind. But of such objects we can always raise the questions, are they real, and can we really believe in them? To what realm are we here referring? If we find a way of answering these questions, we may be led to the sources of our most certain and primordial beliefs. In the main part of the chapter, James tries to show that these sources are to be found in what he calls "the world of sense," in which we exist, pursue our chosen projects, and face death. I have no time here to go over in detail the descriptions on which his argument is based. I can only give a brief and highly selective summary.

According to James, "the mere fact of appearing as an object at all is not enough to constitute reality" (p. 295). My grasp of reality in this eminent sense is gained from my nonobjective self-awareness as I act in the world of sense. Here being is self-revealing and calls forth our surest belief. Hence James can say, "our own reality, that sense of our own life . . . is the ultimate of ultimates for belief" (pp. 296–297). This much of the Cartesian *cogito* he consciously accepts. But why does he call this *belief* and not *knowledge?* (Here is a radical departure from Descartes.) In part because of the vagueness that belongs to the original experience. The self in which I believe with a primordial certainty is not a thinking thing enclosed within itself. It is open to a field of independent persons and things with which I am intimately and really connected by my cares and concerns. Hence by believing in myself, I also believe in them. Or as James puts it, "whatever things have intimate and continuous connection with my life are things of whose reality I cannot doubt" (p. 298).

Here we must take note of another divergence from the traditional Cartesian conception. The self in which I believe with this original certainty is an embodied self, inhabiting a world of embodied persons and things that can be sensed. In such experience the thing, or person, is present to us in the flesh rather than in idea only. Hence we try to connect our ideas and images with something corporeal like a diagram or bodily gesture, or, as James puts it, "all our inward images tend invincibly to attach themselves to something sensible so as to gain in corporeity and life" (p. 305). Who does not "realize" more, he asks, "the fact of a dead or distant friend's existence at the moment when a portrait, letter, garment, or other material reminder of him is found?" (p. 303). Corporeal embodiment is, therefore, a mark of the primordial reality and belief which characterize the sense world.

Another is its inescapability. We may lose ourselves for a time in a work of fiction or in the contemplation of ideal objects, but the sense world in which we exist is always present on "the fringes," as James calls them, of such an experience, and it is always there waiting for us when we return. This cannot be said of the other subworlds and subregions. They are not inescapable. We can live without them. In James's words (p. 294), "other things, to be sure, may be real for this man or for that—things of science, abstract moral relations, things of the Christian theology, or what not. But even for the special man, these things are usually real with a less real reality than that of the things of sense. They are taken less seriously; and the very utmost that can be said for anyone's belief in them is that it is as strong as his 'belief in his own senses.'"

The last mark is perhaps the most important of all. This is the direct feeling which is joined to my own existence and to those things and persons with which "I have immediate practical relations" (p. 296). James speaks of them as "living realities" which we directly feel as having a "higher degree of reality." He refers to "that sense of our own life which we at every moment possess" in the here and now and to "the world of living realities" (p. 297; cf. pp. 305, 200, 321). We may form a concept of this feeling of existence, as we have just done, and we may discourse about it indefinitely. But such discourse presupposes the feeling itself which we know directly by acquaintance, as James calls it, and unless this feeling of existence can be elicited from the reader, all talk about it will be really meaningless. On James's view, it is the chief ground, if we may call it that, for our verbalized belief in "the paramount reality" of the life-world. But to this must be added the others we have mentioned, the indubitability of self-existence and the objects with which it is practically connected, the felt presence of corporeal objects in the flesh, and the inescapability of this world of life.

It is important to recognize here that James is not saying that belief in the life-world is strictly indubitable nor that it is necessarily conscious and verbally articulated. As we have indicated, it is pervaded with vagueness and certainly can be doubted and refused. But when such radical doubt arises, as psychiatrists know, our existence is affected. The agent is paralyzed and unable to act in normal ways. His acceptance of himself and the world in which he exists may never be conceptually clarified and formulated. It may be present only as a "dumb conviction" (*Sentiment of Rationality*, p. 93), or *Urdoksa*, to use a Husserlian term. Nevertheless it is presupposed by all our other meaningful beliefs and activities in the world. What would happen to a mathematician, for example, if in pursuit of an exact demonstration, he were suddenly to doubt the meaningful structure of the world and his existence in it? Would he be able to continue? Not if the doubt were serious. Such doubt may arise, and when it does the whole edifice of knowledge is threatened at its foundations. But this acceptance of the sense world is the most certain of all our beliefs, and the standard by which we measure the rest, as when we say of some conviction that it is as sure as my senses, or as certain as I exist (p. 297).

According to James, since I cannot disbelieve in X without believing in something else, Y, disbelief is not the real opposite of belief. The generic opposite of both belief and disbelief is the mental unrest which we express by such terms as "doubt" and "hesitation" (p. 284). In certain extreme forms, it becomes the questioning mania which the Germans call *Grübelsucht*. In this condition the mind is unable "to rest in any conception" and seeks theoretical confirmation even of waking percepts, such as "This is my hand." The opposite attitude of firm belief also has its pathological manifestations, as in drunkenness, where the sense of reality and truth becomes abnormally intensified. As James puts it, "in whatever light things may then appear to us, they seem more utterly what they are, more 'utterly utter' than when we are sober." As he then indicates, one of the charms of certain forms of drug intoxication is the reaching of a "fully unutterable extreme" of belief, "in which a man's very soul will sweat with conviction, and he be all the while unable to tell what he is convinced of at all" (p. 284). We may add that without artificial stimulants this attitude is often practically expressed in what we call bigotry and fanaticism, and theoretically in what we know as *dogmatism*. These remarks, of course, imply that in justifiable, or grounded, belief there is an element of doubt, and James might have avoided certain misunderstandings if he had indicated this more clearly in what he says of belief in his popular essays on ethics and belief, to which we shall now turn.

With this background from the *Principles of Psychology* in mind, we should be able to avoid certain misunderstandings. Those who now read James's well-known essay *The Will to Believe*, which should have been called *The Right to Believe*, are apt to think that he is primarily concerned with dubious articles of religious faith and patent superstitions which for them are dated and dead. They think he is talking about the faith defined by the schoolboy who said, "Faith is when you believe something that you know ain't so" (*Will to Believe*, p. 60). James anticipated this misinterpretation and gave his answer, grounded on the *Principles*, at the beginning of his essay.

There are many different types of belief. Those which are most basic and most certain are concerned with the real facts of experience. "Can we," he asks (p. 36), "by any effort of our will or by any strength of wish that it were true, believe ourselves well and about when we are roaring with rheumatism in bed, or feel certain that the sum of the two one-dollar bills in our pocket must be a hundred dollars? We can *say* any of these things, but we are absolutely impotent to believe them; and of just such things is the whole fabric of the truths that we do believe in made up—matters of fact immediate or remote . . . and which, if not there, cannot be put there by any action of our own." The most certain of our true beliefs are concerned with those facts and structures of the life-world which are real in a paramount sense. But why, then, is the notion of belief required? Are these facts not merely given as passive impressions of the mind?

James later on sometimes wobbled on this point. But in the *Principles* and in this essay (1896) his position is very clear. ". . . Our non-intellectual nature does influence our convictions," —even the most basic ones (*Will to Believe*, p. 42). According to the *Principles*, the human mind is never purely passive but always active and selective. An empirical fact is never just received. First of all, it must be selected from among a host of others that might be perceived. Our attention must be focused on it. Then, following Brentano, it may be accepted, doubted, or rejected. If I consent to it, this is belief. But my belief in a fact is not the same as the fact that is believed in. It is this intentional structure of experience, clearly recognized throughout the whole of the *Principles*, that makes it necessary to recognize a factor of belief, or acceptance, over against what is believed. The most certain of the realities to which we have

access are the sensory facts with which we are directly acquainted. But these are not passively received impressions. They
are the objects of belief.

Since even these beliefs are not *infallible, because* of their
vagueness, all the other convictions by which we live are at
best uncertain, and run through the vast range of different types
and degrees of possibility and probability which is now beginning to attract phenomenological attention. Hence we can understand the factor of risk involved in any real belief in the life-
world, which is so deeply emphasized in James's moral essays.
This is especially true of those overarching philosophical and
religious beliefs which are his major concern. The *test* of real
belief is *action.* If we are not ready to act in accordance with
what we say, we are expressing an opinion, not a belief. James
argues that in deciding to accept or to reject such overarching
beliefs, the volitional nature of man not only *does* factually
play an important role, but in carefully specified ways it is
entitled to do so.

In these essays, James's attention is focused primarily on the
unique situation of the living human agent, as over against the
detached, objective thinker in facing overall decisions of belief,
and of the peculiar types of option in which he finds himself
involved. In real life we face options that are living, forced,
and momentous, whereas in our dealings with objective nature,
as James says, "the questions here are always trivial options,
the hypotheses are hardly living . . . , the choice between believing truth or falsehood is seldom forced" (*Will to Believe*, p. 51).
What James means by these different types of option has often
been misunderstood. This is especially true of the contrast
between those that are living or dead, which is worthy of some
comment.

Analytical philosophers in particular find it difficult to distinguish between an ambiguous situation in real life and a
problem confronting a theoretical philosopher, and readily pass
from one to the other. It seems especially hard for them to
grasp the difference between what James calls a *living* and a
dead option. They reduce this merely to what does or does
not have a subjective appeal to the agent. Thus according to

John Hick (*Philosophy of Religion* [Prentice-Hall, 1963], p. 66), "the basic weakness of James' position is that it constitutes an unrestricted license for wishful thinking." It is merely "an encouragement to us all to believe at our own risk, whatever we like." Hick is here picturing the mind of a detached thinker who is trying to formulate a theory which will correspond with external facts. It is always against the rules for such a thinker to give in to his desires and to engage in wishful thinking.

But James is not referring to such a theoretical situation. He is thinking of a situation in real life where a man is engaged with limited time at his disposal and is forced to choose one mode of action against another. It is of course essential for one making such a decision to take account of the relevant facts. But he must also take account of his needs and desires— his active tendencies, as James calls them. If a proposed belief has no connection with these tendencies, if it offers him nothing to do in his concrete situation, then it is a mere abstract opinion, or, as James says, a "dead" option. The expression of a mere wish, therefore, is dead, for it gives us nothing to do. To interpret James as arguing for wishful thinking is, therefore, a misconception. The liveness or deadness of a hypothesis are related to the individual's tendencies to act in the real life-world. As James says, "they are measured by his willingness to act. The maximum of liveness . . . means willingness to act irrevocably. Practically, that means belief. . . ." (*Will to Believe*, p. 34).

This statement is correct as far as it goes, but it leaves many further questions unanswered. If James had worked it out further, he might have avoided certain further misunderstandings. So it might be well for us now to look at this phenomenon and to note four distinctive traits of belief which arise from its connection with action and which mark it off from scientific theory. We have just noted the way in which close attention to action leads us back to those inner feelings and desires which are so readily dismissed by objective thought as "subjective." But the world of belief always finds a place for hope, fear, aspiration, lethargy, and other factors of the inner life. At the same time it is always reaching out toward the ultimate horizon for the global pattern of the world as a whole; for action is outwardly directed and always needs orientation. Of course not all beliefs are global. They may be concerned with special objects. I may believe in a friend. But even this must have its place in an overall pattern, for action needs a direction. This may be observed in the mythical beliefs of early men which guided their tribal action and reached out to the uttermost limits of their lived space and time. On the other hand, we cannot expect any science, or all the sciences together, to give us such knowledge. They are abstract and partial, tending always toward further specialization. There is no science of the world.

Now we must notice, in the second place, that science and belief are related to their objects in different ways. The attitude of strict science and theoretical philosophy remains detached. In James's language, they give us not direct acquaintance with, but knowledge about, some object. On the other hand, when we believe *in* something or someone, like a friend in trouble, there is a fusion of the knower with what is known in this way. We are involved *in* him and ready to give ourselves over to him. This is an engaged kind of knowledge, required in the life-world where we exist not merely as spectators but as active agents whose existence, as James specifically says, is always at stake.

This is closely correlated with a third difference in the relation of the knowledge to the knower. Scientific and philosophic theorists remain separate from their theories. As we sometimes put it, they function not as existing persons but *as* scientists and *as* theoretical philosophers. They defend their theories as objectively true, and it is only in special contexts where personal belief is involved that they refer to them as "mine." As scientists they do not assimilate their hypotheses into their lives. Hence we find it odd to hear one say "I *am* my physical theory." Beliefs, on the other hand, are very different. They are incorporated into our existence and belong to us. We defend them not only as objectively true but as our own, and when they are criticized and rejected by others we feel that we also are being attacked. Thus I recognize my convictions as mine, for I am committed to them and act on them. Hence we are not surprised to hear a practicing Buddhist say, "I am a Buddhist," or a real Marxist say, "I am a Marxist," or a philosopher, in speaking not only of the theory as such but of his conviction, "I am a Platonist."

This brings us to a fourth and final difference, also noted by Aristotle, concerning the way in which we judge or evaluate scientific theories on the one hand and convictions on the other. Of the former, we ask simply *is it true or false?* Does it correspond with the objective facts? And this is correct, since the world of the scientist and his own existence in it are not involved. But in the case of a human conviction by which we live, the whole world, including the objective facts as well as our existence, is at stake. So we ask two types of question concerning such a belief: On the one hand, is it true or false? Does it fit the facts? And on the other hand, is it good or bad? Does it fit our human existence? Not only objective truth but other existential values also are at stake. Does the philosopher have any obligation to these other values, aside from telling the truth about them? According to James he does, and James defended this view in his later pragmatic writings.

Thus, in considering a belief, he agreed that we need to ask these *other* questions: Is it or is it not challenging? Is it open or closed? Does it appeal to the whole of our being or only to a part? Is it unifying or disintegrating? Will it support and strengthen our existence or weaken it and break it down? The theorist will regard such questions as subjective, irrational, and irrelevant. But to the living, acting person the soundness of his guiding beliefs is not irrelevant. Furthermore, the answer to such questions is not merely a subjective judgment, for it involves not only our own being but the meaning of the whole world in which we live. Are these compatible? Do they really fit together? This is what we need to know. And the answers to such questions cannot be given by theory alone. As James saw very clearly, they must not only be thought through thoroughly but lived through as well.

Belief is the medium by which "knowledge" is assimilated into existence and enters into the real world of sense. It is

the way man must take insofar as he consciously remakes
himself and the world in which he lives. When actualized and
vitalized in this way, reason is shaken out of the rigid structures
it tends to impose upon itself. When brought into contact with
being, this living reason, which may inhabit belief, may regain
its freedom in wider and deeper horizons. With the requisite
courage, reason need not be afraid of coming to life. The points
we have just made go beyond the specific words of James. They
are implicit in what he says about live options and living
belief.

The distinction between forced and avoidable options and between those that are momentous and trivial refer to a difference
between the temporal conditions of real life on the one hand
and of objective investigation on the other. An option between
belief and nonbelief is avoidable if a decision can be postponed
and a neutral position maintained. Science and objective thought
in general can follow *a waiting logic* of this kind. Since there
is more time to come for this cooperative endeavor, when the
evidence is not decisive on a given issue, it is better to wait
until further evidence may appear. For the individual, however,
with only a limited time, to remain neutral with respect to a
moral value, like freedom, is equivalent to a negative decision.
Hence such overarching issues confront him with options that
are forced.

An option is momentous if it presents us with a unique opportunity. We do not have an indefinite number of lives to live.
Hence any decision concerning the overall tenor of a human
life is irrevocable and cannot be taken back for another new
experiment. A trivial option, on the other hand, is of minor
importance and lacks the element of uniqueness. Hence it is
not irrevocable. If the choice I now make turns out to be
unsatisfactory, I may take it back and try again. Choices concerning what I may like to do in a brief interval of time are
trivial options of this kind.

The options faced by the detached, objective thinker are not
living, in James's sense. They are avoidable and trivial. In real
life, on the other hand, we face options that are living, forced,
and momentous. These are the foundations of James's argument.

They lead him to two conclusions, one concerned with what he calls the right to believe, the other with the verifications of overall beliefs.

According to James, basic questions concerning human existence—such as, Am I free and responsible? Does existence have a meaning? Am I living in a moral universe where choices really matter? Is life worth living? —when they are seriously raised, involve options that are living, forced, and momentous for the individual. To give an affirmative answer to such questions is to believe in the "strenuous life," as James calls it. This is his own moral position. But the factual evidence is so rich and far-ranging that it is ambiguous, and cogent arguments can be marshaled on both sides. In such cases our passional nature, the active powers that "lie slumbering in every man," not only does but has a right to enter into the decision-making process. James sometimes writes as though these powers can then bring forth only a purely arbitrary decision in which the intellect plays no role whatsoever. This has occasioned serious misunderstandings for which James himself is partially to blame. That *he* does not mean this is indicated by his discussion of the way in which such beliefs may be justified or verified.

James distinguishes again between scientific theories and moral beliefs (*Will to Believe,* pp. 51–56). The truth or falsity of the former is decided by the facts, for "in our dealings with objective nature, we . . . are recorders, not makers, of the truth. . . ." (p. 51). We must first discover the facts and then construct our theories to conform with them. Here the facts come first, human theories and action later. But with moral beliefs the situation is different. They are concerned not with what already is but with what ought to be in the future. Man is remaking himself and, by his beliefs and action, bringing new facts into existence. Here human beliefs and action come first, facts later. If men are to bring forth a worthy result of cooperative action, they must first have faith in one another. As James puts it, "there are, then, cases where a fact cannot come at all unless a preliminary faith exists in its coming" (p. 56).

Now let us look at the different ways in which these two

types of theory are verified. An objective theory has its eyes on the objective facts. It begins as a hypothesis. Belief is suspended until the facts have their say. If experiment shows that they support the hypothesis, belief and action in line with the facts will follow. But now let us suppose that man has the power, within certain limits, to remake himself and the world which he inhabits in line with patterns of meaning that he himself orders and chooses. In this case he can become free, and he inhabits an unfinished world that is subject to a degree of moral control. How will he become free and autonomous? First of all by working out a pattern of meaning that takes account of the facts and that challenges his active tendencies; then by believing in this project (which is not a hypothesis); and finally by acting on it in spite of the risk. This is what James calls the strenuous way of life. Unless we back it with all our powers, we will not be giving it a real test, and it will never be falsified or verified.

But how, then, is it verified? Will it be verified by facts already in existence? No, since new facts and situations will arise from our free action. Do these new facts verify the original belief? Who will judge? *We* must judge, for in this case we are responsible in large part for the pattern of meaning, the belief, the project, the new situation, and the judgment. But not altogether responsible, for the world contains beings and powers which are completely independent of us and our fragile forces. What, then, will indicate that our project is true? James gives the following answer: "If you proceed to act upon your theory, it will be reversed by nothing that later turns up. As your action's fruit; it will harmonize so well with the entire drift of experience that the latter will, as it were, adopt it, or at most give it an ampler interpretation, without obliging you in any way to change the essence of its formulation" (*Sentiment of Rationality*, pp. 105–106). But James recognizes that this statement is too individualistic. The content of human history is too rich and its potentialiies too vast. ". . . in a question of this scope," he says, "the experience of the entire human race must make the verification," and "all the evidence will not be 'in' till the final integration of things, when the last man has had his say, and contributed his share to the still unfinished X" (*Sentiment of Rationality*, p. 107).

This in outline is James's theory of belief.

So far I have tried to give an accurate summary of James's phenomenology of belief and to guard it against certain misunderstandings. I have also suggested certain criticisms. Let me now try to restate them and to develop two of them further in a way that is consistent with his own descriptions. First, we have noted how James, in Chapter XXI of the *Principles*, speaks of sensory objects as "more real" than the fictive objects and others that simply appear before the mind. On this view, then, there is no sharp difference between a real thing and a delusion, only one of degree. The real thing is merely *more of the same*. But this would seem to fit better with a mentalistic view than with the pluralism of James. As a matter of fact, he seems to recognize this in his careful descriptions of the distinctive traits of the sense world—indubitability, inescapability, embodied presence of things and persons, and the peculiar tang of existence. This would suggest that we are here confronted not merely with more of the same but with a distinct mode of being. This, I believe, was James's more basic view which he compromised in the *Principles* by speaking of it as though it could be reduced to a mere difference of degree.

James's use of the phrase "passional nature" in stating his thesis in *The Will to Believe*—"our passional nature not only lawfully may, but must, decide an option between propositions, whenever it is a genuine option that cannot by its nature be decided on intellectual grounds . . . " (p. 42) and other phrases like "desire and emotion" in his other popular essays—has led to serious misunderstandings of his meaning. We have already commented on Hick's interpretation of it as a call for wishful thinking. This leads him to say also that James's method "could only result in everyone becoming more firmly entrenched in their current prejudices" (p. 66), which is far from James's intent. He had no interest in this sort of peace of mind. The belief he is speaking of is concerned with projects taking us

far beyond any *status quo* and capable of inspiring both im-
passioned hope and strenuous action. As he says in *The Moral
Philosopher and the Moral Life,* "every sort of energy and
endurance, of courage and capacity for handling life's evils, is
set free" (p. 213). James is certainly critical of intellectualistic
monism and recognizes a legitimate place for "feeling" and
"desire." When associated together, his words sometimes give
the impression that he is recommending an exclusive reliance
on subjective factors with no attention to rational argument and
objective facts. Many passages from his essays might be quoted
to show that this was not his real intent. Thus in *Reflex Action
and Theism,* published in 1881, he says (p. 130): "not a sensible
'fact' of department One (feeling) must be left in the cold,
not a faculty of department Three (action) be paralyzed; and
department Two (reason and meaning) must form an indestruc-
tible bridge." Each of the three departments of the mind, as he
called them—feeling and the perception of facts, rational argument, and action—has its proper role to play. Distortion will
arise if any one is suppressed. It is the whole man who should
decide, believe, and act. It is hard to see how the charge of
anti-intellectualism can be raised against this view.

There is another criticism, however, which is more serious.
As we have noted, James rightly thinks of doubt as the true
opposite of belief and disbelief. This leads him to infer that
belief and doubt are essentially opposed. To doubt an active
belief is equivalent to negating it. Thus in *The Sentiment of
Rationality,* James says, "if I refuse to bale out a boat because
I am in doubt whether my efforts will keep her afloat, I am
really helping to sink her" (p. 109; cf. p. 97, *Will to Believe,*
p. 57).

Now, it is true that a deep-seated attitude of doubt may lead
to disbelief and inaction of this kind, which James is right
in condemning. But this is not necessarily so. The position of
doubt is more ambiguous. It may be joined with active belief
as well as disbelief. Thus in the situation cited by James, one
may imagine a doubter who devotes himself to bailing out the
boat with the last drop of his energies, in spite of his doubt and

even spurred on by it, though he will be more open to other possibilities than the fanatical believer envisaged by James. Belief can be both strong and open at the same time. James's neglect of this possibility prevented him from seeing that the difference between genuine conviction and fanaticism rests on the presence or absence of doubt. It is connected with his failure to make a sharp distinction between belief and opinion which, following Hume, he often joins together, as on p. 43 of *The Will to Believe*. This may be worthy of a brief descriptive comment.

Our shifting opinions come and go and can soon be forgotten, as Aristotle points out in his *Nicomachean Ethics*, Book VI. Our beliefs, however, are different. Being firmly grounded in our active being, they do not so readily change and possess a peculiar stability of their own. Since the time of Plato, influential traditions in Western thought have merged belief with opinion and have opposed them both to science (*episteme*) which is firmly grounded in rational insight and demonstration. Hence we are apt to infer that the stability of belief is purely "subjective" and has no real ground in evidence accessible to all. This is no doubt true of most of our opinions and of *fanatical* beliefs, but it is not true of all.

There are beliefs *well grounded* on empirical evidence gained through direct acquaintance, as James called it, like our belief in our own existence and that of the independent things and persons with whom we are familiar. Certain beliefs, therefore, may have a dual stability. They may be grounded not only subjectively on permanent sets and habits in the believer but also on cogent, though probable, empirical evidence of various kinds. Such beliefs are strong enough to withstand constant doubt, and thus to remain open without losing their active power. Opinions, on the other hand, are too weak to withstand serious questioning and are likely to disappear when faced with pressing doubts. These descriptions could be developed much further. James's failure to develop them leaves him open to these and other criticisms.

But in his *Principles of Psychology* and his moral essays, he worked out a phenomenology of belief which is highly original and in many respects so sound that it will, I think, have a lasting interest for empirically oriented philosophers. Like the existential philosophers of more recent times, James was concerned with the actual problems of living men. Hence he had a special interest in the phenomenon of belief, for even though men now believe in science, they live their lives on the basis of belief, and according to him they always will. Belief is essentially different from science and can never be replaced by it. Traditional thought had neglected this phenomenon, and discounted it in favor of theoretical knowledge. On this view, we know being by reason and theoretical speculation. James reverses this position. According to him, we believe in reality with all cognitive and active powers—feeling, perception, intellect, and will—and unless we believe in it, nothing is real for us now, nor will we bring anything real into being. As to an unrevealed reality in itself, James was wholly skeptical and *Kantian.*

The test of belief is action, and no matter what a man says, his acts speak louder than his words. As judged by this test, the primordial reality in which men believe is the world of sense in which they exist and act, and special theories are verified only insofar as their objects can be shown to be connected with these real objects of sense. In his moral essays James's main aim is to show, against Clifford and others, that the waiting logic of detached observation should not be confused with the logic of real belief, which has to be lived through in time and, therefore, has distinctive features of its own. In science the options are never global in scope; they are avoidable and trivial, whereas in real life we face options which are global in scope, forced, and momentous. In science we can wait for the facts to decide, and then adjust our beliefs and acts to the facts as they already are.

In moral decisions, however, whereby man remakes himself and the world in which he lives, belief and action come first, and facts follow after. The verification of such global beliefs concerning freedom and the meaning of life, therefore, cannot be left to the objective facts alone. We ourselves, our total action and judgment, are also involved. James has supported these theses concerning the logic of belief with painstaking description and concrete examples taken from real life. Whether or not we agree with his tentative conclusions, he has made significant contributions to the phenomenology of belief which should be of primary interest to all philosophers who do not think of their subject as a mere verbal game.

William Leon McBride

SARTRE AND THE PHENOMENOLOGY OF SOCIAL VIOLENCE

In this tumultuous year of revolution and counterrevolution, of the radicalizing of attitudes and the polarization of oppositions in many parts of the world, the phenomenon of social violence, violence between man and man, is naturally an enormous preoccupation of all of us in our everyday lives. But for many philosophers there seems to be no clear connection between this phenomenon and their discipline; the only relationship that they can discern is a purely negative one, that of the interference of an enormous surd with the life of reason. Is it not true, after all, that *inter arma philosophia tacet?*

To certain thinkers, of course, including some of those who might be called philosophical interpreters of the findings of the behavioral sciences, a *kind* of explanation seems readily to impose itself upon the data: it is that social violence is simply a more complex manifestation, typical of the human species, of biological traits characteristic of lower animal forms as well —traits such as an innate impulse to aggressivity or an innate territorial imperative. Like all philosophical reasoning, this sort of approach involves, as I have said, an *interpretation* and thus a going beyond the raw data. But there are at least two especially weighty reasons why such an explanation, taken alone, is inadequate: first, because it is in principle universalist and thus unable to take into account the particular individual or the particular social group, and, second, because, insofar as it treats men as being *just* animals of a peculiar kind, it cannot generate a normative, ethical answer to the barbaric code of ethics implicit in the frequently heard remark concerning certain manifestations of social violence—namely, "They're just animals anyway, and that's the way they ought to be treated."

As both a Frenchman and a Marxist, Jean-Paul Sartre has lived through as harrowing a year of violence as most of us. He was not one of the direct inspirers of the French student revolts that began at Nanterre in late April, but he manifested considerable sympathy for the aims of these uprisings, gave direct encouragement to the student leader, M. Cohn-Bendit, and was proportionately discouraged at the comparative failure of this movement. Later he witnessed with outrage the events in Czechoslovakia. But at least Sartre has the advantage of possessing a highly developed philosophical framework through which to consider these events, a framework that attempts to avoid the inadequacies of the biological approach that I have just mentioned. His *Critique de la raison dialectique* is, from a certain point of view, all about social violence; it sees our world as one in which violence is pervasive, in which, to use a distinction employed by Sartre himself, everything takes place not always *by* violence, but *in* [an atmosphere of] violence.[1]

I

Violence pervades the *Critique*, and it does so in a way that, if I may report a personal reaction, seems far more salient than in the case of *Being and Nothingness*. Many other readers have had the same reaction, and it has upset some of them. Alphonse De Waelhens, for example, wrote a scathing early review of the *Critique* in which the following typical remarks occur:

> Let us not insist. If the totalization of an epoch really has no other foundation of intelligibility—if we even admit that it *is* one—than a dialectic (or a non-dialectic) of this sort, it is better

1. Jean-Paul Sartre, *Critique de la raison dialectique*, Tome I, Paris, 1960, 225.

to give up all hope for the history that this dialectic will produce.[2]

What upset De Waelhens in this particular passage of his review was the connection that Sartre establishes between fraternity and terror in what he calls the group—the progressive, revolutionary social structure which he has contrasted with the passive form of social existence called the series, or seriality. Whether or not one finds it emotionally upsetting, the pervasiveness of violence in Sartre's account is undeniable. Let me briefly try to indicate why this is so.

The key term, as anyone who has heard anything about the *Critique* knows, is *scarcity*. This is Sartre's fundamental ontological concession to Marxism, from which the other aspects of his move toward *rapprochement* with Marx can be seen logically to follow one another. Man, regarded as free sensuous activity, or *praxis*, finds himself in a *contingent* situation in which matter is scarce, there is not enough for all. In a highly dialectical fashion, the resulting necessity for man to work on scarce matter comes to impose upon man some of the inertness and unfreedom of matter, while making it appear, contrary to the basic reality of the situation, that inert matter is a free agent dominating man. Thus, to use the consecrated Marxian phrase, the producer becomes the product. The social structures of *our* world are the complex results of the contingent condition of scarcity; in another imaginable world, according to Sartre, it might have been otherwise.[3]

From this starting point of the discernment of scarcity in our world the phenomenology of social violence follows, as it

2. Alphonse De Waelhens, "Sartre et la raison dialectique," *Revue Philosophique de Louvain*, 60 (1962), 96. (This translation and all subsequent translations from the French are mine, unless otherwise noted.)

3. There are, incidentally, some interesting parallels between these initial premises of Sartre's social philosophy and the very conservative political philosophy of David Hume, for whom the so-called artificial virtues, notably justice and other basic values of the domain of intersubjectivity, are all the result of the contingent condition of scarcity. The parallels between Hume and Sartre here are at least as great as those in Sartre's earliest writings, prior to *Being and Nothingness*, when the influence of Husserl's problematic on him was greatest.

were, immediately. There is not enough for all, and the practical recognition of this fact by individuals in a social setting, the treatment of others as *Others* which can result in any conduct, from the most passive kind of fear and suspicion to the most overt acts of destruction, *is* violence.

> In reality, violence is not necessarily an act . . . ; neither is it a characteristic of Nature or a hidden potentiality. It is the constant inhumanity of human conducts [considered] as scarcity interiorized, in short, what makes everyone see in everyone the Other and the principle of Evil. . . . This means that scarcity as the negation in man of man by matter is a principle of dialectical intelligibility.[4]

In *Being and Nothingness,* it will be remembered, the basic relationship in all possible relations with others, in Sartre's discussion of being-for-others, was said to be struggle or conflict. In his discussion of love, Sartre explicitly acknowledged his debt to the Hegelian dialectic of master and slave. At first glance, then, it might be thought that what he has to say about violence in the *Critique* is simply an extension of the same theme. But this is not quite true. Paradoxically enough, despite the more violent "atmosphere" of the later work, Sartre now seems to regard struggle as much less of a fatality, an inevitability, in human relations, because his new emphasis on scarcity renders struggle less essential to the ontology of inter-subjectivity. To put it very simply, the basis of radical evil has shifted, for Sartre, from the Other in *Being and Nothingness* to matter—or, as it should more correctly be put, to the material condition of scarcity—in the *Critique.*[5] Sartre himself expresses it very clearly, though somewhat less simply, when he attempts in the *Critique* to distinguish his present position, not so much from his own previous philosophy as from Hegel's:

> . . . One would be very mistaken if one were to believe that the goal is the annihilation of the adversary or, to assume the idealist language of Hegel, that every consciousness pursues the death of the Other. In fact, the struggle has its origin in each

4. *Critique de la raison dialectique,* 221.
5. Dina Dreyfus, "Jean-Paul Sartre et le Mal Radical," *Mercure de France,* January 1961, pp. 154–167.

case in a concrete antagonism which has *scarcity*, under a definite form, as its material condition, and the real goal is an objective conquest or even a creation, for which the disappearance of the adversary is only the means.[6]

In short, though the phenomenological descriptions of being-for-others in *Being and Nothingness* place relatively little emphasis on the concept of violence as such, the admitted dependence of all these descriptions on the acceptance of conflict as the fundamental relationship with others could easily lead one to the pessimistic and politically conservative conclusion that violence is *and will always remain* an inescapable aspect of the life of every man who is not absolutely alone in the world; the *Critique*, on the other hand, in providing the lengthy and complicated descriptions of the we-subject that Sartre had dismissed so quickly and negatively in his earlier writing, points to the possibility of a future human society in which violence might no longer be inevitable. It can only do so because struggle is no longer regarded as the rock-bottom relationship in being-for-others.

But let us return to violence in the present. At one point, rather late in the *Critique*, Sartre distinguishes between two kinds of violence, both of which, as he emphasizes, are manifestations of the *freedom* which human *praxis* always is at base, however warped and turned against itself it may become under conditions of material scarcity. I shall quote at some length:

> At the most elementary stage of the *struggle for life*, it is not blind instincts which oppose one another through men, it is complex structures, goings beyond of material conditions by a *praxis* that founds an ethics and pursues the destruction of the Other not as a simple menacing *object*, but as freedom recognized and condemned right to its roots. That is precisely what we call violence, for the only conceivable violence is that of freedom towards freedom through the mediation of inorganic matter. . . . It can take on two aspects: free *praxis* may directly destroy the freedom of the Other or put it between parentheses (mystification, stratagem) by means of a material instrument, or else it may act against necessity (the necessity of alienation), that is to say,

6. *Critique de la raison dialectique*, 192.

exert itself against freedom as the possibility of becoming Other (i.e., of falling back into seriality), and *that* is Fraternity-Terror.[7]

Sartre's numerous descriptions of the first type of violence, that of destroying the freedom of the Other by direct or indirect means, are interesting and often brilliant, but they do not break any very new ground. Marx and many others have gone before him in this matter, though Sartre's descriptions have a thoroughness seldom achieved. The Great Fear traversing France, the presence of the royal troops menacing the inhabitants of the Quartier St. Antoine, the slick imposition by the controlled radio and television networks of the official Establishment policy line on modern audiences listening in silent rage in their condition of serial impotence—these and so many other vignettes provided by Sartre must remain unforgettable, I think, to most serious readers of the *Critique*. But it is in his discussion of the *second* aspect of violence, that within the group itself, the violence that has the dual characterization of fraternity and terror, that Sartre shows himself most philosophically original and no doubt most controversial. I should like to speak about this for a few minutes more, at the same time showing in somewhat more detail what Sartre takes to be the relationship between violence and freedom.

The key term in this phase of Sartre's social theory is *le serment,* the oath. A group once formed (or "fused," to use the more frequent Sartrean term) in order to achieve a specific objective decides to perpetuate itself with a view toward more long-range common projects. And so the members swear reciprocally to remain loyal to each other as a group and to guard against their own and others' defections. That this conception bears many resemblances to old social contract theories is obvious, though Sartre explicitly denies [8] that it amounts to quite the same thing. But what is of interest to us here is the striking way in which Sartre demonstrates the inevitability, in the case of a group that is undertaking to make itself permanent, of a free interiorization—free on the part of each of the mem-

7. *Ibid.,* 689.
8. *Ibid.,* 439, 456.

bers—of the violence that had been directed outward at the
first moment of fusion; it is on this basis that he concludes that
a complementary, dialectical relationship must exist between
fraternity and terror in any genuine group in our world of
scarcity. Let me quote a few sentences from the *Critique* which
will indicate the drift of Sartre's analysis:

> We fraternize because we have shared in the same oath, be-
> cause each one has limited his own freedom through the other;
> and the limit of this fraternity (which at the same time de-
> termines its intensity) is the right to violence that each has
> over the other, that is to say, very exactly, the common and
> reciprocal limit of our freedoms. . . . This violence, born in
> opposition to the group's dissolution, has created a new reality,
> the [potential] behavior of treason; and this behavior is defined
> precisely as what transforms fraternity (as positive violence) into
> Terror (as negative violence).[9]

It is, then, in his discussion of "the oath" that his "cult of
violence" reaches its apogee. There is a direct connection between freedom, the sovereign freedom of the individual that,
though now subdued and placed in a very different context,
remains a constant theme from the earlier to the most recent
phases of Sartre's philosophical development, and violence, since
the free struggle against the enslaving necessities imposed by
the contingent fact of scarcity in our world must by definition
be a violent one. But this struggle, in any setting other than
a Robinson Crusoe situation, first has the possibility of meeting
with some measure of success through group action. And any
group action that is prolonged beyond the first apocalyptic,
revolutionary moment entails guarding against members' back-
sliding into the former condition of serial impotence by in-
teriorizing violence within the group—that is, by creating the
Janus-faced phenomenon of fraternity-terror.

At one point in this section of the *Critique,* Sartre goes so far
as to say, concerning the objectification of the group that is
produced by the oath, *"C'est le commencement de l'humanité."* [10]
At least some of what he means is quite clear from what I have

9. *Ibid.,* 456.
10. *Ibid.,* 453.

already said: if it is only through group action that social man can, as it were, overcome the enslavements of material necessity in order for the first time to exercise his freedom, then indeed the establishment of a group on a permanent basis is precisely that dawn of a new world that Sartre proclaims it to be in this passage. It is, of course, just this section of the *Critique* and just this sort of attitude on Sartre's part that most aroused the disgust of de Waelhens, whose scathing remark I quoted earlier—as it has, no doubt, of many other readers. But I am inclined to think that, whatever the defects may be either of other aspects of his "theory of practical ensembles" or of his manner of presentation, Sartre has made a considerable contribution to our understanding of social violence in general by his rather original analysis of violence within the group itself. It seems to me that his reasoned conjunction of freedom, violence, betrayal, and terror could help considerably in comprehending such divergent phenomena as the historical opposition between Bolsheviks and Social Democrats or, in our own extraordinary present era, the fratricidal rifts that have sprung up within once-united communities and even within political parties. (I do not propose here, of course, to undertake the actual application of Sartre's theory to any such instance, for this would require introducing many complexities and qualifications. No modern community, for example, ever attains the homogeneity of a Sartrean group.) None of the classical social and political philosophers, in my opinion, has provided as penetrating an insight as Sartre does into the interrelationship of group action and violence. Significantly, the closest approximations to Sartre's account among earlier thinkers are to be found, I think, in certain passages of Rousseau's *Social Contract*.

Let me now make a few final comments about the Sartrean theoretical possibility, to which I have already alluded, of a violence-free world of the future. In what he has published thus far, Sartre himself makes very few allusions to such a possibility, and indeed it does, as we shall see, raise very fundamental difficulties. If he were to fail completely to allow it, however, his difficulties would be even greater; the desired connection with the Marxist vision of a future reign of freedom would be irreparably lost, and a pessimistic or attitudinally indifferent conservatism would become at least as reasonable a valuational conclusion as any other to be drawn from the Sartrean analysis.

The conception itself, on the basis of what I have already said, is very simple: the elimination of social violence hinges on the elimination of material scarcity. In a society of abundance there would no longer be any need for violence either between antagonistic groups aware of the fact that there is not enough for all, or within groups that are struggling to maintain themselves against a possible relapse into seriality. In such a society one might be able to conceive of a perpetual but unsworn group *praxis*—that is, a striving for common objectives by a group not bound together by oath; furthermore, this group might eventually become universal—that is, encompass the entire human race. In one of the most frequently cited passages in his introductory *Search for a Method,* Sartre says concerning the condition of social life and the new, post-Marxist philosophy that he foresees as emerging under conditions of relative abundance, "We have no means, no intellectual instrument, no concrete experience which allows us to conceive of this freedom or of this philosophy." [11] Indeed, at one early point in the *Critique* itself, he goes so far as to question whether organisms on other planets in which scarcity did not prevail or biological descendants of ours in an era in which scarcity had been eliminated could conceivably live as *historical* beings at all. [12] He furnishes no certain answer to this question. Nevertheless this intriguing possibility of a violence-free world haunts all the pages of the *Critique,* just as it does, I would suggest, our violence-filled or at least violence-surrounded lives. Near the very end of the volume, for example, Sartre again returns explicitly to this theme, only to turn back quickly to the world with which we are stuck. He says:

> Certainly this does not mean that other practical organisms in other worlds differently constituted (without scarcity, for

11. Jean-Paul Sartre, *Search for a Method,* trans., Hazel E. Barnes, (New York, 1963), p. 34.
12. *Critique de la raison dialectique,* 202.

example) might not have a different consciousness of [the dialectic] (and one without the intermediary of antagonistic reciprocity). But it means that in *our* world, [the dialectic] appears at the moment when the group raises *itself* up against the oppressed series as dictatorship of freedom.[13]

Our world, is short, is a world of struggle and violence, but it might be otherwise. Just as it would have been very misleading for me to conclude this brief summary of Sartre's treatment of social violence without making reference to this important alternative, apparently historically remote but alleged by Sartre to be logically conceivable, of a violence-free future world, so it will be impossible for me not to revert to it when, in Part III, I come to raise some more basic critical questions about the Sartrean theory.

II

I wish now for a few moments to consider the problem of what type of explanation, theory, or indeed philosophy Sartre is confronting us with in the *Critique*. This is a somewhat baffling problem, if one stops to reflect upon it, for the methodology employed in the *Critique* defies assimiliation to those philosophical styles with which comparison is most readily suggested—with the writings of Marx, Hegel, Rousseau, or Kant or even with *Being and Nothingness*. There are, of course, many possible approaches to answering this question; I would like simply to suggest a means of clarifying Sartre's theoretical purposes by contrasting what he is doing in the *Critique* with the biological type of explanation of social violence to which I alluded at the beginning of this paper. But first it would seem appropriate to acknowledge the somewhat controversial quality of my decision to use the word "phenomenology" in my title in order to designate Sartre's treatment of social violence. Is Sartre's account properly to be called phenomenology at all?

Sartre himself seems deliberately to avoid any mention of phenomenology throughout the some 750 long pages of the *Critique*. One might seriously question whether an emphasis

13. *Ibid.*, 744.

on dialectics is compatible with any phenomenology that is traceable to Husserl rather than to Hegel. A few simple points can, however, be made in partial justification of the designation of Sartre's account as a phenomenology. First of all, Sartre has continued masterfully to employ familiar phenomenological *techniques*.[14] The thorough and complex description of the fusing of the group that is eventually to seize the Bastille, a description that occupies a central place both in Sartre's treatment of social violence and in the volume as a whole, is an excellent illustration of this. Secondly, despite some terminological appearance to the contrary, the method remains primarily *descriptive*. No abstract or hypothetical entities are postulated to explain the condition of violence in our world; *praxis*, which might at first sound like such an entity and which is certainly an abstract concept in the Hegelian sense of being, when considered by itself, *incomplete*, is simply a suggestive way of regarding the totality of the sensuous activity either of an individual human being or of a group. There are, then, numerous senses of the word "theory" in which Sartre's *Critique* cannot be regarded as containing a theory, and this is one of the major reasons for persisting in designating his account as phenomenological. Thirdly, and as a natural complement to what I have just said, Sartre remains faithful to Husserl in the *Critique* by undertaking his account without relying on any theoretical presuppositions from the natural sciences, including behavioral psychology, and particularly without reference to presuppositions about the nature of causality. This brings me back to the contrast that I wish to underscore between the Sartrean account of social violence and what I have called the biological type of account.

There are certain obvious senses in which Sartre makes no pretense of beginning his *Critique* with an *epoche*. Those familiar with his introductory essay, *Search for a Method*, will remember his rather uncharacteristically unsubtle insistence on

14. This seems to be what Desan means when he says, concerning the *Critique*, that "the book reveals once again Sartre's unusual phenomenological skill." Wilfrid Desan, *The Marxism of Jean-Paul Sartre*, New York, 1965, p. 243.

regarding Marxism as *the* philosophy of the present era, as well as his reliance on a mixture of Marx and Freud in his discussion of Flaubert. Moreover, in the early part of the *Critique* proper Sartre claims that his book could only have been written after Hegel and Marx and the subsequent abuses to which the very notion of dialectics fell victim at the hands of the Marxist vulgarizers,[15] and he further criticizes "the dream of absolute ignorance which discovers the preconceptual real." "Far from presupposing," he says, "as certain philosophers have done, that we know nothing, we should at the limit (but that is impossible) suppose that we know everything." [16] (He is referring especially to knowledge of *cultural* facts.) All these comments seem to add up to a rejection of some of the central themes of Husserl's method, and indeed they are. But what Sartre has retained from that method seems to me to be of at least equal importance, especially in his treatment of social violence, and that is precisely the unflagging search for meaning and rationality at the basis of even the most apparently nonrational human actions. Social violence is a prime case in point.

We sometimes, of course, speak of the violence of a storm or of the sea; that sort of thing is not our concern when we discuss *social* violence. But often enough, writers who should know better delight in comparing, let us say, violent mob action to just such inanimate phenomena. Sometimes, of course, their purpose is political: if, for example, a revolutionary mob can legitimately be regarded as a flood or some other such natural phenomenon which, at least in our era, may be subject to control by technology, then a sanction has been provided for counter-revolutionary repression. Often, too, even when a writer does not consciously intend to take an ideological stance in his treatment of social violence, he simply finds analogies with nonrational entities to be very facile and convenient for his purposes. So, for example, the late Crane Brinton, in his now undeservedly popular *The Anatomy of Revolution,* latches onto the analogy of pathology (i.e., revolutions are like diseases) for reasons that he claims to be primarily of this utilitarian

15. *Critique de la raison dialectique,* 141.
16. *Ibid.,* p. 145.

sort.[17] Pathology has the additional convenience of straddling conceptual lines: it straddles the line between the organic and the inorganic (since diseases are diseases *of* organisms, but their sources are often inorganic), and it is also applicable to mental as well as to nonmental phenomena (since the word "pathological" is commonly applied to psychological disorders). And so even our very language abets us in thinking of occurrences of social violence as acts of God, or as epidemics of widespread physical disease, like the plague, or as outbreaks of mental illness, or even, in what seems by contrast with these analogies to be a far less invidious approach, as the manifestations of alleged tendencies to aggression, to defending one's territory, or what have you, that are said to be innate in human, as in animal, nature.

Let me now indicate what I take to be the fundamental Husserlian insight, in the light of which Sartre has eschewed all such explanations of social violence as these. From his very earliest published writings on, Sartre has taken as his own, though of course after his own fashion, the Husserlian struggle against "psychologism." Today, when the relationship between behavioral psychology, on the one hand, and physiology, biology, and the other physical sciences, on the other, has become perhaps just a little bit clearer than it was when Husserl's career began, it can be more fully appreciated that the danger, pointed to by Husserl, of eliminating human meanings by reducing them to subhuman mechanisms exists as a constant threat to *all* the sciences of man. The search for causalities, primarily of a psychological nature, in the social sciences, though often a frustrating one in light of the avowed goal of augmenting our predictive powers, must go on, and its thus far modest successes deserve applause and encouragement. But this search must not be allowed to replace or overshadow the simultaneous effort of social philosophy at illuminating the human, rational *meanings* of social phenomena. Ideally there should be cooperation between the two enterprises. Sartre, though his general attitude toward the *Kausalwissenschaften* seems, from his writings, to be somewhat more hostile than mine, accepts the reality of

17. Crane Brinton, *The Anatomy of Revolution*, New York, 1958, p. 17.

this basic division :of labor and continues in the *Critique* to be engaged in the *philosophical* enterprise of which I have spoken, the enterprise upon which Husserl's lifelong polemic with psychologism and its descendants shed so much light. Sartre's field of investigation has shifted from the psychological and individual to the social, intersubjective; and in the meantime he has undergone and responded to many new intellectual influences. But his inquiry remains, in sharpest contrast with the shallow and dogmatic "scientific" pretensions even of many of those self-proclaimed Marxist thinkers with whom Sartre would now like most to engage in dialogue, an inquiry into meaning and rationality. The very title of his book proclaims this.

And so, in dealing with the phenomena of social violence, Sartre is no closer than he was at the time of his writing, let us say, *The Transcendence of the Ego* to relying on reified mental states, such as emotions and passions, as explanatory agents. Nor does he, of course, appeal to an allegedly fixed human nature; the strong denial that there is such a thing in a humanly relevant sense, a denial for which Sartre is justly famous, is an especially salient point of agreement between his earlier and later loves, existentialism and Marxism. A particular instance of social violence, for Sartre, can only be satisfactorily understood as dialectical reason at work: it is a complex interplay of the free *praxis* of individuals and groups in a particular, concrete set of circumstances and in a world of scarcity. The inert matter which is scarce, and on which human *praxis* works, is not itself, of course, dialectical or rational; it is, rather, the "antidialectical" moment within the dialectical process. Social violence, like other aspects of the social lfe of man, must for Sartre be understood in terms of reason's encountering and working on the nonrational, the antidialectical, and not, as explanations of the opposite sort would have it, in terms of the internal structure of the nonrational itself. A mathematical relationship—for example, the figures that express the ratio between the value of available resources and the population of a particular country at a particular time—is given, not subject to challenge by reason. But the diverse possible human responses, relatively violent or relatively nonviolent, to an unfavorable ratio of resources to persons are in principle intelligible and questionable in a way in which the given ratio is not. The *Critique de la raison dialectique* is concerned with explicating in greatest detail this *human* sort of intelligibility, an intelligibility that is not dependent on considerations of causal mechanisms.

Viewed in this way, the *Critique* deserves, I think, enormous praise. For it constitutes a sustained theoretical insistence (to put it in terms immediately applicable to our contemporary American situation) on treating demonstrations or riots as human actions that are in some way rational, a sustained refusal simply to regard violent protests with the distance, disengagement, and contempt of the laboratory technician observing the behavior of his rats. Sartre's social philosophy does not propose that violent events be understood solely or primarily in the participants' own terms; far from it, for Sartre constantly stresses the necessity of referring to the larger, often hidden, processes of totalization of which single events may be mere parts. On the other hand, it also succeeds admirably in indicating how very violent in reality may be the *praxis* of those in positions of dominance who decry the more overtly violent acts of the protestors. Although the *Critique* itself is a descriptive rather than a hortatory exercise, Sartre's theory points to the *possibility* of a progressive, humane, and rational approach to violence at a time at which, among our fellow citizens, calls for brute repression seem to receive far greater publicity. But this latter kind of violence, too, as Sartre has shown, has its own peculiar dialectical intelligibility.

What I have now said about the type of social theory that is contained in the *Critique* suggests one more capital point of contrast—a point that I mentioned at the beginning of this paper—between Sartre's social phenomenology and the opposed type of explanation that I have cited. It is that Sartre wishes always to refer us to the concrete situation in all its detail, whereas contrasting theories content themselves with explanatory concepts that are universally applicable. The "aggressive instincts" stressed by many such rival theories, for example, are thought to exist wherever the human and any of a number of other species are present; Sartre refuses to allow himself to rely on any psychological or sociological constants of this sort. In one short passage in the *Critique* he is quite explicit in labeling as "metaphorical" the "Gestaltist" attempt to find in the conjunction of certain types of groups, such as soldiers and workers under certain conditions, what comes to be called a "typically revolutionary" situation. Such allegedly typical relationships, he points out, are *"too universal* [and] must be specified in each case."* He goes on to say that, for dialectical reason as contrasted with what he calls "analytic reason," universality is usually a misleading appearance that requires to be dissolved in order to reach an understanding of the concrete situation—though there is, he admits, another sense in which universality can be said to be the final goal of the whole dialectical endeavor.[18] This heavy emphasis, within a highly abstract and general theory, on referring to the concrete and specific circumstances in order to render events intelligible naturally creates a considerable tension within that theory itself. There is at least one crucial point at which I wonder whether the tension may not become too overwhelming, with the result that Sartre has yielded, with unhappy consequences for his theory, to the temptation to fall back on a universal and non-human force as the basis of explanation. That is why I wish to consider the nature and role of *scarcity* in the first of my two sets of concluding critical comments.

III

Scarcity will be the focal point of my first set of critical considerations; some *ethical* implications of Sartre's theory will be the subject matter of the second set, which will be more appreciative and constructive than negatively critical. The following remarks will be rather impressionistic.

In giving material scarcity such a central place in his theory, Sartre has of course taken a major step toward *rapprochement* between his earlier philosophy and Marxism. Since Marxism is, whatever else may be said about it, a form of materialism and since Sartre inveighed against materialism while accepting many

18. *Critique de la raison dialectique,* 518–519.

of the ethical and political goals of Marxism, as recently as his
"Materialism and Revolution" (1946), the concept of scarcity
can be seen as a crucial theoretical bridge across which Sartre's
reconciliation with Marxist materialism was able to be achieved.
And yet, as Sartre himself acknowledges, Marx and Engels
seldom speak explicitly of scarcity, and when they do they
often seem not to accord it quite the place of centrality that
Sartre does. Sartre is, I think, essentially correct when he says
that "Marx . . . takes the thing for granted." [19] Furthermore,
Sartre points out, Marx optimistically believed not only that the
revolution was very near but also that the ensuing socialist
society would be able to absorb scarcity within itself and to
eliminate it. Of course, this has not happened; contemporary
societies that call themselves socialist are still undertaking, as
Sartre puts it, "the giant struggle . . . against scarcity." [20] Thus,
although he can give good reasons for the difference of emphasis
between himself and Marx and Engels on this point, Sartre
displays considerable uneasiness about it.

But I am not concerned here about how good or bad a
Marxist Sartre is; rather it is the use made of scarcity by Sartre
himself that troubles me. Scarcity, it will be remembered, is the
single most important key to Sartre's treatment of violence,
since he says that social violence *is* inhuman human behavior
considered as "scarcity interiorized" and since he has suggested
that social violence would no longer exist in a world without
scarcity. But it seems to me that Sartre has nowhere, throughout
his extremely lengthy *Critique*, come squarely to grips with the
fact, so readily recognized by Marx himself, that scarcity is a
highly relative concept.[21] I cannot, of course, conclusively prove

19. *Ibid.*, 220.
20. *Ibid.*, 221.
21. "The number and extent of [the labourer's] so-called necessary
wants, as also the modes of satisfying them, are themselves the product
of historical development, and depend therefore to a great extent on the
degree of civilisation of a country, more particularly on the conditions
under which, and consequently on the habits and degree of comfort in
which, the class of free labourers has been formed. In contradistinction
therefore to the case of other commodities, there enters into the determination of the value of labour-power a historical and moral element." Karl
Marx, *Capital*, I, Moscow, 1961, 171.

this contention of mine, but there is one simple phrase in *Search for a Method* that seems to me especially indicative of Sartre's problem. At the point at which he speaks of the impossibility of our foreseeing the form that the post-Marxist philosophy of freedom will take, he says that Marxism will have ceased to be relevant "as soon as there will exist for *everyone* a margin of *real* freedom beyond the production of life." [22] Contrary to many critics, I think that Sartre is usually a very clear, though complicated, reasoner; but the just-cited phrase concerning "a margin of *real* freedom beyond the production of life" strikes me, I am afraid, as being rather vague and rhetorical. How, in short, would we ever be able to recognize a state of affairs in which scarcity no longer existed? Though we might, at least for purposes of argument, concede Sartre's contention that we do not have the intellectual tools at present for adequately conceiving of the structure or the new philosophy of the possible future society of abundance, it seems to me essential that we should have the intellectual tools for recognizing its *approach*, if the concepts of scarcity and abundance are to have much theoretical usefulness. But the thus-far-published part of the *Critique* does not furnish us with such tools.

It would be rather superficial, no doubt, to conceive of social scarcity solely in terms of individual wants and their satisfaction or nonsatisfaction; moreover, to confine the concept of scarcity to this dimension would again be to make a *psychological* category determinative for all dialectical reason. We are all parts of what Sartre calls a "totalization in course"; we have intersubjective relationships with our fellowmen, and it is our interactions with them that are the stuff of history. Thus scarcity and abundance must be *social* categories, not intelligible if one limits oneself to the isolated analyses of individual cases. If this is so, then the fact that it is the students, coming primarily from middle-class families, who have been more active than any workers in recent social upheavals should not seem like the sort of practical refutation of a proletariat-oriented theory such

22. Sartre, *Search for a Method, loc. cit.*

as Sartre's that some critics have seen in it and that even
seems somewhat to concern Sartre in a brief published conversation between him and Cohn-Bendit.[23] It is obviously not of
capital importance whether the protesting individuals themselves come from penurious circumstances; the crucial fact,
rather, is the penury of the societies in which they live. But
this still throws us back on the question of what constitutes
a state of scarcity in a whole society. Perhaps one would want
to say—and I am sure that this is the case with Sartre [24]—that
scarcity in any part of the world affects the *praxis* of *all* of us, in
one way or another, today. Granted. But again, under what
circumstances, we want to know, would it ever be possible to
speak of an *end* to worldwide scarcity?

The point is that neither Sartre nor I nor, I think, most of
us would wish to define scarcity and its potential elimination
in purely quantitative terms—for example, the possession by
each individual of at least x dollars or their equivalent buying
power, calculated with 1960 as the base. That would be
grotesque. But what, then, is the qualitative alternative? To
speak of "a margin of *real* freedom" for all is not wrong, but
it leaves us most unsatisfied. I would suggest that, despite the
tremendous meticulousness of so much of Sartre's analysis in
the *Critique*, the central concept of scarcity constitutes such a
concession to intellectual indolence and to a type of theoretical
universalization that would treat concrete human events in
unspecific and nonhuman terms as to give it a role analogous
to the roles played by aggressive instincts, territorial imperatives,
and so on in the theories that I have contrasted with Sartre's.
Yes, a defender of the *Critique* might reply, but scarcity is
precisely what has been defined as the inhuman interiorized in
man, which manifests itself as social violence. But to leave
the definition at this level, I contend, is much too simple; for,

23. *Atlas,* 16, No. 1 (July 1968), trans., from *Die Zeit,* 22.

24. In a recent interview, Sartre seems to find the greatest hope in
the *international* character of recent student protests; he is very much
impressed by the students' worldwide solidarity. Cf. "Die Revolution
Kommt wieder nach Deutschland," interview with Jean-Paul Sartre, *Der
Spiegel,* 29/1968, 58–64, esp. p. 64.

as *Being and Nothingness* has established very clearly, judgments
as to the nonexistence of a quality such as scarcity are themselves the products of human *praxis*. Inert matter, considered
as such, is uniform and undifferentiated, but *praxis* is always
directed to a concrete, particular situation. Beyond the most
extreme cases in which immediate survival is at issue, judgments may differ. We can all concede that, because of the
special circumstances of a war, scarcity exists in its most blatant
and horrible form right now in Biafra. But how could it ever
be said to have ceased existing entirely? If every human being
were, at some time in the future, guaranteed the possibility of
living until the age of 120, but medical experimenters were able
at the same time to envisage a possible extension of this limit
to 150, would not the individuals of that era still, in a certain
very real sense, be living in a regime of scarcity? I think so.
And so the possibility of violence—of violence, let us say,
against some administration's refusal to allocate more resources
to medical technology—would surely remain. Well, then, is
a violence-free world truly conceivable at all, on Sartre's account or any other? Perhaps not. Judgment will have to be
suspended at least until our understanding of the meaning
of scarcity and its relationship with abundance and with freedom has undergone considerably more clarification.

Meanwhile the ideal of a scarcity-free world can stand—
like, perhaps, Sartre's conception of freedom itself in his earlier
writings—as a valuable limiting concept capable of guiding
ethical and political actions. Constant reference is made to
Socrates' concession, in the *Republic,* that the ideal may be
laid up in heaven and unattainable in this world; but far too
little attention is paid to his less poetic but equally important
remarks, in Book Five, to the effect that parts of his model
may still be useful to actual states that are unable to adapt the
whole. These remarks might well be applied to Sartre's conception of scarcity as the basis of violence, and it might serve
as a point of orientation for the ethical appraisal of social
violence in our own or any other time. This will be my
final consideration in the present paper.

Elsewhere I have written about the possibility of eliciting an ethical orientation from the *Critique*,[25] and I cannot repeat most of that here. I believe that the *Critique* provides a valuable complement to Sartre's earlier emphasis on individual freedom and authenticity and that the hints made in the *Critique* to a conceivable future society of freedom, of group *praxis* without constraint, and, of course, of abundance provide the outline for a systematic approach to ethical questions. The issue of a Sartrean ethic is complicated by his reported Marxist abandonment of ethics properly speaking (in 1949) as "a combination of idealistic tricks," [26] but I do not think that we have to enter into the intricacies of that particular problem at this point. All that I wish to emphasize here is not only that social violence is accepted by Sartre as a very central and logically explainable phenomenon of our world, but that the employment of violence as a means of bringing about a desirable future society simultaneously receives implicit justification within Sartre's theory. Simone de Beauvoir's *Ethics of Ambiguity* contains some particularly forceful expressions of this point.[27] Within the Sartrean universe there are no Camusean qualms about the approval of violence directed toward genuinely progressive social goals. In this regard, at least, it is in the spirit of Sartre, and not in that of the author of *The Rebel*, that the main forces of the New Left act today.

Nowadays the justification of overt social violence directed toward the achievement of a better society may rightly be condemned in many places as impractical and impolitic, and Sartre's expressions of solidarity with the May student revolutionaries in Paris had something of the ring of impracticality and self-deception to them. Political efficacy has never been Sartre's forte, and it may be that his treatment of violence in the *Critique* suffers from his frequent misapprehension of the

25. "Jean-Paul Sartre: Man, Freedom, and *Praxis*" in George A. Schrader, ed., *Existential Philosophers: Kierkegaard to Merleau-Ponty*, New York, 1967, pp. 261–329, esp. pp. 307–320.
26. Mentioned by Simone de Beauvoir in *La Force des choses*, Paris, 1963, p. 218.
27. Simone de Beauvoir, *Pour une morale de l'ambiguïté*, Paris, 1947, esp. pp. 139–166, "Les antinomies de l'action."

immediately, politically feasible. From a theoretical point of view, on the other hand, Sartre's own recent self-criticism in his interview with Cohn-Bendit suggests just the opposite failing —namely, a certain lack of imagination about the extent of the field of possibilities. Sartre is quoted as saying:

> What is interesting about your activities is that they put the imagination in power. To be sure, your imagination has limits, but you have many more ideas than your fathers had. We of the older generation were educated in such a way that we had only one notion of what was possible and what was not. I'd like to describe what you have done as extending the field of possibilities.[28]

In particular, Sartre's Marxist fixation on the proletariat as the necessary bearer of the brunt of revolutionary activities today, while perhaps not *entirely* misguided, may have led to a certain impoverishment in his view of the constructive possibilities of social violence, though this emphasis is not obtrusive in the *Critique* itself. Despite the experiences of last May, he still seems unwilling to abandon it.[29]

While one may have many reservations, therefore, about Sartre's abilities as a drawer of blueprints for fundamental social change and about the agents that he considers most likely to effect it, it seems to me that his acceptance and implicit theoretical statement of the justifiability of social violence under certain circumstances is, as hard as we may find it to admit, essentially sound. This is so despite the impression with which Sartre leaves us, to the effect that the regime of abundance and freedom which serves as the horizonal ideal toward which justifiable violence is ultimately directed may in historical reality be almost as unattainable as Plato's Republic itself.

I could never understand, and still cannot, how an absolute ethic of principled nonviolence could be built on the onto-logical discovery of the contingency or the "absurdity" of our universe. Sartre, especially in his later writings, has turned from the narcissistic contemplation of the absurdity of our condition, an attitude that colors at least some parts of his earlier works,

28. In *Atlas, loc. cit.*
29. Cf. interview in *Der Spiegel, op. cit.*, p. 60.

312 William Leon McBride

to the attempt to elaborate an understanding of human society that at least leaves open the possibility of developing a positive, future-oriented social ethic, even if he himself refuses explicitly to do this.[30] In the course of enriching that understanding, he has discovered violence everywhere in our world, and it is therefore no surprise if one can extract from his descriptions no injunction against the employment of overt violence, in particular circumstances, to oppose the overt or covert counterviolence of the various forces of reaction. On the other hand, there is not in Sartre the same romantic glorification of violence for its own sake that characterizes the mediocre philosophic efforts of one of the few earlier thinkers to have concentrated on the problem, Sorel, or that has even given some unfortunate discoloring to the more astute treatment of the subject by the late Frantz Fanon (a treatment that was prefaced, significantly enough, by Sartre himself).[31] The phrase an "ethic of violence" has a harsh ring to it. Yet philosophers today must deal with such problems instead of pretending that they do not exist, for, in the famous epigram of Maurice Merleau-Ponty, "We do not have the choice between purity and violence, but between different sorts of violence." [32] And Sartre's work provides a more promising beginning of such an ethic than does, for example, that either of the protofascists or of the integral pacifists who have turned their attention to it.

In conclusion, however, we as individuals and as philosophers may judge particular manifestations of social violence in this present period of our history—when, as always in the past, reaction seems intent on wreaking its revenge on hope—we can at least be grateful to Sartre for having dared to deal with

30. As Francis Jeanson, one of the best interpreters of the early Sartrean treatment of ethics, says in his 1965 Postface to the new edition of his study: "I know: [Sartre] has also said that he had wanted 'to make an ethics' and that he no longer dreamt of it. But I, for my part, am definitely of the opinion that he still dreams of it. . . . " *Le problème moral et la pensée de Sartre,* Paris, 1965, p. 346.

31. *The Wretched of the Earth,* trans. Constance Farrington, New York, 1966.

32. Maurice Merleau-Ponty, *Humanisme et Terreur,* Paris, 1947, p. 117.

and to clarify the bitter social realities which even the first half of this century, despite all its wars and turmoil, failed to unmask fully for us in the West. After the bourgeois optimism in which we all, even through the Depression, down through my own, younger generation, were raised, Sartre comes to present us with the truth of our times, the truth of the pervasiveness of social violence, in the light of which a nonrepressive or classless society, or one in which group *praxis* might prevail forever, seems only a very distant, though certainly very useful, ideal.

Zygmunt Adamczewski

KANT'S EXISTENTIAL THOUGHT

Of many conquests achieved in the *Critique of Pure Reason*, not the least is Kant's decisive stand on the question of existence. Without it, existential thought beginning with Kierkegaard could not have emerged, whatever its inspiration antedating Kant. The purpose of this essay is to clarify an understanding of Kant's thought about existence, interpreting it only as it appears in demand. Understanding any thought is surely prior to all legitimate criticism of it.

For this purpose it will be necessary to correlate Kant's main statement on existence in the last chapter of the "Transcendental Dialectic" with other relevant statements. References in English will be to Norman Kemp Smith's translation, but it will also be advisable in some cases to refer to the original German. The only basic notion to be introduced, other than Kant's own, will be the traditional contrast between existence and essence: while the assertion of the former claims that something is, the description of the latter states what or how it can or must be.

The well-known main statement occurs in the section which demonstrates the invalidity of the "ontological" argument for the existence of God. This essay is not concerned with that demonstration. Let it simply be remarked in passing that the invalidity is more easily seen if the argument is understood in Heidegger's terms as not "ontological" but "ontic," as dealing not with being as such but with the existence of some determinate being or something. Thus:

> the existence of this thing can never be represented by me as absolutely necessary. . . . I cannot think any particular thing as in itself necessary. (A 615–B 643)

Two further preliminary remarks are due. First, when in a crucial passage Kant's text has the word "being" instead of "existence," its immediate application in the context is, in accordance with the reflections just quoted, to the existence of some entity. But his reason for the verbal noun, or infinitive, "to be" quite apparently lies in the wider consideration of the sense of the word "is" in thought. Second, whether or not his text is ambiguous, contemporary readers sensitive to the distinction between use and mention of words may miss the indication—as by use of quotation marks some of which are supplied by the translator—when Kant thinks of words and when of what they signify; but this difference need not be obliterated in his thought.

The discussion of the "ontological" argument, although ostensibly devoted to the existence of the most real among beings, consists largely of statements about existence of beings or widely understood things in general. It contains three successive and connected stages (beginning A 593–B 621, A 596–B 624, A 598–B 626).

In the first stage, considering the relation of existence to necessity, Kant contrasts things to concepts and judgments or propositions. The latter can indeed be characterized by necessity in the way they are confronted by the human mind, and the logical guidance to such necessity consists in the avoidance of contradiction. But this has no sufficient bearing upon the existence of things to which judgments and concepts relate.

> If, in an identical proposition, I reject the predicate while . . . if I take the concept of anything, no matter what, I find that retaining the subject, contradiction results; and I therefore say that the former belongs necessarily to the latter. But if we reject subject and predicate alike, there is no contradiction; for nothing is then left that can be contradicted. To posit a triangle, and yet to reject its three angles, is self-contradictory; but there

is no contradiction in rejecting the triangle together with its three angles. The same holds true of the concept of an absolutely necessary being. If its existence is rejected, we reject the thing itself with all its predicates; and no question of contradiction can then arise. (A 594/5–B 622/3).

To postpone for the time being the weight of the important word "posit," the following points result from this passage. To undertake geometrical thinking at all, it is necessary to comply with logical requirements: a triangle may not be conceived as nontriangular. But geometry can be undertaken with no existential commitment: as a Platonist I can assert that there are triangles; as an anti-Platonist I can reject their existence and think only of what they would have to be if they existed. The geometrical doctrine need not be affected by my attitude in either case. The laws of logic are existentially relevant only up to a point: I am indeed unable to assert the existence of a square triangle—but noncontradiction is only a necessary and not a sufficient condition for my asserting any existence, and, further, to say that what I am unable to assert does not exist is to commit myself to an ontological principle which is by no means compelling. This holds quite generally: to think of a unicorn that would have no horn and of a lion that would not be a cat contravenes the logical demands in the same way, although lions exist and unicorns do not. Logic, as Kant often says, abstracts from the object, which means here, from its existence.

Necessity, then, can emerge in conceiving and combining concepts to form judgments. The contemporary formulation of it says: if anything is—or were—such-and-such, then it must be so-and-so. And this formulation shows clearly that such necessity pertains not to existence but only to the essence of things as the mind thinks of them. Essential thinking, however, is not always bound by necessity: e.g., thinking of a lion which could be blue or of a unicorn with a transparent body involves only possibility. In the former relation of essences, thought is logically constrained; in the latter it is imaginatively spontaneous, at the risk of vacuity. But the factor common to both is that thinking of essence—necessary or possible—is a happening of the mind:

what man must or what man can think. This is distinguishable from the question of what exists. Thus Kant, opposing the trend of Leibniz, also issues a "warning against arguing directly from the logical possibility of concepts to the real possibility of things." (A 596–B 624 footnote)

The point about asserting and rejecting may be now developed this way: existence is not arrived at by thought. To cite a seeming counter-example, asserting the existence of a new planet as end result of a complex mental calculation: it will be acknowledged on reflection that this result is not reached by thought alone but relies on data of what Kant calls "empirical intuition." Implicitly at least, essential philosophy was deserted before Kant with the rise of empirical science, which rebelled against just thinking with the maxim: Go and look! By data gathered in going and looking, lions are found but not unicorns. But if thought by itself does not reach existence, how does it relate to it? The alternative is that thought must start with existence. In order to proceed it has to entertain something as hypothetically existing, thus: suppose that there is a triangle, a lion, a unicorn, then . . . Such mental entertaining or supposing has led to confusion involving the existence of mental entities, e.g., as between God and the idea of God; the text under discussion has been written partly to remove such confusion. The conceiving and rejecting, as of a triangle, i.e., of the subject with its predicates, may be understood as undertaken by the mind thinking as it can or as it must. So arises the question concerning Kant's word "posit"; it will be explored in the context of the third stage of his statement.

In the second stage Kant turns more specifically to the argument about God as *ens realissimum*, which contains by definition the maximum of any reality, including, allegedly, existence. If this were so, then what is claimed as proof would amount to "but a miserable tautology": the most real being—*qua* real—exists. But Kant by no means grants any such analytic inclusion. Of general import is the contrast he introduces here between reality and existence or, in the present context, actuality. This may not be directly appreciated in translation and requires explanation because in English, also in philosophical English,

the words "reality" and "existence" are not infrequently used
as synonyms.

> The word "reality," which in the concept of the thing sounds
> other than the word "existence" in the concept of the predicate,
> is of no avail . . . for if all positing (no matter what it may be
> that is posited) is entitled reality, the thing with all its predicates
> is already posited in the concept of the subject, and is assumed
> as actual; and in the predicate this is merely repeated. But . . .
> all existential propositions are synthetic. (A 597–B 625)

Connected with this should be the following sentence:

> If we think in a thing every feature of reality except one, the
> missing reality is not added by my saying that this defective
> thing exists. (A 600–B 628)

Once more there is a mention of "positing" which can pro-
visionally be taken as at least entertaining or supposing something in thought, e.g., that there is a triangle or an *ens
realissimum;* I shall comment further on it later. Now, in the
last sentence quoted Kant clearly denies that the word "existence" can be used as a substitute for any kind or "feature of
reality." And before that he says that something posited is
assumed as actual. The sentence begins conditionally, stressing
"if" all positing is entitled reality—that antecedent he does not
admit as correct, but regardless of it he asserts the consequent
about actuality. Perhaps his intent can be made clearer if these
clauses—significantly in the second person—are here retrans-
lated more literally, with parenthetical emphasis supplied: "For
if, at that, you call all positing reality (which I would not do),
then ('I believe you should notice) you have the thing posited
already and assumed as actual." What should transpire from
this elaboration is that in Kant's thought "reality" must not be
taken as equivalent to "actuality," or to "existence." The relation
of the latter two terms will be brought out in later discussion.
At this moment, especially in view of the English usage, the
question arises: what, then, does Kant mean by "reality"?

That word so common in ordinary and philosophical English,
"reality," has an equally common equivalent in German, *Wirklichkeit.* Yet this term is in the *Critique* translated as "actuality"

—and rightly. Because Kant himself departs from ordinary usage, introducing a less common word from Latin, *Realität:* it is this word that is now being considered. It will be easily remembered that the Latin noun *realitas* derives from the simpler *res* meaning thing, object, matter (*res publica* is a public matter). Reality, then, in Kant's intended use would seem to be understandable as, roughly, "thingness" or "somethingness." But philosophically this will not quite do, because through a long historical tradition originating in Aristotle particular "things" such as stones, trees, houses have been regarded as relatively independent, self-contained bearers of qualities or attributes, viz., "substances." And this is precisely what Kant, aware of the tradition, avoids in his use of the word *Realität*. Rather, his thinking moves even farther back in history, to Plato's ontological viewpoint which sees the reality of anything in this world as what it essentially consists of, what Ideas it participates in: the reality of a stone is nothing but its general qualities such as shape, hardness, weight, heat, color. In this view reality is tied to what an object is (*quid*) or what it is like (*quale*), and amounts to quiddity or quality.

To show that this is how Kant thinks about reality, it might be sufficient to recall that the term *Realität* is listed in his table of categories under the heading of "quality." An even more convincing reference is available. Sensations, according to Kant, provide the matter or content of appearances as man empirically encounters them; thus experience alone brings them forth—i.e., they are unpredictable *a priori*. And yet an aspect of empirical consciousness or perception can be anticipated, in the second type of "Principles of Pure Understanding." In that section Kant speaks of appearances containing "the matter for some object in general"; this may be noted as unlike the particularity of a thing or substance. The principle of the anticipations alludes to "sensation, and the REAL which corresponds to it in the object." (A 166) There is significance in the "and" which cannot be discussed here; but attention must be called to the "in," signifying that the real is not identical with the object, general or particular, but belongs to, or inheres in, it. And the text is even more unequivocal:

> Between reality and negation there is a continuity of possible
> realities and of possible smaller perceptions. Every colour, as
> for instance red, has a degree which, however small it may be,
> is never the smallest; and so with heat, the moment of gravity,
> etc. (A 169–B 211)

The instances of reality Kant cites are none other but instantiations of Platonic Ideas such as weight, heat, color. These are
not things as substances but what things possess or are characterized by. To clinch the point, this is how the section concludes:
". . . in all quality (the real in appearances) we can know A
PRIORI nothing save . . . that they have degree. Everything else
has to be left to experience." (A 176–B 218) The parenthesis
equates "the real" with "quality"; the preceding quotation gave
qualities as kinds of reality. And while no particular thing's
experience can be anticipated, man knows *a priori* of what
in general all his experience consists. The result is adequately
clear. In Kant's terms, "reality" (*Realität* but not *Wirklichkeit*)
means quality; it can be explicitly rendered as "whatness" or
"somewhatness" that gives determinable character to things
as substances. In strict accordance with Plato—and with reference to what was said at the outset of this essay—when Kant
speaks of reality, he describes or determines essence. It should
no longer be surprising that he strenuously objects to any
inference from it to existence. To connect with the first stage:
the conceiving and correlating, now also the comparing in
degree, the conjoining toward a maximum, of any essences or
realities belong to the power and discipline of man's mind.
This is not so with existence.

In the third and final stage of his main statement about
existence Kant, having prepared the ground, comes to establish
it in terms of "positing," which is contrasted with "determining."
All sorts of misunderstanding have arisen in the reading of this
text; it will therefore be better to consider it in parts.

> . . . the confusion of a logical with a real predicate (that is,
> with a predicate which determines a thing) is almost beyond
> correction. Anything we please can be made to serve as a logical
> predicate; the subject can even be predicated of itself; for logic
> abstracts from all content. But a DETERMINING predicate is a

predicate which is added to the concept of the subject and enlarges it. Consequently, it must not be already contained in the concept. (A 598–B 626)

The following points emerge: First, the passage deals at least primarily with words and their use in judgments. About words, all words grammatically suitable—to exclude, if someone insists, e.g., conjunctions—Kant says: any of them can serve as logical predicates, even, rather vacuously, those which are subjects. To rephrase: "serving as logical predicate" is a potentiality or a dispositional property of words in human use. Second, if this is so with all words—as qualified—then the relation of potential logical to any other predicates is not that of two different classes but of a main class and its subclass, nothing being said about any other subclass. According to the text's parenthesis, a "real predicate" and a "determining predicate" are synonyms. Such predicates then can form a subclass of logical ones. Third, if words' service as logical predicates is a matter of their potential use, so is their service as determining predicates. This must be noted in view of their functioning as explained by Kant, viz., of essentially enlarging the meaning of the subject. No predicates are absolutely and forever determining; e.g., "round" can very significantly serve as enlarging knowledge of what something is like in "The earth is round," but it does not so serve in "The sphere is round" because a "sphere" is not meaningful unless understood as round. It serves there, say, as analyzing or explicating the essence of the subject, and such an analytic function could thus be a basis for forming another subclass of all predicates that can be used as logical ones; note, however, that Kant calls existential propositions not "analytic" but "synthetic." And last, if someone should object that no predicate —*qua* word—can literally be "added to the concept of the subject," let it be hoped that this rephrasing will do: a determining predicate is a word used so that its meaning adds to and enlarges the meaning of the word used as subject of the given proposition. This was the reason for saying above that the passage quoted dealt with words at least primarily, i.e., with words considered as meaningful in reference to using them in propositions, hence conceiving and understanding them. Such a consideration should be kept in mind with regard to the sense of the central part now to be quoted:

> "BEING" is obviously not a real predicate; that is, it is not a concept of something which could be added to the concept of a thing. It is merely the positing of a thing, or of certain determinations, as existing in themselves. Logically, it is merely the copula of a judgment. (A 598–B 626)

Three sentences only, but with much weight—and much misunderstanding having been read into them. First of all, some linguistic comments are due. In the first sentence, as remarked at the beginning, the German word *Sein* is both verbal noun and infinitive; and for various reasons many readers might prefer its text to start: "TO BE is obviously . . ." (Kant has no quotation marks). In the second sentence, which will have to be looked at again, the word *bloss,* translated as "merely," can also be rendered as "only, exclusively, purely, simply, clearly" and need not be taken, as it has been, in a derogatory sense; a different word, *lediglich,* in the third sentence is a more unequivocal "merely." And in that third sentence the translation "logically" is not quite adequate to the literal German: "in logical use." These points concerning words of the text are not irrelevant to the understanding of it.

The first and worst misreading, that has unfortunately spread wide, claims: "being" is no predicate, none at all, no possible one. It is a genuine enigma how thoughtful and acute readers could have fallen prey to it. The immediately preceding sentences of Kant tell what he means by "real" or "determining" predicates; and now, as plain as day, his words are: "to be" is not a real predicate. The continuation of the paragraph, still to be cited here, may cause some perplexity about "is" and predication, but surely not as much as to dismiss forcibly the word "real" that Kant takes pains to explain. However, this has been elaborated above and Kant's intention is clear: "is" by itself cannot be used as a word so as to enlarge the meaning of the proposition's subject. It can, as all grammatically suitable words can—and it is eminently so—"be made to serve as a logical predicate." But here emerges a second, less glaring misunderstanding. Does

Kant say that it must so serve? Not at all. Yet some say, "being" is just a logical predicate, "merely the copula." Here the translation's ellipsis in the third sentence is relevant. The original text reads: "in logical use it is merely the copula of a judgment." The logical use of words is potential, not exhaustive, by no means compulsory; it is sometimes empty and sometimes puzzling. Hardly anyone would preempt the word "rose" for logical use, being able to say, "a rose is a rose"—a subject predicable of itself, to recall Kant's own allusion. Therefore, while granting that "to be" can, and abundantly does, serve as a copula for logical use, it is necessary to reflect on the middle sentence: "to be" is purely. the positing. . . . Unfortunately, this is not quite a "pure" thought. Kant's hope is not so easy to share.

The difficulties are partly terminological, even semantic; they have to be faced. From the foregoing clarification, this result at least may be affirmed: Kant distinguishes, speaking of words, between determining and positing. Earlier it was pointed out that words as such are not absolutely and forever determining but can on some occasions be used to fulfill the determining function; now it appears that the word "to be" is absolutely and forever disqualified from that function, not ever a real predicate. The distinction is for this word quite sharp. It may also be said that positing need not at all be equivalent to a word's service in logical use. Kant ties the word "is" to positing without restriction, then adds that it can serve as copula in logical use—which is thus restricted only to some, even though very many, occasions. But the next step, while tempting, is rather risky: to say that as Kant earlier spoke of a logical predicate and of a real or determining predicate, so now he introduces a third type—a positing predicate. There are two reasons for caution here. One, that in his further text the relation of positing and predication is not entirely clear; and two, more importantly, that the question can be raised: why can the word "is" never determine? The first sentence continues: "it is not a concept of something which could be added to the concept of a thing." Why? In the examination of the first stage of the whole Kantian statement it was said: thought does not reach existence but rather must start from it. Such understanding of Kant agrees well with his present denial that "it" could ever be added to the concept in thought. But—as even the reading of the last cited clause suggests—this makes questionable whether Kant is still dealing with words primarily. Existence with which thought starts, and which it cannot add to the concept, is not the word "existence" or "to be." If it were a matter of words, obviously thinking could start with and add any of them. On the other hand, if positing were understood as putting forward, introducing, almost creating by fiat, it would not do for existence of anything other than myself: such positing of a unicorn could not make it exist. Thus the question whether it is legitimate to speak of a positing predicate relates to this: to what extent are Kant's three central sentences concerned with words?

To answer "exclusively" or "not at all" is in either case extreme and implausible. To avoid such extremes, this paraphrase of the central part may be offered: when something is posited, a form of the word "to be" is used, a word suitable for logical predication as copula in judgments but not suitable for real or determining predication which could add to conceptual meaning. It should be noted that this paraphrase does not assert a synonymy between "to posit" and "to use the word 'to be,'" only their concurrence. But, someone may ask, does not the text read: it (being) is the positing? The translation reads so, admittedly; it also supplies the quotation marks around "being," absent in the original. This absence, provoking contemporary readers as only a semantic inadequacy, may, however, also be significant for the understanding of Kant's thought. Kant may have thought here on two levels and expressed them simultaneously, which no doubt contributed to the difficulty of understanding. One, he said, as paraphrased above: we use the word "to be" when we posit; and this is a metalinguistic statement. But two—and this must be a metaphysical or ontological statement—he could have wished to say, having none of the hostility against such statements that his readers might have: being is position. For a reason to be explained later, the form "position" is employed rather than "positing." This is quite faithful to the German text, which contains the word *Position,* elsewhere clearly taken by Kant as equivalent

to *Setzen* (or *Setzung*) and reminiscent of the Greek *thesis*.
I shall not explore the weight of such a statement at this
point; nor is the status of the word "posit" clear as yet. With
this in mind, it is now proper to consider the subsequent text,
the last part of Kant's main section dealing with existence. The
sentences which immediately follow those already quoted can
corroborate the trend of the foregoing discussion:

> The proposition "God is omnipotent" contains two concepts,
> each of which has its object—God and omnipotence. The small
> word "is" adds no new predicate, but only serves to posit the
> predicate IN ITS RELATION to the subject. If, now, we take the
> subject (God) with all its predicates (among which is omnip-
> otence), and say "God is," or "There is a God," we attach no
> new predicate to the concept of God, but only posit the subject
> in itself with all its predicates, and indeed posit it as being
> an OBJECT that stands in relation to my CONCEPT. The content of
> both must be one and the same; nothing can have been added
> to the concept, which expresses merely what is possible, by my
> thinking its object (through the expression "it is") as given
> absolutely. Otherwise stated, the real contains no more than the
> merely possible. A hundred real thalers do not contain the least
> coin more than a hundred possible thalers. . . . By whatever
> and by however many predicates we may think a thing—even
> if we completely determine it—we do not make the least addi-
> tion to the thing when we further declare that this thing is.
> (A 598/600–B 626/628)

In the remainder of the section there are still expressions
relevant to the present examination, but the general Kantian
statement on existence is here completed. One marginal linguistic
remark: the word "absolutely" above has no special application, is not even there in German—*schlechthin gegeben* means
just simply given, given indeed.

The above text can perplex readers, mainly because Kant
deals in it partly with the use of words, viz., the subject-
predicate relation in judgments, and partly with something
quite different, e.g., the subject-object relation in thought.
Here is the probable cause of the bad confusion claiming that
"being" is no predicate, and perhaps of the misreading: "being"
is only a logical predicate. The latter can be easily corrected:
"God is omnipotent" has as its subject-term the word "God,"

of which logically predicated is the term "omnipotent" by means of the copula. The copula thus is not the logical predicate; this is sufficiently clear. In the other case, "God is" has no copula as such; hence, recalling that "in logical use 'to be' is merely the copula," it can be concluded that this is no logical use because no term is logically predicated by means of a copula. Alternatively, reading this as "God is existent," it can be said that the word "existent" serves here as logical predicate—as all grammatically suitable words can—but still not the copula. Whether existential assertions do or do not belong to "logical use," in either case "being" need not be a logical predicate. On the other hand, readers might have been misled into saying that "being" is no predicate at all by the twice-occurring phrase "no new predicate." Yet to reflect on this—once Kant says: "is" adds no new predicate but relates the available predicate "omnipotent" to the subject; and then he says: in "God is" we attach no new predicate to the concept of God. Surely his word "new" must be intended for the denial of any novelty in our conceiving of the proposition's subject "God," i.e., of its enlarging? Implicitly Kant here only repeats that "to be" cannot fulfill a determining function, is not a real predicate, adds nothing to the quality or essence of whatever is conceived. The last sentence in the quotation is quite decisive: "however many predicates," let us say all of them, can "completely determine" something; Kant is here clearly considering predicates as determining ones. Once more, in this sentence "determining" refers to knowledge of what a thing is like; by hypothesis, when our mind is in complete possession of the thing's whatness, reality, quality, we can still "further declare" that it is. Existence remains outside the most complete listing of qualities or essences. If, and only if, all predicates were always considered as determining or essential, "to exist" or "to be" would not be one of them.

One other correlation can be pointed out, with an important correction of the translation. In the famous illustrative allusion to the hundred thalers, the differentiating word in German is *wirklich*, which certainly should have been translated as "actual." Also in the preceding principle, the original reads: "The actual contains no more than the purely (*bloss*) possible." This is quite important because, as the English translation stands, it makes no sense in view of the preceding explanations of Kant's use of "reality." For him the real is the possible, even the "purely" possible, in the sense of what the human mind can and must deal with purely, i.e., nonempirically. Existence is not so "pure." The principle can be expanded: the actual contains no more essence than the possible which is somewhat to the mind, somehow qualitatively real. Essentially, a hundred actual thalers are no different than a hundred possible thalers: existentially they are poles apart, in the relation of something to nothing.

Into this difference enters the question of the Kantian word "posit." The last quoted passage has three occurrences of it: "posit the predicate" in relation to the subject, "posit the subject" with all predicates, and "posit it as being an OBJECT that stands in relation to my CONCEPT." Instead of the latter two, in Kant's original sentence structure there is only one occurrence. This shows clearly that there Kant considers one case alone: to posit the subject with predicates is to posit an object for my concept. In the previous occurrence he considers the predicate posited relatively to the subject. This is secondary, almost metaphorical, because it means that the subject must have been posited already when in relation to it (italicized by Kant) the predicate is posited. Understandably if not literally, the translator alludes to the primary positing in thought as absolute. The two cases, then—positing the predicate as secondary, the subject as primary—differ in "logical use," in the role words play in a proposition; and logicians today may argue about this difference. But to understand what Kant means by "positing" as such, it is more important to concentrate on his latter identification. Described logically, it is positing the subject for a judgment of proposition (*Satz*, in German very close to *setzen*—"posit"). The same is described in a way other than logical, viz., as positing an object for my concept, my thought. It would seem that "position" yields "proposition": I must posit, i.e., think something (*setzen*), in order to have it capable of logical analysis in the form of subject-predicate (*Satz*). This confirms the secondary and relative importance assigned to the subject's predicate. Primary is my thinking or conceiving of anything whatsoever: a God, a triangle, a unicorn. But in this context Kant says that my concept "expresses merely (purely) what is possible"; it concerns a thinkable somewhat, in his sense real. This was earlier alluded to in this essay as mentally supposing. A proposition about a unicorn is surely but a supposition; to undertake it no one need posit anything as an existent object. Such "position" must attain more and in that sense come after a mere "proposition." The interrelations are complex, but they show that it would be wrong to equate positing and mentally entertaining or conceiving. In previously introduced terms, this can be said: in a sense legitimate but not sufficient for Kant, "position" of a mental entity as the inception of thinking enterprise is logically prior to "proposition" as its explicit development—this is so with regard to any essence the human mind may contemplate or manipulate. In contrast to that, Kant understands "position" with regard to existence, to an "object" for a concept, about which more than one "proposition" may be already available, if not posterior to, it is more than what lies in the domain of essential thought. Yet this relation is not logical but ontological. The contrast is between something dependent on the mind, in Kant's terms "subjective," e.g., the idea of God—and a being independent of the mind's control and thus "objective," e.g., God. This contrast is not logical, if logic regulates thought by laws of identity and contradiction, because "the content of both must be one and the same": i.e., the concept and its object are identical as far as thought is concerned.

Still, in that sentence Kant alludes to "my thinking its object as given." This link between "thinking" and "given" may be a not uncommon instance of Kant's vague usage of words, in view of the statement binding the whole critical doctrine: "Objects are GIVEN to us by means of sensibility . . . thought must . . . relate ultimately . . . with us, to sensibility, because in no other way can an object be given to us." (A 19–B 33) But for that matter, the above interrelations are also vague as yet. With regard to existence, what Kant condemns is more definite than what he affirms. It is necessary to ask further:

What is the relation between positing and predicating? How far is positing of existence a happening of the mind? Where in the conceiving of existence shall fit its pure, categorical conceiving? What modes of being can and must be posited? And thus: how does Kant's thought stand with regard to ontology?

In order to explore these questions, it will be proper now to retain the insights gained in the section on the "ontological proof," and so armed to move on to some other decisive points of the *Critique*. Three separate directions will be pursued in strict connection with Kant's thought about existence. These will be three instantiations of what Kant's thought implicitly requires to be posited; not explicitly, though, because the word "posit" is not much used by him outside of the main section examined already.

This is not a serious handicap. Thus, in spite of missing the word, hardly any reader of the *Critique* can deny that if any existence is to be posited in Kant's sense it is that of appearances, objects of possible experience, or phenomenal objects. The phrases just used are meant as synonymous references to the same mode of being; any doubts of such synonymy are not in scope of this essay. The existence of phenomenal objects is most unambiguously asserted by Kant; it is also that existence about which most can be known by man.

Knowledge of existing objects as appearances is due to the fact that they can be not only posited but also determined. Man knows about their existence and their essence: that they are and what they are. The former is here of direct interest, but it must be seen in relation to the latter. If existence is to be held apart from determination, as the main statement emphatically asserted, a difficulty arises on recalling that "existence" is a word listed in the Table of Categories, naming one of modality (A 80–B 106), because it may be argued generally that pure concepts or categories are for Kant ways of determining objects of possible experience. It might have been better if Kant had not listed that word there, but the confusion possibly resulting is not irremediable. His listing amounts to saying that man must think of existence and is intellectually equipped to experience it. Does it also imply that "existence" is a determining predicate in the sense explained, viz., of enlarging a concept? Certainly not:

> The categories of modality have this peculiarity that, in determining an object, they do not in the least enlarge the concept to which they are attached as predicates. . . . No additional determinations are thereby thought in the object itself; the question is only how the object, together with all its determinations, is related to understanding. (A 219–B 266)

Not only does this statement agree with the others in denying the "enlargement" of the concept; it also confirms that not all predicates are determining: words used for modal categories, i.a., "existence," are predicates but provide "no additional determination." If someone objects to the phrase "categories . . . in determining an object," let him blame the translation; the original reads: "The categories of modality are as such peculiar in that they do not in the least enlarge the concept, as determination of the object, to which they are attached as predicates. . . ."

Next, it should be remembered that no categories as such are sufficient for determining objects; this may have been forgotten by readers who avoid the difficult but important chapter on schematism, which concludes:

> The schemata of the pure concepts of understanding are thus the true and sole conditions under which these concepts obtain relation to objects and so possess SIGNIFICANCE. . . . The categories, therefore, without schemata, are merely functions of the understanding for concepts; and represent no object. (A 146/7– B 185/7)

To connect this with earlier discussion: the use of pure concepts is a happening of the mind, pertains to its potency and discipline but is "formal" only; categories are "nothing but FORMS OF THOUGHT, which contain the merely logical faculty." (B 305) It appears legitimate to connect them with the "logical use" of words and with logical predicates but not yet with those which can determine objects. Even if Kant lists "existence" among them, this use of the word is far removed from positing, perhaps a kind of formal basis for it. But what is of prime weight in the schematizing of pure concepts? To stress only the main link of relevance: the distance of nonhomogeneity between the mind's formal category and, on the other hand, the concrete object of experience must be bridged by some third intermediary, which Kant finds in time. The point is that only when a category is thought of as temporal does it become referentially significant. With that in mind, it is possible to appreciate this interesting statement:

"The schema of actuality is existence in some determinate time." (A 145–B 184) First, the name of the category is here, perhaps preferably, "actuality." Second, "actuality" and "existence" are not strict synonyms if the latter enters into the schematizing of the former. Third, existence is not here completely circumscribed, because, e.g., the next listed schema of necessity alludes to existence "at all times." Fourth, in contrast, the immediately preceding schema of possibility contains in its description no mention of "existence"; this accords well with the earlier discussed correlation of possibility with essential thinking only, illustrated with the "hundred possible thalers." Fifth, if the question is raised, what enables the category here to relate to an object?, the answer is: not existence but time. It is always the schema that makes any category significant, and "the schema of modality and of its categories is time itself." (A 145–B 184) Although Kant's phrase speaks of existence in "some determinate time," this appears equivalent to "some particular time"': as ostensibly available, time renders the category applicable or schematizes it; problems with necessity of existence in the "ontological proof" can be linked with the fact that "all times" are not available to man. And the part of existence in the thought of this regrettably brief statement? It is, to amplify, existence of an object in appearance—only such can be in question for categories. The existence of such an object provides the datum in time without which a category has nothing to apply to. Explaining when, to which data of experience causality becomes relevant, Kant says: "The object is THAT in the appearance which contains the condition of this necessary rule of apprehension" (A 191–B 236), i.e., the condition of the necessary application of the category as schematized. Existence alone does not make categories applicable; schematized categories can apply to, and determine, existing objects as to what they are.

But asking whether existence is or is not a category, how it is related to actuality, and how positing is to be understood in regard to phenomenal objects can only be further clarified by reference to the Postulates of Empirical Thought, specifically the second one. It states:

> That which is bound up with the material conditions of experience, that is, with sensation, is ACTUAL. (A 218–B 266)

And its exposition contains remarks most clearly anticipating the later main statement about existence:

> In the MERE CONCEPT of a thing no mark of its existence is to be found. For though it may be so complete that nothing which is required for thinking the thing with all its inner determinations is lacking to it, yet existence has nothing to do with all this. . . . Our knowledge of the existence of things reaches, then, only so far as perception and its advance according to empirical laws can extend. (A 225/6–B 272/3).

The last sentence definitely circumscribes the field of objects of possible experience; it will be considered further. The preceding two can be paraphrased: existence has nothing to do with concepts referred to by all determining predicates, nor even with the pure concept of actuality or, if someone insists, of existence. Paradoxical as this sounds, existence is here thought of by Kant in terms of positing, and that, as observed already, is unlike the use of a category. If this is so, what does the postulate mean? It postulates "material" conditions of experience; these complement the "formal" ones, i.e., those contributed by the mind, such as the categories, even schematized—since the intermediary of schematism, time, is also a form of intuition. The material conditions in sensations are those which cannot be anticipated except for their general "reality" or "somewhat-ness," as shown earlier. Any particular something as object of sensation affects the mind's receptivity as it comes forth; it is not mind-made. Once more, "reality" must not be taken as synonymous with "actuality"; yet in this situation they happen to coincide: the appearance must generally share in reality, be somewhat, of some kind—and if given to sensibility "in some determinate time" is something actual. The three postulates, Kant says, explain the categories of modality "in their empirical employment," or more literally "in their empirical use." (A 219–B 266) The phrase is parallel to and distinct from "in logical use." It warrants this interpretation: "actual" does not serve here simply as a logical predicate but as an empirical one; this empirical predicate is not used to determine the object—this is explicitly denied by Kant—and "determining" is the same as "real" predicate, i.e., it pertains to reality or essence. How, then, is the word "actual" empirically used here? The answer is not in the text and therefore must be cautious: it is only reasonable to connect this use with positing—if any positing occurs at all—but it need not be claimed that "to posit" is a synonym for "to predicate actuality." That would be quite inadvisable, if earlier positing was correlated with "to be" or "to exist" and in the statement of schematism "existence" and "actuality" were seen as nonsynonymous.

The situation with which the second postulate is concerned clearly yields empirical knowledge which is also "knowledge of the existence of things"; known here is both what a thing is, i.e., its essence or reality, and that it is, i.e., existence. There are two corollaries to this. First, the use of the word "actuality" is restricted by Kant to refer to existence which is knowable, in his sense of what knowledge amounts to. Second, throughout the *Critique* knowledge is taken by Kant as attainable only if the mind is active—although not all activity of the mind yields knowledge; positing, therefore, should be understood as an act of the mind, which may or may not be verbalized. Positing of existence is more than just mentally supposing; when this act of the mind occurs in awareness affected by something materially or sensibly given, it yields knowledge and its verbal expression consists in predicating actuality. Needless to say, such predicating concerns only objects of possible experience, and so actuality is a category applicable to determinately real objects. But the sense of "existence" is certainly not exhausted here: "to be" may be used not of determinately real and knowable objects.

It is therefore better to leave still open the question how properly existence is tied to categories. On the other hand, the situation justifies this limited statement on predicates: "to be" in case of actuality legitimately serves for empirical but not real predication.

No separate discussion is provided by Kant of the existence of mental entities. Data of introspective psychology can be accommodated phenomenally "as I appear to myself"—whether thoughts, e.g., of God or triangles, can be is more debatable—but the main point is that they are all "inner" and belong to myself as a thinking and intuiting subject. Consequently, for Kant the question of their existence as self-dependent objects does not arise; rather, a reserved attitude toward mental entities can be read in lines such as "to understand the possibility of things in conformity with the categories, and so to demonstrate the OBJECTIVE REALITY of the latter, we need . . . intuitions that are in all cases OUTER INTUITIONS." (B 291) To whatever extent inner entities are a real somewhat, they must not be confused with outer objects; "outer" meaning, if not "spatial" at least "other than myself." But the existence of that self on which they wholly depend requires separate consideration that will also concern mental "objectivity."

From this exploration directed to the existence of objects as phenomena, there is a point of transition to the next direction. The postulate speaks of actuality as "bound up" with material conditions, and discussing it Kant alludes to "perception and its advance." Actual is not only the immediately perceived; we can "know the existence of the thing prior to its perception . . . if only it be bound up with certain perceptions, in accordance with" the analogies. The analogy in question is probably the second, viz., of causality, and Kant illustrates: "from the perception of the attracted iron filings we know of the existence of a magnetic matter." (A 225/6–B 273) This constitutes a more vague extension of the sense of "actuality" demanded by the binding, connecting, synthetic advance of human knowledge. Whether "magnetic matter" is taken as an "actual" cause of attraction or the iron filings are themselves understood as "magnetic matter," i.e., whether it is an instance of causality or of identity, the direction of advance here may be essentially not explored. In terms of contemporary empirical advance, the question whether actual existence in Kant's terms is to be predicated of entities not even indirectly accessible to "the grossness of our senses," is debatable; at least it can be claimed that we know what they are, or should be like—atoms and their constituents, microorganisms, etc. But at any stage of "advance according to empirical laws," such as the present one, there are problems, e.g., the causes of cancer or the quasi-stellar sources of radio waves. With regard to these (examples being ever variable) it appears proper to say that they are but we do not know what they are. However, such thinking is "problematic" in Kant's own sense: it moves in the direction of noumena.

Do noumena exist? "Doubtless, indeed, there are intelligible entities corresponding to the sensible entities." (B 309) This sentence is cited only to show that in the letter of the text this question of existence emerges indeed. But its apparent assurance must be carefully qualified, and first the literal term "intelligible entities" must be queried. Such terms as "intelligible entities," "intelligibilia," "entia rationis," "noumena," meant as synonyms of Greco-Latin derivation, are in the Critique a rather unfitting heritage from the rationalist tradition according to which the intellect, unlike sense, penetrates into the very nature of things with determinate clarity of knowledge. But this doctrine Kant decisively rejects (see A 42/46–B 59/63 and A 50/51–B 74/75); thus his use of such terms does not accord well with his denial of any existing objects knowable by the intellect alone. Of those cited, only the term "noumenon" is too frequent and too much accepted historically to be disregarded; but it must be read as equivalent, with qualifications, to "transcendental object" —more used in the first edition—and strictly synonymous with "thing in itself," which is critically distinguished from "appearance" or "phenomenon."

In order to justify more directly the need for considering existence in regard to noumenal "objects" or things in themselves, it will be well to look once more at the second of Kant's three central sentences about the "ontological proof" and to retranslate it with parenthetical explication. "It (being or 'to be' or existence) is only (or purely) the positing (or position) of a thing, or of certain (perhaps: of its) determinations, in itself." Whether the "determinations" are or are not dependent on the "thing"—the former is reasonable, as determinations are hardly free floating—the sentence ends in German with "*an sich selbst*," a phrase grammatically indifferent to singular and plural and thus legitimately connectible with "a thing," not only with "determinations." With this reading the text affirms the possibility of positing a thing in itself. A further instance of such textual usage, not grammatically doubtful, may be quoted: "The knowledge of the EXISTENCE of the object consists precisely in the fact that the object is posited in itself, BEYOND THE THOUGHT OF IT." (A 639–B 667) Here, from earlier examinations, the question naturally arises whether Kant, in alluding to existence as known, does not intend the "object" as phenomenal, also existing "beyond the thought." Both quotations suggest the need to pursue the sense of positing existence by asking next about the relation in Kant's thought of how phenomena and noumena "are."

In the text's first introduction of the relation, Kant says:

> . . . though we cannot KNOW these objects as things in themselves, we must yet be in position at least to THINK them as things in themselves; otherwise we should be landed in the absurd conclusion that there can be appearance without anything that appears. (B xxvi/xxvii)

The latter clause reads more literally: "that appearance would be without that which there appears." The stress lies on the conditional "would be"; the English "anything" or "something" with the component "thing" had better be avoided, as will be explained later; and "there appears" might be expanded: "is there on its own and enters into an empirical relation to the human mind." The point is that in this early reference Kant announces the principle that nothing can ever appear unless it already is; or more briefly: being is the ground for appearing.

That such is indeed the principle of Kant's thought can be shown in the context of his main discussion of phenomena and noumena:

> The sensibility (and its field, that of the appearances) is itself limited by the understanding in such fashion that it does not have to do with things in themselves but only with the mode in which, owing to our subjective constitution, they appear. The Transcendental Aesthetic, in all its teaching, has led to this conclusion; and the same conclusion also, of course, follows from the concept of an appearance in general; namely, that something which is not in itself appearance must correspond to it. For appearance can be nothing by itself, outside our mode of representation . . . the word appearance must be recognized as already indicating a relation to something . . . which . . . must be something in itself. . . . There thus results the concept of a NOUMENON. (A251/2)

Such Kantian phrases as "appearance can be nothing by itself, outside our mode of representation" are sometimes taken as idealist in the Berkeleian vein. But the sequel in this quotation disallows such interpretation. In Kant's "appearance," *esse* is certainly not equivalent to *percipi*, if that word of his is to indicate a relation to something in itself. How, then, is "appearance" to be interpreted? On the one hand, phenomenal objects are appearances "for" man's subjective constitution in possible experience. On the other hand, as both the above quotations assert, they are appearances "of"—what? The phrase "must correspond" does not clarify enough. Yet the preceding sentence states "they appear," the pronoun standing for "things in themselves." If so, phenomena are appearances "of" noumena" "for" the human mind. The principle remains: whatever is to appear, must be. And the relation of phenomena to noumena, suggested in the phrase "must correspond," is not that of causality, which is among the categories and like all of them—except for the Third Antinomy—consistently applies to phenomena only. Strange as it may sound, that relation is approachable through identity.

This assertion must be substantiated, especially since passages of the first edition in the chapter on Phenomena and Noumena are often taken as less definitive. Here is a statement from the second edition:

> . . . if we entitle certain objects, as appearances, sensible entities (phenomena) . . . we thus distinguish the mode in which we intuit them from the nature that belongs to them in themselves. (B 306)

All that is required in the reading of this sentence is careful attention to the pronouns, viz., the same "them" pertains to appearances as to things in themselves: "they" are identical. But some understandable difficulties in appreciating any such identity stem from the plain fact that such disparate assertions can and must be made by Kant about phenomena as against noumena. On this account, it might be argued, identity makes no sense here. This has to be explored reflectively.

To distinguish names, references, descriptions does not imply denying identity in whatever those are applicable to. Various sentences containing "Evening Star" are not proper to the "Morning Star"; yet their object is one and the same. Or again, all sorts of legitimate statements might have been made about Dr. Jekyll by people without an inkling that he was also Mr. Hyde. Such distinctions and contrasts are relative to available knowledge, and nothing necessarily follows from them about existence—single, double, or multiple. To be sure, the single existence or identity of Evening-Morning Star and of Jekyll-Hyde was made known, but in other parallel cases it may not be known. Epistemological discrepancy is no bar to existential identity. With this in mind, Kant's following sentences become significant:

> The division of objects into phenomena and noumena, and the world into a world of the senses and a world of the understanding, is therefore quite inadmissible (second edition adds "in the positive sense"). . . . We must not, in place of the expression MUNDUS INTELLIGIBILIS, use the expression "an INTELLECTUAL world." . . . For only modes of knowledge are either intellectual or sensuous. (A 255–B 311/2)

The subtle adjectival difference "intellectual-intelligible" need not be considered, because under either title Kant denies the existence of objects accessible only by the intellect. But it must be noted first that for him distinctions in "modes of knowledge" need not be ontological, and second, more definitely, that he condemns the Platonist ontology of two worlds—the addition "in the positive sense" means: there are not two worlds of objects that man could positively and determinately assert. Putting together these two observations, it can now be said that Kant's division of phenomena and noumena is epistemological; thus it does not prevent his referring to "them" as identical. This can be confirmed by reiterating phrases from the preceding two quotations: we "distinguish the mode in which we intuit"; we deal "with the mode in which" they appear to our subjectivity. These are modes of human phenomenal knowledge and nothing else.

Intellect and intuition having to cooperate to yield knowledge, we do not reach any "noumenal" knowledge. The word "noumenon" must be understood in the "negative" sense, i.e., not as naming any determinate object accessible in any special way. "The categories . . . think objects in general. . . . But they do not thereby determine a greater sphere of objects." (A 254–B 309) It is perhaps advisable to recall some earlier explanations. The quoted sentence says: no determining predication applies to things in themselves; the categories fail to render for them any determinacy, n. b., including causal; consequently they have no reality—but in Kant's sense—which does not mean they are not there. On the contrary, in the negative sense specified, thinking of them is "indispensable" and "no arbitrary invention." When Kant asserts that we "must" think them, this demand is stronger than just granting what we "can" mentally suppose, e.g., triangles or unicorns. The question remains, how do we fulfill this demand, how much or how little do we think here?

> If the objective reality of a concept cannot be in any way known, while yet the concept contains no contradiction and also at the same time is connected with other modes of kowledge that involve given concepts which it serves to limit, I entitle that concept problematic. (A 254–B 310)

The notion of "problematic concept" is thus introduced immediately to fit thinking about noumena; with one exception, to be mentioned, it is fitting nowhere else in the *Critique*. It specifies three criteria. First, thinking of noumena is not self-contradictory; it would be that only if it were a necessary truth that whatever is, must appear to man—which it is not. Second, such thinking connects with and limits human knowledge; it connects with phenomenal knowledge by the principle that any given appearance relates to "something" that is in itself, and it is limiting in a twofold manner. For one thing, as often reiterated, knowledge is possible for man only if understanding cooperates with sensibility in synthesis of concepts and intuitions; it is limited, then, to intuitible appearances. But out of that emerges another limitation. Knowledge covers both that things are and what they are; the former factor is supplied in the "material conditions" of the sensibly given, the latter in the "formal conditions" of the mind which determine objects. Therefore, there is no knowledge beyond the limits of those conditions; still, man thinks of and beyond such limits. And thus the third criterion: thinking of noumena yields no knowledge of objective reality. Again, there are two points here. Noumena have no knowable reality because they cannot be rendered determinate by forms of intuition or those of thought, the categories. This is, in Kant's terms, another way of saying that man has no knowledge of their nature or essence; it has no bearing upon existence. But Kant denies their reality as "objective," suggesting thus that noumena are not objects in relation to the experiencing subject. The expression "noumenal objects," if convenient, can only be used metaphorically. Courting the risk of a paradox, it may be said that things in themselves are not things. Things as objects can only be determined in the field of possible experience.

Thinking of noumena amounts, then, to thinking of existence without essence, indeterminate and nonobjective. And still, according to Kant, it is not thinking that the mind is free to undertake or not as it pleases.

> [The understanding] by applying the term noumena to things in themselves . . . sets limits to itself, recognizing that it cannot know these noumena through any of the categories, and that it must therefore think them only under the title of an unknown something. (A 256–B 312)

In view of the remarked "non-thingness" of noumena, it may be pointed out that the last word of this sentence, in German *Etwas,* contains no "thing" root; the English translation, "something," while it can hardly be bettered, may be avoided as slightly prejudicial. Even so, it has to be acknowledged that in this discourse Kant was groping for terms. "Noumena," synonymous with "things in themselves," mostly replaces the term of the first edition, "transcendental object." Kant's reason for eliminating the word "object" is now clearer. There is another interesting point in this change. Unlike the plural "noumena," the "transcendental object" is throughout used in the singular, parallel to "an object in general" and equated with "x"; possibly to correlate it with the "transcendental unity of apperception," Kant even speaks of it as "always one and the same." (A 108/9) But this unity replaced by plurality need not produce any puzzlement; the dominant critical doctrine forbids the application of the categories to the indeterminate "x" under any title, clearly including those of quantity. The grammatical form is therefore irrelevant simply because it is not subject to quantification: neither "one" transcendental object nor "many" noumena can be determined numerically—or in any other formal way. And just to remark in passing, any "negative" use of the categories is equally inapplicable; in that all too concise conclusion of the Transcendental Analytic (A 290/2–B 346/9), Kant provocatively compares noumena to "nothing." For human knowledge, they or it is neither one nor many; "x" is no thing— and yet in contrast with *nihil negativum*. Those who agree that philosophy deals with more than words will not wonder why Kant was here groping for linguistic expression and found it mainly inadequate.

Taking, after these qualifications, "the transcendental object" as an expression of Kant's noumenal thought, it is possible to clarify further its "problematic" character. It was said that such thought concerns indeterminate existence rather than essence. Here is a confirmation and a contrast:

> . . . the transcendental object lying at the basis of appearances . . . is and remains for us inscrutable. The thing itself is indeed given, but we can have no insight into its nature. But it is quite otherwise with an ideal of pure reason; it can never be said to be inscrutable. . . . On the contrary, it must, as a mere idea, find its place and its solution in the nature of reason. (A 613/4– B 641/2).

The German word translated as "basis" is *Grund;* thus the phrase alludes to the principle: that which is "x" is ground for what appears—but not cause. "Inscrutable" (*unerforschlich*) can also without license be rendered as "indeterminable." "Ideal of pure reason" is Kant's systematic term of reference to the idea of God whose knowable existence he questions at such length. This is the contrast, then: the concept of God is determinable "in the nature of reason," like the concepts of a triangle, of a unicorn, of a hundred thalers; the mind here thinks hypothetically of what they should be like, of their reality or essence which it can determine—"yet existence has nothing to do with all this." In strict opposition, the transcendental or noumenal "x" is not to be determined essentially—yet the mind "must" think it. Even granting that the word "given" may not be taken quite literally, it is clear that the mind must think the "x" as being there, as existence though not as actuality which is categorically inapplicable. Such thinking is less than knowing, but as "indispensable" it is more than "arbitrary" inventing or supposing. Only terminological and rather sterile objections can now remain against the claim that, with regard to the transcendental ground of appearance, Kant's thought amounts to positing of existence.

If this is so, thinking of noumena "problematically" has no kinship, in spite of verbal likeness, with "problems" man can set for himself in essential thinking, e.g., in theology or in mathematics. The latter can solve its problems without positing the existence of numbers or triangles; the former can systematically arrange its conceptual structure; yet if Kant is right in denying that its proofs yield knowledge, it requires not another essential problem but another kind of "positing" of existence, viz., of God, through faith which is voluntary. On the other hand, Kant's "problematic x" is a nonvoluntary provocation to philosophical thought: there is what appears to me and I am there and I cannot determine what is there that does not appear to me, yet I have no reason to deny that there is such. This is why I am not entitled, unless in content-less logical use, to employ the terms "possible" or "impossible" of that which transcends and grounds the scope of human experience; these terms but name my forms of thought employable within that scope. Or, if I visually symbolize "all there is" in a great area, I cannot tell how much of that appears to man—perhaps a narrow section only, perhaps, though not likely, the whole area. Even this attempt oversimplifies, since quantitative answers "how much" are categorically illegitimate. Yet the awareness of the limit to the field of appearances, which means the availability for thought of some domain, be it empty on the other side of that limit, remains an "indispensable" need. Thus Kant's "problematic" thought concerns not so much the problem as the mystery that there is whatever there is. The idea of God has been historically a way of confronting but hardly eliminating the mystery of existence, which provokes philosophy from Thales to Wittgenstein.

In such indeterminate positing of existence, clearly the word "to be" does not serve as a real or determining predicate. Nor does it serve, as it does for actual appearances, as an empirical predicate—although the principle that if anything appears "it" is (something in itself) relates it implicatively to such predication. The question of logical predication is more complex. To take Kant simply as saying, "There is (are) the transcendental object (noumena)," can be equivalent to "The transcendental object (noumena) is (are) existent." Here, as observed earlier, "is" must remain only a copula in logical use, and "existent" can be understood as the logical predicate, which is logically almost like any other predicate—almost, because this likeness obtains only in abstract symbolic formulations. If these are interpreted, substituting for letter symbols predicates such as "red," "straight," even "actual," a difference emerges: while any of those predicates cannot be seen as redundant, the predicate "existent" can, after the copula. And this must cause suspicion about its purely logical use. Further, if in accord with the preceding examination, Kant's noumenal thought is also expressible in "There is an x," it must be noted that in logical formulations this corresponds not at all to predication but to the introduction of the so-called "existential" quantifier, e.g., "There is an x such that x is red." But such correspondence is nominal and conceals an opposition. In contemporary logic, "there is an x" symbolizes the arbitrary mental supposing of somewhat, quite indifferent as to how genuine its existence, and immediately determined by the

logical predicate, even "such that x is a unicorn": hence the
claim that logic can proceed without any ontology. For Kant,
on the contrary, "there is an x" expresses the nonarbitrary positing of existence which is not determined at all. To put it drastically, the word "is" serves him there for antilogical or, better,
for prelogical use. Yet he would certainly not grant that these
words, "there is an x," say nothing significant. The remaining
point is therefore rather terminological; but it can be proposed
that "to be" with regard to noumenal positing serves for transcendental predication. The distinction between transcendental
and general logic is here relevant (see A 55/7–B 80/2).

An objection may have occurred to the course of the preceding pages, viz., that they contain no further elaboration of the
identity asserted between phenomena and noumena, that they
even move away from it toward noumenal indeterminacy and
nonobjectiveness. Granting this, it must be stressed that the
question of identity, unless treated only linguistically, is not
simple enough to be dealt with fully in the scope of this essay.
But a few comments can be added. It sounds simple to say that
identity is asserted if some terms, nonsynonymous, refer to identically the same entities, as in "Evening Star-Morning Star,"
"Jekyll-Hyde," "phenomena-noumena." Identity of meaning, or
synonymy, is of course different, although that also depends on
some entities such as words. But if the question is not about
terms, it is less simple to ask: how to understand that which is
asserted in identity, even in the case of "A is A"? In addition,
when and how is man able to assert identity? Words are not
the answer; astronomical observations of the planet Venus and
detective pursuit of Mr. Hyde must be undertaken. Perhaps,
then, it can be suggested that asserting identity is based on
identification, and this is accomplished in the course of possible
experience. Now the difficulty about noumena is clear, and considered by some insuperable.

Yet it may be still asked: what is the presupposition for any
identifying? The answer to that is: in a variety of modes,
existence—of words, of physical bodies, of imaginary characters and of their imaginative human authors. Because its determinable modes vary, therefore existence is indeterminate as

presupposition. On its ground takes place all experiencing and thus determination and identification of entities, of objects—and equally all thinking and thus formation and logic. Once more, existence is pre-logical and pre-objective. In the logical supposition, it seems that existence may be disregarded as it conforms to laws of thought; in the Kantian position or presupposition, all laws of thought must conform to existence. If now it were asked what determinate objects are identified and then variously referred to as identical, the true common-sense answer would be: the same as there are. It is their sameness in "there are (is)" that must be posited in asserting identity, e.g., of planets; while in the case of mental or fictitious entities "there is" and must be their thinker. This is Kant's transcendental thought on existence. While the usage of "identity" for the relation of phenomena and noumena is not as simple as among determinable things in possible experience, it is not illegitimate if identity only emerges from existence, if "to be identical" implies "to be," if to say that "x" is the same under various descriptions it is proper to start with "there is an x." Existence is not reached by thought; thought has to begin with it as "indispensable." Be it noted, however, that no determinate existence is known as necessary, not even that of God.

The objection may not have been removed entirely. Thus, looking from the logical point of view with Quine, "to be" is seen as a value of the logical symbol or variable "x such that . . ." or as within a range of pronouns "such that it is . . ." Yet general and contemporary symbolic logic may not, unlike Kant's transcendental thought, inquire into the setting up of the range for the pronouns or variables, leaving "there is an x" not only in indeterminacy but in existential limbo. This cannot be so with ontology. Identity is logically no "problem"; ontologically it is. The logician may disapprove of identity of noumena with phenomena as pronominally dubious—it or they or neither—even though his "existential" quantifier is also numerically indeterminate in scope. It may not be inapposite to reiterate that, according to Kant, existence is determinately known only phenomenally; noumenally it is thought—but indispensably. This distinction is not accessible to logic. But those who insist that indispensable thinking cannot be other than knowing are not very sensitive philosophically. Transcendental philosophy thinks of the ontological ground of man's cognizing objects of experience, or the way such objects come "to be" for man. (A 12–B 25)

One more point should be mentioned in this section: the relation of existence to the categories. It might be wondered whether, with regard to noumena, existence could not be conceived as a category unschematized, since time, the intermediary of pure schemata, does not bind noumena. But apart from repeated assertions that categories have only phenomenal scope, it must be remembered that unschematized they are but logical forms of thought. And it has been explored above how unlike purely logical thought is Kant's positing of noumena. The conclusion, therefore, is that noumenal existence in the transcendental "there is an x" should not be tied to any category, schematized or unschematized. But that this conclusion is legitimate in Kantian terms will be substantiated in the following section.

Two senses of "positing" existence have been examined: determinately knowable, and indeterminate hence unknowable. These correspond to two ways of using the word "is." But to whom or what does such positing and using belong?

> I find that a judgment is nothing but the manner in which given modes of knowledge are brought to the objective unity of apperception. This is what is intended by the copula "is." (B 141)

The statement echoes the earlier cited determinate positing of "an object in relation" to my thought. In a parallel vein it can be said that in "there is an x" the word "is" intends relation to my indispensable thought. Thus emerges the third factor involved in human thought of existence: the thinker, the subject, the self. This is an important ontological conquest of Kant. Unlike Descartes, he sees clearly that such existence requires consideration entirely unlike that of objects, things, or substances. He deals with this matter in the chapter on Paralogisms; and his terms there, introduced already in the Transcendental Deduction exclusively for this mode of existing, are "transcendental subject" or "transcendental unity of apperception," also symbolized simply as "I think."

Although Kant's textual expressions vary in scope and precision, it is first necessary to realize that his thought here concerns the prerequisite of all conscious experiencing, thinking, representing by concepts and intuitions. Thus: "The abiding and unchanging 'I' (pure apperception) forms the correlate of all our representations" (A 123), or: "It must be possible for the 'I think' to accompany all my representations; for otherwise something would be represented in me which could not be thought at all." (B 131) In other words, nothing is represented, experienced, thought unless by someone or something termed "I." This is not to say, however, that the nature of this "I" must be well known; on this point the doctrine of the paralogisms differs sharply from that of Descartes.

The word "representation" is used by Kant to name the genus to which belong both intuitions of sensibility and concepts of understanding or reason (see A 19–B33 and A 320–B 376). The two preceding quotations, therefore, make clear that the "I" of apperception "correlates with" or "accompanies" all intuitions as well as concepts. This should be noted because in discussing the paralogisms Kant links it much more explicitly with concepts; yet his stress is understandable in view of the critical teaching that no intuitions, no human experience or consciousness can take place without being synthesized in the unity of the thinking or apperceiving "I." It would be a strange view indeed that kept all concepts as "mine" and left all intuitions unowned.

With this in mind, here are some pertinent statements concerning this transcendental "I":

> This is the concept or, if the term be preferred, the judgment, "I think." As is easily seen, this is the vehicle of all concepts . . . and is itself transcendental . . . the mere apperception "I think," by which even transcendental concepts are made possible . . . we cannot even say that this is a concept, but only that it is a bare consciousness which accompanies all concepts. Through this I or he or it (the thing) which thinks, nothing further is represented than a transcendental subject of the thoughts = x. It is

known only through the thoughts which are its predicates, and of it, apart from them, we cannot have any concept whatsoever, but can only revolve in a perpetual circle, since any judgment upon it has always already made use of its representation. (A 341/6–B 399/404)

First, to avoid semantic confusion, it is proper to keep apart the symbolization as concept, judgment, or whatever (on this the text hesitates) and that for which it stands; the latter alone is here under discussion. Second, with regard to that entity, Kant is not hesitant but intentionally vague: "I or he or it." Third, he uses here the term "transcendental" in its primary meaning, viz., as that which exceeds yet originates modes of known consciousness, experience, thought. Fourth, he introduces the mysterious "x" which has stood already for the transcendental object, but here equating it with the transcendental subject, with the clear intention of suggesting its unknown nature. And fifth, lest this point be misunderstood, in the next sentence he immediately separates these two significations of "x," intimating the main principle of the paralogisms: that the transcendental subject cannot ever be object to itself, because to make itself object it would have to remain active as subject. Thus objective knowledge of it is barred.

More explicitly, this principle is enunciated further:

> The subject of the categories cannot by thinking the categories acquire a concept of itself as an object of the categories. For in order to think them, its pure self-consciousness, which is what was to be explained, must itself be presupposed. (B 422)

For better or for worse, the subject-object distance is thus well assured in the *Critique*. Another way of emphasizing the above principle is to assert that the transcendental subject or self cannot be counted among the "objects of possible experience." But this assertion does not cut it off from possible experience, which after all is "its" or "his." It rests on a careful observance of the simple grammatical polarity between the experiencing and the experienced (or experienceable). It is quite evident in this sentence, translated here so as to restore the Kantian emphasis: "Not the consciousness of the DETERMINING self, but only that of the DETERMINABLE self . . . is the object." (B 407)

The transcendental subject is the self active in determining, experiencing, apperceiving. Whatever of the self is object— and this will be explained further—has to be determinable and experienceable. These two approaches to human consciousness must not be confused, as they are not only by outdated Cartesians but by contemporary behaviorists.

The point reached now makes it possible to see the unique perspective in which Kant views the transcendental apperceiving self. On the one hand, *qua* subject of possible experience, it must correlate with its objects which are "phenomenal." On the other hand, *qua* nondeterminable and thus unknowable, it correlates with the negative "noumenal" mode. This Kant confirms, arguing that if we could acquire determinate objective knowledge of it, "we should have taken a step beyond the world of sense, and have entered into the field of noumena." (B 409) Consequently he takes care to specify that its unique status is strictly neither "phenomenal" nor "noumenal":

> . . . in the transcendental synthesis of the manifold of representations in general, and therefore in the synthetic original unity of apperception, I am conscious of myself, not as I appear to myself, nor as I am in myself, but only that I am. (B 157)

The contradistinction is twofold. A human subject's transcendental apperception is not equivalent to consciousness of his nature or reality as it appears, i.e., as phenomenal object. Neither does it break through the noumenal limit of knowledge, viz., of even his own reality in itself, although it reaches that limit. That which is elsewhere symbolized in "I think" is here singled out as my consciousness that I am—but not, once again, what I am, either "apparently" or "really." Kant's perspective on the transcendental subject quite unequivocally aims at existence without essence.

But a linguistic complication arises immediately. The preceding sections explored two senses of positing existence and using the word "is." It cannot be strictly claimed that here is a third one, because in Kantian thought it is the thinking subject who does the positing for the other cases. A play on words like "positing of positing" is neither illuminating nor adequate. In another approach, the word "is," appropriate for "appearance" or "thing in itself," is not appropriate here. The seemingly superficial grammatical difference would falsify Kant's ontological intent, which could certainly not be rendered in "The thinker is" or "Human subjects are." "I am"—or even stressing the self's unknown whatness in an awkward "X am"—resists third-person objectification with reason. This fact may confirm that the existential status of the transcendental subject must not be confused with that of the transcendental or noumenal "object," even though verbal expression there also formulates only existence without essence. While this is not accessible to contemporary logic in its symbolic uniformity, for Kant "there is an x" is critically distant from "there am I (x)." If possible experience is the field in which alone emerges determination of knowledge about essence and existence, and if it is wholly encompassed by the subject-object distance, then this demands two existential presuppositions, both indeterminate, indispensable, and irreducible: "There is an x" and "I am." Within this frame of reference can be fully understood Kant's statement:

> Certainly, the representation "I am," which expresses the consciousness that can accompany all thought, immediately includes in itself the existence of a subject; but it does not so include any KNOWLEDGE of that subject and therefore also no empirical knowledge, that is, no experience of it. (B 277)

Man's existence and experience are like root and fruit.

Concerning linguistic expression, the irreducible first- versus third-person difference in the intransitive verb "to be" corresponds to that of active versus passive voice in the transitive verb "to posit." For the moment it is advisable to leave it at that: "posited" is determinate actual existence of objects of possible experience and indeterminate existence of the transcendental "object(s) x," but such "positing" is due to the existence of the indeterminate transcendental "subject I."

In addition to the improper confusion between the transcendental and the "noumenal" self, there can be another: the failure to distinguish it from the "phenomenal" self. Why, it might be asked, should the subject-object distance be preserved within the self's inner unity, or why could not inner intuitions—never

denied by Kant—be taken as determinate "subjective" knowledge? Part of the Kantian reason has already been cited: intuitions of inner as of outer sense, to amount to knowledge, must
be synthesized in categories, and the categories do not apply
to the transcendental self-consciousness which is their presupposition. There is a further reinforcement. In the paralogisms
Kant criticizes the "rational psychology" which attempts a dogmatic doctrine about thinking beings and their independent
existence as "being able, in and by themselves, to determine
that existence in respect of the permanence which is a necessary
characteristic of substance." (B 417/8) This claim of substantiality for the "I think" he considers as empty. Permanence is
the pure concept of substance schematized by time; and "the
subject, in which the representation of time has its original
ground, cannot thereby determine its own existence in time."
(B 422) In other words, the self as it appears consists of inner
intuitions sequent in time; this is its elusiveness in Hume's
pursuit. In contrast—and this cannot be fully explored in the
present essay—the "abiding I" of apperception, if not atemporal,
at least originates time, its form of intuition, as it does the
categories, its forms of thought, therefore is not bound by them
or by time. To put this rather simply, it makes for temporal
occurrences which do not occur to it; or, to hazard metaphors,
it is the eye which looks but does not naturally see itself in
space, it is the author in whose "own" play he is not an active
figure. However proper these simplifications, clearly in Kant's
thought the essentially knowable "phenomenal" self and the
transcendental subject cannot coincide. Thus the paralogisms
attempting to derive from "I think" four determinate conclusions
in fact yield "nothing whatsoever towards the knowledge of
myself as object." (B 409) Although they are there introduced
in a somewhat loose fashion, all four types of categories are
thereby denied application to the transcendental subject, their
vehicle or bearer.

And that leads directly to the question of the category of
existence. This was partly postponed at the end of the previous
section and can be now reconnected with it. While the distinction between "There is an x" and "I am" must be maintained,

both these expressions are alike in being used by Kant to allude
to bare indeterminate existence. But what is their relation to
thought, in particular to the pure concept of existence? Also, how
is to be understood the replacement "I am" for "I think"? These
matters are dealt with in a long and interesting footnote, presumably written as later reflection even on the revised text
of the second edition. It is possible there, once more, to observe
Kant striving for more adequate expression and succeeding but
to intimate his thought. The understanding may be easier if
the passage is taken up in parts.

> The "I think" is, as already stated, an empirical proposition,
> and contains within itself the proposition "I exist." But I cannot
> say "Everything which thinks exists." For in that case the property
> of thought would render all beings which possess it necessary
> beings. My existence cannot, therefore, be regarded as an infer-
> ence from the proposition "I think," as Descartes sought to con-
> tend—for it would then have to be preceded by the major
> premiss "Everything which thinks, exists"—but is identical with
> it. (B 422)

First of all, the passage agrees with Kant's main statement
on existence in denying the existence of particular necessary
beings and in objecting to the treatment of existence as a conclusion arrived at by inference. Second, it confirms the point
elaborated earlier, viz., that "I am (exist)" is not transformable
into an objective "There is (are)," adaptable as a syllogistic
premise. Third, the identity mentioned amounts at least to the
proper reading of the formulation as "I exist thinking" (this
having been suggested in B 420); incidentally, Kant is wrong
in suggesting that Descartes did not see that. Fourth, the existence in question is not completely indeterminate, as in "There
is an x," but restricted to my thinking existence, i.e., as transcendental subject. Fifth, the phrase—however it is read: "I am,"
"I think," or "I exist thinking" —is an empirical proposition; this
is to be explicated further in the last sentences of the passage
along with the opening words of the continuation:

> The "I think" expresses an indeterminate empirical intuition,
> i.e., perception (and thus shows that sensation, which as such
> belongs to sensibility, lies at the basis of this existential proposi-

tion). But the "I think" precedes the experience which is required to determine the object of perception through the category in respect of time; and the existence here (referred to) is not a category. The category as such does not apply to an indeterminately given object but only to one of which we have a concept and about which we seek to know whether it does or does not exist outside the concept. (B 422/3)

There is some terminological inadequacy here, hastily taken by some critics as inadequacy of thought. The reason why Kant chose to omit fuller explanation may have been shortage of time and space in revising the second edition (see B xlii). For greater lucidity he could have reiterated the earlier cited contrast (B 407) of determining and determination. Thus, keeping in mind that "I think" symbolizes the active self-subject, the terms "intuition, perception, sensation"—which that phrase "expresses"—can only be meant as "my intuiting, perceiving, sensing." This is "indeterminate" or, if another word be permitted, pre-determinate. Why? Because Kant speaks of a transcendental presupposition, of the subject's existence which "precedes the experience which is required to determine . . ." Such an understanding means that "I exist thinking" expresses the transcendental subject's simply being there, but as himself, viz., capable of determining, i.e., both of thinking and of sensing. The clause in parentheses concerns the basis of this "proposition" *qua* "existential"; therefore —evoking echoes of the second postulate—it stresses that for any experience not the formal but only the material conditions in sensation, hence also in "sensing," have anything to do with existence. This tie between "formal" thought and "material" sensibility is alluded to at the end of the passage. Now, confirming the statement of B 277, the transcendental subject's existence "precedes" experience, not temporally but ontologically. Even apart from that, categories apply, schematized "in respect of time," only within experience but not "to an indeterminately given object," not to a "transcendental x"; this is reiterated. Consequently—and this is for the present purposes the climax of the whole passage—"existence here is not a category." Problematic but indispensably presupposed existence of what is indeterminably symbolized in "x," whether it stand for object or for subject, remains beyond the scope of any category even schematized. It transcends the forms of essential thought and logic.

The concluding sentences of the passage aim at more elucidation:

> An indeterminate perception here signifies only something real that is given, given indeed to thought in general, and so not as appearance, nor as thing in itself (NOUMENON), but as something which actually exists, and which in the proposition, "I think," is denoted as such. For it must be observed, that when I have called the proposition "I think" an empirical proposition, I do not mean to say thereby that the "I" in this proposition is an empirical representation. On the contrary, it is purely intellectual, because belonging to thought in general. Without some empirical representation to supply the material for thought, the ACTUS, "I think," would not, indeed, take place; but the empirical is only the condition of the application, or of the employment, of the pure intellectual faculty. (B 423)

First, in accord with the above understanding, the first sentence says: "Indeterminate perceiving here signifies a real somewhat that is given, namely, for thinking as such, therefore not as appearance, nor as thing in itself (noumenon), but as somewhat that exists indeed" ("actually," referring to the schematized category, is not in the text). It explicitly prohibits both phenomenal and noumenal approaches to the unique existence of the transcendental subject—and its only doubtful term is "given." Second, however, the following two sentences are meant to remove the impression that the "I" is "given." The word "I" does not stand for "an empirical representation"— to supply the explication—"of anything given"; rather, Kant repeats, it "pertains to thinking as such." Third, now there is some imbalance in favor of an intellectual "I." Accordingly the last sentence—as the translation unfortunately omits—begins: "However, without some empirical representation that gives over material for thinking . . ." Now the intent is clearer: the "I" is not only formally "thinking" but affectable by what "gives" material; man's intellect applies ever "conditioned" by sensibility, i.e., his faculty for "having given" sensible intuitions (compare the very opening of the *Critique* in A 19–B 33: "But all thought must . . . relate ultimately . . . to sensibility"). And fourth, for man such unity of the formal with the material, the intellectual with the sensible is involved in the *actus*. Kant preserves the Latin word; thus it is not out of place to connect it with the Thomist *actus essendi,* translatable as "existence." The *actus,* phrased fully in "I exist thinking," is the existing human subject's transcendental unity of apperception.

If it is now well understood that this complex Kantian expression means existence which is uniquely mine and not any other, then it must be clearer that the epistemological modes, "phenomenally" positive and "noumenally" negative, are not pertinent to it because they belong to knowledge, strictly: my knowledge of—whatever is other than my simply existing. In undertaking to know, I objectify, from the indeterminate "x" which is—yet other than I am—to determine objects. All that other is at a distance, viz., in Kant's subject-object relation, insuperable for any knowing relationship. Thus anticipating some of Sartre's analyses, Kant regards even the data of my inner sense as phenomenally objective, "as I appear to myself," i.e., as at a kind of alienating distance from that "me" active in the endeavor to know myself, introspecting. Such data are mine *qua* "inner" as opposed to "outer"; yet in their objectification they cannot constitute me, the cognizing subject. But if distinctions of knowledge fail to bind the knower, then in discourse concerning "him or me or it" there must be failure of adequate application of epistemological terms like: "representation, given, proposition" and also "category"; hence the questions about existence which "is not a category." Kant seems to have been aware of this deficiency but not in time to supply a remedy—which did not come until 1927 with *Being and Time.* Most seriously, the inadequacy touches the *Critique's* central concepts: *"a priori"* and "empirical." References to the latter in the preceding quotations are perplexing, since they must not weaken that which is *"a priori"* to all *"a priori* knowledge": the thinking, apperceiving subject. It might be suggested that Kant stresses there the word "empirical" in view of the fact that *"a priori"* throughout signifies but formality of thought or intuition, while subjective existence is certainly not just formal but must be taken materially in simply being there, as "empirically" as anything whatsoever. And still, "I exist thinking" fails in the *a priori* criterion of universality, as not transformable into the logical "Everything . . ."; and it fails in the "empirical" criterion of being conditioned and contingent, as the indispensable precondition of experience itself. The concepts undeniably fall short—and rightly, in this unique case.

One more point may be derived from the conclusion of the passage quoted, which can read: "The empirical is but the condition for the application or the use of the pure intellectual faculty." The last phrase may allude to the purely logical use, i.a., of words. What about the logical use of the word "to be," particularly in predication? In accordance with both this phrase and earlier considerations, "I am" is not to be taken as an instance of logical predication; nor is it one of empirical predication, such as was found proper for actual objects of possible experience. It is, because uniquely nonlogical, more parallel to the case of "There is an x," which has been taken as transcendental predication. But in that case, as in the present one, it does not seem fruitful to engage in a debate as to whether the term "predication" is applicable at all. Yet these two elusive instances of word use are, as explained, to be kept distinct. Also, the transcendental predication was thought of with regard to Kant's Transcendental Logic, which is concerned with the mind's relation to "objects entirely A PRIORI" (A 57–B 81); and this does not fit here. Therefore, as an exclusive term for what is still, according to Kant, a kind of proposition, it may be suggested that in "I am (exist)" the word "to be" is used inflexibly for subjective predication. In a wider sense, though, this is also transcendental. It should be added that in other passages, e.g., A 396/405 and B 428/431, Kant speaks of the apperceiving subject's existence in various even more perplexing statements. It is believed that they do not depart from his main intent as explicated here, but to show this would demand more scope and patience.

In the preceding three sections of this essay some suggestions were made about existence and predication, with constant regard for Kant's central view: "to be" is not a real predicate; in logical use it is the copula. In addition to those explicitly mentioned by Kant, viz., logical and real (determining), three other modes of predication have been proposed: empirical, transcendental, and subjective. All have to do with "to be." These terminological proposals are intended to bring out Kant's own thought. They take "predication" in a sense wider than "determination"; this covers all expression of man's thinking powers, whether or not this is also "logical" by a more rigorous criterion. Through the *Critique* all the syllogisms of reason and all the compound judgments of the understanding rest on simple judgments in the form of subject-predicate; from these is also derived the list of categories in whose completeness Kant firmly believes. The conclusion is easily supplied: Kant was convinced that to formulate properly anything thinkable is to predicate. In this respect he was clearly an Aristotelian. The uses of the word "to be," formulating what is not only thinkable but critical for him, belong to this wide scope of predication. Such thought may be today questioned by logicians, but that does not matter. This is said not in disrespect for logic but in rejection of its contemporary claim to straitjacket the creative thought of philosophers as great as Kant.

[To men courageous and clearheaded enough] I leave the task of perfecting what, here and there, in its exposition, is still somewhat defective; for in this regard the danger is not that of being refuted, but of not being understood. (B xliii)

If such presumption be forgiven, the aim of this essay has been to clear an understanding of what in the exposition of Kant's existential thought is not entirely without defects, especially of omission. *An* understanding, not *the* understanding, because other and more clearheaded men may reach elsewhere. But the conviction that prompted the writing of these pages is that Kant's existential thought can surmount the danger "of not being understood." This again does not mean that it leaves no serious questions unanswered. If it did, it would not have belonged to philosophy—whose reflecting endeavor must cope with oncoming time. *Veritas filia temporis.*

At the outset it was affirmed that without Kant nothing like "existential thought" could have emerged. Now may be re-affirmed those points of Kant's decisive stand which constitute such a foundation.

Existence of any entity whatsoever is unlike its essence: the question whether, and answer that it is, must be distinct from questions and answers as to what and how it could and should be, provided it was there. The latter, but not the former, man has power to determine by thinking alone. This discovers insights epistemological, logical, and ontological. The first is that knowledge concerning existence—or simply knowledge—is not attainable without some sensible immediacy of the given and thus must "begin with experience." Yet all knowledge does not "arise out of experience" which itself presupposes something like human existence capable of having it given and thought. The second is that existence is not to be arrived at exclusively by inference. Such inference cannot be undertaken without some existential premise, but specific origins of such premises may not be logically investigated. The third is that processes of determining, identifying, forming are rooted in the ground of that which is, indeterminate; whatever can appear within experience of man and give material for his thinking must, to begin with, somehow be. And all these insights point in this direction: the human being, which not only thinkers share, "precedes" all questions on other entities, whether and what they might be. While philosophy may attempt to abstract from this transcendental "precedence," to forget, and even to obliterate it, the truth remains that the existence of the subject is as mysterious as that of his object; yet the latter—for all the ambitious immersion in knowledge that is to be "mine"—stays on at a distance from the former which any "I" am.

It is not claimed that all these points are in every respect novel in Kant's philosophy, but their significant configuration is. The available text of St. Augustine has not prevented historians of philosophy from discussing the "Cartesian" *Cogito ergo sum.* In a similar vein has been understood here the "Kantian" thought on existence. Tracing its antecedent inspirations would be an entirely separate task; so would be listing its subsequent exploitations and explorations by more recent "existential thinkers."

They and others have raised a host of questions tied to reflections presented above. Unpredictably more will be raised in the future, because eminent thought is eminently questionable. Purely as indication of interest, a couple of questions might be mentioned now. For instance, what is the status of existing "objects"? This concept must be kept carefully apart on the one hand from the subject's, on the other from indeterminacy in existence without accessible "objective reality." As suggested, it indicates apparent distance of any otherness with an opposed stance (*Gegenstand*); and yet that covers "inner" as well as "outer" appearance. The word "objectify" has been used in the exegesis for the actively thinking movement among those limits; but if proper, this word must serve both Kant's impulsion toward critical, not naive, realism and his own chosen title of transcendental idealism. This is not a simple matter. Another question, not unconnected: What, after all, is the relation of thinking to existence? The general trend in the *Critique* considers human thinking accommodated in the allegedly complete list of categories; this may have motivated Kant to include "existence" on that list. Yet its schematizing covers only determinate actuality; and, as shown, Kant explicitly visualizes existence as beyond the category—still thinkable. It has been suggested that his epistemological notions, i.a., the categories, cannot suffice for all Kant's purposes. If so, thought of existence, which neither yields knowledge nor consists of "mere ideas of reason," needs to be pursued on its own, perhaps with another criterion of "purity." This brings up one more question which ostensibly departs from the textual goals: Is it sufficiently appreciated that in the central statement on existence Kant uses the word "to be (*Sein*)"? His reason in the context is understandable, but this means taking for granted—and so it has been throughout these pages—the interchangeability of "to be" and "to exist." However, is this always required? And is it a matter of conventional word usage alone? With the authority of tradition, in this essay the contrast has often been stressed: existence versus essence. Yet speaking of essence is also impossible without at least the words "to be." Why? The existential thinkers after Kant tend implicitly to restrict "existence" to the human being. There is full explication in Heidegger, in whose usage "existence" is not a synonym for "ek-sistence" (human) or for "being"—to which "essence" (*Wesen*) also pertains. Without going into it, there is an aspect of Kant's term "pure," as emphasized over anything "empirical," that is also relevant. Suspending problems of thinking, of the mind, of any idealism, "empirical" is for Kant existence limited as conditioned, contingent, particular, fleeting. May there not be a sense of "purity" disposing of these characteristics, thus freeing the ground for unlimited use of the words "to be"? Would not, then, transcendental philosophy, asking for that which is in itself—I and he and it and x— ask about being? Did Kant entertain this?

As much in question, then, as in correlation with the earlier cited reading, this essay must conclude with a final reflection on Kant's thought about *Position* (German as well as English). This is exposing what Kant may have thought, and is exposed as questionable. But whatever the risk, in question is Kant's ontology, not his terminology. With regard to the latter, three types of predicate were named: empirical, transcendental, subjective. These, if desired, can be taken as "predicates of position" in strict contrast to "predicates of determination." And still, *qua* linguistic forms, they are but singled-out expressions. How did Kant think of what they express?

If the structure of the present essay renders a proper understanding of Kant, there are three perspectives for thought about positing (*setzen*). Posited are empirically actual objects, posited is indeterminacy from which they acquire a stance in experience, and positing is due to the apperceiving subject. To embrace them all in the statement: "Being is position (*Setzung*)" means: "Being is the positing (*das Setzende*) and the posited (*das Gesetzte*)." Such a formulation brings to mind echoes of Berkeley: *esse est percipi et percipere*. Yet, Kant's transcendental idealism notwithstanding, it would be hard and one-sided to take Kant's ontology in such a mental or idea-founded way. Elaboration is due.

Positing is of existence rather than essence. That which is posited or does the positing, because it is, cannot be devoid of essence; but it is not essence which, so to say, makes up the positing relation. Essence or reality is for Kant's de-Platonized thought within the mind's province and privilege; brute and "impure" existence is not. Therefore, while positing must be understood as an act of the mind, its "situation" must not be forgotten, that which Kant alludes to as "indispensability"; in other words, whenever positing emerges, it is not entirely spontaneous but forced or affected in some way. This may be implied in the unity of apperception being intellectual-plus-sensible or in the inseparability for Kant as for Aristotle—except for purposes of analysis—of form-and-matter, whenever anything is "given" or exists. What has to do with positing or being posited must not be founded on conception or even on perception *qua* mental. This may also correspond to Kant's reason for the expression "in itself" as opposed to "for the experiencing mind." To be is more than to be perceived-or-perceiving, more than to be thought-or-thinking.

Still, to say "Being is the positing and the posited," with its conjunction, can raise the question of a split or bifurcation within being. And that is due to the pervading subject-object distinction or distance, throughout the *Critique*. These two shall never meet as far as knowledge is concerned: such is Kant's doctrine. But what of their being "in itself"? The terminology of "things in themselves" and of "the transcendental object" is not entirely adequate and causes Kant some difficulties. But the subject also "is" in himself, endowed with a noumenally unknown nature. Kant never denies this point, which is pertinent to his second *Critique*. To put it otherwise, "I am" and "There is an x" are not to be merged; still, they belong together and not just verbally as formulations of the same word. The indeterminate ground for knowing pertains to both "the positing" and "the posited"; it originates both, transcending them. The embracing, therefore, of both subject and object can only be thought with Kant's word "transcendental," taken widely and seriously. It is significant that he entertained the long-range undertaking of his genius under the title: "transcendental philosophy."

Existence is, traditionally conceived, unlike essence in that the latter unifies under a universal heading; from this viewpoint even to speak of "indeterminate existence" may be suspicious as universalizing it; this had to be spoken of because Kant's thought clearly tends in that direction. But that feature of it also indicates that his thought was more than existential; it was ontological, if but implicitly. The present exploration leads the writer to believe that while he did not express it so, Kant would not have turned away from this end: "Being is purely transcendental position of the positing with the posited."

Frederick A. Olafson

HUMAN ACTION AND HISTORICAL EXPLANATION

The events that historians recount and seek to explain are extremely heterogeneous. They include executions and famines,
rebellions and depressions, discoveries of continents, and de-
clines of empires. If one wishes to argue, as I do, that history
has as its preferential subject matter human actions, this thesis
can evidently draw no unambiguous support from the way in
which historical events are—at least superficially and initially
—named. Even in the short list above, there are designations
of types of historical events which plainly refer to them as
actions of some kind, and there are others which just as plainly
do not. Thus if a historian talks about the execution of Charles I,
this very way of referring to that event implies that someone
executed him and presumably also that someone ordered or
authorized that execution, i.e., that two distinct but related acts
were performed by assignable persons or groups of persons.
But if the historian's interest focuses on the depression of 1929
or the Irish famine of 1846–49 it is not at all obvious that these
concepts of "depression" and "famine" are names of actions; nor
is it clear what actions, if any, are necessarily included in what
we mean when we speak of depressions and famines. We know
of course that in the case of famine there is usually, as there
was in Ireland in 1846, a crop failure that reduces the food
supply to the point where people go hungry and die. But a

crop failure is a natural event, not an action, and its consequences
—people going hungry and dying—are not actions either in the
sense that is relevant here. It seems, then, that a history of the
Irish famine would have to be an account of certain natural
events—the successive crop failures of 1846–49—and of the suffering and death they caused. How, it may be asked, can one
claim that such a history of the Irish famine would be in any
special sense an account of what men did, especially when
the event itself is named after that element within it which
is simply a natural event?

Considerations of this kind have led many philosophers to
assume that history is not merely superficially heterogeneous but
profoundly and unalterably so, and that it is a mixture of actions
and nonactions in which the former enjoy at best a priority of
interest and attention while the logical form of the explanations
given remains that of the subsumption of events—whether
actions or nonactions—under relevant laws. In fact, however,
even such examples as those given above do not, under closer
inspection, really support these conclusions. For while the potato
blight in Ireland certainly explains why the principal food
supply of the Irish people was reduced to a small fraction
of its normal quantity, that fact by itself does not explain the
occurrence of a famine. If it did, the work of historians of the
Irish famine would be easily done—much more easily and
quickly than it in fact is. To be sure, historians take due note
of the destruction of successive potato crops by the *Philophthora
infestans* fungus; but they are not satisfied to explain the
famine—the suffering and death that followed upon the crop
failures—simply by reference to the latter as their cause. As
any reasonable person would, they ask, "What could have been
done in the circumstances to prevent starvation?" If nothing
could have been done by anyone at any time to prevent the
deaths that occurred, then the famine would have to be regarded
as an act of God or as an event similar to the collision of the
earth with another planet. It is quite clear, however, that the
famine was not uncontrollable or unpreventable in that sense.
Various things could have been done by various persons and
institutions; and the historian who wishes to explain the famine

and not just a crop failure must ask whether any of these things were done and, if they were, why they failed to prevent large-scale starvation. If they were not even attempted, he must ask why this was so and whether they were considered and then rejected; and in the latter case, why they were rejected. Accordingly Mrs. Cecil Woodham-Smith, in her admirable book *The Great Hunger,* pays only passing attention to the causes of the crop failures and a great deal of attention to the attitude of the British government, especially as formulated and expressed by the permanent Undersecretary of the Treasury, Charles Edward Trevelyan. Since that government was aware of the magnitude of the disaster and had direct responsibilities in the area, it was in the best position to take action *if something was to be done.* This fact explains and justifies Mrs. Woodham-Smith's close attention to the attitude of the British government in spite of the fact that the latter did not intervene in any significant way. At the same time Mrs. Woodham-Smith shows why it would have been very difficult to distribute food on the required scale, even if a decision to make the effort had been made, by reason of the primitive system of communication and transportation in Ireland and the absence of a highly developed governmental apparatus for carrying out welfare functions. But she also shows why the British government was reluctant to make this effort at all and why in fact it did not. Now all this is clearly in the nature of a consideration of the matter from the standpoint of a person—especially certain persons with the means to intervene—in the situation itself, and from this standpoint the Great Hunger cannot be explained until it has been shown what courses of action might have prevented starvation in spite of the crop failures, and also why they failed if they were undertaken and why they were or were not undertaken. Among these remedial courses of action are, of course, those that were open to the victims of the famine themselves, and Mrs. Woodham-Smith very properly raises such questions as why the Irish did not take to fishing when potatoes were unavailable, although it is not clear that she really explains this.

It would appear, then, that in these cases at least the historian shows a certain *a priori* selectivity in his analysis of the

causes of such an event as the Great Hunger and that this
selectivity is based upon a priority assigned to actions—possible
and actual—over nonactions. In a period in which plant bacteri-
ology and related prophylactic measures did not yet exist, a
potato blight and the resultant crop failure were clearly nonactions, i.e., they were not actions even in the marginal sense
of being partially attributable to someone's negligence or folly.
The potato blight was, moreover, a necessary condition of the
famine, since if it had not occurred there is no reason to think
there would have been a famine. At the same time this occurrence and its likely effects were known to many persons
inside and outside Ireland, and so the possibility of doing something to prevent a famine unavoidably suggested itself to those
persons at the time, as it does to the historian of the event.
A famine follows necessarily upon the destruction of the food
supply only if nothing effective is done to provide food from
other sources. In the Irish case nothing effective was done, and
the decision of the British government not to attempt to supply
food on a large scale can properly be regarded as a further
and necessary condition for the famine's occurrence. But it was
not just *another* condition, at least from the standpoint of the
historian. It was the *decisive* cause of the famine and as such
the event which the historian has a particular interest in
explaining. I have already noted that the historian pays some
attention to the causes of the potato blight; but he draws his
explanations of this event from other, nonhistorical sources,
and it is not his responsibility to discover its causes if they are
not such as are already clear to the relevant branch of natural
science. The specific scientific explanation which the historian
borrows in this way will very likely have little or no connection
with the rest of his narrative, and if it were to be revised by the
plant bacteriologists, that change too would very likely have no
impact on the historian's work. Certainly the fact that a potato
blight had an identifiable natural cause is important if only as a
means of warding off explanations that appeal immediately to
the will of God and also as an indication of the area in which
long-range solutions to the problem were to be sought. But
in the main the occurrence of a potato blight is simply a fact

that serves as an essential premise in the kind of explanation which the historian is really concerned to give. What has to be explained is what human beings did in the situation in which they were, in their different ways, confronted by this fact which was also a premise of *their* practical deliberations and of *their* actions. Those actions, as it turned out, were such as to make it inevitable that famine would follow upon the potato blight. The historian's problem is to explain not that natural event itself but the course of action and inaction by virtue of which that event was permitted to lead to a famine. My point is that it is not the job of the historian to explain the events which provide the premises of human action but the actions themselves, unless of course these premises deal with events which are, in some measure, at least, the result of human action themselves.

To claim that human actions have a position of special importance in historical narrative may well seem a resounding truism. What, after all, could human history be other than a record of what human beings have accomplished or tried to accomplish during the past ten thousand years or so? Nevertheless this appearance of being a truism is misleading. In saying that human actions have a position of special importance in history, I am not claiming merely that human actions are the subject matter of history, although they are that. The point I wish to make is rather that the form of historical narrative and historical explanation is dictated by the structure of the human actions which are the subject matter of history. In other words, human actions are not merely picked out of the whole domain of past events as the special subject matter of historical inquiry; but the way in which these actions are depicted in their relationship to one another and to the relevant nonactions that are included in an historical account is adapted from the way in which human agents construe their situation for purposes of action. I am claiming also that the "causes" that historians are interested in are primarily human actions and that these actions are isolated from the other causal conditions of the event to be explained and given a position of special prominence among the *necessary* conditions for the occurrence of that event. Understood in this way, the claim I am making about the place of human actions in historical narrative may be false but it is not truistic.

The kind of organizing influence on the form of historical narrative that I am attributing to human action has an analogue in the field of law which casts a good deal of light on the parallel case of history. In the law, as in history, it is necessary to explain what caused certain events. While it is accepted that the events of the type to be explained *may* stand in invariant relationships of succession to some set of the conditions that obtained at the time of the event's occurrence, this fact is not of any special relevance for purposes of determining the cause of the event in legal contexts. Usually the sufficient conditions for producing the event are not known, and even if they were, that would not permit us to make the all-important distinction between normal or usual conditions and the abnormal and unusual events which are typically regarded as intervening in the normal course of events and are therefore designated as the cause of the event to be explained. More importantly, since the purpose of legal inquiries into causes is to fix responsibility for them as a preliminary to reward or punishment, voluntary human actions have a special place among the conditions required to produce a certain effect. Especially when these actions are intended to produce the effect in question, they are treated as the decisive cause of the event, and all the other conditions necessary for the production of that event are reduced to the status of means or background conditions which are utilized by the action or on which the action supervenes, as it were, from outside. But even when the action is *not* intended to produce the effect, as in the case of a match dropped in a forest, it may well be treated as *the* cause of a forest fire, since the latter is among the results of such an action that a normal person might reasonably be expected to bear in mind and seek to avoid. On the other hand, if the result was produced only because of certain exceptional conditions that could not be anticipated, then the action of dropping the match may no longer be ranked as a cause but be demoted to the status of a precondition. What is important in all these cases is the fact that a distinction is made *among* the conditions for the occurrence of an event—a distinction between cause and conditions —and it is made on the basis of an interest in the control of the outcome by human agency.

There are several points of special interest in this legal treatment of causation. When a human action is segregated from the "conditions" for the occurrence of an event and is treated as *the* cause of that event, in the manner just described, the person performing the action will normally have reasons for acting in that way and those reasons will typically include certain states of affairs that either precede or are contemporaneous with his action. Now this action can be designated as the cause of the event in question *without* our being committed thereby to any claim that there is some invariant relationship between it and *either* the conditions that are utilized by the action *or* the states of affairs that are the motivating reasons for that action. The only requirement with respect to these conditions is that they be such as jointly to make it possible for the event to occur if the action in question is performed. There need be no suggestion that, whenever these conditions are satisfied, the action regularly follows and thus the event itself. Such a claim is, of course, precluded in the first instance simply by virtue of the fact that a great many of these conditions will be unknown to us. But even if they were exhaustively known, this would merely represent a complete characterization of the conditions which make it possible for the agent's action to produce the event to be explained; and when the action assumes the importance that is assigned to it in these legal contexts, we will normally have reason to believe that the event to which it leads would not occur simply as a result of the presence of what we have been calling its conditions. But it is even more important to see that the action need not itself be imbedded in a sequence of regular connections for which the "conditions" for the occurrence of the event are its own sufficient conditions as well. There is, in other words, a certain looseness or contingency in the relationship between conditions and action which permits us to speak of the latter as utilizing the former to produce an effect which may be predictable on the basis of conditions plus action.

Exactly the same observations apply to the relationship between the reasons for the action and the action itself. From the
standpoint of the law at least, as Professor H. L. A. Hart has
observed, "the statement that one person did something because, for example, another threatened him, carried no implication or covert assertion that if the circumstances were repeated
the same action would follow. . . . the assertion that he acted
because of the threats carries no implication that, given similar
circumstances, he would act again in this way or that in similar
circumstances he or other persons had always acted in this
way." (Hart, *Causation in the Law,* p. 52.) All that is needed
in order to show that a consideration was a reason for acting
in a certain way is some indication that from the standpoint
of the agent it made the action in question eligible and was
relevant to the promotion of some purpose he is presumed
to have. Just as in the case of the conditions which make the
desired result of the action possible, so in the case of the
states of affairs which are considerations in favor of the action
from the standpoint of the agent, there need be no claim that
the action must stand in a relationship of causal dependence
and uniform succession if it is to be regarded as the cause of
some event. What is necessary is simply that actions of this
kind be known to have a tendency to produce this kind of
result and that there be no set of conditions present which,
excluding the action itself, may be expected to produce that
result. In effect, then, the explanation of actions in the law is a
mixture of explanation through exhibition of the necessary conditions for the action or for its success, and of rational or
teleological explanation in which the agent's reasons for acting
in this way are set forth. In neither case is there a claim that
the action itself is imbedded in a causal sequence that is an
instance of a general law. The perspective of the explanation
thus remains essentially that of the agent himself, who sees the
conditions that make an action possible, as well as the reasons
for performing it, but surely does not subsume his action under
any general law in which that action would be declared to follow
regularly upon these conditions, whether enabling or good-
making.

In spite of important differences, there is a suggestive parallel between history and the law in these respects which I have been considering. While the law usually has to determine the cause of one event or of a group of closely related events, the historian's task is rarely so confined. Particularly in narrative history it is necessary to deal with a very large number of events which may be distributed over a considerable period of time and to explain them, i.e., to exhibit some intelligible relationship among them so that we come to understand why they occurred. This problem of intelligible continuity or colligation among the events with which the historian deals is one of the most difficult questions to which the philosophy of history must address itself. The example of the law is suggestive here because it raises the possibility that historical narrative is organized as a sequence of actions, each of which is understood and explained in the manner described above. That is, history in the primary sense would be an account not of what happened but of what was done, and it would therefore take as the organizing foci of its narrative human actions whose relationship to their context would be understood in teleological terms. In other words, the historian, like the lawyer, would have a special interest in one kind of necessary condition for the production of some result he seeks to explain—namely, the voluntary actions of human agents. These he treats as the decisive causes of that result as distinguished from the conditions that make the action (and the result) possible. Historical events would thus be a sequence of such actions whose relationship to their context is understood in the same (teleological) way as it is by the agents themselves. The problem of colligation in historical accounts would accordingly become a question of how these actions are related to one another, both when they are the acts of the same agent at different points in time and when they are the acts of different agents at either the same or different points of time. As in the law, where, as we have seen, the deliberate human act is "something *through* which we do not trace the cause of a later event," so in history each action would be understood in its own terms, i.e., under the description the agent may be assumed to have given it. Its relationship to its environment would in the first instance be the one which it stipulates itself by organizing the situation for purposes of action. Then the further question of colligation and continuity would concern the extent to which these actions are taken into account by other actions, i.e., how one person's action is understood and interpreted by other persons and how this understanding or misunderstanding is then incorporated into the programs of action of these agents. Here again the guiding assumption of this conception of historical process would be that the relationship between these different agents and their actions is to be understood in teleological terms rather than in terms of some scheme of lawlike regularities. That is, the actions of others and, as we shall see, the consequences of these actions would be themes of interpretation for each historical agent and as such would become elements in the historical environment of that agent's own programs of action, i.e., considerations or reasons bearing one way or another on what he tries to accomplish and not causes standing in an invariant relationship to an undertaking such as his.

Here again the law offers an interesting parallel to the analysis sketched out above, in its treatment of interpersonal transactions. These are transactions in which one person's action has as one of its necessary conditions the action of some other person of the kind that might be described by saying "He made me do it," "He persuaded me to do it," or "He advised me to do it." Admittedly, in most legal contexts the contact between the persons involved is likely to be immediate or at least much closer than it often is in historical cases, but in both cases one action takes the form of an influence on another person, to which the latter's performance of some further action is referred by way of explanation. The interesting feature of these cases from our standpoint is that while we will very likely say in such cases that one person acted as he did because of the action of the other, we do not say that the first action caused the second unless the first action is of a very special character that tends to limit or entirely to cancel the voluntary character of the second. In cases where this last is not the case, the law treats the first action, which the second agent is assumed to be aware of and to understand, as his reason for behaving as he does. Furthermore, just as in the case where the reason for his action has to do with some state of affairs not involving another's action, so here the assertion that the second action was a response to, and motivated by, the first carries no commitment with respect to any regularity of connection between the first action and the one that responds to it. Similarly in the case when one person's action does not directly attempt to influence the other's, but instead creates or denies an opportunity for the other to act in a certain way, perhaps quite unintentionally, we may use causal language to describe the effect of the one action on the other. But again, the generalizations that may be involved are designed to show that the opportunity afforded or denied was a necessary condition for the success of some further action but not that such opportunities are always exploited in the way this one may have been by the following action.

Thus far I have been presenting a fairly simple model of the way events are colligated in historical narrative. First events are sorted out into actions and nonactions; then the latter are further subdivided into those states of affairs which are known to the agent and those which are not. Among those which are known to him, some will have the status of reasons bearing one way or another upon the realization of the intention in terms of which his action is identified. Actions will be explained in purposive or teleological terms by reference to goals which their agents intend to achieve, as well as to the beliefs of the agent about certain features of his situation and the likely effects of acting upon them in certain ways. The fact that a person desires to achieve a certain goal can be explained by showing that this goal is related in some positive way to another goal or goals of the same person and thus fits in to the latter's general life policies, but his having either of these desires need not be explained in the sense of being shown to be an instance of some general law about what people desire under what conditions. Events of interest to the historian are thus explained through the exhibition of one type of condition that was necessary for their occurrence, i.e., the human action or actions in the absence of which the event would not have occurred on that particular occasion. Such a condition is not, of course, an absolutely necessary condition for the occurrence of events of the type in question, since on other occasions they may well occur without it. At most the action that is singled out by the historian is a necessary condition in the sense of being a member of one subset within an open disjunctive set of conditions which are jointly necessary—in a stronger sense—for the occurrence of this event.

If one were to seek a single word that would adequately describe the type of continuity which I am ascribing to the historical process, "dialectical" is undoubtedly the most appropriate, in spite of the fact that it has been used for so many different purposes and has consequently become a kind of symbol of a wide variety of philosophical theses that are highly controversial. Historical dialectic is typically thought of as a mysterious sort of engine that remorselessly grinds out events in a predetermined pattern of triplets, and it is also regularly associated with a panlogistic and deterministic view of history. Whether this conception of dialectic is a correct interpretation of the view of Hegel, to whom it is imputed, is a matter which I cannot go into here. What is clear, however, is that this interpretation misses altogether the close relationship between dialectic and purposive human action which is a very important element in Hegel's theory. It may be that he conceived of all human action as being organized toward an eventful convergence and harmony with itself in a way that we are powerless to alter, but this should not blind us to the fact that dialectic is in the first instance an instrument for the analysis and description of human action itself. Here the first and simplest of the notions suggested by the term is perhaps the most helpful: I mean the notion of dialectic as conversation. To understand the parallelism on which a dialectical view of history rests one must first understand the sense in which a human action is like saying something, making an assertion. Thus, to appropriate a physical object for one's own use or consumption is to say, implicitly at least, "This is mine." Perhaps Hegel's most important and original insight is just this point—that distinctively human actions involve corresponding forms of conceptualization and assertion and that the latter are in some sense elements of the action itself. But then it follows that many actions performed by different agents are like the assertions that are made by the several parties to a conversation; and so, both when these actions come into conflict with one another and when they are cooperative, we may, by extending the metaphor of conversation, speak of relationships of contradiction or compatibility among them. What is important, however, is not the full application of this metaphor but rather the notion of interaction among rational beings that underlies it. In a conversation a number of persons make statements which deal with some common subject matter that is distinct from the statements themselves and which purport to be true accounts of some aspect of that subject matter. Furthermore, these statements take account of one another and respond to the claims made by earlier speakers by acknowledgment, agreement, disagreement, and so on. In a well-conducted discussion each new statement will be as much a response to earlier ones as it will be a commentary on the subject of discussion; and while it would be foolish to expect that the progress of such a conversation must lead to the common acceptance of a fully satisfactory and internally harmonious account of the matter under investigation, it is very often the case that agreement does emerge in a cumulative way from such exchanges.

Now, the parallel to conversation in the case of human actions—the parallel that underlies the application to the latter of the term "dialectical"—is not hard to discern. An action seeks to make a change in the world, and very often this is observable physical change by which some human need or desire is satisfied. In the simplest cases this change is effected by one person in his natural environment. Inevitably, however, the individual agent must reckon with the actions taken by other persons, especially when they are such as to block or facilitate his own, and the same holds for those other agents in relation to him. Each agent's action must be a response not just to his natural situation considered in relation to his own needs and desires but a response also to the intentions implicit in what other persons are doing. When these agents can communicate with one another as human beings can, they will offer one another descriptions of what they are doing and why; and in this way, especially when there is a possibility of conflict among their actions, they will attempt to justify what they are doing to one another. Naturally these justifications will not always be accepted, and there may also be serious differences in the estimate different persons make of the likely outcomes of specific actions. On the whole, it is even less likely that this dialectic of actions will lead to a harmonious resolution than it is that conversations will do so. But to the extent that the interests and needs of human beings are convergent and to the degree that their satisfactions must be either cooperative or at the expense of one another, they do compose a dialectic just in this very simple sense of taking one another into account and of being thus internally related to one another. The thesis I am seeking to defend is that these relationships in which individuals and groups, considered as systems of action, stand to one another provide the thread of continuity in historical narrative.

In order to clarify this view, it is necessary to make a distinction between different ways in which human actions and their consequences can be described. An action can be described simply as a change in the state of the agent that brings about a change in the state of some object or objects (which may be persons) on which, as we say, the action is performed. No reference is made in such a description to any further purposes which may be achieved, or partially achieved, or not achieved at all through the change that this action brings about; and this is true whether those purposes are imputed to the agent or to someone else who is affected by the action. When the consequences of the action are described in this way, that abstracts from any larger system of purposes in which it may be situated, they may be called the "natural consequences" of the action. In the simplest cases, these natural consequences will be physical changes; and such actions as a political assassination could undoubtedly be described in terms of the movements of the assassins, the guards, the victim, the action of the pistol, the trajectory of the bullet, its impact, etc. In this way we can describe a man's being killed, a church's being built, the siege of a city, or the depopulation of a rural area through malaria. In each case certain physical processes bring about an end result that is described simply as an alteration of a previous state. In general, although we may not know what laws are instantiated by this change, we feel sure that there are such laws that govern the action of the physical modalities that are employed; and there are plenty of rough everyday generalizations that are available for projecting the likely outcome even in the absence of laws that fit the situation exactly. To be sure, the movements effected by the agents involved in these transactions are purposive, but in the case of this kind of description that fact is really disregarded and the actions in question are treated just as physical transactions.

It is quite another matter to describe the consequences of an action in a way that relates them, positively or negatively, to the achievement of some purpose. In the first example cited above, the description given— "political assassination"—is of this type, since even this summary designation indicates the capacity in which the victim became the target of the bullets which struck him and also suggests the general area in which the more specific ulterior purposes of the assassins are to be sought. From another point of view, this same act or its consequences might be described as a threat to constitutional government in a given country or in some other way, depending on the context of purposes and intention within which it is envisaged. The point is that no one would describe a set of consequences of his own or someone else's action in this way unless he also had a practical stake in it one way or another and had projected further goals of action that would, at least in his opinion, be influenced one way or another by it. A purely contemplative observer of the previous events and their consequences would not be practically concerned—even vicariously—in this way, and he would therefore lack the indispensable context of purpose and concern that is characteristic of human commentators on the consequences of action. Again, if human beings were solitary and isolated creatures and if the resources of the earth that

supplied their needs were not in scarce supply, so that com-
petitive relationships become inevitable, there would be no
reason for us to evaluate the consequences of the actions of
others in terms of our own practical concerns, since *ex hypothesi*
they would be most unlikely to make any difference. But as
things are, we are thrust into one another's company; and since
we compete for so many of the same things, what one of us does
has fateful consequences for the undertakings of others. The
consequences of action, considered from this standpoint, might
be called "moral" or "practical" consequences; and the characterization they receive reflects the principles and policies—that is,
in some sense the decisions and choices—of the person whose
characterization it is.

The natural consequences of an action, then, are the consequences that are describable by the historian without his
assuming—even vicariously—any framework of purposes that
might be affected by the outcome that he is describing. "Moral"
or, as I wish to call them, "historical" consequences are outcomes that are described in the context of some practical interest
that may not, to be sure, be shared by the historian himself but
is imputed to some participant in the historical transaction
of which the action itself forms a part. Considered as natural
consequences, the outcomes of actions are changes effected in
the situation which further actions—by the original agent and
by others—will have to take into account but which do not yet,
under this "natural" description, reflect the practical orientation
of any agent toward them. The difference between these two
modes of description is in some respects comparable to the
difference between the accounts that would be given of the
actions or moves of the players in some rule-governed game—
by persons who are familiar with these rules and can appreciate
the point of a particular maneuver, relate it to a certain strategy
for "winning," or detect the opportunity it creates for an op-
ponent—and, on the other hand, accounts of those actions given
by persons who are not familiar with the rules of the game,
who do not know what constitutes winning or losing, and who
must therefore describe what they observe principally in terms
of the physical movements made by the players. A history writ-

ten in this manner would truly deserve to be called a chronicle in the rather unusual sense employed by analytical philosophers of history since it would describe events at a level that gives no hint of the animating motives or goals of any of the actions that may be involved—in other words, as just one damn thing after another.

A NOTE ON THE CONTRIBUTORS

JAMES M. EDIE was born in Grand Forks, North Dakota, in 1927, studied at the University of Louvain and the University of Paris, and now teaches philosophy at Northwestern University. He is the editor of *Invitation to Phenomenology* and of *Phenomenology in America*.

SAMUEL J. TODES was born in Stamford, Connecticut, in 1927, has taught at Massachusetts Institute of Technology, Yale University, and Brandeis University, and is presently Associate Professor of Philosophy at Northwestern University. He is the author of "Comparative Phenomenology of Perception and Imagination" and "Knowledge and the Ego: Kant's Three Stages of Self-Evidence."

ALPHONSO LINGIS was born in Crete, Illinois, in 1933, has taught at Duquesne University, and is presently Associate Professor of Philosophy at the Pennsylvania State University. He has translated *The Visible and the Invisible* by Merleau-Ponty and *Totality and Infinity* by Emmanuel Levinas.

STEPHEN A. ERICKSON was born in Fairmont, Minnesota, in 1940, has taught at Claremont Graduate School, and is presently Associate Professor of Philosophy at Pomona College. He is the author of "Leibniz on Essence, Existence and Creation," and "Wild's World: A Study in Existence."

DON IHDE was born in Hope, Kansas, in 1934, has taught at Boston University and Southern Illinois University, and is presently Associate Professor of Philosophy at Southern Illinois University. He is the author of "Some Parallels between Analysis and Phenomenology," "From Phenomenology to Hermeneutic," and "Some Auditory Phenomena."

ROBERT GOFF was born in Buffalo, New York, in 1937, has taught at Hamilton College, and is presently Assistant Professor of Philosophy and Fellow of Cowell College, University of California at Santa Cruz. He is the author of "The Tillichian Symbol: An Essay in Philosophical Methodology," and "Wittgenstein's Tools and Heidegger's Implements."

CYRIL WELCH was born in Los Angeles, California, in 1939, he taught at Antioch College and Northwestern University, and is presently Assistant Professor of Philosophy at Mount Allison University. He is the author of numerous articles and reviews in learned journals.

ALBERT HOFSTADTER was born in New York in 1910, has taught at New York University and Columbia University, and is presently Professor of Philosophy at the University of California at Santa Cruz. He is the author of *Locke and Scepticism, Truth and Art* and editor of *Philosophies of Art and Beauty.*

EDWARD S. CASEY was born in Topeka, Kansas, in 1939, has taught at the University of California at Santa Barbara, and is presently Assistant Professor of Philosophy at Yale University. He has translated *The Notion of the A Priori* by Mikel Dufrenne.

JOHN J. MCDERMOTT was born in New York in 1932 and received his Ph.D. from Fordham University. He is presently Professor of Philosophy and Director of the Honors Program at Queens College, City University of New York. He is the author of *The American Angle of Vision* and "To Be Human Is To Humanize: A Radically Empirical Aesthetic" and editor of *The Writings of William James* and *The Basic Writings of Josiah Royce.*

JOSÉ FERRATER-MORA was born in Barcelona, Spain, in 1912. He has taught at the University of Chile, Bryn Mawr College, and Princeton University. He is presently Professor of Philosophy at Bryn Mawr. He is the author of *Man at the Crossroads, Philosophy Today,* and *Being and Death.*

STANLEY ROSEN was born in Warren, Ohio, in 1929 and is presently Professor of Philosophy at the Pennsylvania State University. He is the author of *Plato's Symposium.*

ARTHUR C. DANTO was born in 1924 and has taught at Columbia University, the University of Pennsylvania, and Princeton University. He is presently Professor of Philosophy at Columbia. He is the author of *Analytical Philosophy of Knowledge, Nietzsche as Philosopher,* and *Analytical Philosophy of History.*

GEORGE L. KLINE was born in Galesburg, Illinois, in 1921 and has taught at Columbia University, the University of Chicago, Swarthmore College, and the Johns Hopkins University. He is presently Professor of Philosophy at Bryn Mawr College. He is the editor of *Alfred North Whitehead : Essays on His Philosophy*, editor and contributor to *European Philosophy Today*, and author of *Religious and Anti-Religious Thought in Russia*.

THOMAS HANNA was born in Waco, Texas, in 1928 and has taught at Hollins College, Duke University, and the University of North Carolina. He is presently Professor and Chairman of the Department of Philosophy at the University of Florida. He is the author of *The Thought and Art of Albert Camus*, *The Bergsonian Heritage*, and *The Lyrical Existentialists*.

PAUL G. KUNTZ was born in Philadelphia in 1915 and has taught at Smith College, Grinnell College, and Emory University. He is presently Professor and Chairman of the Department of Philosophy at Emory. He is the author of *Philosophy, the Study of Alternative Beliefs*, *The Concept of Order*, and *Santayana and Lotze : George Santayana's Lotze's System of Philosophy*.

CARL R. HAUSMAN was born in St. Louis, Missouri, in 1924 and has taught at Kansas State University, Northwestern University, and the University of Colorado. He is presently Chairman of the Department of Philosophy at the Pennsylvania State University. He is the author of "Art and Symbol," "Spontaneity: Its Arationality and Its Reality," and "The Existence of Novelty."

ROBERT R. EHMAN was born in Los Angeles, California, in 1934 and has taught at Yale University and Vanderbilt University. He is presently Associate Professor of Philosophy at Vanderbilt. He is the author of "Freedom," "Privacy," and "Moral Objectivity."

JOHN WILD was born in Chicago, Illinois, and studied at the University of Chicago and Harvard University. He is at present Professor of Philosophy at Yale. His most recent book is *The Radical Empiricism of William James*.

WILLIAM LEON McBRIDE was born in New York in 1938 and is presently Assistant Professor of Philosophy at Yale University. He is the author of "Jean-Paul Sartre : Man, Freedom and *Praxis*," "The Acceptance of a Legal System," and "Towards a Phenomenology of International Justice."

ZYGMUNT ADAMCZEWSKI was born in Poland in 1921 and has studied at Innsbruck, London, Columbia and Harvard Universities. He is the author of *The Tragic Protest* and a contributor to *Phenomenology in*